ARTHUR
CAPPER

Publisher, Politician,
and
Philanthropist

by

HOMER E. SOCOLOFSKY

University of Kansas Press, Lawrence, 1962

© Copyright 1962 by the University of Kansas Press

L C C C Number 62-13869

PRINTED IN THE U S A BY THE
UNIVERSITY OF KANSAS PRESS

TO MY MOTHER AND FATHER

MARY RENEAU SOCOLOFSKY AND ABRAHAM L. SOCOLOFSKY

Preface

By the time of his death in 1951, Arthur Capper had gained national prominence as a publisher, politician, and philanthropist His birth in 1865 came shortly after the end of the Civil War During a fairly typical boyhood he learned the printing trade and soon after high-school graduation he was employed as a printer by the Topeka *Daily Capital,* a paper he eventually owned

The job as printer was soon dropped for one in journalism, and after nine hectic, busy years of training and experience, Capper took his first plunge into the publishing field with the Topeka *Mail,* which had a weekly circulation of about one thousand During the next thirty-five years his publishing empire expanded through the purchase and consolidation of almost thirty newspapers and magazines, so that by 1930 he owned and directed the activities of half a dozen farm papers, several dailies, and other publications Circulation continued to climb until the time of his death, when it stood at four and a half million

Capper's success in journalism enlarged his interest in partisan politics, especially when he became involved, with other Republican progressives, in their fight against "boss" rule in early twentieth-century Kansas Although he had never served in an elective public position Capper became the Republican candidate for Governor of Kansas in 1912, only to lose by twenty-nine votes, the narrowest margin on record for such an election in the state His winning the governorship in the next election inaugurated an impressive chain of seven consecutive political victories for the highest offices available in Kansas politics Two terms as Governor were followed by five terms as United States Senator

The source of Capper's "mysterious" power over Kansas voters baffled the political professional, for Capper's modest and even humble bearing did not seem in keeping with his political ambitions He was impressive neither physically nor as an orator, but his "lone wolf" political tactics inspired faith in his own sincerity and drew voters to the polls who were rarely impressed by the party regulars

In many ways the mild-mannered Capper was a paradoxical character, but he considered his role as Governor or as Senator to be that of a direct and willing spokesman of the home-state majority. Ever alert to mirror "grass roots" sentiment, he successfully braved the dissident winds of political vagary for more than a generation

Capper's interest in Kansas youth led through a series of youth clubs to philanthropic assistance for crippled children The major beneficiary of his will was the Capper Foundation for Crippled Children, now his chief memorial in Topeka

From the time of beginning this book till its completion innumerable cases of helpfulness and kindness have made a long road easier. It was first proposed, at the time of Capper's retirement from the Senate, by Elmer Ellis, the suggestion being seconded by Lewis E Atherton, both of the University of Missouri Capper associates, particularly the late Marco Morrow, Rod Runyan, the late Leland Schenck, Clif Stratton, and Julia McKee, proved an invaluable aid to a more thorough study of Capper and his life Nyle Miller and the staff of the Kansas State Historical Society provided their usual courteous assistance Additional support and encouragement came from the Kansas State University Bureau of General Research, and from Fred L Parrish, James Carey, Philip M Rice, and A Bower Sageser, all of them colleagues in the Department of History, Kansas State University Thanks are also due to the directors of the Capper Foundation for Crippled Children, to Frank McGrath, its executive secretary, and to Mark Plummer, now at Illinois Normal University The final typing was done by Jan Miller and Mary Wiersma The Editor of the University of Kansas Press has provided skillful editorial assistance

Through it all my family and my wife, Penny, have created an atmosphere favorable to the progress of this study, and I am eternally grateful

HOMER E SOCOLOFSKY

19 May 1962
Kansas State University
Manhattan, Kansas

Contents

I	"Nerve to Be Born in Kansas"	1
II	Growing Up	9
III	The Young Apprentice	19
IV	New Horizons	29
V	The Emerging Publisher	42
VI	New Links in a Chain	53
VII	Involvement in Politics	63
VIII	Two Races for Governor	74
IX	The Meek and Mild Governor	87
X	Capper Is a Committee	106
XI	The Capper Youth Clubs and Promotion of Rural Life	115
XII	Capper and the World War I Peace Treaty	126
XIII	A Publisher's Shifting Fortunes	135
XIV	The Farm Bloc and the Twenties	145
XV	The New Deal Years	166
XVI	Capper Publications, Incorporated	187
XVII	Senator Capper and the Forties	202
XVIII	Capper and Kansas	215
	Bibliographical Note	231
	Notes	233
	Index	271

Illustrations

ARTHUR CAPPER   *frontispiece*

BIRTHPLACE OF ARTHUR CAPPER   7

                                                        facing

MRS HERBERT CAPPER   20

THE CAPPER CHILDREN   20

MR AND MRS ARTHUR CAPPER   21

CAPPER BUILDING AND RESIDENCE   36

CAPPER IN WASHINGTON AND AT WICHITA   37

KEY CAPPER PERSONNEL WITH THE SENATOR   164

CAPPER IN 1944   165

CAPPER IN 1948 AND IN 1919   180

THE CAPPER FOUNDATION   181

Chapter I
"Nerve to Be Born in Kansas"

After a dreary winter of fighting the curtain fell on the Civil War at Appomattox Only minor engagements marred the peace that was celebrated in most Northern states by the ringing of church and fire bells, accompanied by long-winded speeches, booming cannon, and kindled bonfires. But spontaneous joy was soon turned to righteous wrath and grief with the announcements that President Lincoln had been assassinated

While the nation anxiously followed the news stories concerning the assassin and his accomplices a young couple in Garnett, Kansas, Herbert and Isabella Capper, were anxiously awaiting the coming of a child The report of the execution of four of the Lincoln murder party reached Kansas on the same day the child was born, July 14, 1865 The Cappers named their young son Arthur, after the son of a boyhood friend An earlier daughter, Mary, had died in infancy, and the young parents were relieved to find their son vigorous and healthy.

Herbert Capper (1833-1897), the second son of Thomas and his second wife Elizabeth Capper, was born in Longton, Staffordshire, England. Thomas Capper was a worker in the metal trades as a tinner, and Herbert learned the trade as a youth He had the usual schooling and excelled in penmanship and spelling After Herbert's mother died, his father remarried and for Herbert his home had disintegrated [1] The new mistress in his father's house did not endear herself to her new charges, and when Herbert was barely nineteen years of age he left home because of the treatment of his brothers and sisters The rupture was a serious one, and because of it young Capper migrated in 1853 to Philadelphia, where he soon found employment in a wholesale house. After a few months he wrote a friend that he was impressed with the "fine country but so hot I can scarcely bear it   . I have had little else but trouble since I left Longton, yet when I remember the treatment of my kindred before leaving I cannot say I have any desire to return to stay "[2]

The following year, 1854, found young Capper in southern Iowa, first at Drakesville in Davis County, then at Cincinnati in neighbor-

1

ing Appanoose County He was becoming acquainted with the strange ways of Americans, and he was particularly attracted by the "Wesleyans or True Wesleyans They are thorough Anti-Slavery, Anti-War, Anti-Secret-Societies . believing in goodness of God for the future and not to the oaths and provisions of secret societies." He later joined an anti-slavery society but not the Wesleyan group [3] In Iowa he "found better friends than . relations in England," and he was pleased to record that "folks call me the Tinner here" He set up a tin shop and was advertising in the local journal A leading impression for the young tin-smith in 1854, which he disclosed to his transatlantic correspondent, was his experience in "eating breakfast with two fine fellows, (fugitives) a few weeks since. I was at one of the stations of the underground railroad and was right glad to see them I suppose they are safe in Canada by this time I cannot give you any further particulars here about this road for fear my letter might come to light "[4]

One of Capper's Iowa acquaintances was the Reverend Samuel B McGrew, who encouraged him to go to Kansas [5] McGrew's brother, Simon, had migrated to Linn County along the eastern Kansas border in 1855 There he erected a log cabin at the head of Elk Creek, about three and one-half miles southwest of Mound City, and in 1857 he brought his wife and seven children into the new territory Either that year or the next—old records are indecisive—Herbert Capper journeyed to Westport Landing and walked with J P Harris and others to Ottawa [6] From there he continued south into neighboring Anderson County, and settled on a claim located on the North Fork of Pottawatomie Creek Only a year or so earlier, along the lower reaches of this same stream, the indescribable horror of the Pottawatomie massacre of pro-slavery settlers was carried out by John Brown and his men This action and Brown's subsequent appearance at Harper's Ferry would eventually stamp the "Old Brown" name indelibly on American hearts Here, in the same vicinity, many of Major Jeff Buford's Georgians had settled and, according to abolitionists, could not keep their hands off free-state cattle herds The clashing of rival interests—violence, excitement, opportunity— was in the air With apparent resolution Herbert Capper came to Kansas as a part of a larger movement that soon dominated the political scene in the territory. For in territorial Kansas a little civil war between slavery and abolition died before the national Civil War was born

If there was anything Herbert Capper stood for it was abolition He was a mild person, but he had strong convictions His birth, background, religious belief, and economic views all led him to look upon slavery as a detestable practice He had few direct experiences with that "peculiar institution," but these only strengthened his basic attitude. His birth in England came on the eve of abolition of slavery throughout the entire British Empire His religious views were never orthodox and exhibited the individualistic traits which eventually led him into the Society of Friends He did not enjoy or seek violence, but he came to the scene of recent outrages when he took up his "claim" six miles northwest of the new town of Garnett

It is evident that Herbert Capper went to Kansas because of his convictions in favor of abolition But of equal importance was his desire to settle on the frontier The troubles in Kansas had been on everyone's lips the past few years Reports from the new territory emphasized violence, but they also laid stress on the opportunities of the new frontier and on the dream of squatter sovereignty Those who went to Kansas would share in making the crucial decision involving slavery Capper went to Kansas to provide one more vote for abolition, and he also was looking for opportunities in frontier real estate.

Herbert Capper's first homestead in Anderson County was bisected by the swift-flowing waters of the North Fork of Pottawatomie Creek The high bank of the stream, almost blufflike in proportions, sloped steeply down from the rolling prairie from which Garnett could be seen in the distance This area, a frontier region in 1857 and 1858, abounded in wild game and small animals and was well provided with timber and spring water This first farm was built up through four transactions to 240 acres before it was sold by Capper in 1868 [7] That he possessed a "money sense," an ability to perceive and to take advantage of increasing land values, is evident in his extensive dealings in real estate By 1861, he was already the holder of 640 acres of frontier farm land Of this amount, one-quarter section was in Bates County, Missouri, and the rest was in Kansas, 280 acres in Bourbon County, and 200 acres, some with patent incomplete, in Anderson County [8] In the eight years he had been in the United States Herbert Capper had done quite well for himself. He had accumulated property of increasing value. He had traveled over much of the northern United States and had even returned to England on at least one occasion. His skill as a tinner had provided him a needed occupation, but in 1861 he was "working at farming" on his Anderson County land, with the hope of paying his way through "the winter and no more, perhaps not that."[9] At other times he lived at Cincinnati, Iowa.

Also of long standing was Herbert Capper's commitment to abstinence from alcoholic beverages. That contact with drunkenness was one of his reasons for leaving home is apparent from a comment he made about his foster mother. "Oh, that cursed drink, it has made her a miserable lot."[10] Later he wrote, "The American women at least a many of them have sense enough not to have any man without he is a total abstainer."[11] His belief in abstinence and prohibition stayed with him all his life.

By the time the Civil War began Herbert Capper was a naturalized citizen of the United States. He was a "radical Republican in [his] views of government," and he had "no doubt but the north will win,"[12] Early in the war he believed that "Fremont is the chap to do something if they would let him alone, but he is too much of an anti-slavery man for this administration and for the masses of the people."[13] From Iowa he wrote that "my friend and agent in Kansas, tells me they see fighting within 12 miles of his place, things are not favorable for peace, [and he] says the people of southern Kansas are sorely vexed about old Abe superseding Fremont, if some of the ultra one's there had Abe he would be apt to get some tar, others think Abe just the right man,"[14]

Herbert Capper supported the Union cause with gifts and loans rather than his service.[15] For in spite of all his concern for Northern victory, he had "no desire to leave Uncle Sam's Country by a bullet or pruning hook's assistance, neither [did he] wish to kill a human being." "Sometimes," he said, "I would rather be killed myself."[16] So while "all Englishmen [he had] seen espouse the northern cause" and his brother Alfred "enlisted before the draft" Herbert Capper did not enter the Union army. The main reason, other than his antipathy to a soldierly occupation, was the fact that he had married. Even though he had written in October, 1861, that "my aunt says

4

that my visit to England and the sight of English girls has disgusted me with Americans" he was married to an American girl before another year had rolled around [17]

The new bride was Isabella McGrew (1841-1903), the daughter of "the Fighting Quaker" Simon B and Ura Marsh McGrew, and niece of Capper's old friend the Reverend Samuel B. McGrew Isabella, or Belle as she was intimately known, was born in Sewlickley Township, Westmoreland County, Pennsylvania Ancestors in the McGrew family line had migrated to northern Ireland in the seventeenth century and had come to Maryland and then to Pennsylvania in the next century There most of them were members of the Society of Friends and made use of the "plain language" in their immediate family In 1844, Simon McGrew moved his family to Jefferson County, Ohio, where he built and operated a flour mill In 1852, they moved again to the newly formed Quaker settlement at Salem, Iowa [18] In 1857 a final move brought the family to the previously mentioned Mound City location in territorial Kansas During the following year a comfortable and commodious log house was built adjoining the original cabin, and the family continued to occupy it for the next six years [19]

The McGrew family, while possessing more worldly goods than the average settler, found it necessary sharply to reduce their standard of living on the frontier However, a tradition persisted in the family that Mrs McGrew brought to her new home the first ingrain carpet used in Linn County Simon McGrew's energetic support of free-soil activity caused his family to fear attack from Border ruffians Traditionally he was listed as one of the free-state men who barely escaped being a victim in the Marais des Cygnes massacre [20]

Soon after the McGrew migration to territorial Kansas, Isabella taught a nearby one-room school She also taught one term in an abandoned log cabin which was known as the Osborne School Two brothers and her youngest sister were among her pupils in that school [21]

After their marriage Herbert and Isabella Capper resided for a short time in Mapleton, just over the line into Bourbon County But prospects for a thriving community were not good, and in 1863 the young couple moved to Garnett, with about 600 inhabitants [22]

There they retained their family home during most of the remainder of their life In Garnett, Herbert Capper soon was established as a tinner He gained a reputation for industriousness and was held in high respect by leading citizens of the community But incomplete records seem to indicate that he was a follower rather than a leader in his community Although a man of growing wealth and the possessor of serious convictions he did not seek or hold public office, nor can he be found among a list of prominent settlers for the years he arrived in either Anderson County or in the county-seat of Garnett Local histories of Anderson County first acknowledge his presence some ten years after he settled in the county.

Apparently Capper was inherently modest or had become so through the influence of his wife She seems to have been the guiding hand in his propensity toward the Society of Friends He wrote soon after their wedding "My wife is 7 or 8 years younger than myself, of quaker parents which suits me to a T as I have had a hankering that way a long time Thee says I am getting quite expert in theeing etc already, to very intimate friends I use what Quakers term the plain language, in writing, and to my wife in conversation, tho I make blunders sometimes "[23]

But given enough provocation, Herbert Capper would overlook his Quaker attitudes and take up arms in defense of his home Basically a peace-loving man, he responded to such a challenge when a Kansas State Militia unit was organized at Garnett to act as a Home Guard. Capper was enrolled by G W Iler, justice of peace at Garnett, on October 10, 1863. When Sterling Price's command approached the Kansas border in its raid across Missouri, Capper "was ordered into active military service as 1st Sargeant in Co 'I' Tenth Regiment" under the immediate command of Captain McLaughlin, on October 9, 1864. His service was brief and he was relieved from duty on October 28, 1864, after being "absent sick from October 20 per certificate of surgeon "[24] He never claimed veteran status because of this brief military venture Years later he recalled that he had lived on "Price Raid crackers and worms," but he seemed to consider his contribution insignificant [25]

At other times during the Civil War years in Garnett, Herbert Capper was busy at his trade as tinner This was also a period of active real estate transactions for him Between October, 1863, and

May, 1865, he purchased a dozen town lots in Garnett Half of these came to him from the town company, probably in return for service or in compensation for starting a business in Garnett The two separate transactions involved a total payment of $2 The other six lots he obtained in three transactions at a total cost of $220 Some of the lots faced the courthouse square, and at least three of them were desirable corner lots Most appear to have been without improvements at the time of purchase However, four lots at the corner of

Birthplace of Arthur Capper, Garnett

From a sketch in Margaret Whittemore's *Historic Kansas*

Cedar and Fifth, acquired on March 1, 1864, for $135, may have been improved If they were, these four lots contained either a partly built or newly completed house. The following year a small red brick house existed on one of these lots at 508 Cedar [26]

This small house, built of locally made soft red brick, was the birthplace of Arthur Capper. Furnished in modest fashion and enlarged from the initial two rooms with a lean-to addition to the side, it served as the home of the Cappers for only a few years Eventually, when rail service came into Garnett, the track and main roadway of one line occupied the Fifth Street right-of-way beside the little house After World War II a factory was built on the same lots, and the original brick part of the house was left standing, although the addition was removed Almost a century after his birth, the house where Arthur Capper was born still stood at the corner of Cedar and Fifth in Garnett Efforts to restore the building to a condition suitable for housing a small museum were initially unsuccessful Because of its dilapidated condition it is doubtful whether without extensive care or renovation the Capper birthplace can survive much longer

Recalling the conditions in "Bleeding Kansas" and the Civil War, Arthur Capper would frequently say, "It required nerve to be born in Kansas " Because of respect for his parents, he would hasten to add, "If I had it to do all over again, I'd want it to be the same way "

Chapter II

Growing Up

By mid-1865 issues of peaceful and individual interests were more and more claiming the attention of Americans The battle could now be directed to developing new factories, expanding commercial activity, learning to live with peace, and conquering the endless prairies One example of new activity occurred on July 12, 1865, when a railroad meeting was called to order by Senator James H Lane at Ottawa, Kansas, on behalf of the Leavenworth, Lawrence and Fort Gibson road Plans were developed for rapidly pushing the new railroad south through Ottawa and Garnett and on to Indian Territory, but countless delays held up completion of the line for many years

The year 1865 was also a time for taking a state census in Kansas Tucked away in the manuscript census returns for Anderson County is the enumeration on August 30, 1865, of the young Capper family Herbert Capper was listed as thirty-one years old, and as a tinner possessing real estate to the value of $2,400 and other property valued at $400 Isabella Capper was recorded as twenty-three years old, and a son, not named, was credited with an age of 1/12 year

Little is known from contemporary accounts of Arthur Capper's life during these early years Other children, Mary May, usually called May (1866-1939), Bessie (1870-1909), Benjamin (1874-1887), and Edith (1879-1953), were born to the Cappers Arthur, as the oldest child, had responsibilities and privileges generally accorded to a person in that position

Arthur Capper later remembered that his father was "physically not a strong man" but that he possessed a "quiet persistence" in his task The family was "not rich but classed as well-to-do " They "lived well but not extravagantly or ostentatiously " Belief in work, honestly and industriously carried out, was an article of faith to the members of the Herbert Capper family [1]

Isabella Capper was also fondly remembered by her son Arthur She was gentle and ambitious for her children She impressed on them the necessity of obtaining a good education She gave them a desire to read good books and to live "according to the Bible."[2]

Devoted to her children, she was still concerned about their health and welfare when they were gone from the family home Such motherly anxiety is shown in a letter to her eldest son "I told Pa when I commenced this I didn't intend to write much only to give thee a scolding for not writing but I find I am scribbling quite a good deal "[3] Some twenty years after her death Arthur Capper wrote, "There was nothing of passive non-resistance in her Quakerism She was inflexible in her adherence to her conceptions of righteousness "[4] Her ideas of proper conduct included abstinence from the use of tobacco and intoxicating liquors [5] Her children also remembered that she had a W C.T U pin but that she "did not like to wear it as she did not like any jewelry "

Evidence points to a happy youth for Arthur Capper, each member of the household contributing warmth and human understanding. Grandfather McGrew wrote his grandson in 1876 recalling some of the experiences of the previous decade He remembered, "When I used to go into the room to rest on the carpet and thee would play over me and then fall asleep on my breast and sleep so sweet and then thee don't remember how when awake thee used to make believe thee was going to snees [*sic*] and then laugh so cute all these little things grandfather has not forgot   ."[6]

After the Civil War Herbert Capper expanded his business activities in Garnett By 1868, he had a line of stoves and was known as a stove dealer [7] He also continued his purchases of Garnett town lots, and in 1868 bought 360 acres of land from school sections in Anderson County It is interesting to note, in view of his son's future, that the patents for the school land obtained by Herbert Capper were signed by Samuel J Crawford, then governor of Kansas Valuable town property was secured later by Capper, but these transactions of 1868 and 1870 terminated for a short time his real estate activity in Anderson County [8]

The census information taken on July 1, 1870, listed Herbert Capper as a retired merchant with real estate valued at $3,800 and a total personal estate of $11,940 [9] Capper had apparently disposed of his business to make a move, with another Garnett man, C P. Alvey, to a new town which was located about eighty miles southwest of Garnett.

In the summer of 1870, the Capper party made the tiring, hot, dusty journey by covered wagon to the recently established community of Elk Rapids in newly organized Howard County There Herbert Capper quickly set up the town's first hardware store Since Elk City had been located about twenty miles down the Elk River in another county and since Elk Falls was about ten miles west, postal authorities refused to approve the name of the new town So Herbert Capper's suggestion that the town be renamed Longton, after his ancestral home in England, was accepted [10] However, the Elk Rapids Town Company, chartered August 23, 1870, did not formally change the town corporation name for almost two years.[11]

Contacts between the Cappers and Garnett were not broken The editor of the Garnett *Plaindealer* on September 16, 1870, published a lengthy letter from Capper telling of the bright prospects for Longton. Capper began his letter by stating that "no actual misrepresentation of mine will ever add one to the population of Longton " His letter told of the surrounding country and the improvements on the town site By September, 1870, the first schoolhouse in Howard county had been built and had been in use through the summer He also told of other activities and of his own enterprise, which he described as a "large stove and tinning concern [that] will blaze away when the building is ready " A local need was expressed for lawyers, doctors, a hotel, a furniture store, a boot and shoe shop, a drug store, and blacksmiths and carpenters Capper cautioned, however, that those who come "should be men of grit who can stare the little annoyances of pioneer life out of countenance, and patiently await the bright and comfortable future,   "[12] When the *Howard County Ledger,* Longton's first newspaper, was published, it carried business cards under the "Merchants" column One of them read·

Herbert Capper
Dealer in Hardware, Tinware and
Stoves All kinds of tinware made
to order on short notice [13]

Arthur Capper was about five years old when his family moved to Longton He later reported that he "went to school there when . . about 7 years of age," and it was there that he had his "first ambition to be a newspaper man "[14] Stories that he played around the newspaper shop in Longton tend to verify this reminiscence of later years.

11

He also reported that a life of Ben Franklin was the first book he read and that his first essay grew from his reading [15] Apparently the Cappers lived within the boundaries of the town, in spite of assertions that they lived on a farm or ranch

Since Herbert Capper had subscribed to the New York *Independent* for twenty-four years in 1868, the Cappers were reading news from other than local sources [16] Moreover, Horace Greeley, the editor of the New York *Tribune,* was one of Herbert Capper's heroes He wrote Greeley at least once and received a prompt answer to his inquiry [17] It was a "great disappointment" to Herbert Capper when Greeley was defeated by President U S Grant in the election of 1872 [18]

Just before the presidential election another disappointment came to Herbert Capper when Longton lost in its bid to become the county seat of Howard County [19] This election defeat would limit Longton's opportunity to grow Real estate values in the community would not normally increase so rapidly and business prospects would not be as good And so the Cappers moved from Longton, though a major reason for their departure may have been the fact that Herbert, almost fifty years of age, was in failing health

Contemporary records have not disclosed the movements of the family during the years 1873 to 1875 After two years of residence in Longton they may have returned to Garnett Herbert Capper still had real estate interests in Garnett and Anderson County, although possibly some of the transactions of this period were handled on infrequent trips or through correspondence On the other hand, a purchase, in the name of Herbert Capper of Longton, of two lots, presumably with a house, on March 18, 1872, may have indicated that the family was preparing to return

Stories of almost legendary quality tell of various happenings to Arthur Capper when he was growing up He carved his name on one of the desks in the Garnett public school Years later, with appropriate ceremony, this desk was presented to him, and for a while it occupied the corner of his private office On another occasion he was involved in shooting off a firecracker while seated in a church balcony during Sunday services A parental reprimand quickly followed In a speech, while campaigning for Governor, Capper said in Garnett that the "fellow who pounded the big drum was my school mate in

8th grade who quarrelled with me over a red-headed girl and licked me good and plenty " As a youth he was remembered for always having half a dozen long, well-sharpened pencils in his shirt pocket His companions included many of the youth of Garnett, and the town of his birth always held a special place in his memory

Years later Arthur Capper said that he began selling the Kansas City *Times* in Garnett when he was a boy of ten years, and that he sold the newspaper for about three years [20] A letter from the young enterpriser, published in 1878, tells a little of his other business experience To "Aunt Mary" of *American Young Folks* he wrote. "I could not possibly get fifty cents in currency, so I have to send stamps I made money by raising lettuce and selling five and ten cents worth at a time My father says I could not invest fifty cents more profitably than in another year's subscription to the American Young Folks "[21]

Traditional stories of Arthur Capper's boyhood usually describe a small printing press which was a Christmas gift in 1877 Herbert Capper, in presenting it to his young son, is reported to have stated, "I hope thee will avail thyself of this present It may aid thee greatly in thy future "[22] With his toy press he printed cards and handbills on order for neighbors [23] Herbert Capper was a long-time friend of the editor of the Garnett *Journal,* and Arthur often visited the office of the newspaper [24] In the fall of 1878, Arthur, then thirteen years of age, began his first real newspaper work on the *Journal* as the office "devil " His job involved the multitude of little tasks found around a newspaper office, including the setting of type and eventually the writing of stories He did edit, for some time, a "Young Folks" column for the *Journal* He also had another letter published in *American Young Folks* in December, 1878, illustrating the "Ben Franklin" philosophy of the young Capper [25]

AUNT MARY . have not written to the YOUNG FOLKS for a while I have been working in the office of the Garnett Journal, for over two months, I like the printer's trade very well I am getting along slowly, I set up a column to-day We were very busy printing tickets before election, there were a great variety of tickets Democratic tickets with Greenback men on them, Greenback tickets with Democrats and republicans, and almost every kind you could think of A young man, a printer by trade, told me when I commenced to learn the trade, that it was the poorest trade there was, and that I could not make a living at it I do not think it can be the poorest trade Since I have been at this trade I find that a great many printers chew and smoke and drink I have been figuring it up, if a man spent ten cents a day for whiskey, then in ten years, without any interest it would amount to $365 00, and for tobacco, if they spent only twenty cents a week, that would amount to $104 00 in ten years, and both together would make $469 00 enough to buy a good second hand press and type I am now thirteen years old, and I am going to try to put my savings out at interest, in place of spending them on drinks and tobacco, and by the time I am twenty-one do you think I will have enough to buy a good second hand press, or will it turn out as a young man I mentioned said, that printing was the poorest trade in America?

Yours Truly,
ARTHUR CAPPER

For about a year in the early 1880's the Herbert Capper family lived in New Jersey [26] While there they lived first in Haddonfield, near Camden, and then at Vineland, some twenty-five miles further south For a while Arthur worked in a printing shop after school, on Saturdays and holidays The Capper family also attended the Friends Meeting in Haddonfield [27] From Vineland Herbert Capper returned his family directly to Kansas [28]

Since the Capper family was frequently on the move, the question arises, "Why did Herbert and Isabella Capper move their family so often while the children were growing up?" Only tentative answers can be given to such a query The move to Longton and the moves to a variety of different residences in Garnett seem to have been prompted by the improved financial resources of the family or by a desire for economic opportunity The move from Longton was promoted, no doubt, by Herbert Capper's failing health By late 1884 Herbert Capper had also lived "temporarily" in Galva, Kansas, and he had been in Georgia, North Carolina, and South Carolina, "long enough to know from actual experience or sight" much about the political climate of each area [29] It is unlikely that Herbert Capper took his family with him on all of these distant travels. It is known that he went without his family on an extended trip to California in the spring of 1884 and later on a jaunt to New Orleans [30] After Arthur left home Herbert Capper took his family to Georgia and to California The knowledge that from the early 1880's he was "suffering from diseases peculiar to his trade, at times being able to get about and at others confined to his room suffering agonies that no pen can describe" allows one to conclude that many of these trips were short-lived or ineffectual attempts to regain lost health [31]

Herbert Capper, as a tinner, had contact in his trade with several varieties of solders containing lead compounds His contacts with molten lead may have been similar to those of a printer Prolonged and close association with these materials may have gradually induced in Capper a kind of lead poisoning Proved cases of tin poisoning, on the other hand, are of such rarity that there is even doubt that poisoning from tin or tin compounds is possible If lead poisoning was the pernicious influence on his health, Capper could possibly have gained temporary relief by absence from the source of his infirmity However, such poisoning is cumulative and renewed contact with lead products would decrease his ability to resist the advances of the disease

If Herbert Capper was traveling in the 1870's and 1880's in search of health, he was not alone Travel or new surroundings were leading prescriptions of medical doctors of that time for a variety of complaints The records of history are full of the names of people who followed such advice, with varying results This was also a period when the quality of the water was often severely questioned, and attendance at mineral springs or at a health spa became an accepted pattern of life all over this country or in Europe The value of vacations for health reasons at these nineteenth century resorts might be variously attributed to the new environment or to the rest and relaxation provided But for Herbert Capper, his "thorn in the flesh" persisted as the 1880's gave way to the 1890's

In the meantime, Garnett was developing growing pains In 1880 the reported population was 1,380, and the growth was several hundred during the next two years The St Louis, Kansas and Arizona Railroad had arrived in 1879 as Garnett's second railroad, and for a brief time the community was a terminus for the new line [32] Overnight rail connections to St Louis ballooned the town's pride in its accessibility to markets New additions to the town were being platted, new residences built, and new businesses organized The prevailing spirit of optimism was extended to the Garnett *Plaindealer,* which was delivering 900 copies of the paper each week, reputedly the largest circulation in the county.

This was the Garnett to which Herbert Capper returned his family in the early eighties It was quite different from the community he saw develop in the 1850's, but no other place seemed as much like home to him Here he again made investments in Garnett real estate One of his largest transactions involved an undivided half interest in business property fronting on the courthouse square[33] Additional property was obtained by Capper from later purchases and sales

The Capper children were attending Garnett schools again, and Art, as he was now known, was in high school In addition to his new responsibilities in school he had duties in the *Journal* office During the summer vacation of 1883 he also served as a clerk in the post office The news report of this activity in the *Anderson County Republican* stated briefly that "Miss Allie Gregg will be the new clerk in the post office Arthur Capper, retired, will attend school "[34] Another story explained that "Sam Lindsay and Arthur Capper struck for higher wages at the postoffice They didn't get the wages but did get fired "[35]

Evidence of Arthur Capper's scholastic ability before he reached the senior grade in high school is rare Honor roll lists published in the local newspapers more frequently contain the names of Bessie or Mary May Capper than Arthur's Later reminiscences, made at the age of eighty-four, by a former Garnett high school superintendent, J B Robinson, would tend to refute any assumptions based on lack of contemporary information He reported that Arthur was perfect in deportment and averaged 98 per cent on final examinations[36]

During his last year in high school, Art must have been a busy young man. There were many things to do in Garnett Attending church services two or three times a week was not only a religious experience but a leading social activity The Garnett Opera House was open almost every night with some kind of meeting, local performance, or traveling play In April, 1884, a cantata, "The Blacksmith's Children," was presented under the auspices of the ladies of the Presbyterian Home Missionary Society Arthur Capper was listed as one of the chorus singers[37] A similar program, presented by the Band of Hope, a temperance organization, later the same year had in its cast Bennie, Bessie, and May Capper[38]

"Public School" Commencement exercises for Arthur Capper and his eight classmates were held May 23, 1884, in the Garnett Opera House, and classes had ended a week earlier Reports indicated that the "evening was warm, the ventilation of the room imperfect, and the attendance a perfect jam " Young Art was the "solitary masculine among so many winsome representatives of the fair sex "[39] The news report continued "The theses presented by the young ladies were read in a very correct and effective manner   The valedictory by Mr Capper differed from the other exercises in being delivered without manuscript It was given in excellent style and showed a great deal of original thought, literary culture, and careful preparation " Since Capper's valedictory address, "Public Opinion," filled a newspaper column, it cannot be reproduced in its entirety Briefly, he said

One of the most important elements in the formation of character is public opinion   We should be moderate in our regard to public opinion We should not lay too great stress upon it   neither ought we to be too independent of public opinion   One of the highest qualities a man or woman can be blessed with, is independence, a quality which should always be admired It is the absence of this estimable quality which makes persons unable to withstand the jeers of corrupt and un-principled men It is our duty to do right even though it may be dis-pleasing to our friends, for right will conquer in the end The best ministers, the best statesmen, the best citizens care very little for public opinion, for they do what they know to be right We should mould public opinion, and not allow public opinion to mould us   [40]

The most impressive association with his graduation exercises for young Capper was a poem given to him by his father He memorized it and used it on many occasions in later life The poem was

> Work wins; it always wins
> Though days go slow and night be dark
> 'Twixt days that come and go,
> Still work will win Its average is sure
> He gains the prize who can the most endure,
> Who faces trials, who never shirks,
> Who waits and watches,
> And who always works [41]

Soon after his last class meeting in the Garnett High School Arthur Capper began to put into operation plans that had been made for his future His father and mother did not favor his leaving home immediately His mother encouraged him to attend college [42] He may have started his quest for work before graduation, but shortly after the ceremonies he came down with the mumps, which can be a serious disease for a young man almost nineteen years of age [43]

The usual story of Capper's search for work following graduation emphasizes speed and decisive action After repeated telling it differs in minor details from what can be reconstructed from contemporary records Capper hoped to find work as a printer in one of the larger towns of the Kansas River valley or possibly as far west as Salina If nothing could be found there, he had the feeling that he would have to find a job outside Kansas The first stops in search of employment were either Ottawa or Lawrence, where he found no work So the young printer went on to Topeka [44] There after tramping the street for some time, he was hired by Will Scott, foreman at the *Capital* Though reports as to the exact time of his employment vary slightly, his skill as a typesetter soon made his work as compositor more than temporary Thus, shortly after finishing high school, a young, homesick Arthur Capper had climbed another rung in his career [45]

Contemporary records do not carry the embellishments or the dramatic qualities of the oft-repeated story of Capper's search for work Each of the three Garnett newspapers gave brief mention of the departure of the native son All commended his industry and his potential All reported that he left Garnett on June 12, 1884, and that he already had a position on the Topeka *Daily Capital* [46] Perhaps the Topeka position had been located before graduation and some delay took place because of his bout with mumps The complete story is still somewhat of a mystery, but the facts are evident that Arthur Capper, almost nineteen years of age, arrived in Topeka in late spring or early summer of 1884, and obtained work in the composing room of the Topeka *Daily Capital* Topeka would remain his home for the remainder of his life, and he would be profoundly influenced by the *Capital* and would in turn guide its fortunes.

Chapter III
The Young Apprentice

When Arthur Capper came to Topeka in June, 1884, the Kansas capital had grown to a city of 21,901 people, more than ten times the size of Garnett After Leavenworth, Topeka was the largest city in Kansas, and it was inhabited largely by a native-born population About 70 per cent of the total was made up of native-born, white people and about 18 per cent was Negro The foreign-born accounted for the remaining 12 per cent

The Atchison, Topeka and Santa Fe Railway was the town's largest employer, with some seven hundred men working in its shops, and local flour and feed mills accounted for the second largest capital investment in industry The three printing plants were the next largest In June, 1884, at least four daily newspapers and eight weeklies were being published in Topeka and North Topeka [1]

The *Capital* had a circulation of from three to four thousand when young Capper started working in Topeka as a compositor In later years he claimed honorary membership in the Topeka Typographical Union, but there is no record of his regular membership in this group of forty men.[2] Conditions of work on the *Capital* were considered good in spite of the six-day, sixty-hour week Most compositors were paid for piece work, and a competent man might earn from eighteen to nineteen dollars each week A youth of Capper's experience was probably able to earn around fifteen dollars a week, under these conditions Little is known of Capper's experiences in his first six months in Topeka He did room at 322 Kansas Avenue, in the same rooming house occupied by another printer and a clerk He was making more money than he had ever made in his life, but he was not extravagant in spending it He faithfully attended to his job as a printer, but he also indicated an interest in learning about the newspaper business as a whole. Because he already knew shorthand he needed only an opportunity to expand his working knowledge of journalism

In 1880 the Kansas state constitution was amended to prohibit the sale of alcoholic beverages Subsequent legislation to enforce the provisions of the amendment provided for a complicated Prohi-

19

bitory Liquor Law to regulate the manufacture and sale of liquor for medical, scientific, and mechanical purposes Contradictions between state and federal law and the indifference of some law-enforcement agencies made execution of the law difficult

Capper's opportunity to transfer from printing to journalism came when District Judge John Martin spoke from the Shawnee County Courthouse steps, announcing his stand in enforcing the law against "jointists "[3] Tradition reports that Capper, an ardent prohibitionist, attended the meeting and recognized a good story when he saw it So he took shorthand notes, got Martin's approval on quotations, and wrote an account of the speech, which he had printed in the *Capital* the next morning Judge Martin's investigations of alleged violations of prohibition laws found strong approval in the columns of the *Capital*[4] Major J K Hudson, the editor, was profoundly pleased by the article He encouraged Capper to accept a job on the paper as a reporter The new position paid only ten dollars a week, considerably less than his salary as a printer, but prospects for advancement were much brighter So after about six months as a full-time printer, Capper became the cub reporter on the North Topeka run of the Topeka *Daily Capital*[5]

Arthur Capper's entry into journalism came at the time of the general elections of 1884 Association with his father had given him a lively interest in politics Herbert Capper had supported John P St John, the Prohibition candidate for President against major party candidates Blaine and Cleveland, and the outcome of the election caused the elder Capper to defend his vote in a "letter-to-the-editor" series involving the Garnett *Journal* and the *Republican-Plaindealer*[6] There are indications that Herbert Capper's political interests and views had some influence on his son In general, however, the younger Capper would follow a policy that was closer to that of the Republican party

During 1885 new responsibilities came to Arthur Capper with his increasing experience as reporter He was also telegraph editor, and according to his employer he had a "genuine newspaper ability " In June, 1885, he was assigned to the position of city editor of the *Capital*, and had under his guidance two other reporters[7] The local news events were his primary responsibility and his regular news-gathering sources included the Courthouse, the Statehouse, three-

Mrs. Herbert Capper,
Arthur's mother

Courtesy of the Kansas State Historical Society

The Capper children, 1881.
Arthur, Mary May
Edith, Benjamin, Bessie

Left: Florence Crawford and Arthur Capper about the time of their marriage. *Below:* Mr. and Mrs. Arthur Capper about 1913.

Courtesy of the Kansas State Historical Society

justice-of-the-peace courts, Rowley's Drug Store, the police court, the City Hall, the hotels, and the legislative sessions in season [8] As a *Capital* editor young Capper, not yet of voting age, supplied stories to many dailies and weeklies over the state and soon gained a reputation as an accurate and interesting reporter [9] According to a later analysis, "Capper was a good reporter of local news because his ideals were those of the local majority All the manifest destiny of the agricultural civilization of the great Western States he saw as clearly as the humblest clodhopper   The growing national life to which he and those around him gave thought carried their minds in the same conveyance "[10]

The best contemporary records of the activities of young Arthur Capper in 1886 and 1887 are found in the columns of the *Capital* and in the pages of a small personal diary The diary was obviously a partial listing of the activities of the budding journalist, and the *Capital* carried many of the stories that he wrote

Early in 1886 Arthur Capper moved to a room at the E W Longshore residence and he boarded at the Windsor Hotel, where his meals cost him $4 50 each week. His weekly income at the *Capital* was increased from $10 to $15, and his stories, sold to out-of-town newspapers, supplemented his earnings Capper's fixed expenses for food and lodging were about $30 each month, and his income was usually at least twice that amount [11]

With some of his regular earnings young Capper began to speculate in Topeka town lots in a manner similar to his father's speculation in Garnett town property Many Kansas communities were enjoying a boom in real estate values in the late 1880's, and Topeka was no exception New additions were being platted and developed to be offered at rising prices to an increasingly gullible public Perusal of abstract records would indicate that Capper was able to profit through some of his transactions, but the result of his investment in real estate was likely on the debit side, a fact which influenced his later opinions on ownership of real estate for speculative purposes [12] Nevertheless, promising reports came from real estate activities in Topeka A former Garnett citizen, writing from North Topeka to the *Republican-Plaindealer,* told of the real estate boom in the state capital, as a consequence of which, "Politics seemed wholy [sic] lost sight of in the boom excitement "[13] During these years Capper was also buying a share in an investment company, a practice which eventually enabled him to begin his own business

From the time Capper began work at his first job in Topeka until the Spanish-American War the Topeka *Daily Capital* was published every morning of the week except Monday [14] As a result editorial employees did not have regular duties on Sunday, and social activity, though not exclusively reserved for Sundays, was concentrated on the weekend Capper recorded in his diary infrequent attendance at church services on Saturday evening, and at both Sunday morning and evening services On one occasion he visited an afternoon Sabbath school The attraction of church services for the young man in his twenty-first year may have been the young women who attended. He discreetly recorded in Pittman shorthand the names of a Miss Risener, a Miss Johnson, and several others whom he took home from church or from a temperance concert or some such entertainment His reserve may have been due to a stronger interest in Jennie S , with whom he was engaged in serious and prolonged correspondence After she wrote him a thirty-two page letter in June, 1886, he seems to have written her regularly for about a year, and on two occasions he sent books to her.[15]

Sundays for Arthur Capper in 1886 were also his time for writing letters to his mother, his sisters, or his father Saturday night and Sunday would frequently find him at dinner with friends or acquaintances He also moved his residence from one rooming house to another on Sunday, and many of his real estate negotiations were apparently made on either Saturday or Sunday During the summer months part of his week-end holiday might be used for a visit to Turner Garden, for a swim at Garfield Park or in the river, or for a trip over to the west end of town

Topeka was a proud and growing community Horse-drawn street railways which began operation in 1881 seemed to supply the ultimate in speed and accessibility But six years later a steam streetrailway system was established over part of the city, to be shortly replaced by an electrically driven line Capper was proud of his adopted home town and pleased to show it to relatives, such as Uncle Abner McGrew, and Garnett friends He was discovering the variety in a city much larger than the one in which he had spent most of his life The theft of valuables from his boarding house caused him to buy a small revolver [16] His diary contains cryptic shorthand notes showing his acquaintance with the seamy side of life in Topeka His companions in 1886 included Sam Lindsay, when he was in town, Dick Thomas, Jim Heslet, and many of the local reporters, eight of whom were with him for a studio portrait, taken in September, 1886.[17]

As a reporter and city editor Arthur had freedom to enter into many activities that would have been outside the reach of most newly arrived young men He enjoyed his work, in part because of the interesting people with whom he came in contact, and he also liked the creative nature of his job He was well accepted as a House and Senate reporter and, along with other reporters, he was "presented a valise" during the legislative session of 1886 [18] He also enjoyed his excursions to other Kansas towns and soon had personal friends all over the state. His work took him to Bismarck Grove, at Lawrence, to report the address of General John A Logan to a large gathering on a "very hot day "[19] He also reported the Republican convention which followed The meetings of the National Teachers' Convention were held in Topeka in mid-July when Capper "was 21 years old," but he "was too busy to celebrate " When the Republican county convention was held, he attended as a reporter and enthusiastically wrote about Charles Curtis's being unanimously renominated as candidate for Shawnee County Attorney [20] Capper modestly recorded in his diary in shorthand that he had "acted as assistant secretary" at the convention.

When Capper went to Clay Center to report the Fifth Congressional District Convention, the *Capital* fairly bristled with long two and one-half to three and one-half column articles in support of John A Anderson for whom the "enthusiasm . . is simply wonderful " Opposition to Anderson for the Republican nomination was furnished by a district judge usually depicted by Capper as a "drunken bolter." The judge was reported as describing the residents of Wayne, in Republic County, as a "d - - d set of grangers and don't know enough to pound sand in a rat hole."[21] Anderson's successful race for Congress, although Topeka was not in the Fifth District, was a delight to Capper. To his diary he confided on November 2, 1886, "cast my first ballot, which was straight republican "

When the American Woman Suffrage meeting was held in Topeka, with such notables as Susan B Anthony, Mrs E C Stanton, Mrs Belva Lockwood, and Mrs Helen Gougar in attendance, Capper met Mrs Julia Ward Howe, who dictated her speech to the young editor [22] Reports of other Topeka activities, of political speeches, of the dedication of Snow Hall in Lawrence, and of the State Sanitary Convention in Wichita, consumed much of his remaining time as a journalist for the year

On May 20, 1886, Arthur Capper went "down to Lawrence . . and found [a] house for [his] folks " The Herbert Capper family then moved to Lawrence from California, where they had been for a while [23] Late in November Arthur sent his father "groceries to the amount of $15," and the freight added another $2 25 No explanation was given for this deed, although it may be conjectured that a dutiful son was helping out a father who no longer had a regular source of income [24] The following summer young Bennie Capper died of typhoid fever at the Capper home at 1228 Ohio Street in Lawrence Burial was in Garnett, where the Capper family were guests of their old friends the L K Kirk family [25] Sometime later Herbert Capper returned his family to Garnett, where they re-established their residence

During this early period as an editor of the *Capital,* Arthur Capper served as correspondent for many out-of-town newspapers A partial list would include the Boston *Globe,* the *Missouri Republican,* the Denver *Tribune,* the St Louis *Post-Dispatch,* many of the Kansas newspapers, and eventually the Kansas City *Star* [26] During some months in 1886 and 1887 Capper earned as much from his reporting for outside newspapers as he did for one or two weeks at his *Capital* job [27]

On July 26, 1886, Arthur Capper confided in shorthand to his diary that "F P Baker offered me $20 per week to work for him "[28] He did not accept Baker's offer, and by late August he recorded, "Salary raised to $20 per week " Slightly more than a year later it was increased to $25 per week, but sometimes he was late in getting his expected pay [29]

Throughout his life Arthur Capper enjoyed excellent health, and the year 1886 was not an exception In August, just before leaving on his vacation trip he got some medicine from a doctor He went to a dentist in late September, "who said tooth would have to be pulled,

24

but [Capper] backed out " A week later he went to another dentist, "and had tooth cured "30

His vacation in 1886 was spent visiting old friends in Anderson County, where he stayed at the farm of Phil Hicks There he helped with haying and threshing and went swimming and hunting He visited the county fair and saw a show at the Garnett "opera house with N P " He also visited at Ft Scott and in Linn County before his return to Topeka 31

By mid-1887, Capper, now an ambitious youth of twenty-two, was looking for new worlds to conquer The Stevens County representative in the state legislature, John L Pancoast, wanted an editor for a Republican newspaper in Hugoton, in southwest Kansas Stevens County was just being settled, and all of the other county newspapers favored the Democratic party Moreover, the selection of a permanent county seat, an issue between Hugoton and its rival Woodsdale, promoted by Colonel Sam N Wood, would be a prize tantamount to riches for the promoters of the successful community Most county-seat "wars" in Kansas were settled peacefully at the polls But in Stevens County the state militia was twice mobilized, and five men, including Colonel Wood, were eventually to lose their lives in the bloodiest county-seat war in Kansas 32

So Capper went to Hugoton to look into Pancoast's offer After leaving the Santa Fe at Hartland, he took a stage south through Grant County to Hugoton 33 Although the ponies pulling the stage on this fifty-mile trip broke away and left the travelers temporarily stranded, the party reached Hugoton by sunset It was a raw frontier town, with visitors and new arrivals so numerous that their names were no longer listed in the newspaper 34 Pancoast was offering Capper a newspaper at no cost The young editor also met Wood, who understood the purpose of his trip from Topeka, and he was told of the many disadvantages of pioneering a newspaper in the county As remembered later, by Capper, he left Hugoton and "Without making a final decision, I got a bus back to Hartland On the way we passed through Cincinnatus, in Grant County, the rival of Ulysses for county seat The principal building in the town was a saloon and as we stopped to water our horses three cowboys came riding up with fractious cow horses and rode right into the door of the saloon to have their drinks served "35

This boisterous frontier experience ended Capper's intention of becoming the editor of the Hugoton *Hermes,* which published its first issue on August 12, 1887 [36] So he returned to Topeka from southwest Kansas, and it was almost twenty-five years before he was again in that area

Capper's work on the *Capital* gave him an increasing reputation among Kansans during the next few years His "clear, concise and complete report of the 1889 Legislature" helped to establish him in Kansas [37] An employee of later years reported that Capper possessed the faculty "of carefully approximating the measure of credulity the public mind will sustain "[38] Gomer Davies, the Murdocks, the Becks, and many other newspapermen were among his acquaintances of this period J K Hudson, the owner of the *Capital,* was actively promoting his Highland Park real estate project after 1887, and he was soon in financial difficulties So the business was transferred in 1890 to a joint-stock enterprise, the Topeka Capital Company Capper became a director of the new corporation, and during the next two years also the owner of twenty shares of stock with a reputed par value of $500 per share [39] In 1894, when he had already embarked on other newspaper ventures, Capper owned forty-two shares representing about 8 per cent of the stock in the company When the Topeka Capital Company went bankrupt in 1895, he doubtless lost heavily on his investment [40]

The boom in Kansas town lots and rural real estate, as well as agricultural prosperity, came to a more or less abrupt end in the late 1880's General business conditions reflected the lack of success on Kansas farms Bad growing years were accompanied by foreclosed mortgages, increased business failure, and political discontent Railroad construction of new lines, which had reached a peak for Kansas in the year 1888 with more than two thousand miles built, declined to a mere forty-two miles of new track in 1890 The only recourse, to many Kansans, was through political power to overthrow the economic and political evils of the time

The People's party, which emerged as the legitimate offspring of previous reform movements, became a national third party for the presidential election in 1892 Its Kansas roots were found in a weak Greenback party of the early eighties and in the Farmers' Alliance, not established as a state-wide organization until 1888. Its surprising strength was shown in 1890 when Farmers' Alliance candidates captured five of the seven Kansas Congressional seats and the lower house of the state legislature John J Ingalls, with a growing reputation of forgetting the farmer through his three terms as United States Senator, was turned out, and William Peffer, editor of the *Kansas Farmer,* was elected to that post by the legislature

The Republican party retained Capper's loyalty during this period He served in minor party positions in Shawnee County and learned the characteristics of political-party organization at the precinct, county, and state level In the late 1880's he became secretary of the Kansas Republican League Because of this position he wrote many Republican leaders over the nation, and he received encouraging replies Senator John J Ingalls had responded to a Capper letter by indicating concern over a prospective political upheaval in Kansas He wrote Capper, "I wish you would favor me with letters occasionally, giving me your impression about matters generally in different parts of the State "[41]

Capper's interest in national and Kansas political figures proved an incentive to develop an autograph collection He may have been interested in this hobby as early as his last year in high school, when he wrote John Greenleaf Whittier and received a photograph and letter in reply The following year he received replies from John Robinson, Kansas' first Secretary of State, and from former Associate Justice David Davis of the United States Supreme Court Indiana Senator Benjamin Harrison responded in 1887 to a Capper letter conveying the wish of a Republican club that the Senator should be a candidate for Vice President Harrison, in typical fashion, said that he wanted to "return to the Senate "[42] After this small beginning Capper's hobby of collecting autographs and eventually autographed pictures was to ebb and flow and ultimately to grow stronger because of increasing contacts with the great and near-great

Physically Arthur Capper was now five feet eight inches tall, and he weighed between 125 and 130 pounds, a weight that hardly varied throughout his life Although "more sedentary . . than athletic," he traveled around Topeka in the late 1880's and early 1890's by bicycle [43] He rode his bicycle to Colorado on one trip, but he was too busy to go fishing with his friends [44]

A kind of paradox in the Capper character in his later life was a mild and reserved manner coupled with an active life as a party-goer He enjoyed dancing, card playing, and the company of attractive women, and most stories indicate that these pleasures were a part of his life as a young man His Topeka friends were delighted with his company, and he was a frequent guest at Topeka social affairs in the 1880's

After "playing the field" for half a dozen years, Capper became increasingly attracted to Florence, the beautiful and talented daughter of former Governor and Mrs Samuel J Crawford Florence had been born in Topeka, July 1, 1868, while her father was in his second term as Governor Her brother, George Marshall Crawford, was four years younger, and a student at Yale in the early nineties She had grown up in Emporia, Washington, D C, and in Topeka She attended public schools and the Episcopalian College of the Sisters of Bethany in Topeka, private schools in Washington, and the Conservatory of Music in Boston Florence played the piano, the harp, and other stringed instruments, and had a pleasant singing voice Somewhat frail in appearance, the blond Miss Crawford was a social favorite in the Kansas capital She was the epitome of a proper young lady of the American Victorian era Since she came from a family of increasing wealth, the thought of doing household chores or the necessity of engaging in productive labor had hardly ever entered her pretty head

Florence and Arthur reached an understanding in June of 1891 Both would have their birthday anniversaries the following month when she would be twenty-three and he would be twenty-six But Arthur was due to take a "post-graduate" course in journalism and their marriage would have to be delayed Their separation from each other during the next eight months was viewed at the time as a major tragedy In reality this crisis in the Crawford-Capper romance has proved a great boon in the reconstruction of their story, for they both kept a daily journal during the months they were apart, and these diaries disclose day-by-day events in their busy young lives

Chapter IV

New Horizons

From June, 1891, to May, 1892, Arthur Capper traveled in various eastern states, worked on a New York newspaper, and served as a Congressional reporter in Washington These new opportunities in journalism and adventure in travel produced impressions which were to have a lasting effect on the young Kansan Capper was not alone in going to a large city to obtain new ideas about his profession Many in journalism and in other vocations had advanced their occupational standing through similar experiences [1]

Capper's absence from Topeka was also a time of testing for his romance with Florence Crawford They were not separated during the entire ten and one-half months, however, for Florence went east with her mother in September, 1891, and Arthur shared a week with them at Nantucket Island She was also in Washington near the end of his stay in the East.

Descriptions of this period in Capper's life have often exaggerated the opening of new vistas for the young journalist Though he was traveling into some new territory, he had been in the East before and had lived in New Jersey for almost a year Furthermore, plans for his journalistic experiences were much fuller than is assumed in the usual stories Arrangements were made for letters of reference to help open doors in New York

Topeka and Garnett newspapers recorded his departure, the longest article, in the *Capital,* was copied by the Garnett *Eagle* "Arthur Capper left Friday for the east He will be gone eight to twelve months and expects to work a portion of the time in New York From that city he will go to Boston and then to Washington, during the session of Congress, where he will act as Washington correspondent of the Capital A party of his lady and gentlemen friends bid him good bye at the train "[2]

Upon his departure on June 19, Florence gave Arthur a small journal, or diary When aboard the train he wrote, "It will be one of my dearest treasures and her request that I write in it daily will be faithfully observed "[3] Florence also promised to write every evening in a similar book Her journal, completed in 192 pages, and Arthur's, 134 pages long, lay almost forgotten for many years among other

29

books in the Capper library Their contents provide a glimpse of the lives of Florence and Arthur which is more complete and intimate than any comparable record of any other time in their lives Their journals, though unique to them, contain romantic passages characteristic of the "Gay Nineties"

Capper's immediate destination upon his departure from Topeka was Chicago, where his father "was reported to be dangerously ill"[4] He "found father much better" and attended church services the next morning with his mother[5] His mother asked "a great many questions about Florence She says she fears she will be a little bit jealous," but he thought he had "nearly convinced her that Florence is the loveliest of girls" His comment on retiring at nine that evening was "pretty early for this boy"[6]

From Chicago Capper visited Detroit for the first time, and he went on to Niagara Falls and Toronto before his journey took him to New York City, where he arrived eight days after his departure from Topeka He marveled at "the swift flowing streams of clear water, the wooded hills, the lovely valleys" near Ann Arbor But he could not help comparing the Toronto "street cars . pulled around by one horse" with "Topeka's fine electric road," or the Canadian city's "dingy tumbledown" governmental buildings "which would be a disgrace as a court house for a Kansas county seat"[7] He reported to a Garnett newspaper that he "enjoyed the sight of Niagara more than all else," and that the New York State Capitol was the "grandest building" he had ever seen[8]

Capper's arrival in the "great city" of New York somewhat bewildered him, and he was disappointed in finding no mail from Florence He located a room at 47 West 12th Street and soon began to use his letters of introduction He accidentally met an old acquaintance when he went to Brooklyn to hear Dr T DeWitt Talmage, whose sermons were published each week in Garnett and Topeka newspapers[9]

Capper's first two weeks in New York City were taken up with visits to business offices, to a large number of newspaper establishments, calls upon prominent New Yorkers, and in general sightseeing He also visited the New York Press Club, the headquarters of the Republican League, the offices of the American Press Association, a big "Tammany demonstration in Tammany hall," and the

Y M C A , and attended services at Dr Lyman Abbott's Plymouth Church in Brooklyn [10]

Some of his experiences were reported in the Topeka *Daily Capital,* and Mrs Mary Hudson, the wife of his employer, encouraged him to continue sending letters for publication although she was disappointed that he had not put in more of his personal experiences She warned him that many Kansans believed his trip was a mistake [11]

Also in Topeka Florence Crawford was writing in her journal that "the feeling of desolation and loss that now and then comes over me is almost unbearable " She wrote that she "felt absolutely sick since he left   Why did he leave me when we were so happy together " She also voiced her disappointment because the mails were so slow, but she kept busy going to Ottawa by train, riding around Topeka behind Billy, the family horse, meeting with her book club, attending card parties, "shopping with Mamma," and going "down street" for a walk or a visit [12]

Florence did "not want to do anything that would seem untrue to Arthur," but her close friend, Madge Johnson, and others insisted that she must not drop out of the social activities of the "crowd "[13] So her gentleman escort varied with the occasion, and it was "one thing after another" until she would almost invariably begin her journal entry, "Am so tired tonight   ." Some four months later she re-read her diary and wrote, "I have only known since returning home how very near I came to being seriously ill " According to her doctor's diagnosis, she was "very near to having nervous prostration from going out and keeping late hours so much "[14]

Florence was alarmed when Dick Lindsay told her that "he didn't see how Capper dared go away and leave a girl he was engaged to " If that had happened to him "he would be sure to see some other girl he liked better " Florence responded in her journal by writing, "Now I have perfect confidence in Arthur & know he and Mr Lindsay are not at all alike, but nevertheless I did not feel any the better for the remark "[15]

At times Florence told her journal of an unwillingness to be patient with her many friends Madge Johnson had stayed all night and did not go home until nearly noon the next day Florence "had just commenced a letter to Arthur when Mabel [Johnson] came It seems," she wrote, "as if people just hang around the corner until I commence a letter to him, then all rush in "[16]

For Florence the high point of the first month of "marking time" after Arthur had gone to New York came with the arrival of an engagement diamond [17] Her journal for the next few days shows an extensive use of such words as "pleasant," "beautiful day," and "long delightful talk" Her faith in Arthur had been vindicated by a positive display of his affection for her

On July 10, 1891, Arthur Capper was "put   on for trial" at the New York *Tribune* City Editor Arthur Bowers tried to discourage Capper and assigned him to "a meeting in the West Shore saloon on the West Side about the New York Central tracks" His report was "cut down to about a stickfull "[18]

In the next few weeks Capper had many new experiences and was learning about the operation of a large, successful, metropolitan paper He had his first Sunday work on a newspaper, and he also served on the "night watch" He "traveled all over town" interviewing people about the International Copyright law He wrote in his journal that he "got up a pretty long article and took it to one of the editors who cut it all to pieces right before my eyes It came out Sunday morning however in pretty good shape, and was in a good position "[19]

After a variety of reporting duties during his first two weeks with the *Tribune,* Capper had an experience on July 25 which is legendarily recalled as his "first" assignment with that New York newspaper His comments to his journal that evening were "Today I was sent out to report a yacht race I first thought I had better resign and go back to Kansas I knew nothing about a yacht and hadn't the least idea how to make a report of the race I made a bluff at it, however and got along pretty well I expected to have the editor turn me over, but my report went through all right"

Early in August the Crawford family journeyed to Nantucket Island for vacation On the way Arthur and Florence were together two days in New York Time passed so swiftly that Florence did not even write of the events of the day Afterwards she did write, "Oh, how I hated to see Arthur go again "[20] His record for the same day includes the comment that the "separation from her is my only misfortune "[21]

For the next month, while Florence was in Nantucket and Arthur in New York, they were again separated and their only contact was once more an expected letter every other day Florence slept like "a second Rip Van Winkle" near the ocean She read and enjoyed sailing, swimming, playing cards, pool, and tennis She expected one Sunday to be dull, but it passed pleasantly, because she got a letter and that made her "happy the whole day" One of her pastimes was teasing another guest at the cottage where the Crawfords were staying Florence wrote, "I know I have guyed her fearfully we girls simply could not help it   "22

During the same period Arthur was witnessing a "test of the Sims-Edison torpedo" He also went on the Schnorer Club excursion, with "about 500 Dutchmen on board, and about 100 kegs of beer It was about the most hilarious crowd I ever struck" He met President Harrison's train and "wrote up a half column for the Tribune" He also reported the Park Place disaster for five days in late August and followed that by serving for a week as the city editor's secretary 23

On September 12 Capper found "Governor Crawford at the Gilsey House," and they left for Nantucket the following day 24 Florence wrote speculatively, "Those two—papa and Arthur—are on the Fall River streamer now They are sitting on the deck, papa with his feet on the railing smoking and doing all the talking, Arthur listening, quiet but taking it all in "25 The "delightful week" passed so quickly that "days seemed like hours, and hours like minutes "26 Arthur kept no day-to-day record of his Nantucket vacation, but Florence wrote, "This afternoon Arthur & I went to the mill and then to an outlook on Orange Street In the evening we went to the Nantucket House & looked at the ocean" Again she reported that they went "down to see the Gay Head come in this evening & afterwards went up to the Cliffs just for the walk "27 For her the days while Arthur was there were "going altogether too fast" She confided to her diary that she had come to "grudge each minute as it passes by—wish it was an hour long—but only a day or two now and things will be running the old way—Arthur in New York and I in New Haven, Boston or some place far from him" Governor Crawford left for Washington on September 17 and George had earlier returned to Yale Florence and her mother went back to New York with Arthur, so that the date of their separation was delayed until Sunday, September 20, after attendance at a concert in Madison Square Garden [28] For the next two weeks Florence and her mother visited in New England and in Washington, and then they returned to their home in Topeka

Capper was again on the job with the *Tribune* He visited Gettysburg with a Tammany regiment, he "was sent up to Ex-President Cleveland's house   to write up the new baby," and he spent a number of days on the police bureau staff He had an extensive report on a disastrous fire and wrote in his journal that the "city editor complimented me on my write up of the Belmont fire I had made an error for which I expected to be criticized and was very much surprised when instead he spoke highly" During his last month on the staff of the *Tribune* he interviewed such well-known persons as James A Blaine and Mrs Russell Sage, and he was sent to interview Major William McKinley but did not see him He also wrote an extensive article on "registration frauds" just before the election When his work on the *Tribune* ended he was glad to be "through with New York" and regretted that he could not return immediately to Topeka [29]

From New York City Capper visited old friends in New Jersey, then he traveled to Boston, where he made new acquaintances among newspapermen and refreshed old ones He did some sightseeing in the Boston area, and he attended church services conducted by Phillips Brooks, but he was most impressed by the Thanksgiving dinner for newsboys in Faneuil Hall [30]

Since Congress was about to convene, Capper hurriedly visited George M Crawford at Yale, spent another day in New York, and arrived in Washington on December 1, 1891 He quickly found many Kansans in the national capital and within three days had sent his first dispatches by telegraph to the *Capital* and the *Tribune* [31]

Because of contemporary political developments in Kansas, the owners of the Topeka *Daily Capital* were willing to go to extraordinary expense in maintaining a Washington correspondent during the 1891-92 session of Congress For the first time in the state's history a majority of the Kansas delegation was "other than republican representatives," and the Republican *Capital* was anxious to depose them [32] Results of the United States Census of 1890 also justified an additional Congressional seat for Kansas in 1892, and Republican strategists believed that the surest way to pick up that and other seats was to expose their Alliance or People's party representatives to a full public gaze The mild-mannered and seemingly innocuous Arthur Capper was the logical choice to harass the Alliance "lion" in its lair

Acknowledging this position in general terms, the *Capital* was proud to announce that "Kansas readers are especially interested in the proceedings at Washington this winter by reason of the new role played by the state in national affairs In view of the peculiar position of our representatives the CAPITAL will cover the proceedings of congress, with special reference to the interests of Kansas, more fully than any other paper in the west The special dispatches and daily correspondence from the CAPITAL's Washington representative justify the assertion that from no other newspaper can Kansas readers keep fully informed of the course of the Kansas delegation "[33]

Capper began his service as a Washington correspondent believing that the job would be over in two months Privately he objected to further separation from Florence even for a short time [34]

As a *Capital* correspondent Capper "saw for the first time a session of Congress open It was one of the most interesting scenes" he had ever witnessed [35] Two days later he attended his first session of the United States Senate and considered it "a treat to be brought face to face with great men like Sherman, Allison, Quay, and dozens others "[36]

An interesting but sad chain of experiences for Capper began on December 17, when he "went with Senator [Preston B] Plumb to call on President Harrison at his reception room in the white house and chatted with him pleasantly for ten minutes or more "[37] Two days later while playing cards at Governor Crawford's the talk around the table was "about Senator Plumb for vice president "[38] The following day, after he had gone "on a bicycle to soldiers home for a ride," he "learned of the death of Senator Plumb " Although severely shocked by the loss, Capper "was busy sending the news to the Capital " At the time his dispatch of more than three thousand words was the longest ever sent by wire to the Topeka newspaper [39]

During the following week he wrote for both the *Tribune* and the *Capital* speculative articles about a successor for Senator Plumb [40] He was happy to receive word from Harold Chase, editor of the *Capital,* that "Major Hudson will probably be appointed Senator "[41]

His elation over the prospective appointment was turned to disappointment when he learned that former Congressman Bishop W Perkins, of Parsons, was appointed to the unexpired term

The young Kansas newspaperman was also introduced to Washington society Loyalty to his native state and concern for Florence were reflected in his journal entry He wrote, "I don't like it Too rich for me Kansas is good enough for me "[42]

Florence was writing Arthur that she did not want to wait much longer for his return After almost seven months of separation in 1891 Major Hudson was not inclined to satisfy her heart's desire, because he was asking Capper to remain in Washington throughout the session of Congress Before that decision both Florence and Arthur seemed to feel that his service outside Topeka would end by early February, 1892 She became apprehensive and almost melancholy when her father wrote that Arthur was not well She could "think of nothing else" and she had "almost a stifled feeling" about his illness She wrote her private thoughts in her journal "Oh I don't like to care so much for one person—it is dangerous to place all your happiness in the life of one person for should anything happen the wreck would be complete I who in all my life have been so selfish & regardless of others—who always thought I would never love any man —now to give up so entirely & to feel that life is only worth living if it is to be with that one man I hope—I pray that Heaven will be kind to me & let me have sorrows—if sorrows I must have—of all other kinds & spare to me that one person who is so very very much to me "[43]

In spite of his illness, which proved to be no worse than a bad cold and an infected tooth, Florence was "downright angry with Arthur" because she had not received a letter for four and a half days [44] The indecision on Arthur's time in Washington and the fact that only ten pages remained in her journal caused her to lose interest in writing every night until his return She did record the day's crowded events, but on February 19 she arrived at the "last page in this old book " Her record covered a span of eight months, and it ended on a less "desperate feeling" than the one with which she had written the first page But neither was it the "happy joyful feeling" she had anticipated Realizing that she was not "a very calm patient girl," Florence was ready to complain The journal closed with a

Above: Capper Building in 1919, just after the wing to the left was completed.
Below: Capper residence at 1035 Topeka Boulevard, completed in 1910.

Courtesy of the Capper Foundation

Above: In Washington, 1924.

Below: At Wichita, June 1, 1925.

Courtesy of the Kansas State Historical Society

plaintive note, for she wrote, "I ask Heaven—oh so earnestly to guard him & keep him safe & well & bring him back to me the same honest —true *lover* that he was when he left Topeka so long ago "[45]

Capper's journal, with many shorter items, was continued for ten days after Florence had written her last entry He recorded his desire to return to Topeka in spite of his exciting surroundings in Washington He enjoyed talking politics with members of the Kansas delegation and with Governor Crawford He also talked "to Governor Crawford about having Florence and Mrs Crawford come to Washington," but Crawford did not seem interested [46] He attended all kinds of social functions and spent much time on his bicycle An interesting assignment was recorded when he "Spent a good part of the day hunting up the facts about Jerry Simpson's spelling "[47] The *Capital* stories which he wrote on the basis of this and prior research castigated the spelling of "Sockless Jerry" as "a disgrace to Kansas and its schools " According to Capper, "There are members of Congress from Texas who cannot spell, and there are one or two members from Missouri who are anything but experts in penmanship, but Jerry Simpson is the only one who can neither write nor spell "[48]

Since Congressman Simpson had a secretary who could type correctly, Capper was citing only the endorsement written on a bill introduced by "Sockless Jerry " The worst example he found was the bill, "For the releef of certin Setlers within what was formly the Forte Doge military Reservation in Foord county, Kansas, and to conferm entrees of Public Lands Eroneonly allowed thareon "[49] "Jerry Simpson," Capper wrote in his journal, "is wild again about my article in the Capital and they say he is on the war path Its glorious fun "[50] Much comment in Kansas newspapers came from Capper's attack, and Simpson had the bill producing the fireworks withdrawn [51]

During the remaining days in February, Capper conscientiously made entries in his journal On February 26 he wrote "I wonder if Florence has any idea how lonesome I am tonight I wonder if we really must be separated until next summer I don't see how I can bear it that long I wish I could tell her tonight how much I love her I must write to her, now that I cannot see her, to make me a promise "[52]

Only three more days followed for Capper's journal His unintentional final entry came with the end of February No doubt he was influenced by the fact that Florence had completed her journal ten days earlier, but he may have been apprised that Florence was coming to Washington after all

By late March Florence had convinced her mother of the importance of their presence in Washington, and they left by rail for the national capital Rare notice is given of social gatherings which linked the Crawford-Capper names [53] But Washington in springtime, even before the time of cherry blossoms at the Tidal Basin, had many attractions for young lovers

In fulfilling his duty to the *Capital* Capper wrote long, gossipy stories of Kansas' calamity-howling Congressmen Ben Clover and Jerry Simpson were unwilling recipients of Capper's rapier-like thrusts After Clover had failed to vote on an important free-coinage bill which lost because of a tie, Capper reported that the Congressman was asleep on a sofa When Clover saw the story, he "was boiling over with rage" at his colleague, Simpson, not at the *Capital* correspondent To Capper he said, "Yes, that's one of that fellow Simpson's stories "

"Simpson—what Simpson?" asked the correspondent

"Why Jerry Simpson He's been sending out all sorts of lies about me and this is one of them I heard that he said he was glad I lost my vote on the silver bill and that it would make trouble for me "[54]

To put into the public record the "Bad Blood" between Clover and Simpson, Capper wrote a long story which began "All is not lovely in the alliance family Peace and harmony and brotherly love dwelleth not therein Jerry Simpson and Ben Clover do not speak as they pass by It is no common, little, every-day jangle, but a first-class row, which is mighty serious now and getting more serious every day. It started three or four weeks ago and grows worse and worse, and has got to that point where the [participants] say real mean things of each other "[55]

Capper also reported that the two Alliance adherents no longer stayed at the same boarding house, for Simpson had

engaged rooms at another house on the opposite side of the street Every day for a month past, Simpson, returning from the halls of congress, has been walking down the west side of the street while Clover walked down the east side, but each would snub the other as thoroughly as he would snub one of the plutocrats of Wall street This week it got so bad that Clover said he would not live on the same street with Simpson and accordingly he hunted another boarding house a few blocks northeast of the capitol, to which place he moved his baggage yesterday The friends of the two gentlemen will prevent bloodshed if possible [56]

To the readers of the *Capital* and many other Kansas newspapers Congressman Clover was pictured as a dim-witted, lackluster "clod " The Arkansas City *Traveler,* in taking the cue, stated that Ben Clover, whose post office was only twenty-eight miles from Arkansas City, "doesn't know what he wants, and if he did, he would be asleep when the final issue came "[57]

Jerry Simpson, on the other hand, was presented as a shrewd and calculating schemer, who had little use for the folks back home A report was made that Jerry Simpson did not want the Cherokee "strip opened this spring because all the calamity howlers in his district would leave the state, and consequently cause his defeat."[58] An effort was made to show that Simpson was doing very little to earn his munificent $5,000 annual salary and that he was spending most of his time riding his bicycle around Washington. It was not only his bicycle that classified him as a "dude" to many of his constituents, for the *Capital* later reported that "Jerry Simpson's new spring outfit makes the Washington dudes green with envy He came out last Sunday with kid gloves, a dazzling necktie, striped trousers and a very pretty walking stick Jerry is known in Washington as one of the neatest and best dressers in Congress "[59]

Whether the *Capital* had an influence on the 1892 elections is doubtful Though the Republicans gained an additional Congressman with the increase in Kansas Representatives, the Populists were able to hold their own, since they elected the Kansas presidential electors, captured the Statehouse, dominated the legislature, and named their own candidate to an unexpired term in the United States Senate [60] Perhaps the *Capital* did not keep Capper in Washington long enough, or more likely, the *Capital,* even though it printed 100,000 extra copies during the campaign, could do nothing to change the course of Kansas politics in 1892.

Capper did not stay in Washington during the entire session of Congress His return to Topeka on May 4 had followed that of Florence and her mother by only a few days [61] Erroneously the Kansas

City *Star* reported that "Arthur Capper and Florence Crawford, .
were quietly married in Washington, Monday," May 2 [62] Three days
later, in a retraction, the *Star* said, "Arthur Capper and Miss Florence Crawford have not been married The report was sent West in
a private telegram by a Washington young man as a 'joke' to a mutual acquaintance of the parties in Kansas City The young chump
who sent the telegram is no doubt laughing heartily at his 'joke,' but
he will change his tune when the fool killer gets him "[63]

The report of a Crawford-Capper marriage was premature by
only a half year Although Arthur was absent from Topeka obtaining
political news for the *Capital* for the 1892 campaign, he and Florence
were together a good deal of the time Announcement of the approaching marriage was made after the general election, and the
wedding of Florence Crawford and Arthur Capper on December 1,
1892, was listed as ' foremost in this week's society calendar."[64] The
ceremony, a "charming affair," was held in the home of the bride's
parents before 150 guests [65] The main floor of the residence was
decorated with "huge palms," and "Watson's orchestra" was on hand
to lend gaiety [66]

One report of the wedding stated that the "bride and groom stood
in the bay-window of the drawing room Suspended above them was
a yoke of white chrysanthemums and pink roses .

"Although the invitation announced 'no presents,' the gifts .
were numerous and costly."[67]

The young couple left on the "midnight train for Texas," where
they spent a week at the "Beach House situated on the gulf and two
miles from town" (Galveston) Florence marveled at "the leaves on
the trees and flowers in bloom [so that] it seemed hard to realize that
it was not June "[68] Upon their return they made their home in the
big Crawford mansion There they were honored with a reception,
just before Christmas, which was attended by 200 persons

Kansas in the 1890's was undergoing a profound social, economic,
and political revolution The comic-opera "Legislative War" of 1893
held the attention of much of the Kansas press One comment was
"The Legislative situation at Topeka suggests a new use for Kansas
avenue, too wide for a street and hardly wide enough for a cornfield,
it would make a fairly roomy battlefield "[69] Economic hardship in
Kansas, where drought had already taken a toll, was increasingly

serious Populist agitators and "calamity-howlers" were frequently speaking from sad experience about distressing economic conditions According to the State Bank Commission, "Kansas banks had lost 50 per cent of their deposits" between April and October, 1893 [70]

Following his marriage to Florence Crawford, Capper continued to work for the *Capital,* but he was also looking around for a newspaper he could buy By September 1, 1893, his paid-up stock in Shawnee Building and Loan had a cash value of $1,000, and he planned to use that to purchase a newspaper [71]

Of the many weekly newspapers in Topeka, Capper was most attracted to the Topeka *Mail,* published in North Topeka He began negotiations with Frank Root, editor and owner, and under a contract, dated September 21, 1893, he bought the business, stock, and material and other property for $2,500 [72] Capper borrowed $1,000 from Peter Smith, North Topeka banker, to make his down payment [73]

On the whole the Topeka *Mail* looked like a "good buy" to Capper With 1,650 subscribers claimed, the *Mail* reputedly possessed the largest weekly newspaper circulation within the county [74] The purchase price was also within reach of his immediate and possible sources of revenue He was proud of the fact that he obtained his first newspaper with his own financial resources Neither at this time nor in subsequent business dealings did he rely on the financial backing of his father-in-law, Samuel J Crawford [75]

Arthur Capper took over the weekly Topeka *Mail* after its issue of September 22, 1893 He was "editor, reporter, advertising manager, pressman, mailer, and man of all work," and he employed only two people [76] At the age of twenty-seven, his dreams of a newspaper empire, if they existed, were smothered under the endless detail and ever-present deadlines of a small weekly While politics continued as an important avocation his political ambitions were waylaid by the demands that required his immediate attention Always a hard worker, capable of long hours of concentrated mental labor, Capper was determined to succeed with his Topeka *Mail* He had undergone nine years of extensive and varied training in journalism since graduation from high school, and such experience would become increasingly rewarding

Chapter V

The Emerging Publisher

Twentieth-century Kansas journalism has been described as following a "trend from rags to riches."[1] Journalism's period of "rags," the last half of the nineteenth century, was a time of relatively easy admission to the fraternity of newspaperdom. Equipment was not expensive or complicated, and almost any tramp printer, with a "shirt-tail full of type," could start a small newspaper. In 1889 Kansas had 733 weekly newspapers, a banner year for all time. Altogether approximately 4,500 Kansas newspapers have seen the light of day in a little more than a century.[2] But the mortality rate, as with newspapers elsewhere, has been extremely high. Towns that once had as many as three or four newspapers no longer exist. Most Kansas communities of the latter half of the twentieth century have become one-newspaper towns, or rely on printed news from neighboring communities.

The owner of a struggling newspaper, even in the nineteenth century, often would sell his mailing-list and "good will" to a rival to escape the legal necessity of repaying subscribers for unexpired subscriptions. In an age of general business integration many newspaper consolidations were made in this manner.[3]

The *Mail*, as a weekly political and general newspaper, had a fair circulation throughout Shawnee County, but Capper hoped to do better. He wrote in his first issue that "there is a field in Shawnee, the best county in Kansas, and in Topeka, the best city in Kansas, for a first-class weekly paper,—one that is attractive and always reliable in its news columns, out-spoken and sincere in its editorial utterances, and unceasing in its devotion to the interests of the constituency it attempts to represent."[4]

With his initial issue of the *Mail* Capper instituted changes that were readily apparent. The first page, except for one small display advertisement, was made up like a daily with its one-column headlines. Capper had "no exuberant assurances to make as to its future." He preferred to have his efforts judged on performance rather than promise. He knew there was "no royal road to newspaper success,"

42

and he had hopes of making the best possible newspaper through "hard work and honest endeavor "[5]

The last page of Capper's first issue of the *Mail* had a large display advertisement from Crosby Brothers, a retail dry-goods store then located in the 500 block on Kansas Avenue Years later, after Crosby's had paid him more than one-quarter million dollars for advertising in various publications, Capper remembered the elation he had felt from obtaining this first large advertisement He said, "I was determined to have an ad from that firm It was my first attempt to sell advertising I made the best talk that was in me " And he sold the advertisement for twenty dollars, which was enough to pay "for all the paper and all the ink in the entire edition" and have something left over for office rent [6]

The *Mail* was recognized favorably throughout the state and somewhat boastfully Capper wrote "If pleasant notices in the state press made a success of a newspaper the *Mail* would surely be on the top wave in a very short time We might fill up a page with favorable comments by the newspaper boys but   the merchants of Topeka are demanding all the space we can spare "[7]

New features were used to promote circulation Prominent Kansans were asked to write about their experiences at the Chicago World's Fair Some attention was given to agricultural topics, even at this time, but the *Mail* was centered largely on local news and on politics, of the Republican flavor [8]

The political situation in Kansas in the 1890's was fluid, exciting, almost hectic, compared with the steady, almost complete dominance of the Republican leadership during the earlier years of statehood The Farmers' Alliance in the election of 1890 won important victories in state and national elections Similar Alliance strength was shown in many county elections In the 1892 election their successors, the Populists, captured the vote for the Kansas presidential electors, as well as the governorship Their dominance in the state legislature was reduced, although they controlled the Senate The Panic of 1893 aided the Republican cause in 1894, when Populists were ousted from most major Congressional and state positions But in 1896 Kansas again was a major Populist stronghold, and William Jennings Bryan obtained the state's ten electoral votes

The election of Republican, Populist, Republican, Populist, and

Republican Governors in that order through the 1890's resulted in a display of increasingly partisan tempers in the state's press Wholesale changes were made throughout the ranks of the state's civil service after every election This situation, with its frequent changes in personnel, provoked an "inability of either side to discuss the problems of the day without recourse to abuse and vilification "[9]

Capper participated in the partisan activity of the 1890's and shared responsibility in attempts to ridicule Alliance or Populist political activity As an avowed partisan he could have intentionally disregarded the actions of the opposition party, but to ignore them was not in keeping with journalism of that day Politics not only was an avocation but also had a bearing on his business enterprise

To Capper the changing format of his newspaper and increased advertising revenues were dependent on increasing circulation He actively sought, through appeals to the farmers of Shawnee County, new support for his venture Moreover, a close connection with the Republican party, which dominated Shawnee County politics, enabled the *Mail* to become the official county paper, with expectation of future income through publication of legal notices [10]

Other editors began to compliment Capper's work on the *Mail* as one of the conspicuous successes in Kansas journalism In laudatory fashion, a well-known newspaperman wrote·

The same intelligent and earnest effort would have secured the same result in any other city where a reasonable excuse existed for a newspaper Arthur Capper's methods are those of a legitimate publisher He is honest He knows that he has a desirable paper for home reading, and he tells you so, he knows that advertisers can extend their patronage by using his columns, and he tells them so He has the confidence of the reader and of the business man They rely upon him and he brings them together He has the hands of a printer, the legs of a gatherer and the head of an editor He gives value received, fifty-two weeks in the year, and if you doubt his subscription list, he pulls the books on you [11]

With the *Mail* Capper was not starting at the bottom rung of the newspaper publishing business Since he was persistently interested in improving his own newspaper, he studied trade journals and other publications, "not in an academic way," but to see what was new and who was doing it [12] His editorial instinct told him what his readers wanted, and he succeeded in attracting circulation and in gaining advertising revenue Because of this, unsuccessful competitors apparently offered to sell out to him in order to escape the burden of refunding subscription money Years later Capper maintained that he had never initiated the purchase of any of his papers except for his first publication, the *Mail* [13]

An easy and sure-fire way of immediately increasing circulation figures was to accept the offers of a failing publisher and to buy his mailing list at a give-away price Capper made considerable use of this procedure to advance the standing of the *Mail* In 1894 he took over the Richland *Argosy*, and in the next two years he absorbed the *Kansas Breeze*, the *Sunflower*, and the *Saturday Lance* In 1904 the Richland *Observer* was also sold to Capper [14]

The *Kansas Breeze*, established April 13, 1894, as a Populist newspaper, began to lose its appeal when Editor Thomas A Mc-Neal's interest in Populism died down McNeal and his partner, F C Montgomery, had been successful in obtaining subscribers, but advertisers were uninterested in using their services In late 1895 McNeal offered to sell his paper to Capper—an offer which resulted in the consolidation of the Topeka *Mail* and the *Kansas Breeze* The *Breeze*, with 2,500 subscribers, reputedly cost Capper $2,500 The combined publication claimed a larger circulation than any other weekly newspaper in Kansas [15] The union of the two newspapers, which had occupied different fields, was justified on the ground that the good points of both were to be retained and that the combination would result in a better paper at less expense. The *Breeze*, as the official state paper of Kansas, gave Capper control of both state and county legal advertising [16] While "public advertising" rates brought higher income per column inch than did "private business advertising," no newspaper could exist for long without the advertising support of businessmen

A pattern, followed with some flexibility, developed with Capper's purchase of the *Breeze* Initially he did not have complete ownership, but was listed as manager and editor Every effort was made to retain the subscribers of the journal being absorbed Former owners and staff of the purchased publication were taken into Capper's employ By November 29, 1895, Capper became the sole owner, and he was listed for the first time as publisher of the consolidated *Mail and Breeze* [17] Tom McNeal's association with Capper, which began with the purchase of the *Kansas Breeze*, continued for forty-eight years as editor of the *Mail and Breeze* and the publications succeeding it [18]

The *Mail and Breeze*, in 1895, was a general and political weekly, but an unconscious drift in the direction of agricultural journalism was noticeable Very early McNeal directed his reader's attention to the fact that "Kansas is a great agricultural state and we, of course, shall continue to discuss its agricultural possibilities and give information on agricultural subjects from the proper ceremonies to be observed in breaking up a setting hen and diverting her mind into other channels of thought, to the training of a race horse."[19]

Facilities for complete handling of the newspaper were not available in the office of the *Mail and Breeze* in North Topeka The type was set by hand during the first few years, and "wheeled across the river to be run on the flat press of the Kansas Farmer, wheeled back [and the papers were] folded and addressed by hand by Capper and McNeal "[20] Florence Capper would help occasionally with the addressing of the newspaper, but the staff had more than doubled from the day Capper had become a newspaper owner [21]

Efforts to boost circulation of the *Mail and Breeze* with gimmicks, or the use of outstanding Kansans as editors for a few issues, proved moderately successful [22] Even more venturesome was the special thirty-two–page "Quarter Centennial Illustrated Edition" put out on white paper on May 22, 1896 [23] The entire cost of the issue, including five tons of white paper, was more than $2,000 Capper was not sure that the special edition would be a success, but when collections were in, he discovered that he had made a sizable profit [24] After the skyrocketing circulation for the special edition, regular circulation settled down to almost 10,000 copies each issue

In other ways improvements on Capper's paper were being made He was always interested in the best of printing equipment A new linotype was installed with considerable fanfare [25] A corps of twenty-nine correspondents supplied material for the county-news page Capper also engaged special advertising agents in Chicago and in New York His paper regularly featured national and world news, and boosted Kansas in general, with special emphasis on the Topeka area [26]

Capper was at the same time deeply immersed in a political scramble for the state printing "plum " The State Printer, appointed by the legislature, received a net income reportedly as high as $75,000 a year Approximately half of this money was expected to bolster the political activity of the political party in power In 1898 Capper was chairman of the First District Congressional Committee which managed the successful campaign of Charles Curtis Curtis was expected to support Capper for the position of State Printer, and announcements to that effect were published [27] But Curtis dropped his backing and Capper was by-passed After accepting the 1898 decision Capper again was sacrificed to the Curtis ambition when the senatorial race in 1902 overshadowed the appointment of the State Printer Although Curtis did not then become Senator, Capper had been the victim of "the Mulvane-Curtis-Burton combination" to strengthen Curtis' chances [28] Relations between Curtis and Capper were never quite the same again Capper did not hold grudges, but he was inclined to favor Republican candidates and policies at variance with those preferred by Curtis and he had a growing suspicion of party bosses Capper's attempts to obtain the lucrative position of State Printer were held against him by political opponents in later years, partly because he shared the leadership of a successful fight to make the printer's job elective with a yearly salary of $2,500 [29]

Although he failed in several attempts to gain the office of State Printer, Capper won increasing local political support In August, 1896, he received a petition, originated by the Republican Flambeau Club, urging him to begin the publication of an evening daily in Topeka Capper considered the petition, containing 2,700 signatures, to be "too large and too respectable to be ignored," but he could not be hurried into an incautious act Thorough investigation indicated that there was an "impossibility just now of obtaining a first class telegraphic report in Topeka," and such a difficulty could not be immediately overcome by a daily [30]

Capper's active interest in national, as well as in state, politics, led him to add new features as the *Mail and Breeze* grew in size and circulation One of the first of these was a series of political cartoons by Albert T Reid, then a young man from Clyde, Kansas, who won a prize of $25 for the best cartoon to be published in the *Mail and Breeze* Reid, with some training in drawing, had no ideas for a picture until he saw a neighbor snag a plow in a stump He later said, "A subject for a cartoon hit me squarely between the eyes It was a perfect analogy There was our Populist [candidate for] governor, Leedy with the Democratic mule and the stump was the free silver question A little bundle of straw attached to the end of a pole extending over the mule's head was labeled 'Patronage ' "[31]

The letter about Reid's prize included a request for a weekly cartoon, along with an invitation to visit the Cappers in Topeka This meeting resulted in many years of business association Reid, in later years, was a competitor in the farm-publishing business, but in old age Reid and Capper were again cordial friends [32]

The increasing growth of the *Mail and Breeze* forced a move to larger quarters in the Crawford Building at 501-503 Jackson Street, near the heart of the principal business district of Topeka The Mail Printing House, a three-way partnership between Arthur Capper, Mary May Capper, his sister, and George M Crawford, his brother-in-law, was established in 1897 Job printing and other production work not strictly in the line of newspaper publishing was handled by the new company [33]

For many years after 1897 Capper was operating in an expanding market, and he was able to capitalize on the economic situation so as greatly to enlarge his business enterprise In early 1900, the *Mail and Breeze* reported a guaranteed circulation of 22,800 copies printed and sold, which was raised around the 1900 general election to a circulation of 35,000 [34] Efforts to gain greater reader participation and interest were made through requests for photographs illustrating the "fertility and productiveness of Kansas soil,   picturesque scenes among the hills and valleys of Kansas,   in fact any kind of a Kansas picture that will interest the great army of *Mail and Breeze* readers "[35] Later issues show a hearty response to such editorial requests, and readers of the *Mail and Breeze* began to develop an increasing loyalty to their paper.

Increasing stress in the *Mail and Breeze* on agricultural practices by 1900 may have been influenced by Capper's purchase for $300 of the *Missouri Valley Farmer* in April, 1900 [36] This magazine, a sixteen-page agricultural monthly with a circulation reported as 16,000, was established in 1893 at Atchison, Kansas Like most farm periodicals of this period, the *Valley Farmer* gained most of its advertising income from small advertisements from various mail-order companies [37] Capper immediately set out to obtain a wider audience by reorganizing and increasing the number of departments in the paper By August, 1900, the claim of "largest circulation of any agricultural paper in the Southwest" found its way into the *Missouri Valley Farmer,* as well as the first use of Capper's office address in the masthead There was some duplication of pictures and articles in the *Mail and Breeze* and the *Missouri Valley Farmer,* but they soon developed a completely separate identity

It was clearly stated in the *Missouri Valley Farmer* that "advertisements of meritorious articles needed by the farmer [are] solicited Frauds and irresponsible firms are not knowingly advertised " Since Capper was liberal in his interpretation of an acceptable advertisement, advertising standards were not high, though they were in keeping with the time and the nature of the publication [38]

While the editors of the *Missouri Valley Farmer* were mainly interested in articles of an agricultural nature, occasional fiction and articles of interest to women were added Circulation for 1902 reached 100,000 and was 160,000 by October, 1904 The November, 1905, issue was the first to announce "Published by Arthur Capper "[39]

In the meantime, the Topeka Capital Company, which owned the Topeka *Daily Capital* and its weekly *Kansas Capital,* was in serious financial straits In 1895, Major J K Hudson, who had become deeply involved in his Highland Park real estate activity, was still the owner of 260 of the 500 shares of capital stock in the company When he deposited his 260 shares with John R Mulvane as collateral security for mortgages totaling almost $50,000, other creditors brought foreclosure procedures against him So Hudson sold his majority stock to John R Mulvane and David W Mulvane, of the Bank of Topeka [40]

John R Mulvane directed the activities of the *Capital* until August 5, 1899, when the paper was sold to a newly organized Capital Publishing Company [41] Under this company Charles M Sheldon, author of *In His Steps,* had his famous experiment of editing and managing the *Capital* for a week as he believed Christ would have done it [42]

Even the tremendous response to the Sheldon issues did not help the *Capital* out of its financial rut The Bank of Topeka had a large investment to protect, and someone was needed to get the *Capital* out of debt So in March and May, 1901, contractual agreements were executed to sell the Capital Publishing Company to Arthur and Florence Capper, W B Robey, and two former directors of the company, Harold T Chase and R L Thomas Under this plan, Capper received 251 of the 500 shares [43] No change in the ownership of the paper was reported in the *Capital* for many years, but changes were apparent in the newspaper

The cost of the Capital Publishing Company was $56,529 The new owners made a small down payment of $5,000 They were obligated to pay the balance by January 1, 1907 Because he could draw on other sources of income, Capper was able to buy out his partners by December 30, 1904, when he became the sole owner except for the single share owned by his wife [44] During this period of partial ownership Capper appeared reluctant to do anything with the *Capital* which would jeopardize his or his partners' holdings Not until January 28, 1905, did the masthead of the *Capital,* for the first time, indicate that the paper was published by Arthur Capper Most of the note held by the Bank of Topeka had been paid off and only then, on the eve of a Kansas Day celebration, did Capper acknowledge that he had complete control over newspaper policy Throughout his life he tended to follow this line of action Wherever there were minority stockholders in any of his enterprises, they would receive recognition for their share of the undertaking While he desired majority control, he was interested, at the same time, in protecting the rights of the minority

Although his contacts with politics were increasing, Capper's growing publishing enterprise required most of his time In April, 1903, he acquired a little publication named *Push* Tom McNeal and Albert T Reid had begun this literary, nonpartisan, fun-and-art magazine in September, 1902 Material presented in *Push* was reminiscent of the then dead *Kansas Magazine* and the recently deceased *Agora* [45] Like the *Missouri Valley Farmer,* which he had obtained three years earlier, Capper could use *Push* to carry mail-order advertisements The Post Office Department was lenient in its granting of mailing privileges, requiring only a minimum of 50 per cent paid subscriptions for such a publication Nor was there an Audit Bureau of Circulations to police the publishing industry So publishers of journals having considerable mail-order advertising often continued to send their magazines long after the subscription had expired Since circulation figures were of importance in relation to advertising rates, new subscribers were often obtained who had paid little or nothing for their subscriptions.[46]

Push, as the title of a magazine, did not seem in good taste to Capper, so in February, 1904, *Household,* successor to *Push,* made its appearance [47] Provisionally *Household* was granted the privilege of pound-rate postage, but methods of increasing circulation were questioned by postal authorities [48] Nevertheless, circulation was expanded to 160,000, and in the April, 1906, issue, "Arthur Capper, Publisher" was carried on the masthead for the first time A stated advertising policy, almost identical with that found in *Missouri Valley Farmer,* was first published in *Household* in the same issue.[49]

In the meantime, a growing interest in agriculture by *Mail and Breeze* editors was evident, but much of its development seemed to be haphazard For some time, the weekly *Kansas Capital* and the *Mail and Breeze* may have been competing publications, but Capper always told advertisers that they "don't compete."[50] Increasingly after 1900, the *Mail and Breeze,* which still tried to serve the interests of Shawnee County and Topeka as a weekly paper, was branching out into the field of agricultural journalism. Cartoons by Albert T Reid continued to express a partisan point of view, but the trend in the rest of the paper was away from political discussion Editorial rapport with readers was gained through frequently asking them for suggestions to "make the paper more interesting and serviceable . to make it practical . to have the opinion of readers themselves ."[51]

On October 1, 1904, the *Mail and Breeze* had evolved to an agricultural journal with a subtitle, "An Agricultural and Family Journal for the People of the Great West " By that time the major circulation was over the state of Kansas and beyond. The needs of the Topeka area were handled through a separate four-to-six page insert, which contained "Shawnee County News" and notes on "North Topeka." There was something in each issue that would appeal to every member of a farm family Farm people who had been successful in some phase of agriculture were the new editors of specialized departments Single issues were as long as forty pages and circulating claims of 60,000 were made for the area of "The Great Southwest"—Kansas, Oklahoma, Indian Territory, Nebraska, and Missouri

Advertising revenues continued to provide the major source of income for the *Mail and Breeze* Capper consciously promoted the value of advertising, and every week one or more voluntary letters from satisfied advertisers were published But national advertisers were unaware that the *Mail and Breeze* had taken on the character of a farm paper They were influenced by its name and its previous emphasis [52] To present the new purpose of his weekly farm paper, Capper renamed it the *Farmers' Mail and Breeze,* beginning with the February 17, 1906, issue Claimed circulation by that time was in excess of 62,500, three times as large as "any other farm weekly in Kansas " After twelve and a half years Frank Root would not be able to recognize his Topeka *Mail*

In those twelve and a half years many changes had come to Capper and his prospering business All of his publications had made great gains in circulation, in reader interest, and in advertising In addition to the *Farmers' Mail and Breeze,* the various Capper publications in 1906 were the Topeka *Daily Capital,* with its weekly edition, the *Kansas Capital,* the *Household* magazine, and *Missouri Valley Farmer* With a total circulation in excess of one-half million, Capper and his publications were a growing force Only *Household* and *Missouri Valley Farmer* had extensive circulation beyond the borders of Kansas Thus far, although the growth of his publications was attracting the attention of Kansans, Capper was hardly known outside his native state But that would soon change, for in 1906 his business enterprise was on the eve of a great expansion Advertisers and journalists all over the country would soon know of Capper and his publications The general public also would hear increasingly about him, although his name had almost never appeared in the news columns of his own publications

Chapter VI

New Links in a Chain

By 1906 Arthur Capper had built a publishing empire that enabled him in the next few years, a period of relatively few taxes, low wages, and low raw-material costs, to amass a fortune and to become one of the nation's leaders in journalism After 1914, demands on Capper's time never again allowed him to devote a major share of his energy to his various publications, and after that date, changes that occurred were less dramatic and often resulted less from his influence than from outside forces or from various subordinates in his business

Capper preferred to change according to the needs of a developing situation, not in accordance with an inflexible long-range objective He displayed characteristic opportunism when he changed the name of the *Mail and Breeze* to the *Farmers' Mail and Breeze* As an "insurgent" and "progressive" of the early twentieth century he was early classified as a liberal in politics In developing his large publishing empire it was not his nature consciously to follow any particular trend Sometimes developments occurred in spite of rather than because of things he had done

Capper may have envisaged a future organization of multi-state farm journals because it was his nature to acquaint himself thoroughly with activity in the publication field Even though the typical farm paper was small and independent of other newspapers there were already combinations in agricultural journalism such as the Pierce Publications of Iowa and Wisconsin [1] Capper had no real innovations to offer in the sphere of agricultural publications Other successful farm publishers had done what he was doing He was particularly successful in adapting beneficial practices elsewhere to his own business

Agricultural periodicals, of which Capper had two in 1906, tended to confine themselves to a restricted geographical area Often they limited their interest specifically to a single state, a tendency increasingly followed by the *Mail and Breeze* The *Missouri Valley Farmer,* as a farm monthly, was likewise confined to a geographical region, although it was considerably larger than a single state

Competition for the *Mail and Breeze,* within Kansas, was provided mainly by the *Kansas Farmer* and the *Farmers' Advocate,* which after 1908 operated as a single farm journal The *Kansas Farmer* had been founded by the State Agricultural Society in 1863 and was the old-time agricultural newspaper of the state After severing connections with its founding organization, it was published for some time by J K Hudson, Capper's first Topeka employer The *Farmers' Advocate,* on the other hand, had an existence largely political in nature before 1899 [2] Their combination in 1908 provided more formidable competition for *Farmers' Mail and Breeze,* but Capper's audience was always much larger than that of his competitors The *Missouri Valley Farmer* had as main competitor the magazine *Successful Farming* and circulated in the same area National magazines, such as the *Farm Journal,* the *Country Gentleman,* and *Farm and Fireside,* provided farm news for a still larger, more general area The total circulation figures on any of these magazines were watched closely by others in the field, and an effort was persistently made to keep the figures climbing

Capper's farm papers in 1906 provided him with less than half of his business activity *Household* had a larger circulation than any of his other publications, and the *Kansas Capital* had an extensive coverage for each of its weekly issues But the Topeka *Daily Capital* provided urgent problems and required closer supervision and more of his time than did any of the other Capper journals He would spend each morning at the office of the *Capital* on East Eighth Street Afternoons were spent at the office of his other publications at Fifth and Jackson, some five blocks away In the evenings, after dinner, and usually on Sunday evenings, Capper would again be at the office of the daily

Although he worked long hours, much of Capper's work seemed to be done with a minimum of effort On the surface, he was not systematic, his desk was always cluttered But his marvelous memory always enabled him to find what he was looking for Capper had a faculty for dictating to a secretary so that even when interrupted he could go back easily to the point where he stopped Furthermore, he knew what was going on in the various departments of his growing business His office door was always open, and he enjoyed visiting with employees or friends dropping in His "hunch" about his business and what policy should be followed often proved more reliable than the coolest reasoning of his leading executives He possessed an "intuitive feeling" about elaborate reports which quickly enabled him to get to the heart of the matter The very capabilities which enabled Capper to develop a large business enterprise were responsible for his repeated success in later years as a politician [3]

The growth of the Capper enterprise by 1907 found still in use many of the business practices that had been originated when Capper had taken over the Topeka *Mail* The correspondence for the expanded business with the hundreds and thousands of incoming items of mail were handled by a growing army of women clerks under the guidance of his sister, Mary May Capper Subscribers often mailed stamps or money to pay for their subscription and the clerks would count the monetary contents of each envelope, replace the money or stamps, and give their assembled work to their supervisor Since the business was his, Capper would frequently come out of his office to get some necessary pocket change or stamps He was completely unaware of the embarrassment for a short-changed clerk, but Mary May Capper always smoothed things over When double-entry bookkeeping was installed in the business in 1907, Capper was encouraged by his sister to make withdrawals for his personal or business needs where they would show on the books But even then he still took stamps when he needed them [4]

Even though he owned a large and growing business, employees remembered that in his own building Capper often acted as if he was trespassing Almost every day he would visit the pressroom and courteously ask a boy stacking papers whether he might have a copy He never issued a direct order and he was always soft-spoken He gave his employees the impression that they were working together in an important task He would frequently keep his own counsel, but his method of "command" was to ask whether there was room for a particular news story or whether a particular job should be carried out

With complete ownership of the *Capital* and an assured position in Kansas journalism Capper personally launched a nation-wide campaign to secure advertising for his publications Much of this advertising designed to reach large national companies was written in 1904 or 1905 about Arthur Capper and his "Remarkable Western Publishing House," and "His Five Big Winners," with a listing of Capper publications Later, information about Topeka, "a town of but 45,000 population, [which] ranks thirty-third among the 9,708 post-offices   from which second class matter is mailed," was used to attract attention to the growth of Capper's enterprise [5] The culmination of this advertising series was a group of front-cover "announcements" in issues of *Printers' Ink* In a frank and informal manner Capper wrote

Printers' Ink has sold me this space every other week for a period of one year It will cost me over $2,000—a rather expensive publicity campaign to be sure, but I am confident I can use the space in a way that will be profitable to myself as well as a large number of *Printers' Ink* readers

I have on my desk a carefully prepared list of over 300 important advertisers who, in my judgment, should be using one or more of my publications,   I particularly desire to reach these 300 through *Printers' Ink* I want these people to know more about the advertising situation in this the world's greatest wealth-producing center I have no "hot air" to give them, no buncombe, no cut-and-dried stereotyped advertising effusion to weary them with—simply a candid, honest, explicit, statement of facts and information about five unusual publications and their territory

I have no use for such glittering generalities and bombastic assertions in newspaper exploitation as "you cannot cover Kansas without using the *Capital*," etc   .

In the next issue I shall tell why, in my judgment, Kansas just now offers greater opportunity than any other State for advertising investment [6]

Later issues of *Printers' Ink* carried the stories of the growth of Capper publications and the area in which they circulated Favorable comments about the Capper Publicity Campaign were apparently widespread One editorial comment later stated that Capper "is doing by far the best advertising that is being done by any publication in the country at the present time "[7]

Since he had always personally guided the fortunes of his advertising and circulation departments Capper had developed no leaders to assume the responsibility for the increasing job before him He had handled and directed the activities of these departments with the help of clerks while his printing and editorial departments were guided by capable men in whom he had confidence His business had grown so fast that he had not foreseen the need for trained leadership, so in 1908 he decided to go outside the organization to hire heads for his advertising and circulation departments [8]

The first "outsiders" which Capper brought into key positions in his business were Marco Morrow in advertising, and Frank Ball in circulation Morrow, several years younger than Capper, had had many experiences in journalism that paralleled those of his new employer His special experience as secretary of a Chicago advertising agency and editor of the publication *Agricultural Advertising* would be of great value in the new position Ball had considerable experience in guiding circulation campaigns of leading publications [9] Never before had Capper paid wages as high as those he offered Morrow and Ball, approximately $5,000 per year, so he was cautious in bringing newcomers into his organization But he was already buying other papers, and he wanted a stronger group of leaders to handle the increasing responsibilities [10]

Another plan to help handle future expansion was to erect a building large enough to house all the activities of the Capper journals The growth of the business had resulted in demands for working space that far exceeded the area available in either the *Capital* building or the offices of the *Mail and Breeze* Other Capper offices were scattered all over downtown Topeka Because of his experience in large metropolitan newspaper offices, Capper had definite ideas of what he wanted He desired space to handle adequately all the departments of his growing business and news offices He wanted to create the hustle-bustle of a city room of a large metropolitan newspaper He believed that such working conditions would foster the co-operative endeavor essential to getting out a journal A sincere feeling that people were working with him as one big family rather than working for him always appeared uppermost in Capper's mind

James C Holland, former state architect and designer of many public and private buildings in Topeka, prepared the plans for Capper's new building The site was at the southeast corner of the intersection of Eighth and Jackson, just across the street from the State Capitol grounds The contract was let on June 15, 1907, and Capper, with great interest, followed the progress of construction [11] He was absorbed in the new work He seemed to look forward to activities not within the normal routine of his business Completion of the building by late 1908 enabled all Capper departments to move into their offices by December 10

The new five-story fireproof, steel, stone, terra-cotta, and reinforced concrete home of the Capper papers, considered by its owner to be the best-equipped newspaper publishing plant in the West, was not completed any too soon The Capper organization had grown with such speed that it was difficult to establish efficient business methods so long as the various departments were separated from each other The usable area of almost 50,000 square feet in the new building was obtained at a cost of slightly more than $150,000 New presses, equipment, and other costs resulted in a total expenditure of $355,000 [12] Because of the prosperity of his business Capper was able immediately to pay all but $100,000, which was obtained through a loan from the Shawnee Fire Insurance Company [13]

Because of the space that was available, the fourth annual "Reunion" of the Capper "family" was held in the Capper Building on New Year's night in 1909 Three hundred eighty-six employees in twenty-one departments were then on the Capper payroll in the new building [14] Capper was lauded as the individual employer hiring more people than any other in Topeka, and he in turn vowed that he had "the best printers and pressmen in Topeka, the best reporters and editors in Kansas, the best advertising and circulation men in the United States, and the finest bunch of girls in the whole world "[15]

The formal opening of the completed Capper Building was announced in a special Housewarming Edition of the *Capital* on February 28, 1909 [16] Other Capper publications featured the new building in early 1909, and they, like the *Capital*, noted the special provisions made by the owner for his employees The staff had for their use a professional journalism library, a restaurant, and an auditorium But even before the building was completely occupied the auditorium was cut up into rooms, and the restaurant was reduced to a single counter after the first year [17] In reality the architect who planned the Capper Building created a building lacking in storage space, loading docks, and many other essentials of a high-speed publishing plant Equipment, such as the presses, had to conform to the area provided for them in the building, and almost no provision was made for expansion Although the structure was widely admired and

Capper was proud of it, many flaws in planning and in construction were discovered with use

Following the completion of plans and initial construction of the new building, publications in increasing numbers were being offered to Capper Most of these papers, just as in the case of other Capper papers, had a small circulation at the time he bought them Many of them were in financial straits and as far as he was concerned, "every time it was a gamble" to take on a new publication [18] The price paid, in almost all cases, was low There was no plan of building a Capper publishing empire made up of numerous publications, and Capper was often reluctant to accept a new paper In many cases the staff of a newly purchased paper would go to work for Capper If the main circulation was in some other state than Kansas, editorial offices were maintained in that state, and editorial content was aimed at the readers there Printing was generally centralized in the Topeka plant Competing state farm papers were consolidated in some cases, because most states had too many farm papers for efficient or successful operation

The first of these new Capper publications was *Poultry Culture* This journal, published in the interests of the specialized poultry raiser, was taken over by Capper with its April, 1908, issue, although he participated in its publication earlier [19] Because this publication differed from most Capper papers, which attempted to satisfy wider, more general interests, it was sold on February 1, 1916, to a Missouri buyer, who published it as *Useful Poultry Culture* [20]

Until 1908, all of the Capper journals had the state of Kansas as a primary area of circulation This pattern was broken with the purchase of *Nebraska Farm Journal* in August of that year, due to the urging of W T Laing The publication cost only two hundred dollars, but there was in actuality no paid circulation According to Laing, there would be little trouble in quickly adding circulation [21] So Laing and Capper bought it, and Capper assumed full control in the fall of 1908 [22] The paper was printed in Topeka, editorial and business offices were maintained in Omaha, and Laing served as Capper's Nebraska representative for a few years Feature stories were often written by editors from Topeka, but they were particularly directed at the Nebraska reader Several hundred subscription agents quickly boomed the Nebraska paper's circulation, and it soon gained a formidable position in Nebraska agriculture Circulation by 1911 exceeded one hundred thousand, and the publication was subtitled the "Nebraska Section of The Capper Farm Press "[23] Competition with the *Nebraska Farm Journal* came primarily from the *Nebraska Farmer* and the *Twentieth Century Farmer* Locally owned Nebraska farm publications often based their advertising opposition to the Capper paper on the fact that it was a part of a multi-state syndicate [24]

With this beginning, the invasion of other states to purchase farm publications became easier The initiative for Capper's entry into Missouri probably was taken by Colonel Ed R Dorsey, of Topeka, after he received a letter from the owner of the *Ruralist,* early in June, 1910 [25] Capper made a trip to Sedalia, Missouri, to determine the conditions under which the *Ruralist* would be sold He indicated that he was not "particularly anxious to take on any more publications and   only at the suggestion of Mr Dorsey" he had "figured on this proposition " Capper's offer of $5,000 for the paper and its belongings was accepted with some misgivings, before the end of June, although his first issue of the newly dubbed *Missouri Ruralist* did not appear until August 10, 1910 [26]

The *Missouri Ruralist* followed the Capper prescription of closely identifying the publication with the state in which it circulated Capper announced that the paper would be "Missouri from start to finish, a livestock and farm journal that the Missouri feeders and farmers will be proud of "[27] A complete list of department editors and editorial contributors, most of them Missourians, was soon drawn up, and subscription agents were transferred to Missouri, with a goal of 50,000 new subscriptions within a year This goal was some 10,000 too high, but the paper was growing rapidly *Breeder's Special,* of Kansas City, was purchased on August 16, 1910, and consolidated with *Missouri Ruralist* on December 10, 1910 At that time the editorial office was moved from Sedalia to Kansas City, Missouri [28]

Expansion of the Capper syndicate into Oklahoma came with the acquisition on March 28, 1912, of the Oklahoma Farmer Company of Guthrie, publisher of the *Oklahoma Farmer* Initiative for this purchase came from M L Crowther, a former Capper employee, when he bought the *Farmer* for $1,000 in cash and $2,000 in notes The notes were in turn transferred to Capper, who became liable for them An agreement between Capper and Crowther made the latter manager of the *Oklahoma Farmer* with a stipulated salary and a possible bonus of one-fourth of the new annual profits of the publication [29]

Tactics proved of value to Capper publications in Kansas, Nebraska, and Missouri were applied in Oklahoma The paper was closely identified with Oklahoma in Capper's first publisher's announcement and in editorial assignments Within a month a consolidation had been effected with *Oklahoma State Farmer* and a drive for new subscriptions was under way [30] Editorial offices were subsequently moved to Oklahoma City, and in 1915 the *Oklahoma Farm Journal* was purchased for $24,000 and consolidated with the *Oklahoma Farmer* [31] John Fields, former owner and editor of the *Oklahoma Farm Journal*, became the new editor of the consolidated paper [32]

Another purchase, also made in 1915, was apparently the result of prolonged negotiations initiated by Charles W Bryan of Lincoln, Nebraska, brother of William Jennings Bryan Correspondence in the summer of 1915 had opened the possibility of sale of the *American Homestead*, a monthly farm magazine which Bryan published Bryan's principal interest was to have another farm paper whose reputation he could recommend to the subscribers of the *Commoner*, a monthly newspaper He was therefore willing to accept subscriptions to Capper's farm paper, the *Missouri Valley Farmer*, as his re-return for the sale of the subscription list and good will of the *American Homestead* Negotiations opened on the figure of $5,000, payable in annual subscriptions to the *Missouri Valley Farmer*, but later the price was set at $10,000 [33] Since obtaining new subscribers was expensive, Capper was willing to accept, and the contract with Bryan was formally signed Nov 29, 1915, granting Bryan five years to collect the required number of subscriptions [34] The *American Homestead* expired with the sale, and Capper papers were used to complete the subscriptions of many *Homestead* readers [35]

One other change in the composition of the various Capper publications came before Capper began to devote the major share of his time to public office That was the renaming of the *Kansas Weekly Capital* After September 6, 1913, it was known as *Capper's Weekly* The change of name may have been inspired by a desire for greater recognition, but there were other valid reasons for the new title. The announced reason was that the "Kansas Weekly Capital has outgrown the title given it years ago in its infancy   Its growth was so rapid that the realization that it had so far outstripped its name came as a surprise The word 'Kansas' didn't cover the field at all . . 'Capper's Weekly' seemed better suited than any other name proposed and was adopted "[36]

Thus, on the eve of World War I, the Capper publications included five farm journals—state farm papers for Kansas, Missouri, Nebraska, and Oklahoma, and the *Missouri Valley Farmer*—and they were frequently identified in the publishing field as the Capper Farm Press A closely related publication, still in Capper hands in 1914, was *Poultry Culture* The Capper Printing Company had replaced the Mail Printing House In addition, a woman's magazine, *Household, Capper's Weekly,* and the increasingly important Topeka *Daily Capital* rounded out the Capper list of publications Total circulation had risen to about one and three-fourths million, divided almost equally by the Capper Farm Press and the non-agricultural Capper papers The obvious prosperity of the Capper enterprise was an object of wonder and sometimes jealousy of political opponents or of newspaper owners who were not so fortunate in their own business dealings Unwilling to concede that Capper had obtained his position through the ability to organize and lead a large and growing business whose employees numbered more than a thousand, they professed to see a background of inconsistency and deceit in Capper's march to economic and political prominence The period upon which they usually based their observations, the decade prior to 1914, found Capper branching out into fields that were outside the scope of most of his publications

Chapter VII

Involvement in Politics

Arthur Capper always maintained that his fight against railroad domination of Kansas government through the columns of the *Capital* and his other journals was responsible, more than anything else, for establishing his reputation in the state The battle against "Copeland County Politics" assumed the form of an intra-party fight between the "progressive" or "insurgent" wing of the Republican party and the "standpatters "[1] Under Capper's benevolent leadership, both the Topeka *Daily Capital* and the *Mail and Breeze* were active organs in support of progressive "boss-busting" views and tactics of Walter Roscoe Stubbs, Lawrence contractor turned legislator and later Governor The "trust-busting" activities of Theodore Roosevelt found a ready response from Kansans such as William Allen White, Edmond H Madison, Joseph L Bristow, Victor Murdock, Stubbs, Capper, and others "T R " had captured the Kansas imagination, and support for reform in opposition to entrenched "interests" was the popular order of the day

As an inexperienced, unproved politician, Stubbs had innocently opposed machine politics in his first term in the state legislature in 1903 An effort to humiliate him backfired for the bosses because Stubbs provided a strong point behind which opponents and those not favored by the machine could rally Capper, as a two-time loser in the race for State Printer, was attracted by Stubbs's promise of reform more than for any other reason In a letter written in 1911 Capper held that he was supporting and had supported Stubbs "because he was fighting for progressive principles which we have advocated consistently ever since the paper came under my control "

"If you will take the trouble to investigate you will find that the Capital was making a fight for Direct Primary, Elimination of Free Pass, and other reforms, long before Stubbs had entered Kansas politics "[2]

It was the combination of leading railroad officials and the control of various public officers in Kansas that brought steady and increasing opposition from the reform wing of the Kansas Republican press, of which the *Daily Capital* under Harold T Chase, its editor, was a leading Topeka spokesman For a while, when the battle over the two-cent rail fare and the anti-pass issue was at its highest pitch, Capper instructed his advertising manager to solicit no "advertising from the Santa Fe "[3] Even earlier an effort was made to buy the *Capital* from Capper at more than double his investment in the paper Believing that the money behind the offer was supplied by various railroad corporations, Capper preferred to run his own business rather than sell out and "be branded as a demagogue and . . forever lose his influence to do anything more "[4]

Close associates of long years' standing held that Capper was no meddlesome "do-gooder " He had a "Jeffersonian confidence" in what the masses of people thought [5] His interpretation of public opinion included perfecting the form of government through extension of suffrage to women and a provision for closer party participation through the use of the direct primary election And he became a confidant of a large and growing group of well-known men [6] Another long-time Capper employee had the impression that Capper was "fundamentally good" and right but that he "also believed that it paid to be so "[7]

Along with his growing prestige and increasingly important public position in the early 1900's, Capper became an obvious target for political opponents and jealous competitors The high standards his editors were proposing for public officials and for governmental practice did not seem consistent with Capper's former efforts to gain the position of State Printer or with the contents of some of his advertising columns Since people are prone to emphasize one or two characteristics to the exclusion of others, the apparent inconsistency between Capper editorial and advertising policy attracted considerable attention

As a matter of fact, Capper was most liberal in interpretation of advertising acceptable for his publications He was never a leader in throwing out advertising Before 1908 his usual standard for inclusion of an advertisement was whether or not Jim Pierce of the Iowa and Wisconsin farm papers was also running it [8]

Some advertisements rejected on the basis of instructions given to the advertising department of Capper publications were later restored by direct appeals to Capper He could not say "No" easily when an advertiser wanted to use his journal

Perhaps the most vicious attack on the content of Capper's advertising columns was made in 1905, a half dozen years before a widespread plan to improve the quality of advertising was accepted by a large number of American publishers, including Capper[9] This attack, the product of the vitriolic pen of Henry J Allen, then of Ottawa, had arisen over a fight for the position of State Printer According to a neutral observer Capper had credited Allen's support of Capper's opponent in the race for the office of State Printer to a promised share in the profits Supposedly Capper called Allen a meddler and "lathering boodler "[10] Allen responded with an editorial, "The Human Vampire," in which he attacked Capper's character and business [11] Salient points in the Allen editorial were

At Topeka there are being published by a well known man who is getting rich at it two of the most monstrous publications that ever disgraced and violated the United States mails   These papers are published for the sole purpose of carrying a lot of filthy advertising, such as can not gain entrance into legitimate papers   The most regrettable feature of these filthy advertising circulars is that they make a special effort to reach homes under the pretense of being family papers   the sharks who prey upon the human race by patent nostrums are given entrance to the columns of these so-called house and farm papers, and in return for their money the publisher offers to reach the guileless public by circulating these papers practically free   that any man should so far forget the moral obligations which rest upon him as to seek to make money by publications such as these is sad beyond expression The jointist has a better business than this He strikes generally at the adult male The man who provides a sewer through which the horde of sharks and patent medicine quacks can reach and poison all the members of the family is a vampire, compared with whom the joint keeper becomes respectable The man whose greed for money leads him into a business like this may make an effort to keep his respectability by getting out one publication which makes pretensions to decency, he may even pretend to be a reformer, but he's an enemy of society and no amount of sham or hypocrisy will prevent the public from eventually reaching a just conclusion in his case

The papers indicted by Allen, the *Missouri Valley Farmer* and the *Household,* were used as mail-order journals in 1905, and they actually carried some very questionable advertising The public did not in justice turn against Capper's papers as Allen had prophesied Allen had selected material deliberately to distort his editorial so that Capper would appear in as bad a light as possible Capper apparently made no comment on Allen's editorial and he held no grudges because of this attack Allen soon cooled off, and when his old editorial was dusted off for use against Capper in a later political campaign he wrote a new one which said "All of this silly emotionalism about Arthur Capper not being a proper man for governor of the state, is not having any effect upon the public mind Arthur Capper is a Kansas boy, he grew up in this state and has made his life a success He has stood for the decent things in public life and in private life and will make a splendid governor in every way

"There is no occasion in this campaign for the vituperation and abuse which is being spread about him   ."[12]

The D R Anthony temper was vented on Capper in 1909 in an argument combining the political and advertising issues that divided the two men Tom McNeal had entered the Congressional race against the incumbent Anthony, who was angered by the publication in the *Capital* of a letter-to-the-editor criticizing Anthony and his newspaper "for publishing the advertisement of a Brewery Company " "Does it not strike you as being just a little hypocritical," wrote Anthony,

for you to criticize me for carrying what nine out of ten newspapers in the country consider honest advertising, when your own newspaper carried advertisements which are known to be both immoral and dishonest in their purposes?   what am I to think when you attack me in your newspaper for my standards of business morality when I have a letter signed with your name in which you boldly ask me to intercede with a United States judge to save a swindler, a man who buncoed widows and orphans, from the penitentiary after he had been convicted in court, and simply on the ground that he was a large advertiser in your newspaper [13]

Further threats were made by Anthony, who said that "it may be necessary to see whose hide is the toughest, yours or mine   "

Capper replied immediately to Anthony's charges He remembered "having received only one other letter as insolent as yours,   "[14] In direct answer to each charge Capper wrote

The matter you complain of was from a subscriber of this paper, a reputable business man, who signs his name and stands for the statements and opinions the letter contains   In the same column, in the same issue, you will find a letter criticizing the present state administration on account of increased taxes and urging the nomination of a farmer for Governor to succeed Stubbs next year . Not every man can own a newspaper, but he should have a chance to be heard   You   always have an opportunity to "come back" at these people in our columns if you desire   I take it from your letter that you want me to cut out everything that is not wholly complimentary to you—that you want everything cut off that may be in the nature of criticism   . . you ought to know, Dan, that that is an unreasonable view for you to take of it   I am not running a newspaper particularly to please Congressmen, or governors, or senators, and I don't believe you are either   The people I am under obligation to (and the only ones I am under obligation to) are our friends who "pay the freight"—the farmer and other good folks who send in their five dollars every twelve months for a year's subs   and as long as I am in the game I am going to give him a paper that won't be dominated or bulldozed or frightened by Congressmen or anyone else   The Capital is in that fortunate condition where it does not have to take orders from anyone   It will try to be fair, but I realize that we cannot please everyone

I am, of course, for Tom McNeal

I note your statement that there are immoral and dishonest advertisements running in my paper   This is not true

I note your statement in which you say you have a letter from me asking you to intercede with a United States Judge   That is not true   You had a letter from me, stating that the Kansas City Ad Club, of which I am a member, had requested me to put up to you their request that you co-operate with two Congressmen from Missouri, already interested in the matter, in securing leniency for Horn, but I told you that so far as I was concerned, you could do as you pleased

Now, Dan, your letter is a very evident attempt to "scare" me   I don't know where you got the notion that I am that kind of a rooster   I don't believe you are entirely familiar with my record here the last five or six years, if you were, I don't think you would plan to work me in just this sort of style   .   Anything you might print in the "Times" denouncing myself or my paper would influence me in the slightest   I am not a candidate for office—never will be—have nothing to ask of politicians or anyone else.   I am giving my subscribers and advertisers a full dollar's worth for every dollar they pay me, and any articles you might print in the "Times" would not affect me, or my business in the least [15]

In ending his letter Capper suggested that Anthony talk it over with him sometime   Anthony immediately sent Capper a much subdued blast which stated that he did not believe that Capper would publish falsehoods even when signed by a third party   He specified the immoral advertisements in Capper's journals as "advertisements for the sale of information or methods to prevent conception and such immoral uses, and also advertisements for fraudulent land concerns against which the Government has issued fraud orders " But he also agreed that they should talk it over and he set the date for a meeting [16]

Another attack inspired by a political campaign linked the Capper name with that of Allen, William Allen White, and Joseph L Bristow Albert T Reid, a former Capper employee and a conservative Republican, wrote

And speaking about this new outfit who will undertake the fumigation of politics in Kansas, recalls some interesting statistics Arthur Capper twice tried to connect with the state printer "graft", as his paper now refers to the old arrangement He was beaten by Henry Allen who made an air-tight arrangement with George Clark, and they split the pot Will White had a nice little side line, also An arrangement under the Roosevelt administration made it necessary to ship all the pension vouchers to Emporia for Bill White to print Somewhat expensive, impractical, and occasioned much delay, but Bill was one of the "ring" in those days Well, one day Cy Leland who became pension commissioner, kicked this arrangement upside down, brought the printing to Topeka and gave it to Arthur Capper, who was also quite "regular " Then White went after Cy, who was henceforth an "undesirable " Yesterday Cy was chairman of the credentials committee in Bill White's convention Also there is Bristow—the "lean and hungry" one who wanted Senator Long to get him an easy job with a good salary, so he could loaf around Kansas and look after the interests of the "ring " Gentlemen, we are saved![17]

Sometimes editorial or advertising copy carried in the pages of Capper's journals stirred up a hornet's nest for other than political reasons For example, in 1908 the *Mail and Breeze* presented a symposium on the value of mail-order houses as pictured in letters from readers As a consequence, the *Mail and Breeze* became the target of both mail-order companies and local retail merchants, an indication of the fairness of the symposium At that time, bitter feeling existed between local and mail-order merchants Merchants in small communities were prone to organize catalog-burning days to vent their wrath on the under-cutting mail-order houses, and citizens were expected to show their local loyalty by supplying the necessary fuel [18] Capper did not intentionally avoid these controversies, nor did he seek to continue them once they had begun.

Although the Topeka *Daily Capital,* under the editorship of Harold T Chase, was providing editorial "Opposition to Bosses and Trusts" before Capper took over, the frequency of demands for reform and in support of "boss-busting" shows a decided upturn after 1905, when Capper had complete control of his paper.[19] Evidence is available to support the position that such editorial combat was costly in a business way, but compensations in reader interest and in circulation were probable One of Capper's advertising agency men wrote him in 1907 that "I am compelled to write you this morning a letter which affords me as much sorrow as it can by any possibility afford you This is to notify you that, by reason of the publication of the article 'The Machinery Trust,' you have lost between $1,500, and $1,600, worth of advertising of this company, for 'The Mail and Breeze ' . "[20]

The advertising agency offered the threat "that if anything more of like character appears in your publication, it will be impossible for us to send you the advertising which we had already scheduled for the Missouri Valley Farmer "[21] If Capper responded as he did in later years—and it was ever his policy to provide independence and backing in their independence for his editors—he would say to his editor, "We don't like to lose legitimate advertising Can you prove the truth of the statements made?" If the editor could, "That's all I want to know All I ask of my editors is to write the truth We'll get more advertising But . you don't need to deliberately try to drive advertising away or lose what we do get "[22]

The business side of the Capper publications did not govern the editorial content of the various journals, although the advertising might be able to limit space for editorial copy Editorial and business departments were separate portions of the entire enterprise under Capper's guidance as publisher And this guidance was extremely light-handed When Capper put a man in charge of a department he delegated authority and he "never let a fellow down within the organization and without "[23] Having been a reporter and an editor, Capper respected his editors' position and strongly proclaimed an editorial conscience for all his journals Each editor and publication would have "a sense of duty to society The obligation of truth and honor bear with increasing directness on all who have to do with the press these papers have stood for the uplifting view, for civic optimism They have turned away from life's meaner side, have preferred to speak good rather than evil And above all else they have been clean papers, free from scandal and filth I want that policy continued "[24]

It became a well-known fact that Capper was openly grateful for the plaudits of his friends, but he never let the barbs, even from one of his own writers, bother him [25] The "Dodd Gaston affair" provides an excellent example of the restraint with which Capper dealt with his editors Jay E House wrote a column "On Second Thought" under the pen name of "Dodd Gaston" for the *Capital* House had no limits on the choice of subject matter for his column, and he criticized the public policies of his publisher and even discussed Capper's choice of suits No order ever came to pull the punches or soften a jab [26] Unknown to the general public Capper even defended House's right to express personal views in his own column When a *Capital* reader wrote Capper complaining of House's opposition to policies supported by the newspaper Capper replied

I am aware that on many matters Mr House does not hold the same views that I hold Politically and otherwise he quite frequently is at variance with the policy of the paper, but I think the people of Kansas very thoroughly understand this They know that it is a free lance column and represents the ideas of no one other than Dodd Gaston, and from its very nature the writer of it must be given free rein

It is the function of a newspaper paragrapher to "shoot folly as it flies" and it inevitably happens that an occasional shot goes astray and hits a mark not aimed at But for all that the good paragrapher serves a useful purpose even when he appears most cynical Mr House, personally, is a clean man of good intentions, though often prejudiced and sometimes irritating [27]

In writing to his correspondent that he hoped he would "not take Dodd Gaston too seriously," Capper was consistent with his long-time views on editorial responsibility He had written, "To my mind, there is no idea more vicious than the notion that an employer or firm or corporation may 'control' its employees on election day, or in the expression of individual political opinion "[28]

One of the "Dodd Gaston" articles of 1909 revealed something of the relationship between Capper and one of his "notorious" employees "Dodd" confessed "Although I have worked for him for more than seven years, and although our relations have always been the most friendly and intimate possible between employer and employe, I frankly admit he has me scared to death   I have never understood the psychology of the 'buffalo' which he unconsciously holds over me   Now, the question is, why am I afraid of the soft spoken, retiring man who wears a little round hat and whose pockets bulge perennially with newspaper clippings?"[29] And "Dodd" did not have any ready answer

If Capper had established a goal for himself by the first decade of the twentieth century—and he never discussed or counseled with anyone on such matters—it is obvious in retrospect that he was aiming for a broader or "wider horizon" than had been the case in the 1890's At first he had been engrossed in establishing his business, although he had a lively interest in partisan politics and he had served his party at the precinct, county, and state level He had sought an appointive public position but had been repulsed, and he seems to have vowed that never again would he seek public office

His marriage to Florence Crawford and his growing wealth opened the doors wide to Topeka society, and he increasingly enjoyed the company of the leading socialites of the community He was a "joiner" and a dues-paying member of innumerable organizations His enthusiasm, as a young man, for bicycles was easily transferred to automobiles at the turn of the century, and his first car, little more than two bicycles bolted together, was one of the earliest, possibly the second, automobile brought to Topeka It was a one-cylinder affair and Capper had difficulty in learning how to operate it After rudimentary experience he told Florence, "If you will be out here about two o'clock I will come along and take you a ride " They were living at Eleventh and Topeka, where they later built their mansion Capper drove "down Topeka Avenue and tried to slow up," but the brake would not work "Mrs Capper was sitting on the front porch waiting, ready to get in." He waved and went around the block Unable to stop the car after several trips around the block, he waved goodbye and went off "wondering what would happen" on arriving home that night [30]

Capper's second car, a Winton, was the fifth or sixth automobile in Topeka Horses were frightened wherever he went and, with no self-starter, it "was an awful job to start out " Whenever possible he would park at the top of an incline to ease the starting problem [31]

In later years Capper still had a considerable enjoyment in the use of an automobile But after they ceased to be a novelty his regard for automobiles was dependent on their service to him

Capper's expanded goals show up in the period of more than a year when the Capper Building was being constructed His business still demanded many policy decisions, but he felt free to devote much time to other matters A recognition of Capper's growing ability and influence is seen in an exchange of letters with Senator Joseph L Bristow in 1909 Bristow wrote that Secretary of Agriculture James Wilson would "not remain in the cabinet a great length of time" and that Capper was "the only man in our state   to push for the place "[32] To Capper's plea of lack of experience in public affairs Bristow replied, "You are very modest   I know the character and type of men that make cabinet officers   I would be glad to exert all the influence that I may be able to accumulate to get you in the cabinet "[33]

About the same time Governor Stubbs finally found a way to put Capper into a public office First notification of his appointment as a regent of Kansas State Agricultural College came to Capper through the pages of the rival Topeka *State Journal* [34] There was no single Board of Regents for the state colleges and universities in 1909, and William Allen White was nominated as a member of the regents at the University of Kansas at the same time Several members of the Senate Committee on Education balked at the White and Capper nominations because of their previous criticism of conservatives in the legislature, but all of the Governor's appointments were ratified [35]

Capper's appetite for political office seemed to have been whetted by this appointment, for in less than a year he was discussed as a Republican candidate for Governor to succeed Stubbs But the Cappers were engaged in the construction of their new "Mansion" at 1035 Topeka Boulevard, and for some time Arthur did not give serious consideration to such talk In fact Capper was corresponding with Representative Edmond H Madison, of the Seventh Congressional District, and with William Allen White in an effort to persuade Madison to enter the race [36] Times had changed in Kansas politics The reform "broom" of Stubbs had swept out the "Bosses," only to have Stubbs installed in the position of political power within the state In his fight for progressive reform, Stubbs had lost a larger number of supporters than he had gained, and many Republican leaders in late 1910 and 1911 were fearful that they could not win the next election In declining to be a candidate for Governor, Madison had reminisced about the political scene of the past decade He wrote Capper, "We were not all progressives at one time in the past Instead, I can remember the time when you were Senator Curtis's right hand man and I was a member of the 7th District machine, and while we have accepted the new order of things and in fact have done what we could to bring it about yet, of necessity, there are certain personal claims and friendships arising out of the older order that cannot be disregarded "[37]

Curtis had become more conservative and "standpat," if that was possible, while Capper was supporting the position of the "progressives" and "T R " Republicans Although they remained on friendly terms, and though a few years later the Curtis family occupied the house across Eleventh Street from the Capper mansion, Capper was personally critical of the Curtis position in the Senate of almost always supporting the "Aldrich program "[38]

As late as February, 1911, Capper was still resisting the thought of becoming a candidate for Governor In response to a letter from Will Beck he wrote that "I have been so busy building up my newspapers that I have had little time to give to politics "[39] But in response to a variety of personal conferences Capper "little by little reached a state of mind where office holding . ceased to be entirely objectionable "[40]

Capper's interest in public office had run a whole cycle He had actively sought the position of State Printer on two occasions Repelled by his defeats, he had reversed his position and opposed any idea of public office During the first decade of the twentieth century his economic and political position in Kansas was greatly strengthened, and in 1909, against his expressed wishes, he was appointed Regent of the Kansas State Agricultural College His minor role as a regent stirred his interest in public office, and the opportunity which presented itself in the Republican party in 1911 re-awakened old political ambitions This new political role was to furnish wider horizons and a broader perspective to Arthur Capper throughout the remainder of his life

73

Chapter VIII

Two Races for Governor

Partisan politics, during the early twentieth century, was more prominently displayed in leading newspapers and magazines than was true fifty years later A candidate for the position of the Governor of Kansas might announce his candidacy almost as soon as the man he hoped to succeed had been inaugurated for a full two-year term When Stubbs was re-elected in 1910 with half the plurality he had received two years earlier, Kansas Republican leaders were anxiously surveying potential candidates for the office of the Governor for the next election Someone was needed to retain the support that had been given to Stubbs and at the same time regain the votes of Kansans who had disowned their progressive, reform Governor

One "straw in the wind" was a story in the St Louis *Republic* supporting Arthur Capper as the logical candidate When D O McCray, the author of this story, showed Capper a copy of the newspaper, Capper responded, 'McCray, I'm very grateful to you for this, but there's nothing to it I am no more fitted to be governor than I am to be a Methodist bishop" Mrs Capper was also shown the boom story, and with displeasure she told McCray, "I want you to know that I do not thank you for writing about Arthur in this way I don't want him to mix up in this nasty, dirty politics—and I don't want you to write anything more like this "[1] Additional newspaper comment and general discussion of a possible Capper candidacy resulted in additional support for Capper in all parts of Kansas

One afternoon early in 1911 Capper was visited by Joe N Dolley, Joe Longshore, and other Republican leaders After they had departed, Capper asked Morrow, his assistant publisher, "Do you know what they want me to do?" "Something you shouldn't," answered Morrow, and Capper told him of their desire that he enter the race for Governor Mrs Capper had not heard of the afternoon conference, but she had become reconciled to the idea and approved the candidacy of her husband After considering the effects on the business, Morrow was also inclined to favor the Capper campaign because of the obvious advantage of having the Governor's name on the masthead of every Capper paper [2]

74

Until he had sought the advice of a wide number of acquaintances Arthur Capper was not ready to announce that he would be a
candidate for the position of Governor William Allen White assured Capper, "You are absolutely sure of the support of every man
in the so-called square-deal camp, if you decide to run," but he also
had some words of caution "The Capital is as permanent as an[y] institution in this state It has done more than any other one force in
this state to bring us up to our present progressive standard and during the next four years, it seems to me we cannot well afford to have
the influence of the Capital crippled, as necessarily it must be crippled if you run for governor .   its activity would be discredited
by the fact of your candidacy   you may depend upon me to do
all that I can to help you "³

By mid-1911 Capper's decision to enter the Republican gubernatorial race in 1912 seemed assured, but outside forces were setting
the stage for an interesting presidential race in 1912 that was to have
repercussions in Kansas ⁴ Senator Bristow was increasingly concerned
about the "presidential situation" as a consequence of his falling out
with Senator Charles Curtis He suggested that Capper "go easy" in
his support of Taft, since that support might later prove embarrassing, and White readily approved of this plan ⁵ Bristow reported
"Taft is a reactionary, through and through From now on until the
election, he will talk progressive ideas stronger than LaFollette or
myself, but his acts will all be reactionary   no one with whom I
talk thinks there is more than one chance in ten for his election, and
I fear with his defeat he will take down the entire party with him,
state and national "⁶

Capper readily accepted the Bristow suggestion that "Arthur
Capper, as the editor of the progressive Topeka Capital, is much
stronger in Kansas than Arthur Capper, as an advocate and promoter
of the candidacy of William H Taft "⁷ William Allen White was
also advising Capper to "continue to say what good things might be
said of Taft without reflecting upon LaFollette " He felt that it
"would be a mistake" to take a definite stand this early and that a
newspaper committed to reform should continue toward its goal and
"keep right on sawing wood   "⁸

When the Capper candidacy was formally announced, W T
Beck, an ardent supporter of Capper, was asked to write an introduc-

tion for a newspaper commentary about the proposed race Beck's flowery remarks sounded the keynote of widespread backing, describing Capper as "the one man who can unite the several factions of the party " The prospective candidate was also pictured as remarkably "free from bigotry He is never arbitrary nor dictatorial "

Capper's announcement in the *Capper Bulletin,* a combined house organ and advertising periodical, stated "My determination to become a candidate for Governor really means that I have decided to let you folks run the Capper newspaper business, while I try to run the state I don't doubt for a minute that you can handle YOUR part of it all right and I have just enough self-confidence to feel that some way or other I can manage to make a tolerable good Governor "[9]

National magazines, such as the *Saturday Evening Post* and *Collier's,* reported the Capper candidacy and recognized his close association with William Allen White, Victor Murdock, and Walter R Stubbs in the progressive wing of the Republican party in Kansas [10] Almost three hundred newspapers in Kansas commented on Capper's decision to run, the vast majority approving his action. Almost from the first announcement he was considered a "harmony" candidate by the various Republican factions [11] But early in 1912 Capper indicated his sympathy with the progressive conspiracy to obtain the Republican nomination for Theodore Roosevelt, an action that no doubt cost him votes in November He also favored a presidential primary in Kansas so that the people could express their wishes to the convention [12] In spite of his backing of "Roosevelt as the most available man" in the party, he had "no desire to say anything in disparagement of President Taft, who has in many respects made an admirable record "[13] Nor did he favor the formation of a new political party [14]

When the twenty Kansas delegates went to Chicago to the Republican convention in 1912, eighteen were pledged to Roosevelt and two to Taft Most delegate contests were decided for Taft under an arrangement that Roosevelt had helped install in 1908 The Taft steamroller relentlessly defeated efforts of Roosevelt backers to establish a stronger position, and they, including William Allen White, Henry J Allen, and Walter R Stubbs, bolted the Republican convention In the state Republican primary election Roosevelt electors easily triumphed over those supporting Taft, and it appeared likely that the pro-Roosevelt electors would appear on the general election ballot in the Republican column But William Allen White, Progressive national committeeman, after he had resigned a similar position in the Republican party, urged the Roosevelt men to resign and run as presidential electors in the Progressive column [15]

As a Republican candidate for Governor of Kansas, Capper was urged by "standpatters" to declare for Taft if he was to continue under the Republican party label [16] Publicity was given in rival newspapers to political leaders who could no longer back Capper because he would not support Taft, but he had no trouble in the primary Frank J Ryan, of Leavenworth, protégé of Congressman D R Anthony, was Capper's only opponent in the primary election Capper received 70 per cent of the vote, while Curtis was narrowly defeated by Stubbs for the party senatorial nomination "Progressive" Republicans, however, lost only one state-wide contest, the one for Attorney General [17]

Capper's Democratic opponent in the general election was George H Hodges, lumberman from Olathe, who had been his party's candidate in the previous election Hodges, with an able eight-year record in the state Senate, had handily won his nomination over two other candidates He was characterized as a "pleasant, agreeable man, a good citizen, a good neighbor, a good businessman and a good politician of average candle power," while Capper was described as "singularly inexpert in the part of blowing his personal horn," and "so modest and self effacing" that he did not look like a political campaigner at all If such observations were accurate, a Hodges-Capper contest, should it become fiery or marked by "mud slinging," would more likely be carried on by subordinates [18]

While Hodges had a positive program for the improvement of Kansas government and Capper was proposing a continuation of the "progressive reform" of the Stubbs administration, most of the heat of the 1912 election campaign was generated by the national election or by those who were supporting the main participants in the battle. Even before Capper had become an active candidate, a widespread rumor was circulated in Kansas to explain the Capper support for reform as due to the fact that "Governor Stubbs held a mortgage of

$40,000 on the Capital " Capper endeavored to correct the rumor by writing to the reputed source of this statement [19]

The chief charges brought against Capper by the Democratic party were that Capper was printing and had printed indecent advertising in his publications Although evidence was drawn almost wholly from advertisements in *Household* magazine, his enemies damned his advertising policy as a whole One leading Democratic politician held " 'men only' meetings in every section of the state "[20] Pamphlets containing advertising culled from the vast files of various Capper publications over the previous decade were distributed with a printed note saying "WARNING Don't risk prosecution under the Federal law by mailing or offering for mailing any of the matter on this page."[21]

Printers' Ink, the outstanding journal of the advertising profession, defended Capper's advertising policy, but its influence in Kansas was not strong An effort to still the attack was made by J N Dolley, Republican state chairman, and by Marco Morrow, Capper's advertising manager Both recognized that advertising standards had risen within recent years and that Capper had actively supported the higher standards Morrow showed contempt for the "pure-minded patriots who are making this attack," and he reported that Capper was declining "advertisements amounting to $30,000 or $40,000 a year Were it not for Mr Capper's restrictions we could easily increase the revenue of our publications something like a thousand dollars a week I know that as far back at January 1, 1908, Mr Capper notified the advertising agencies throughout the country that he would not accept objectionable advertisements for his papers and that has been his policy ever since."[22]

Morrow's explanation could not undo a Capper responsibility if the advertising was truly questionable While the attack on Capper's advertising morals no doubt influenced some voters, he faced a much more serious loss from within the ranks of his own party from his unequivocal stand, taken after the national Republican convention, "I SHALL Vote for the Roosevelt Electors "[23] Full-page advertisements, put out by the pro-Taft Republican Party League, appeared in *Kansas Farmer* and many other Kansas newspapers throughout the two months preceding the election The final blast against all backers of Theodore Roosevelt was in the last issue before the election.[24]

Condemned as "candidates in this campaign who have betrayed the Republican Party" were Stubbs, Capper, and many others Specific charges were brought against "Arthur Capper and W. R Stubbs . conspicuous figures in the development of the Bull Moose conspiracy to betray the Republican Party   When the Bull Moose electors were driven from the Republican column, Capper and Stubbs refused to follow them as decent politics demanded " Many Republicans who had always opposed Stubbs were now against Capper [25]

A Democratic attack on Capper in the closing weeks of the campaign was contained in a circular to all retail dealers in Kansas, endeavoring to show that he was a special advocate of the mail-order system and thus opposed retail merchants Capper quickly prepared a rebuttal, "not in defense of my papers or the policy which governs them, because I do not feel that they need defending, I am writing this to point out the unfair and the demogogic [sic] methods employed in the interest of the Democratic candidate "[26]

The primary charge against Hodges was his membership in the "Lumber Trust " The Hodges Brothers' Lumberyard was reputedly a member from 1896 to 1908 of a "dealers' combine" which made use of the "black list" and "maintained prices and eliminated competition and restricted territory "[27] The denial was not long in coming, and Capper was chided because Hodges could not buy space in either the *Farmers' Mail and Breeze* or the Topeka *Daily Capital* [28]

Much of the Capper campaign was carried on through personal correspondence and in trips around the state Never considered an orator, he endeavored to be seen and heard as the sincere, eager-to-please person that he was Hodges made much the same type of personal campaign, although he was considered a better public speaker than Capper

Never in Kansas history has the outcome of a gubernatorial election been so long undetermined as in 1912 Long after it was known that Kansas had given its electoral vote to Woodrow Wilson, that Kansans had approved woman's suffrage, and that the Kansas House of Representatives and Senate would have a Democratic majority for the first time, the decision in regard to Governor was still in doubt News on November 8, indicating that the race for Governor was still uncertain, was changed the next day to Capper's being "slightly over 100 ahead " Ten days after the election a headline "Hodges 11

Ahead" was replaced in a following issue by news of Capper's winning "by 26 votes "[29] It is no wonder that an editorial on November 15, almost two weeks after the election, responded to the question, "Who's elected?" with "God only knows "[30] Almost three weeks after the election when Secretary of State Charles Sessions gave out an official finding of Hodges by 31 votes, attorneys for Capper brought test suits before the Kansas Supreme Court against the county commissioners of Wabaunsee County to force the counting of ballots which election judges had not counted because of the manner in which they had been marked In addition to the narrow margin for election the issue causing doubt was the "party column" type of ballot used in Kansas in 1912 Instructions at the top of each column instructed the voter to "vote a straight   ticket, as shown by the cross X mark in the circle thereon, except as otherwise indicated by the cross X mark opposite the names of other candidates elsewhere on the ballot "[31] These directions allowed a voter to cast his vote in the Republican party circle and cancel his vote for the Taft electors by placing an X in the square behind each of the Roosevelt electors. "In 1905 the law was so amended as specifically to require the counting of ballots marked in that manner,   "[32] Capper attorneys held that invalidating such ballots in Wabaunsee County alone involved approximately 124 votes and that between two and three thousand such ballots were rejected in various parts of the state [33] The court acted quickly and filed an opinion December 7, 1912 A majority of five justices held that the ballots in question "were in fact valid, but which the election board failed to count and returned as void." But the court could not compel the county canvassing board to "reconvene and count ballots," since it had "passed out of existence and can not be revived by its own action or by that of a court "[34] Dissenting Justice West, with Chief Justice Johnston concurring, held "Few rights are more sacred than the one to have an honest ballot properly counted It is setting the hands of the clock backward to hold that such right can not be protected in this case "[35]

In the meantime the final election figures gave Hodges a total of 167,437 to Capper's 167,408, which was a plurality of 29 votes for Hodges, who received the certificate of election [36] Kansas law provided one other corrective for a disputed election, an election contest Notice of intention to contest an election would have to be filed

with the secretary of the state Senate on certain days after the legislature convened [37] The Senate would be the ruling body to pass on an
election contest, and in 1912, for the first time in Kansas history, a
majority of Senators were Democrats Taking these facts into consideration, along with the observation that the House of Representatives was also dominated by Democrats and that Hodges would be
inaugurated by the time the legislature convened, Capper announced in mid-December that he would "not appeal to a Partisan
board" and would not contest the election [38] Instead he took his appeal to the "court of public opinion," where a more sympathetic
hearing could be predicted Newspapermen throughout the state
commended the Capper action A folder, "Why I shall not enter a
contest though undoubtedly elected governor, a statement to my
friends," was prepared for widespread distribution throughout Kansas [39] Capper noted that his attorneys were well-known progressive
Republicans, while those representing Hodges in the appeal to the
Supreme Court were both "standpat" Republicans He felt that the
decision was "not on the merits of the case " Not one to harbor hard
feelings, Capper wrote "Mr Hodges, working with a legislature of
his own political faith, will have an ideal opportunity to serve Kansas I feel it is now for the best interest of the state that Mr Hodges,
and the party he represents, be given that opportunity Mr Hodges
has my best wishes for the next two years and I shall be glad to assist
in any way I can in making his administration one that will be helpful to the state "[40]

Well-documented arguments have been presented that Wilson
would have won the presidency in 1912 even without the split in
Republican ranks [41] The split in Kansas was more obviously responsible for the Hodges victory If there had been no "Bull Moose"
party in 1912, it is difficult to visualize a loss for Capper, considering
the fact that his margin of defeat was only 29 votes Without a split,
the political complexion of the state legislature could have taken a
different hue Capper's personal popularity in the state explains why
he polled as large a vote as he did

The outcome of the election and Capper's decision not to contest it brought a letter from D O McCray to the defeated candidate McCray, one of the first newspapermen to suggest a Capper
candidacy two years earlier, was disclaiming credit for advertisements

circulated by the Democratic Committee against Capper "This is an absolute lie," wrote McCray, " this document was printed by the Kansas Farmer, and you ought to be able to guess from that where it was instigated " McCray further indicated that he had supported Taft "Had you taken my advice early in the campaign you would have been elected by 30,000 majority But that is past history "[42] And for Arthur Capper there was no looking back He had his eye set on the 1914 election

Early in January, 1913, Capper was active in the organization of a harmony movement in preparation for the election of 1914 Contacts were renewed over the state, and commitments were obtained for support in the forthcoming election [43] Drew McLaughlin, of Paola, observed the "Harmony" program being backed by Taft Republicans at the Kansas Day meeting at Topeka in 1913 Since "there was tension in the party" due to the loss at the polls, Capper was not warmly greeted when he attended, by invitation, a meeting to plan a bulletin which would publicize state affairs Capper volunteered to handle all publication details of the bulletin, and the "Comeback of the Republican party in Kansas was under way "[44] But backers of a program of reconciliation with the Republican party in Kansas did not have the ready assent of such Progressive party leaders as White, Stubbs, and Murdock There were suggestions that Capper wavered in his choice of the party he would back Responsible for this view was a speech Capper made on December 4, 1912, to the Montgomery County Progressive club at Independence [45] Later reports, as the campaign got under way, stated that Capper "has not decided to join the third party," and more than a year later, "How Time flies! Capper changes colors since declaration of 1912 Ugh! How he hated the G O P Two Years Ago! 'Tis a different story now "[46] In a letter to the editor Capper preferred to emphasize his Republican connections when he wrote, "You republish a garbled report of a speech made by me at a dinner given by the Independence Progressive Club

in which you say that I had left the Republican party I did not on that occasion, nor at any other time intimate that I had left or that I intended to leave the Republican party There was no Progressive party in Kansas at that time "[47]

As Kansas Day (January 29) approached in 1914 the "harmony route" to public office through the Republican party included "progressives" Arthur Capper, Joseph L Bristow, and Fred Jackson Stubbs, White, Murdock, and Allen supported the Progressive party, which sought to survive until the presidential election of 1916 by placing a state ticket in the field in 1914 Conservative Republican newspaper editors, "tongue in cheek," felt it was strange to see the new alignment in state's politics One wrote· "Capper went down with the Bull Moose ship in the election Since that time Capper has done much thinking on his own account He has concluded that he will travel awhile with his old friends and now they are making faces at each other White and Stubbs have sorrowfully said good-bye to the Topeka publisher by throwing a brick at him and Capper has retaliated by printing Bull Moose news ninth page, next to Lydia Pinkham advertising "[48]

Kansas political news in January, 1914, was juicy and gossipy Senator Bristow was denounced by William Allen White and Victor Murdock [49] Former Governor Stubbs charged Capper, Jackson, and Bristow with offering to guarantee no opposition for Murdock in the Eighth Congressional District if Murdock would stay out of the senatorial race William Allen White, in righteous indignation, editorialized that it was a plot to steal the Progressive party Capper denied that any such proposal had been made, and in typical fashion he did not attempt to strike back in kind [50]

Instead of becoming involved in antagonizing battles with old friends in 1913 and 1914, Capper sought to win new ones The change in the name of the *Kansas Weekly Capital* on September 6, 1913, to *Capper's Weekly* was in part politically motivated Additional publicity from various "Capper for Governor" clubs was printed Capper was responding to invitations from all over the state to attend Memorial Day services, address state conventions, and share in lodge functions Having attained his oratorical experience, as some said, "through correspondence courses," he usually appeared before an audience as a shy and unassuming man who soon evoked a sympathetic understanding from the group he addressed Attempts were made to acquaint potential voters with the Capper advertising policy which had been followed since 1908 [51] Announcements that he would again run for Governor were made in February, 1914, along with this statement "I am firmly convinced that the third party movement recently begun in this state is a serious mistake because it can accomplish nothing except possibly the perpetuation of Democratic misrule in Kansas There is a wide-spread belief that a majority of the legal votes cast for governor at the election of 1912 were in my favor But a technicality of law considered binding by a majority of the supreme court defeated the plainly expressed will of the people "[52]

Capper was confident that the people, including a large number of women who would be voting for the first time, would clearly express their desire for him in 1914

Since the candidates for Governor of Kansas in 1914 were unopposed in seeking their own party nomination, little actual campaigning occurred before the August primaries, in which Capper, as the Republican candidate, received 105,800 votes Incumbent Governor Hodges and three other minor party candidates received a total of less than 92,000 [53]

As far as Capper was concerned, the major issue was the record of the Hodges administration, which he considered unduly extravagant, poorly organized, and responsible for making more new state jobs and raising taxes more than ever before in the history of the state He criticized the number of pardons and paroles handed out by the Democratic Governor Republican supporters were also critical of the 294 new jobs on the state payroll, at a cost of $10,000 each month [54] Capper did not "promise to reduce . taxes, but   that every dollar of the state's money would be expended honestly and economically and that taxes would be held to the lowest possible figure "[55]

Capper was again attacked because of his advertising policy Newly enfranchised Kansas women were told that he was a man who "sneered at everything sacred to women by publishing and circulating lewd, obscene and suggestive postcards" and that he was responsible for other corrupting practices [56] One of the big sidelines of the Capper business was the sale of post cards, some of them locally produced The post cards described in Democratic literature were not carried on the regular stock shelves, and Capper had no knowledge that his business carried stock which he personally opposed The employee responsible for handling the questionable post cards was warned but not dismissed, contrary to advice Capper received from his leading executives.[57]

When Republican leaders were directing their campaign attack against Governor Hodges, the Governor responded with a challenge to debate the issues involved in the election with his Republican opponent Finally, after he could avoid answering no longer, Capper issued a statement saying "Personally, I have paid little attention to the governor's clamor for a joint debate I have neither the leather lungs, the adroitness of tongue, nor the impudent assurance of the wind-jamming spellbinder Within the last two years the people of Kansas have learned, if they did not know it before, that I am unskilled as a stump speaker, which probably accounts for the governor's clamorous ardor for a debate "[58]

When Hodges complained "that his administration has been systematically misrepresented by the Capper publications and that their columns are closed to him,   " he received only a mild reply from Capper Capper maintained that the *Capital* alone had "printed for the benefit of its readers 342 columns of political speeches, news matter, and other information given out from the office of Governor Hodges or his appointees   " Large numbers of other columns were tabulated to show that much had been published on the Public Utilities Commission, the Bank Commission, the State Grain Department, and other state administrative departments We have "even printed," said Capper, "the best part of the governor's famous Columbus speech in which he informed the prohibitionists of Ohio that he was elected two years ago because he was the candidate of the preachers and the law and order element, while his opponent (Capper) was the candidate of the liquor interests " Capper felt that his columns had been open to Hodges, and he reiterated his offer to the Governor to make additional use of them [59]

Capper was influenced by reaction to the outbreak of war in Europe in 1914 and he spoke out most strongly against "war profiteering," which was evident through increases in general wholesale prices in the United States This was one of the new issues in the 1914 campaign, but, on the whole, the campaign did not become as heated as the one in 1912

With Kansas women casting their initial vote for their Governor, the vote in the general election surpassed the half million mark for the first time in Kansas history Capper, with 209,543 votes, led his ticket and had a plurality of 47,847 over his closest rival, Governor

George Hodges Capper and Hodges together accounted for 70 per cent of the vote, since the other four candidates received almost as many votes as did Hodges Hodges' vote from 1912 to 1914 declined almost six thousand while Capper's was increasing by more than forty thousand Moreover, Capper's state-wide strength in 1914 gave him the lead in 86 counties, whereas he had carried only 65 in 1912 [60] A comparison of election returns in the first two Capper races shows that he gained ground in 95 of the 105 counties, even though there were six candidates in the general election of 1914 Capper was quite willing to give credit to those who he felt were responsible, the women who were voting for the first time He was proud to maintain that he had the "honor of being the first native elected governor and the first elected at the time when intelligent women had something to say about who should be governor "[61]

Soon after the 1914 election William Allen White responded to a Capper letter by writing

I was indeed pleased to get your letter I presume sometimes in throwing the loose portions of the landscape around during the campaign, a fellow may inadvertently grab ahold of something and let drive things that should not be thrown

Because you seemed to want the job, I am glad you got it, but I cannot see why in the world you did want it, or what in the world there is in it to attract you However, you got hold of the tail of the bear and cannot let loose for two years at least

I do not suppose there is very much I can do to help you I am cast in outer darkness politically

In the meantime, the Gazette is going to back you up in every good thing, and I cannot imagine you doing any other kind of thing . [62]

In analyzing the election White wrote less than a week later.

It pays to be gentle and kind Arthur Capper won because he said nothing to offend anyone His victory is a victory for the man who takes the line of least resistance That he will make a good governor seems to be a foregone conclusion He will be fair with everyone He will treat all classes fairly and know no factions or crowds He will call about him the wisest, best men in Kansas as his advisers The great problem of his administration is so to reason with a Democratic majority in the state senate that it will put the state's welfare over the party's welfare For if the Democrats care to play politics they can postpone for two years the fruits of this victory [63]

Chapter IX

The Meek and Mild Governor

The tempo of the times was greatly changed by January, 1915, when Arthur Capper assumed the position of Governor of Kansas. The European war diverted attention from the domestic scene and offered a threat to advances which Americans were making in their standard of living Improvements in communications and transportation accented speed, gone was the leisurely life so frequently associated in nostalgic memories with the days before "the Great War " In the dawn of the age of the automobile, business activity was growing far more complex, and citizens were expecting and receiving additional services from increasingly expensive local, state, and federal governments Progress was being hailed as "bigger," "colossal," and even "stupendous " Progressive liberals were no longer compatible with Theodore Roosevelt, and the Progressive party, which had caused Capper so much grief in 1912 and no little concern in 1914, was on its deathbed

In the transition period between peace and war Capper paid almost no attention to national or foreign affairs His only mention of war during the campaign was to express gratitude that we were not involved as a nation He had strongly opposed possible war profiteering, but the campaign for him hinged on local matters which were little influenced by a distant war

Throughout the campaign Capper spoke of the need for a "business-like" government, and after his election he reiterated his stand in favor of "modern scientific business methods, in the elimination of useless positions and in requiring the highest efficiency on the part of every public servant "[1] His first Inaugural Address delivered in Representative Hall, January 11, 1915, expanded on that theme He was aware that the "second decade of the Twentieth Century   . [was] a time of unrest, of change," but the burdens of taxation had "increased at an alarming rate without commensurate benefit to the public " He proposed a serious "scientific study" to eliminate "useless red tape" and "cumbersome, expensive and wasteful methods" in government He recognized that there were many "material tasks which need money for their accomplishment " Constructive legislation according to Capper included the prohibitory law, the equal suffrage law, the "blue-sky" law, and similar reforms which showed the "progressive, forward-looking spirit of the Kansas people" Optimistically he prophesied that the next two years would find Kansans making a "slow but sure advance in human progress, for loftier ideals, for a wider and deeper justice, for a quickened sense of public honor and public duty, toward making our beloved state a little cleaner, a little more decent, happier, and more God-like."[2]

At the same time Capper found it necessary to lay down certain policies for his private affairs No employee was permitted to go to the Governor's office to talk business Capper would attend to his private affairs in his own office in the Capper Building after five o'clock He was deeply engrossed in his new role as Governor, and he had little time or inclination to consider needed expansion of his various journals When plans for enlarging or drastically changing any of his publications were brought to his attention during this period he usually responded negatively[3] His interest in his business continued, but politics provided many new and exciting experiences to him, and while he was Governor it gained a prior claim on his time On the other hand, as one of the last of the breed of personal publishers he was unwilling to relinquish his position in private enterprise It was a time for change in government, a transition period from peace to war, but for Capper Publications the major interest was in holding the line, and there was little opportunity for variation or new developments

Capper was well aware that the duties of a Governor were time-consuming and likely to separate him from the masses of people all over Kansas So he took his "open door" policy from his own business over to the Governor's office At no time, as Governor or later, did Capper want seclusion from his constituents He wanted to know what they thought and how they felt about questions of public policy Through the pages of his publications he showed a sincere interest in the attitudes of the common man Encouragingly he asked all "Kansas men and women and western men and women for suggestions of any kind whatsoever that they think will tend toward bettering the public service in any particular, or to improving our laws or rules of government"[4] His appeals brought a heavy response, and his mail was large throughout his public service.

A problem not usually faced by Republican Governors in Kansas was confronted by Capper during his first term The hold-over forty-man state Senate was dominated by a narrow majority of twenty-one Democrats They naturally organized the Senate committees to their own liking, and rumors soon persisted that they were determined to scuttle the Capper platform of economy and efficiency Sixty-six Republicans were soon joined by nine Progressives to give Capper a substantial majority in the House Midway through the legislative session Governor Capper appeared before the assembled legislature to remind them that Kansas was "facing an absolute necessity for stringent economy," due to "world-wide uncertainty and depression " He observed that a "niggardly policy of dealing with public affairs is not expected nor demanded of us To impair the usefulness of any state institution or retard its growth is not economizing " But the appropriation bills in the Senate were already one and a half million dollars over appropriations of the previous legislature, and they were one million dollars higher than corresponding bills offered by the House of Representatives Capper did not openly "question the motives of those who now advocate this abnormal increase in appropriations," but he pointed out that "some of the members who are now urging this increase are the very ones who were most deeply concerned two years ago in keeping down appropriations Then they reluctantly appropriated $166,982 for new buildings at state educational institutions, while now they are urgently insisting that $960,350 be appropriated for the same purpose "⁵ Perhaps this move had some influence on his political opposition in the legislature, however, Capper felt obliged to veto seven items in appropriation bills totaling $129,000 ⁶ In spite of these reductions direct appropriations of the 1915 legislature and funds reappropriated were approximately ten million dollars for the biennium, almost a million more than for any previous Kansas legislature

Among the more than four hundred laws passed by the 1915 Kansas legislature and signed by Governor Capper were the laws for creation of a state Civil Service Commission, a stronger "Blue Sky" Law, rural credit loans from building and loan associations, pensions for widows with dependent children, an industrial welfare commission for women, provision for city courts in smaller Kansas communities, virtual elimination of the fee system for compensating public officials, penalties for "fee-splitting" of physicians and surgeons, transferring the duties of the Board of Irrigation to other agencies, and development of a stronger State School Book Commission [7] Radical changes in the administrative affairs of the state, including consolidation of various agencies, reduction in personnel, and provision for a more efficient and economical administration would have to await a more co-operative legislature and the report of the newly created legislative Efficiency and Economy Commission

Capper was not wholly pleased with the results of his first legislative session, 106 of the 421 new laws were passed on the last day But in his typical fashion he waved aside numerous invitations to engage in political squabbles and won the increasing confidence of the state Tirelessly he sought to know the will of the people and so far as possible to make it effective

With almost a hundred separate offices, commissioners, bureaus, and boards in the Kansas Executive Department, Capper soon discovered that the position of the Governor in Kansas, as in other states, was mainly that of a figurehead [8] Leading executives in state government were elected and were responsible to the people, not to the Governor Many of the members of boards and commissions were appointed by previous Governors and owed no allegiance to the incumbent Intentionally the authors of the Kansas constitution, with typical American suspicion of a strong executive, had created a weak one, and Capper came to understand that his platform pledges could not be easily fulfilled in the course of a single term Nevertheless, he continued to publicize the need for "strictest economy on the part of every department head" and the need for less waste and more business efficiency Administrative leaders were urged to review their budget carefully and to eliminate "every superfluous or time-serving employee "[9]

Midway through Capper's first year as Governor his supporters were beginning to recall that he had declined to contest the election two years before in order to give Hodges the benefit of a united Democratic legislature As they pointed out, "Notwithstanding his generosity then, Governor Capper now finds his hands tied and his efficiency program being blocked at every turn by Hodges Democrats The same cabal which resorted to mudslinging in the last campaign, which worked against his economy program during the legislature, now declines by means of Democratic holdover boards, to inaugurate reforms that are clearly in the interest of efficient and economical management of the state institutions "[10]

A break in the barriers insulating the various state institutions from the Governor's office came in July, 1915, when Warden Jeremiah D Botkin of the Kansas State Penitentiary was suspended pending an investigation of charges of inefficiency, misconduct in office, and inattention to duty [11] Botkin, a Hodges appointee, had a checkered political career, first as Prohibition candidate for Governor in 1888, chaplain of a Populist-dominated state Senate in 1895, Congressman-at-large as a candidate of the Democratic and People's party in 1896, followed by three successive defeats for the same position In 1908 Botkin was the Democratic candidate for Governor and was defeated by Walter R Stubbs As a leading supporter of Hodges, it was Botkin in 1912 who led some of the most violent attacks on Capper with his "men only" meetings throughout the state [12]

On September 16, after finding Botkin guilty on eleven counts, the investigation closed [13] In an official letter to the Warden, Capper wrote that the committee found that the "charges so made against you are true, and have recommended your dismissal from the public service as such warden "[14] A week later the Governor "chastised the State Board of Corrections for conditions" that brought Botkin's dismissal [15] The Governor's control over appointive boards, previously weak and ineffectual, was being strengthened

Generally the publicity originating in the Governor's office was well received Kansans were writing their Governor not only about public policy but also about private matters Many letters came to Capper's desk in which correspondents sought advice concerning land problems, divorce, and family relations Capper provided prompt courteous replies, sometimes advising the letter-writers to seek the counsel of the county attorney or a good lawyer

Frequently the Governor broke into the news by calling a meeting to discuss methods for prevention of flood losses, or to ask the U S Department of Labor to investigate conditions causing southeast Kansas coal miners to be unemployed Proclamations, emanating from the Governor's office, included a "Good Roads Day" and a multitude of other "days " Even the Topeka *Daily Capital,* under orders to provide no publicity for the owner in his pre-political days, increasingly told the story of Governor Capper in prominent leading articles But on the whole, Capper's recognition by his own newspaper was probably less extensive, although more friendly, than that accorded to his immediate predecessor

The Panama-Pacific Exposition, held in San Francisco in 1915, provided Kansans with an opportunity to publicize their state The legislature voted $20,000 for a state exhibit, and Governor Capper appointed a large number of official delegates, including the ten Kansans elected to the National Top-Notch Farmers Club The Governor, accompanied by Mrs Capper, left Topeka July 12 to be present for the Kansas Day ceremonies on the 16th These delegates, like those appointed by the Governor to a vast number of other regional and national meetings, traveled at their own expense, but they were frequently gratified by the recognition they received as official delegates from Kansas Throughout his four years as Governor, Capper reputedly named more delegates to out-of-state meetings than any of his predecessors [16]

While Governor Capper preferred that the office, particularly high appointive offices in the state, should seek the man rather than the man seek the office, he was burdened by an abnormal number of applicants for state jobs He reported that more than 4,000 persons applied for one vacancy, and he acknowledged that "Grover Cleveland was probably right—a governor makes 19 enemies and one ingrate for every appointment   "[17] Many people wrote him for their share in the political spoils, and his office systematically maintained two notebooks, one listing the names of persons and the jobs they asked for and another listing individuals and their positions in state government [18] No doubt the issue of political appointments and his inability to satisfy all constituents strengthened his desire for a merit system for all civic servants

The Governor of Kansas, like most other Chief Executives, has a dual capacity of chief administrator and ceremonial leader of the state The symbolic role as chief representative of Kansas, although interesting to him, was a time-consuming and mile-covering task for Capper During his first eleven months in office he had more than 120 major appointments with commercial and business groups, religious, patriotic, and fraternal organizations, local, county, and state fairs, high-school and college commencements, and attendance at sports contests and cultural events [19] More than half of these activities were carried on outside Topeka, and the Governor was expected to give a speech at a great many of them [20] Numerous delegations also visited him in the Governor's office

Kansas in 1915 still had something of the frontier spirit when the 302,087-acre National Forest Reserve south of Garden City was restored to homestead entry Kansans, numbering one and two-thirds millions, were primarily dependent on agriculture The great wealth of underground minerals, of which coal production was then most valuable, was virtually untapped, and industry was in its infancy This rural, largely native-born citizenry, from the heart of the nation, was opposed to anything suggesting intervention in the European war They completely agreed with President Wilson's position on neutrality, and Governor Capper fully endorsed such a position as consistent with his own long-time view

In close co-operation with Governor Hodges, Governor-elect Capper served as chairman of the Kansas committee to provide relief for war-devastated Belgium Six and a half million pounds of wheat flour were collected and shipped in a few brief weeks Within a month after his inauguration as Governor, Capper responded to local World Peace groups and called a state-wide conference into session at Topeka [21] After the establishment of the nation-wide League of Nations to Enforce Peace in June, 1915, Capper became chairman of the Kansas branch, and national stationery of the League listed Capper as a sponsor Still later Capper became a member of one of the committees of the National Security League To advocates of preparedness in 1915 he would respond, " 'Preparedness for war' was powerless to stay this great war in Europe "[22]

Because of his official position and his announced conviction on world peace Capper was a recipient of Henry Ford's invitation to sail aboard the *Peace Ship Oscar II* to mediate the end of the war [23] When Capper courteously responded that the laws of Kansas would not allow him to be absent from the state for the length of time required for the trip a concession was made to allow him to "return to America sooner than rest of expedition "[24] But Capper did not go with Ford and his "aggregation of neurotics" sailing on what was facetiously described as a "loon ship "[25]

By late 1915 Wilson was beginning to change his views on strict neutrality Congress received his comprehensive plan of national defense on December 7 In late January he began a preparedness tour which brought him to Kansas on February 1, when he spent five hours in Topeka Most Kansans were not prepared to depart from their neutral and isolationist position The meeting of the Woman's Kansas Day Club on January 29 had resulted in condemnation of militarism and the preparedness program On the following day Governor Capper, in his address to the Peace and Equity League, again advocated a recurring theme of his, that "manufacture of munitions be taken out of private hands so that individuals and corporations could not profit from war "[26] By the time President and Mrs Wilson arrived in Topeka Capper received a letter which was intended to strengthen his opposition to the preparedness program The writer, Oswald Garrison Villard, told Capper, "I note that you are going to entertain President Wilson when he comes to speak in Topeka He seems to have captivated everybody in Cleveland, according to our correspondent who is with him I hope that Kansas at least will stand fast, and not give in to his plausible arguments "[27] Perhaps Capper's introduction of the President at the City Auditorium was influenced by the letter In part he said "Many of us are not in accord with the program of vast armament, with all its hazardous consequences, and the theory of a chance or a possible foe But we welcome the fullest discussion, and we feel the deepest respect and sympathy for the head of the nation in this grave hour We sincerely desire to avoid embarrassing him, we earnestly wish to do all we can do to help a policy that shall result in the greatest good to our people and to the world "[28]

A presidential address was also made at the high-school auditorium, and the Wilson party had luncheon in the Capper Mansion While he was courteously received, the impression made by the President in Kansas was not as effective as the one he had made in Ohio In an interview following the departure of his guests Capper declared that "President Wilson was the best dressed president" he had ever seen His comparison was with Presidents Harrison, Cleveland, McKinley, Roosevelt, and Taft [29] Two days later another Kansan, Senator Charles Curtis, presented a petition to the Senate containing nearly 11,000 names opposing the preparedness plan of the President Within less than two years such foot-dragging actions would label Capper, Curtis, and others as "peace-at-any-price" pacifists [30]

For a year following the President's visit to Kansas, Governor Capper devoted nearly all his attention to domestic affairs, giving little time to the European war When it was implied that foreign-born people in Kansas were disloyal, Capper defended them as "thrifty, honest and industrious" and he had no doubt of their patriotism [31] He was proud to announce that Kansas was officially out of debt after January 1, 1916, that the state was the third largest contributor to the Belgian Relief fund, and that per capita wealth was twice as high in Kansas as in the nation [32]

Of major interest to Capper was the approaching election He announced as a candidate for re-election His campaign speeches in 1916 were shorter than they had been in previous campaigns Often he spoke about moral standards, the importance of prohibition, the value of universal suffrage, the methods of achieving democracy, and the need for maintaining peace To him the "four great issues before the world today are universal prohibition for nations, universal franchise for men and women, universal democracy and universal peace "[33] Humorously he stated that the "shorter my speech, [the] larger my majority," and in 1916 he received a record-breaking 61 per cent of more than 580,000 votes [34] In spite of a Republican landslide for state and local offices, Woodrow Wilson won the Kansas electoral vote, and five of the eight Congressional seats went to Democrats Wilson's victory in Kansas was variously attributed to the slogan "He kept us out of war" and to $1 75 wheat and other issues, but Capper got a legislature more to his liking, with approximately three-fourths support in each house

The second inaugural address of Arthur Capper as he assumed the office of Governor of Kansas, in January, 1917, was similar to his first, except that his recommendations were more specific After dealing with state affairs he made reference to the war in Europe by saying that "of the several plans proposed, the League of Nations to Enforce Peace, headed by former President Taft," was the "most feasible and practical," and he urged "every man who loves humanity" to support such a movement [35]

The Governor's message to the 1917 Kansas Legislature was more optimistic and more explicit than the one he had made two years earlier Kansas had never been so prosperous, and the legislature was inclined to respond to his wishes The recommendations by the Governor in 1917 included a more simplified and more efficient government and consolidation of bureaus and departments, reduction in the number of judicial districts, development of an executive budget system, four-year terms for state and county officers, reorganization of county government, provision for city managers, reform in receivership laws, elimination of tax-dodging for intangible property, better, more practical schools, more state-published texts, better roads, stricter prohibition, industrial development, provision for a state oil department, provision for flood prevention, more productive state institutions, development of workmen's compensation and other welfare reforms, further reforms in the merit system, abolishment of the State School of Mines, and correction of certain existing laws Capper recognized that expenses in government were increasing rapidly and he urged economy and efficiency To him it was evident that "retrenchment in public expense can not begin and end in economy in the state's business alone," because other levels of government were showing far greater increases in spending than was true of the state.

The legislature, responding quite willingly to the Governor's suggestions, finished their task in fewer days than the session of two years earlier Perhaps the best-remembered act passed by the 1917 legislature was the "Bone Dry" prohibition law which was signed by the Governor on February 23 before 150 legislators who serenaded him with "How Dry I Am " This law was described as one of the "most drastic prohibition measures ever enacted . in any state "[36] Other legislation provided for a State Highway Commission, a Board of Administration to supervise state institutions, stricter regulation of cigarettes, a more comprehensive workman's compensation law, and a wide variety of local and state corrective legislation The state of Kansas almost completely reformed the manner of purchasing supplies for state activities [37]

Since Capper had long been interested in automobiles and motor travel, it was not unexpected that his administration would advocate an improved road system for Kansas The State Highway Commission, as an answer to federal defense legislation, began operation in April, 1917, and a definite program was formulated with the assistance of a Good Roads Association.[38] In a practical frame of mind, Capper could not expect that farmers would tax themselves for improved country roads, and he had no other alternative for such construction. Since the state could not go into debt for such improvements, he became an advocate of good roads within reason.[39] He expressed the belief that when a paved road "becomes a part of the State's highway system, the state shall reimburse the county for the cost of building the road."[40]

Though vetoes were fewer in 1917, Capper felt impelled to oppose some bills. Five of these would have allowed automatic increases in certain public utility rates, required inmates of the State Industrial Reformatory at Hutchinson to work for the Kansas State Fair at the discretion of directors of the fair, repealed a law which Capper considered protection for shippers and farmers, required return to the "party column" election ballot in use in 1912, and provided for a minimum term of three years for stealing a chicken.[41]

Midway through the legislative session the death of Major General Frederick Funston, fourth-ranking Army officer, gave an opportunity to eulogize a famous Kansan. Memorial services presided over by the Governor were held in the Hall of the House of Representatives on February 24, five days after Funston's death.

When former President William Howard Taft came to Topeka in late 1916 to address Kansans on behalf of the League of Nations to Enforce Peace he was pleased with the preparations engineered by the Governor. Capper had not moved as far toward intervention in the European war as Taft. Taft told his audience, "From a purely selfish standpoint it will be much better for the United States to be in a league of nations to enforce peace than to be on the outside in our fancied isolation."[42] Taft predicted that the people of the United States would have to support such a League, otherwise they might "commit the country by a treaty, and then suffer the humiliation of a dishonorable breach of our formal obligations."[43]

That the nation was steadily marching to war was becoming increasingly evident to onlookers, but Capper, strongly pacifist and unwilling to see the nation enter the blood bath, was still waiting for a miracle. Since he had hardly discussed national issues during the 1916 campaign, charges were brought that he was "the captain who deserted the ship."[44] Capper expected "Kansas to lead in peace

Bleeding Kansas has long given way to Leading Kansas " He felt that Kansas was "an enlightened State where many values are so high" that no "material advantage can serve to change" its opposition to war [45] To help stem the rush toward war, "Peace Sunday" was observed on January 27, 1917, by Kansans in accordance with a proclamation issued by Governor Capper [46]

When Germany resumed unrestricted submarine warfare on February 1, 1917, Capper conceded that the "patience of this country is exhausted" and that the President had the "united support of the people of Kansas in the severance of diplomatic relations " But he still hoped that "war will not be necessary "[47] Editorially, a leading national newspaper later criticized him for his persistent support of "our century-old policy, and tradition of pacifism and disarmament

But although Mr Capper is Governor of Kansas, he does not fairly represent the sentiment of his State or that of any State " War had not yet been declared when the editor held that pacifists "constitute in the present hour a much more dangerous element than the Copperheads of the North in the war between the States," and Capper was characterized as a 'misplaced Governor" who, like the Copperheads, was "obviously foolish and misinformed "[48] But Capper sincerely believed that, in spite of obvious division in Kansas over prospective war, he was truly interpreting the wishes of a majority of his constituents He had excellent channels of communication with citizens all over the state, and he had no reason to doubt the authenticity of the reports he received His reluctance to support war caused criticism that he was disloyal, which may have been responsible for his proclamation several days later fixing April 6 as "Loyalty Day in Kansas "[49] Thus, when Congress convened to declare war on Germany formally Kansans were involved in "Loyalty Day ceremonies" complete with patriotic speeches, parades, and pageants The day was observed in many communities throughout the state, and the Governor spoke to the crowd at Topeka.[50]

As long as the issue whether or not the nation would go to war in 1917 was subject to debate, Governor Capper, fundamentally a pacifist, opposed any steps which might be interpreted as warlike For him the debate was ended and the issue was settled in the last weeks immediately preceding the declaration of war Many who had supported or opposed his earlier position could not fathom his 'about-face " Actions which had been previously branded by advocates of war as disloyal would, now that the nation was at war, be considered disloyal by the Governor of Kansas Wholeheartedly he would support the national goal to win the war, and his only reservation would be the means sometimes employed to achieve that goal Extremists on the right or the left were dissatisfied with the Governor, but the vast majority of Kansans accepted Capper as a sincere and willing interpreter of public feeling in the state

The duties of the Chief Executive of Kansas "were quadrupled by the entrance of the nation into the war "[51] A food conference convened in Topeka on March 15, 1917, became the basis for a state Council of Defense organized on April 17 A national council had been organized for six months, but little had been done at the state and local level to mobilize full support for the war effort [52]

War was declared on "extravagance, luxury, unused land, gophers, chinch bugs, Hessian flies, hog cholera, bad marketing facilities, marketing gambling and grasshoppers   " An effort was made to alleviate prospective food shortages by urging a "vegetable garden in every back yard, a potato patch in every vacant lot, and an extra half-acre of potatoes on every farm "[53]

During the first year of the war, never-ending requests for Capper's attendance at patriotic meetings in all but three Kansas counties resulted in his giving "more than 300 patriotic addresses " Capper was zealous in his appeals to President Wilson, members of the President's Cabinet, and other wartime administrators, that servicemen be given clean and wholesome surroundings Likewise, he was fervent in his opposition to inequities suffered by farmers, vicious profiteering, and price gouging engendered by the war activity [54] The Governor appealed to Kansans, in the name of loyalty and the good name of their state, to do the utmost for the war effort "Antidraft" meetings spurred on by small groups within the state caused Capper to write an article for a national magazine declaring that Kansas was truly living up to her obligations under the conscription laws [55] He also reported to the President that "the people in every section of Kansas are loyally accepting the provisions of the conscription act The few professional agitators and secret enemies of the government who have come into the state have served only to arouse and intensify patriotism "[56] When Kansas troops were consolidated into larger units along with personnel from other states, Capper protested that it wiped out "state identity and as a matter of state pride it is unfair to the people who assisted in organizing these troops."[57]

Goals that Capper had fought for before the war were now supported with renewed vigor in the name of the defense effort. Letters were sent to all state governors on April 14, 1917, urging them to prepare petitions for the President and Congress to prohibit the liquor traffic as a war measure. The favorable response helped to strengthen the march toward wartime prohibition and ultimately the Eighteenth Amendment.[58] In November, 1917, Capper headed a group of businessmen on the "Prohibition Special" which went to Washington to support the cause of prohibition. Although Kansas was expected to lead, Capper did not convene a special session of the legislature to ratify the Prohibition Amendment, because of advice of legislators who preferred to wait for a regular session. Not as vigorous as Joseph L. Bristow, who regarded excessive contract prices for munitions and cantonments as "grab and plunder," Capper, nevertheless, was unsympathetic with the reports of rapidly increasing coal prices and other evidences of inflation. Coal producers called to a conference in Topeka by the Governor failed to offer any positive solution.[59] Ceiling prices then set by the national government were denounced by the same coal dealers in the state.[60] Capper also was active in his denunciation of profiteering in flour milling, and he stood his ground when one of the millers disputed his statement.[61] His suggestion as chairman of the Farmers' National Committee on War Finance to draft capital or to conscript all surplus income to provide for major war expenses did not meet with ready response in metropolitan areas.[62]

As a wartime Governor, Capper was an active participant in military ceremonies at Kansas Army installations and at Camp Doniphan, Oklahoma, where large numbers of Kansas troops were trained. He had an extensive correspondence with Major General Leonard Wood, of Camp Funston, on both personal and public matters.[63] Official denials that venereal disease rates at Camp Funston were climbing did not satisfy him, and throughout the war such reports became a source of never-ending concern for him.[64] A major topic of his war speeches was the maintenance of a strong and moral manhood in Army camps, and he asked Kansas citizens to support their servicemen with substantial purchases of war bonds and with their contributions to Red Cross and other wartime organizations [65] Personally, Capper was a heavy contributor of both time and money, and he also made substantial gifts to each Kansas regimental unit to help equip recreation rooms or to provide other forms of relaxation [66]

Governor Capper was criticized by uninformed superpatriots because they felt that he encouraged people over the state to write him about waste in Kansas resources and disloyalty found among Kansas people and that then he would do nothing with the information In almost all cases, even when information came anonymously, he immediately referred complaints to the United States Attorney in Kansas City for investigation by the Secret Service Usually he would write the informer a thank-you note, and to the person accused of disloyal conduct he would write a personal letter, "not in an official capacity," but as a friend who wanted "no slackers in Kansas." An interesting series of personal conflicts is apparent in the "Slacker File" maintained by the Governor Occasionally the person whose name was signed to a letter of complaint would reply to the Governor that he had written no such letter More frequently the person accused of misconduct would write at length to defend his loyalty or to explain that he refused to buy Liberty Bonds from the regular solicitors who were "personal enemy's [sic] but he never for one minute refused to subscribe" from his local banker Similar disputes broke out over local Red Cross drives, and some citizens tried to send their contribution to the Governor rather than face a neighbor who was the acknowledged solicitor for their district [67] Once complaints were filed with the U S Attorney, the matter was out of Capper's hands Capper was tactful in handling these often explosive personal letters, in which one writer complained that her neighbors were "Kaiser borned" and hence could not be trusted Almost no record of the contents of the letters to the Governor ever reached the Kansas press As far as Capper was concerned, Kansas was loyal almost to the last person

During World War I harsh attacks on freedom of speech and the press were so common as to be almost expected [68] People were convicted and imprisoned for criticizing the President, for failing to support bond campaigns or to subscribe to the Red Cross, and for being conscientious objectors In World War I conformity represented loyalty, and most Kansans were conformists Suspected of disloyalty because of the wartime hysteria were persons with German names or anyone who spoke German The Kansas State Council of Defense acted to forbid the use of German in any public meeting, and German was almost completely dropped from secondary and collegiate curricula [69] Local citizens often sought to eliminate the use of German over telephones or in any public or business place, and when compliance was not automatic they would frequently direct their complaint to the Governor, who in turn referred the question to the Council of Defense Actually Capper was not in sympathy with the use of German, and he saw little of value in foreign-language instruction [70] His frequent plea for more practical education included a decrease in such instruction, to be replaced by manual training, domestic science, and vocational agriculture But if the quantity of information about World War I intolerance is a reliable index, Kansas was an island of calm in a sea of bigotry.[71] Some of the credit should go to the Kansas Governor who, with all his patriotic fervor, was certainly no extremist

Another example of intolerance developed during wartime was the reaction toward the Non-Partisan League in Kansas On December 28, 1917, organizers of the League, using references from Arthur Capper and Tom McNeal, established headquarters in Topeka [72] When an official from the Federal Reserve Bank in Kansas City requested information about the activities of the Non-Partisan League in the state and suggestions for dealing with them, Capper wrote to many chairmen of county Councils of Defense [73] Within a week he was able to report that he had heard "nothing in regard to the operations of the Non-Partisan League in this state   . [It has] not gotten much of a foot-hold in this state. I can hardly believe that there is much foundation for the reports that they are circulating anti-government propaganda in Kansas   "[74] Some League members, hearing that Capper was requesting information about their organization, wrote that the "League stands with our government, *right or wrong,* as against a foreign power," and its membership includes "men of unquestionable character and Loyalty " Another wrote, "To think of me as a pro german, is ridiculous and you know that farmers are not I W W 's. If I as an organizer for the League, have ever taken a pro-german into the League, I don't know it .. "[75]

As a result of his investigation of the Non-Partisan League, Governor Capper remained neutral in his opinion of the new farm organization But this did not satisfy the opponents of the League, who were ready to brand it as disloyal because of past actions of its founder, Arthur C Townley, or, as Capper analyzed it, largely because of "the fact that Senator LaFollette made his pro German speech before the organization "[76] Even when Capper wrote these critics that up "to the present time no reports have come in containing tangible evidence of disloyalty on the part of members of the League in Kansas," "though I have made every possible effort to secure it," they tried further to smoke out a condemnation of the League from the Governor To a direct question Capper responded that he "would not accept the Non-Partisan League endorsement for Senator if it were offered " It was further necessary for the Governor to make clear that "Non Partisan League people have no authority for stating that I endorse the League principles There are probably some things in their program that are all right, but I have never lined up with the Non Partisan League in any shape or form and will not do so . "[77]

Capper's attitude toward the League was interpreted as a tacit endorsement and became responsible for a feeling, evident in what was written on the subject, that he was a League supporter [78] He claimed in later years that his handling of the League matter in Kansas led to its early demise in the state [79] Other factors, such as distance from the Non-Partisan League "hot-bed" in North Dakota, growth of the Farmers Union in Kansas, and development of the Farm Bureau, all played a role in keeping the Kansas membership small Capper could not condemn the Non-Partisan League, because his information did not warrant it His position by no means meant automatic approval But some agricultural spokesmen, moulded by their prejudices, unrealistically linked Capper with Non-Partisan League activity in Kansas

A leading Socialist newspaper, the *Appeal to Reason,* of Girard, Kansas, was denied the use of the mails after war was declared, and in September, 1917, it was refused a state charter Editor Louis Kopelin wrote Capper several months later asking why advertising from Capper Publications had been withdrawn from his paper Capper explained that advertisements in the *Appeal to Reason* cost 32 cents per reply, whereas 20 cents was considered high He was not criticizing the anti-war editorial policy "As you know," he wrote, "I have been for many years very much opposed to militarism, but I feel now that we are in war we must all subordinate our political and economic views to the one great purpose of winning the war "[80] Within a week Kopelin had outlined a new editorial policy supporting "the government's war program" and Capper wrote him commending his "fine, patriotic statement "[81] Later Kopelin was drafted and was sent "to allied countries to counteract German influence among laboring classes "[82]

Among the letters in Capper's Governor files are many which show an evident confusion between the powers of the state and federal government, especially in matters connected with rationing, defense, and conscription And well they might, for offices and agencies had pyramided with rapidity during the war years. Additional confusion was added by the announcement on May 12, 1917, that Capper would seek the position of United States Senator in the coming election Only one other Kansas Governor had advanced to the senatorial position previously and he had not made the jump while he was serving as Governor [83] Furthermore, Capper would have to defeat formidable and well-known opponents in order to gain the Republican nomination Other Republican candidates for United States Senator in the Republican primary of 1918 were Walter Roscoe Stubbs, two-term Governor of Kansas, Joseph L Bristow, a one-term Senator, and Charles F Scott, who had served as a Congressman for ten years During 1918 Capper made some 400 Liberty Loan and campaign speeches He often covered four counties in a day of campaigning, and to him they were "pleasant and restful vacations "[84] The overwhelming vote for Capper in the primary was a great surprise to most observers [85] Again accused of disloyalty to the Republican party Capper carried every county but one, which he lost to Stubbs by only twelve votes [86] With 103,120 votes cast for him in the primary, Capper not only won the nomination but received almost 60 per cent of the total Republican vote

The Democratic campaign against Capper in the fall general election was primarily leveled against his anti-war posititon before the United States was officially involved in the war [87] Again the election on November 5, 1918, was a walkaway, with Capper receiving almost 64 per cent of the total votes against the incumbent, Democratic Senator William H Thompson, who had defeated Stubbs in 1912 [88] Kansans had elevated their popular Governor to the United States Senate in a very decisive way, and they increased the number of Republican Congressmen from Kansas by four. Henry J Allen, although on a Y M C A mission in France, had even less trouble in being elected as Governor [89]

With the end of the war's hostilities shortly after the election, Governor Capper wrote many letters urging quick discharge of service personnel He also had time to present his views on "Our After-the-War Program," in which he felt the first two "years after peace are likely to test us almost as severely as the war itself."[90] After properly caring for the veteran, Capper proposed better country roads, positive laws to prevent a depression, selective immigration, the English language for all, opposition to the "epidemic of Bolshevism," and he backed most strongly a "rebirth of Democracy at home " When he left the Governor's office on January 13, 1919, there was an important job waiting for Capper as United States Senator. Mrs Capper and he took a lengthy trip to Miami, in January and February, and returned to Washington early in March From 1919, Washington would be as much a home to Capper as Topeka Topeka and Kansas would share a warm spot in his heart, but the scene would now shift to Washington and national affairs Capper would cut his senatorial teeth on some of the most crucial issues of the twentieth century

Chapter X

Capper Is a Committee

By the time he was elected to the United States Senate, Arthur Capper had developed an able administrative organization for his business which enabled him to devote his attention to the political career before him In a sense he was the chairman of a "committee" which he had picked to help him run his business No man, even one who worked long hours with an exceptional mastery of the profession of journalism, could do all of the things which were credited to Arthur Capper After 1915 his role was at least a dual one, as politician and publisher.

Capper employees or "associates" were loyal and devoted to their publisher, and he willingly gave them credit for their efforts Next to his own family he felt his primary duty was "to the people who are loyally working" in the Capper business [1] He maintained that "it is the policy of management to avoid friction, to keep peace and harmony in the family, and to settle all difficulties and misunderstandings without rupture "[2] The "Capper family" became his term for employees soon after 1900, and in 1905 he began the practice of providing an annual banquet, dance, or picnic for his growing list of employees

With increasing attention to a political career as Governor of Kansas from 1915 to 1919, and as a United States Senator for thirty years after 1919, Capper, of necessity, placed a heavier reliance on his "committee" to carry on the functions of his business The heads of the various departments in Capper Publications were people in whom Capper had complete confidence The loyalty of Capper to these employees and his restraint in dealing with them became proverbial in Kansas [3]

No mere listing of the leading members of Capper's "committee" for both his private business affairs and his public activities to 1920 would give an idea of the talent available to the Capper business and his public career Their background and the manner in which they came to work for Capper help to provide an understanding of the relationship Capper had with his associates

Thomas Allen McNeal, editor of the *Mail and Breeze* from the

106

time Capper purchased the *Kansas Breeze* in 1895, was the oldest Capper editorial worker in point of service [4] McNeal was born in Marion County, Ohio, October 14, 1853, and of necessity worked on a farm in his youth [5] He attended college at Ohio Central, Oberlin, and at Hillsdale, Michigan, but did not graduate After farming, teaching, and reading law, he followed his brother to Medicine Lodge, in south-central Kansas, in 1879 There he continued his study of law, helped to edit the *Cresset,* and was active in politics [6] He served on the city council and was elected to the state House of Representatives for the annual legislative sessions of 1885, 1886, and 1887 [7] McNeal then sold his share of the Medicine Lodge newspaper to devote full time to the practice of law and in 1890 he was elected mayor of his community.[8]

In 1894, McNeal moved to Topeka because he was "practically busted " His first issue of the *Kansas Breeze* was put out on Friday, April 13, 1894, and "it soon achieved rather a wide circulation for an infant It seemed to be going almost everywhere except to hell," and he had "hard work to keep it from going there "[9] In 1895, McNeal and his partner sold out to Capper and McNeal soon became the editor of the *Mail and Breeze* with responsibility for the editorial page [10] His relations with Capper were more like that of an elder brother than that of an employee Theirs was a "working partnership which held thru the years without controversy or dissension "[11] McNeal could do virtually as he pleased on and off his job [12] For example, in addition to his work as editor of the *Mail and Breeze,* he served as private secretary to Governor Edward W Hoch during the first half of 1905 and for the next six years he was State Printer He entered the race for Congress from the First District several times, and in the August primary of 1922 he ran third in a seven-man race for the Republican nomination for Governor.[13]

Never a "joiner," McNeal belonged only to the Saturday Night Club, whose interests provided his favorite recreation He was chairman of the Unitarian forum in Topeka for many years Well known in Kansas, not only as an editor but also as a speaker, he was in almost constant demand at nearly every kind of meeting for forty years Audiences were particularly delighted by his sense of humor and homely philosophy, which also permeated his editorials With the development of the Capper Farm Press McNeal served as head of the legal inquiry department, from which he extended an enormous amount of free advice to readers He was recognized for his interesting and moralistic "Truthful James" stories in many of the farm papers and for his "Sunday Forum" in the *Capital* As an editorial hobby he stressed the idea of small subsistence farms for everybody who earned less than an average salary He had a personal acquaintance with every Kansas Governor and supposedly knew every prominent man in the state His tolerance for political views contrary to his own was widely recognized He had been an early settler in a frontier community and he had seen the state of Kansas grow and develop A key man in Capper Publications for many years, McNeal, through his wide activities and personal acquaintance in the state, had much to offer in ability and experience As an inveterate worker, a man of broad interests and one who rarely took vacations, he helped to develop a loyalty found among Capper employees to their publisher His established position over the state, likewise, aided in increasing the circulation of the Kansas Capper newspapers [14]

Another trusted editor was Harold Taylor Chase, who came to work on the Topeka *Daily Capital* in April, 1889 From 1895 for forty years he served as an editor of that publication [15] Chase was born in Wilkes-Barre, Pennsylvania, on April 13, 1864, and received his bachelor's degree from Harvard in 1886 His early newspaper training was in Wilkes-Barre and from there he went directly to the *Capital* in Topeka For four years he worked with Capper as a reporter and editorial writer, and he stayed with the *Capital* when Capper bought the *Mail* Their journalistic careers were re-united when Capper, together with Chase and others, purchased the *Capital* in 1901

Like his employer, Chase was a person with whom it was difficult to become intimately acquainted He was never a "hail-fellow, well met " Through direct association with him or through his editorials people were impressed with his elegant and scholarly diction [16] A lover of the classics and student of history, he made extensive use of his studies in producing two columns of editorial matter each day, seven days a week and fifty weeks a year Chase had few outside activities and was wedded to his editorial position Like McNeal he helped to build loyalty in the Capper organization [17]

Arthur Lon Nichols, like McNeal and Chase, served many years on the editorial staffs of Capper papers Unlike these contemporaries, Nichols acted in various capacities on different Capper farm and general newspapers and magazines He was born in Leavenworth, January 20, 1865 He left school at an early age to work on the Leavenworth *Standard,* where he rose to the position of managing editor In 1897 he moved to the Omaha *Bee,* where he served as telegraph editor, and on August 15, 1900, he became managing editor of the *Mail and Breeze* Through his newspaper work Nichols developed a vigorous style, and his literary abilities came to be recognized After a period as managing editor of the *Mail and Breeze* he held the same post with the *Missouri Valley Farmer* and finally with *Household* In 1915, he was made editor of *Capper's Weekly,* and a few years before his death in 1936 he was given general charge of the Capper Farm Press [18]

Though Nichols had little personal contact with agriculture, and though most of his work was done without conferences with the publisher, he had wide discretion in his job as editor When he was editor of the *Household* he bought many stories by English authors, which he then condensed and edited to a length of about 100,000 words [19] He had a great capacity for work in spite of a chronic semi-invalidism from which he suffered much Nichols is sometimes regarded as the "father" of the Capper Farm Press because he more than anyone else originated the title [20] Because of his physical condition Nichols had few contacts outside his work and his home and his leisure was devoted to reading His various positions were ones of influence in Capper Publications and there he had a peculiarly close association with Capper

As Capper Publications grew, so did the responsibilities assigned to McNeal, Chase, and Nichols It was a point of personal pride for Capper to produce in his organization "men and women who are competent to assume the positions of large responsibility Preference is always given to old employes Some of our best-paid men have risen from the lowest ranks "[21]

Outside the editorial field was Marco Morrow, a close adviser on advertising and business matters, who came to Topeka as Capper's director of advertising in 1908 Morrow was born in Foster's Crossing, Ohio, July 18, 1869 He graduated from high school in Springfield, Ohio, in 1888 and spent almost a decade in journalism in the same city [22] Although little known outside the newspaper, advertising, and farm publishing field, he was well thought of and even identified "as great" in comparison with others doing similar tasks [23] His manner was often more intellectual than businesslike and on many occasions, in the period before 1930, Morrow served as a "ghost writer" for Capper Working from suggestions or an outline Morrow would prepare a speech or article in a style that Capper desired Morrow was a "student of the classics," and an inquisitive and courageous idealist [24] The fact that he stayed with Capper the remainder of his active working days and spent his years of retirement in Topeka was a surprise to those who knew him intimately, and it was something Morrow never expected [25] Morrow's former employer told Capper that Morrow would leave him at a moment's notice if he was reversed on any decision Morrow soon learned the Capper way of doing business, especially his light touch when dealing with employees. At first Morrow had "felt like cleaning house" in the advertising department, but similar wholesale removals in the Hearst papers had disgusted him So changes were made slowly, closer relations were established with advertising representatives through the country, and finally Morrow was following the "Capper policy of making suggestions rather than giving orders " This pattern seemed best for the temperament of the Capper organization at the time. A man fired from the advertising department for good cause would usually "bob up in another department " Major changes in departmental personnel were not difficult, because the whole Capper enterprise was growing rapidly and fresh talent could be brought in without displacing anyone [26] When Capper went to Washington as United States Senator, Morrow became his assistant publisher, and for many years thereafter he held responsible positions in Capper Publications [27]

Charles H Sessions came into Capper Publications from his political connections with Capper Although he worked as a newspaperman for fifty-four years, only the last twenty-two were spent in the Capper organization Born in Woodstock, Ohio, February 1, 1868, Sessions went to a job as reporter for the Kansas City *Times* after completing high school In 1892, he began work as reporter for the Kansas City *Journal,* eventually operating the Kansas City, Kansas, and Topeka bureaus of the paper [28] He also spent two years in the Washington, D C , office of the *Journal,* and in 1906 he served Governor Edward W Hoch as private secretary for six months [29] In 1910 Sessions was elected Secretary of State and gained re-election in 1912 [30] During Capper's first term as Governor, Sessions was his private secretary During the seond Capper administration, he was a member of the State Utilities Commission After 1919, Sessions was managing editor of the *Capital,* although he took out three years in the early twenties to be Postmaster of Topeka He greatly aided Capper's political career, and it was said that Capper and Sessions "thought alike upon all public and private affairs "[31] Other Capper employees sensed the close contact between Capper and Sessions after 1914 Like other leading Capper editors, he tried to see things as Capper saw them [32]

Several other editors in the "Capper family" had leading positions in his enterprise before Capper had fully committed himself to a political career They were A G Kittell, editor of the *Nebraska Farm Journal* from 1914 until Capper sold it, John Francis Case, editor of the *Missouri Ruralist* for many years after 1913, and John Fields, who began editing *Oklahoma Farmer* in 1915.

Kittell had gone to Capper Publications in 1909 as associate editor of the *Mail and Breeze,* upon his graduation from Kansas State Agricultural College After the Nebraska paper was sold Kittell served successively as associate editor, managing editor, and editor of *Capper's Weekly* [33]

John Francis Case had been a successful rural newspaperman in Missouri when he was drafted in 1913 to edit the *Missouri Ruralist* He was closely identified with Missouri, although he was born in Minnesota in 1876 [34] He held many appointive positions in Missouri and was president one year of the American Agricultural Editors' Association [35]

John Fields, born in Iowa in 1871, had considerable specialized training and experience in agricultural pursuits After graduation from Pennsylvania State College in 1891, he served in various technical positions for Pennsylvania and New York agricultural experiment stations In 1899 he went to Oklahoma as director and chemist of the agricultural experiment station and he was soon editing agricultural newspapers in the state In 1915 Fields became editor of Capper's Oklahoma paper When Capper sold *Oklahoma Farmer,* Fields went into the banking business, first in Oklahoma City, then with the Federal Land Bank and the Federal Intermediate Credit Bank, both of Wichita He was actively associated with Oklahoma affairs, and in both 1914 and 1922 he was the Republican candidate for governor [36] In 1916 he was a delegate-at-large to the Republican National Convention [37] Fields held responsible positions in experiment stations in several stations, and he knew both eastern and western agriculture He was widely considered for the position of United States Secretary of Agriculture in both 1921 and 1925, but Capper failed to support him, and the position went to other agricultural leaders [38]

All of these leaders in the "Capper family" were members of the Republican party Some of them were almost indifferent to individual political activity, while others ran for political office. Two of them, Sessions and McNeal, were frequently successful in achieving that goal Capper did not stand in the way of the political ambitions of his editors, but generally he refused to endorse their candidacies publicly This was particularly true of the political ambitions of Case and Fields, who were not among Capper's most trusted editors As a virtual "lone wolf" in Kansas politics with a large personal following, Capper did not like to interfere in the political contests of his own party He avoided political battles in neighboring states, and in Kansas he would publicly support only the nominated candidates of his own party, especially after the debacle of 1912

Among other Capper "old-timers" by 1920 were Mary May Capper, John E Griest, Charles J Dillon, Harry Wright, Conrad C Van Natta, and Robert Maxwell Each in his own way made important contributions to the enterprise before Capper went into the United States Senate

Capper's sister, Mary May, had worked as cashier in the business office from the early days of the *Mail and Breeze* She was also a part owner of the Mail Printing House and its successor Because of profitable investments which she made in the business of her brother-in-law, A L Eustice of Chicago, she retired from Capper Publications in 1916 [39]

As a boy John E Griest had migrated to Pawnee County, Kansas, from Pennsylvania After entering the service of the Union Pacific he became chief clerk of the Ellis, Kansas, office and was employed in Capper's business office about the time Capper took over the *Capital* Although some of his associates felt he lacked business vision, Capper wanted him back when he resigned to enter the service during World War I, and in all he worked twenty-three years for Capper [40]

Charles J Dillon went to Capper Publications in 1913 as managing editor of the five Capper farm papers Previously he had served as head of the Department of Industrial Journalism at Kansas State Agricultural College for three years, and as a member of the staff of the Kansas City *Star* for eleven years [41] His primary contribution to the farm press was "bringing the technique of the daily newspaper into the business "[42] In the mid-1920's Dillon became a public relations man for the Western Railways, with headquarters in California [43]

Harry Wright, "trouble shooter" for the *Capital,* was an able interpreter of "grass roots" sentiment for Governor and Senator Capper Within seven years after his family had moved to Labette County, Kansas, in 1874, when he was five years old, Wright was helping to support his widowed mother After various positions in newspaper offices and in job-printing establishments he moved to Topeka, where he had his own newspaper He worked for the Capper Printing Company for a time and resigned to serve as manager of a good roads association He farmed for a while and actively entered Republican precinct politics Eventually he returned to work for Capper as "outside contact man" for Capper's political campaigns [44] Senator Capper was nationally pictured as a man with an ability to keep both ears to the ground to hear the "grass roots" speak Almost no one realized that Harry Wright was one of those "ears "[45]

Conrad C Van Natta was born August 20, 1876, in a farm home beside the Santa Fe Trail near Council Grove. He learned the printing trade on the *Osage County Chronicle* and spent eight years before 1893 with various Topeka printing firms and newspapers Just before Capper purchased the *Mail* Van Natta went to the Salina *Journal,* only to return to Topeka about 1899 as foreman of the composing room of the *Mail and Breeze* He was one of Capper's closest friends from the mechanical department of the business He worked closely with Capper in various charitable activities from the distribution of Christmas baskets to the more substantial programs inaugurated after 1919.[46]

Robert Maxwell was another Capper "old-timer" whose service on the *Capital* antedated Capper's ownership of any paper. Born in Mt Vernon, Ohio, June 6, 1866, he began work on the *Capital* as a printer in February, 1888, while Capper was serving as city editor of the paper [47] As an expert technician, Maxwell was invaluable to Capper in helping to install and properly operate new printing presses. For many of his fifty-four years of service on the *Capital* he was superintendent of the pressroom Because Maxwell knew Capper when he was one of the rank-and-file and had worked for him so long a close mutual admiration existed between them [48]

In a sense, these Capper "old-timers" were all among the first-generation employees of Arthur Capper Their loyalty to their employer was reciprocated by him He appreciated their untiring work, and he told them so and tried to see that their income would be comparable to their duties There were others who were members of the inner circle of Capper employees Some were the advertising executives serving in the Chicago or New York offices, or were like William H Souders, who was Capper's private secretary for almost thirty years Some were people Capper saw almost every day, while others had rare personal contact with him When Capper Publications was incorporated, 114 of these long-time associates received shares of stock in the enterprise, and some of them were remembered in the Capper will

No doubt Capper had employees whose ability he failed to recognize When he disapproved of anyone in his employ there was little that person could do to gain advancement Some, aware of their relationship to Capper, left for greener pastures, but others stayed with Capper in positions below their experience and ability all of their working lives.

The "Capper family" continued to grow after the boss left for the United States Senate A second generation began to make itself felt in the business, and as the first generation was dying off in the thirties, others were moving in to positions of leadership A more formal relationship for the "Capper family" came into being in this later period, but that is all part of the Capper story after 1920

Chapter XI

The Capper Youth Clubs and Promotion of Rural Life

The desire of Arthur and Florence Capper to have their own children was never realized [1] Increasingly, as the Capper enterprises developed, there were provisions for recognition of children and youth activities Capper promotional projects for such activities eventually had a considerable annual budget and as he grew older they were a larger and more important source of personal satisfaction to him Attempts to analyze Capper's interest in children generally emphasized the economic value to his business or the strengthening of his political support His own explanation was much simpler He usually told youth groups, "One man took an interest in me, and introduced me to the publisher of the newspaper with which I am now connected, and I began to get along I made up my mind then that I would help boys and girls if I ever had the chance, and I take more pleasure in   [this] than in any other activity of my life "[2]

Although contests or stories by young people were included in the earliest issues of the *Mail* under Capper's guidance, at this time nothing of any formal nature was used as a foundation for later youth-work activity About 1901, when the *Mail and Breeze* was still a general newspaper with circulation in urban and rural areas alike, a "Mail and Breeze Golden Rule Club" for boys and girls came into existence [3] Through the Topeka *Daily Capital* a Juvenile Flower Club came into being about 1908 Free flower seeds were given to members who agreed to "plant and care for them, and take bouquets of flowers   to a hospital or home where there are sick people "[4]

Another youth activity, almost as permanent on the Topeka scene as Arthur Capper himself, was the annual Capper birthday party held on or about July 14 from 1908 until the disastrous flood of 1951 forced its premature cancellation After beginning in a small way, the "birthday parties" eventually assumed a gala, carnival-like atmosphere Street car and bus transportation was free for those going to and from the party held either in Garfield or Ripley Park Picnic lunches were brought by the guests, and dessert, usually ice cream, was provided by Capper Crowds, which eventually swelled to the fifteen to twenty thousand mark, enjoyed the Ferris wheel, merry-go-round, and special games and contests For more than thirty years no rain fell on the Capper birthday party [5] Arrangements for most of the events were handled by Charles Johnson, a Capper executive, and expenses amounted to as high as "$5,000 or $6,000 in the day when things were cheap "[6] A Topeka institution for many years, the Capper birthday party always received local and sometimes national publicity [7]

In many other ways Capper made provision for the youth of his city Remembering his visit to Boston in 1891, he provided an annual Thanksgiving dinner for all the newsboys in Topeka He willingly supplied almost all requests for a plaque, a cup, or a banner, to serve as awards in youth activities His interest in Y M.C A activities, through his contact as a member of the board of directors of Topeka Central 'Y,' caused him to encourage membership for his employees by paying half of their membership fee His first contact with Boy Scout activities came through the position of a vice president of the first group in Topeka to promote the Boy Scout organization Within a few years he was a member of the National Council of the Boy Scouts of America, and actively served on its publicity committee He also belonged to many fraternal organizations which were engaged in youth work, and he was sometimes attracted to them because of this important sideline

A leading promotional activity of the Capper state farm papers was the sponsoring of rural youth clubs Plans made by Kansas State Agricultural College in early 1906 for an extensive Boys' Corn Contest caused *Farmers' Mail and Breeze* to promote a Boys' and Girls' Corn Raising Contest in 1907 [8] A Boys' Corn Club grew from this beginning and in 1910 it reorganized under the name Capper Boys' Corn Club [9] Expansion of the corn club in 1911 made possible granting additional state prizes in Oklahoma, Kansas, Nebraska, and Missouri Members were encouraged to enter all other corn-growing contests in their own area, such as the one sponsored by Senator Thomas P Gore for Oklahoma farm youth, which offered as the grand prize a free trip to Washington [10]

Eventually Capper's clubs, considered the first boys' corn clubs in the West, were expanded into separate organizations for specific states after Capper purchased the *Nebraska Farm Journal,* the *Mis-*

souri Ruralist, and the *Oklahoma Farmer* Prizes were given in each state for the best acre-yield, the best ear of corn from seed of the contestant's own raising, and the champion ear of corn Each contestant was expected to record the number of hours of work performed by himself and his team and to give a detailed report on this [11]

Only in Kansas was the Capper name used frequently in the promotion of youth club work The early development of an outstanding state agricultural youth program in Oklahoma caused the Capper paper there to go along with the already functioning system [12] In Nebraska, the *Nebraska Farm Journal* name was associated with a large number of medals given to winners of state achievement contests for boys and girls [13] Likewise, *Missouri Ruralist,* or the name *Ruralist* alone, was most often used in promoting club activity in Missouri [14]

In order to satisfy a widespread demand for additional activities in Kansas a Capper Girls' Tomato Club was started in 1910, and a Boys' and Girls' Poultry Contest the following year [15] In 1912 there was also a Capper Boys' Baby Beef Club [16] The following year the Capper Boys' Swine Club was organized so that boys could take a purebred pig, farrowed on the home place after March 1, 1913, and feed him until State Fair time, when cash prizes would be given for the biggest increases [17] For a few years premiums were also offered to showings of the Capper Boys' Colt Show at the Topeka State Fair [18] A regular department soon became necessary in the various Capper farm papers to keep people informed about the activities of the Capper clubs [19] Most of these early organizations had only brief careers, however, and few people remembered them in later years

More widely known were the Capper youth clubs founded in 1915 and later The first of these newer organizations was the Capper Pig Club, which offered financial backing to farm boys anxious to obtain purebred livestock The original Capper Boys' Swine Club was still operating in 1915 when Capper, then Governor of Kansas, received a letter from a farm boy which said, "Please help me buy a pig "[20] This request led Capper to organize the new Capper Pig Club in 1915 and to lend members the necessary money to start with purebred livestock Initial membership was limited to one boy in each of the 105 counties in Kansas [21] Capper willingly lent each boy the money to purchase a purebred sow, and the boy agreed to care for the sow and litter properly and to keep a complete record of all feed used In a business-like manner the borrowers signed a personal note, agreeing to repay the loan on or before January 1, 1917, at 6 per cent interest [22] Prizes were given for the best achievement, and Capper doubled the value of all premiums won by members at agricultural fairs in home counties

In later years the pig club was expanded to a maximum of ten boys in each Kansas county, and a similar club was promoted by Capper's Missouri paper [23] In Kansas organized county clubs were encouraged, and "pep trophies" were given to the more successful organizations Enthusiasm for such clubs reached a peak during World War I and the early 1920's County clubs held regular meetings, and members looked forward to special gatherings at the state fairs In 1917 the members of the Capper Pig Club met Governor Capper on his return to Topeka with the yell

> Who are, who are, who are we?
> Capper Pig Club boys you see
> Rah, rah, rah, sis boom, ah,
> Capper Pig Club
> Rah, rah, rah! [24]

Motivation for such enthusiasm may have come from the success achieved by the first club members During 1916 the average profit of club members was $75 on an initial investment of $30. In the 1918 club work the average net gain for each member was $150 During that year club members also began selling purebred breeding stock through a co-operative club catalog, and the major swine record associations voted to admit the Capper Pig Club boys to full membership and to register their stock [25]

In 1917 Capper's organization set up the Capper Poultry Club for girls, with membership limited to ten girls per county in Kansas and five in Missouri [26] In 1920 the Capper Calf Club was opened to boys and girls alike, but it failed to prosper Returns were slower on calves than on pigs or chickens, and declining cattle prices of the post-war years also hampered the organization [27]

An unique quality of these Capper youth clubs was the willingness and ability of the founder to lend the needed funds to the members of the clubs Through this program club members were said to have borrowed more than $100,000 from Capper, yet bad loans over the years amounted to only $200 [28] However, the general agricultural depression of the 1920's was reflected in Capper's decision to cease lending money to participants in club work This change was justified on the grounds that loans "encouraged the habit of going into debt," an unsafe practice for young people who might not know the true value of money [29] Club policy thereafter permitted boys or girls to enter contests only if they could obtain the necessary livestock or poultry through their own resources If they could not buy an expensive animal, Capper club managers recommended that they enter the baby chick department, since the required number of chicks could be purchased for two dollars or less In an effort to attract members a wide variety of new departments were organized for club activity A farm youth could enter the small pen department, for purebred pullets or hens with one cock or cockerel, the gilt pig department, the sow and litter department, or the beef calf department The mother or guardian of a club member could enroll in the farm flock department Seventy-nine cash prizes, totaling $341, were available in 1928 In addition six silver trophies and free trips to the American Royal Stock Show, in Kansas City, were awarded to outstanding groups and individuals [30]

Absence of dues or membership fees for entering Capper clubs and county membership limits meant that county quotas were frequently full Total membership in such clubs through all the years to 1928 was 8,749 [31] Thereafter annual participation in the various Capper youth clubs declined because the Kansas and Missouri 4-H plan was beginning to offer a much more varied and more attractive program than that of the Capper clubs There was an apparent attempt in 1936 to provide greater competition for the 4-H program when Capper advertised twelve different departments for club activity during the year Youngsters could take advantage of such opportunities and still remain in 4-H work, sometimes even using the same livestock project in more than one organization [32] After 1936 the Capper organization relaxed its efforts to promote Capper clubs Finally, as an economy measure, in 1938, Capper reluctantly agreed to abandon the clubs he had founded more than twenty years earlier. Though it was a sentimental jolt to him, he found the action easier to take by recognizing that his work had pioneered the way for the

4-H organization Nevertheless, the disappearance of the Capper clubs was not publicized in various Capper publications other than through the increasing amount of space given over to the activities of the 4-H Clubs [33]

Capper's personal interest in the 4-H program was exemplified by his participation in the group which organized the National Committee on Boys' and Girls' Club Work in 1919 This organization aided greatly in obtaining governmental backing for 4-H Clubs, and Capper remained a key member for many years A law which bears his name, the Capper-Ketchum Act, was passed in 1928 to provide permanent federal appropriations for agricultural extension work and financial support for the 4-H Club movement [34]

Beginning in 1932 Capper recognized the outstanding Kansas 4-H club boy and girl with college scholarships valued at $150 each He also contributed $5,000 to help buy Rock Springs Ranch, near Junction City, when it was purchased for the Kansas 4-H Club Camp [35] As a result of his untiring support and helpful encouragement to rural youth throughout the state and nation, Capper received the first Kansas "citation for outstanding service to 4-H Club work "[36]

Through the years Capper Publications, individual Capper farm papers, and Capper, personally, gave a great many gifts and scholarships to rural youth and to 4-H organizations on a random basis No permanent record of what these gifts total or even when each was made was kept No basis exists for making an accurate estimate of the value of such gifts made by Capper to promote youth work, but it easily came to tens of thousands of dollars [37]

In addition to the use of generous space in the Capper farm papers for various rural youth projects, attention was directed to the promotion of the Master Farmer movement The first awards of this kind were given to twenty-two farmers of Indiana, Illinois, and Wisconsin, by the *Prairie Farmer* in 1925 [38] Capper state farm papers soon followed the example of the Illinois-based *Prairie Farmer* In 1926 *Ohio Farmer* and *Michigan Farmer* inaugurated their Master Farmer program, followed the next year by *Pennsylvania Farmer* and *Kansas Farmer* and in 1928 by the *Missouri Ruralist* [39]

Selection of farmers to be honored with the Master Farmer award was a long, difficult, and expensive process Farmers were nominated by their neighbors, and they were evaluated in an elaborate score card on their farming operations, business methods, general farm appearance and upkeep, home life, and public spirit The farmer with a "high technical and business competence combined with high quality as husband, father, and citizen" was the kind of man the makers of the score card had in mind and wanted to honor [40] Care was taken not to call Master Farmers the best in their respective state, since others were worthy of the award and might win recognition another year

By 1935, about 1,400 Master Farmers, including five or six women, had been named in twenty-eight different states and in the four western provinces of Canada [41] Thereafter the program disappeared in some states, and in others smaller classes of Master Farmers were selected Wartime and postwar disturbances further prevented selections for many years

Closely allied with the Master Farmer movement was the Master Farm Homemaker contest, begun in 1927 by *Farmer's Wife* In 1939 *Kansas Farmer* began a regular practice of selecting outstanding farm women as Master Homemaker, but no other Capper farm paper sponsored such a project [42]

Early in 1954 a combination of the Master Farmer and Master Homemaker program was developed through the Kansas Extension Service, with the co-operation of the *Kansas Farmer* editorial staff. Annually since then six couples, two from each of the extension districts, have been designated as Master Farmer and Master Farm Homemaker [43] Most of the other state farm papers abandoned the Master Farmer awards because of the expense involved and a reasonable doubt that the best farmers had always been selected Master Farmers were chosen in a few other states than Kansas in the 1950's, but the former strong interest in the program was no longer widespread [44]

Another promotional project, employed by most of the Capper farm papers, was support in varying degrees of the National Corn Husking Contests in the year preceding World War II Such contests were started in Iowa in 1922 and by 1924, husking champions from Iowa, Illinois, and Nebraska, competed in Iowa in what has been officially listed as the first National Corn Husking Contest [45] The *Missouri Ruralist* sponsored its first "Corn Shucking" contest in

1926, but neither the champion nor runner-up appeared in that year's national contest [46] In 1927, the *Missouri Ruralist* and the *Kansas Farmer,* and farm papers in five other states, promoted state husking contests, with the winners competing in Minnesota for the national championship [47] *Ohio Farmer* soon joined her sister publications in sponsoring state contests, but *Pennsylvania Farmer* and *Michigan Farmer,* located in areas where corn was a less important field crop, provided less regular support [48]

The national husking contests, attended by huge crowds, were rotated among eight leading Midwestern corn states. Capper state farm papers in Kansas, Missouri, and Ohio each sponsored a national contest within its own state The attendance at the national contest in Ohio in 1936 was variously estimated at 140,000 to 160,000, supposedly a national record for a single agricultural event of a sports nature [49] In 1942, the state and national contests were abandoned for the duration of the war The manual skill of husking corn became less of an asset as a result of subsequent mechanization of Corn Belt farms, and the contests were not revived after the war

For many years another service provided by various farm papers of the Capper syndicate was the planning and managing of low-cost tours for farmers *Ohio Farmer* initiated this practice, and eventually all members of the Capper Farm Press organized and managed their own tours [50] Sponsoring papers provided a tour manager, made all arrangements, and obtained special rates [51] Wartime restrictions caused even *Ohio Farmer* to abandon this service, but after the war such plans were again an annual activity of many of the Capper journals

In 1929, shortly after the stock-market crash, Arthur Capper announced an ambitious undertaking, the annual Capper Award for Distinguished Service to American Agriculture The award, open to any living American, consisted of a gold medal and $5,000 in cash as "a concrete expression of gratitude to some of the people who make contributions of national importance to American agriculture and to assist in stimulating public appreciation of unusually fine service to the country's basic industry "[52] In setting up this generous prize, Capper gave only general instruction to the selection committee. He had in mind such men as G Harold Powell of the California Fruit Growers' Exchange, James L Reid, producer of Reid's Yellow Dent corn, and M A Carleton, who introduced Durum wheat into the United States, these men would have been eligible for recognition had they been living [53]

When the Capper Award committee met at Chicago in June, 1930, they chose Dr Stephen M Babcock, Emeritus Professor of Agricultural Chemistry at the University of Wisconsin, from the more than 350 nominees for the first award [54] Of national importance to American agriculture was Dr Babcock's invention of a test for determining butter-fat content in milk and cream He was eighty-six years of age when he received the Capper award and was much praised for having given his invention freely to the world without patenting it [55]

In 1931, the Capper gold medal and the cash award went to Dr Leland O Howard, former chief of the Bureau of Entomology of the United States Department of Agriculture, for his long, active governmental service, and the development of insect controls which benefited the whole world [56] Capper expressed a hope to "continue in our selections to merit the commendation of the scientific world," but in 1932 the selection committee was on the verge of announcing its choice when the project was abandoned precipitously Poor business conditions caused Capper to take action to eliminate that worthy project Later correspondence indicated that a leading candidate for the 1932 Capper award was Dr Marion Dorset, who was active in developing hog cholera serum, but he received no official recognition and no part of the award [57]

Another service assumed by members of the Capper Farm Press as an aid in attracting additional patronage, was designed to help farmers eliminate thievery on farm property Earlier farm papers had generally "guaranteed" all advertising claims, but during the latter half of the 1920's an alarming increase in thefts from farms provided agricultural papers and their subscription salesmen with an appealing idea, first exploited by *Wallaces' Farmer* [58] *Kansas Farmer* followed suit with the inauguration of the Kansas Farmer Protective Service in February, 1927, and similar services were soon provided by other members of the Capper Farm Press [59] Rewards were offered to persons responsible for the capture and conviction of thieves stealing from farms where protective-service signs were posted [60] Eventually this service proved so popular that subscription salesmen stressed it rather than the editorial merits of the paper in seeking new patrons [61] A variety of methods were developed for marking livestock and property subject to theft, and the protective service was expanded to include the answering of business questions, and handling legal claims of certain kinds, as well as the provision for rewarding the captor of farm thieves [62] In the thirties a combined "Capper's National Protective Service" was organized by certain of the farm papers, and another publication, *Household* magazine, sponsored an Anti-Crime Association for small towns [63] By 1939 these two anti-crime agencies, and their predecessors had paid out more than $100,000 in rewards for 4,210 convictions [64] During World War II the protective service continued under its own momentum, with provision for a "four-fold service" of helping to prevent loss from theft, helping patrons to obtain adjustments for damages, warning them of "crooks," and supplying them with requested information [65] During the prosperous postwar years farm thievery ceased greatly to concern farmers, a much smaller number of rewards were paid, and the service became largely dormant [66] The employees of Capper Publications in Topeka also had their own state-charted credit union, which provided them with means of quickly obtaining a small loan [67]

Through the years a large number of groups and individuals were the recipient of the Capper bounty The various Capper youth clubs were eventually crowded out by other activities, but in their day they served an important purpose Their design and organization emphasized quality, not quantity, yet their appeal was widespread Most former Capper club members were favorably disposed to the Topeka publisher and when they were able to cast their ballot in the regular election of public officials they were usually for Capper Many would use their former membership as an excuse to visit with Capper in Topeka and in Washington Capper enjoyed the attention and the friendly conversation The positive benefits that came from the youth clubs were an indication to him that they were good business

Capper and his various publications also sponsored a wide variety of other projects, including the granting of college scholarships, support for the International Farm Youth Exchange, the granting of prizes for rural youth contests, contributions to worthy rural projects, support for the Flying Farmers' organizations, the granting of prizes for state safety contests, support for state spelling contests, and similar activities Such activities often remained a vivid memory to people having contact with Capper and his enterprise

Chapter XII

Capper and the World War I Peace Treaty

With an experienced show of humility and appreciation Capper thanked the Kansas electorate for their "overwhelming vote of confidence" in his election in 1918 to the United States Senate Indicating that it "was a serious mistake on the part of the President to issue a partisan appeal, especially just before election," Capper believed that "the Republicans in Congress will be broad enough to give" the President "the strongest possible support in putting thru the war and the peace program, and in meeting the problems of readjustment and reconstruction."[1]

The task facing any member of Congress after World War I was immense, as Capper knew Armistice Day came less than a week after the general election Republican majorities in both houses of Congress were widely interpreted as a repudiation of the program of President Wilson The unremitting tensions of war were replaced by the encumbering complexities of peace In Congress partisanship would be the major difference between wartime and the peace after the war Partisanship was at a minimum during war, but when peace came with a majority in the opposition it was renewed with increased vigor

After the Republican victory of 1918 Henry Cabot Lodge, then Senate minority leader who expected to become majority leader, wrote all of the newly elected Republicans about the problems facing the narrow Republican majority in the new Senate. Capper replied that he was not asking that as a "tenderfoot" he be given precedence in committee assignments He was "fully in accord" with the Republican leader's wishes to organize "our control of committees" in the oncoming Senate [2]

As important as were the internal affairs of the United States in the days following the war, the Senate of the sixty-sixth Congress would devote its major effort during the Special Session called to order on May 19, 1919, to full discussion of the prospective treaty with Germany There was no doubt that a vast majority of American citizens were in favor of eternal peace How it was to be achieved was the great question.

126

Capper and the World War I Peace Treaty

From the time of its formation Arthur Capper was a member of the League of Nations to Enforce Peace and chairman of the Kansas branch Many were the times he had spoken and worked in its behalf, and after the war he still proclaimed a belief in a future "permanent peace thru a federation of nations . . This must be the last war," he said, "the world can and must find some other way to settle its differences "[3] Throughout the war Capper had maintained his connection with the American League of Nations to Enforce Peace, which had a close relative in a similar organization in Britain The members of the American organization, according to one observer, were mostly Republicans, with leaders such as former President Taft, Elihu Root, and Charles Evans Hughes [4]

In a friendly manner Capper sent two messages to President Wilson in October, 1918, when Germany appeared ready to surrender under certain conditions Capper applauded Wilson's "rejection of the latest German overtures for an armistice," and he appealed for an "unconditional surrender   . [as] the first step toward a permanent peace   " To emphasize his feeling he suggested that "the allied armies should give the German people a vision of the meaning of a world in arms by marching thru to Berlin and camping on German soil while the peace terms are being concluded "[5]

Capper had always cloaked his partisan leanings during the war But he was distressed by what he considered unfair treatment of such military leaders as Major General Leonard Wood, which he suspected was based on politics To him politics seemed to enter the war picture in many unlikely ways Thus, when peace was assured with the Armistice on November 11, Capper had a variety of reasons to be suspicious of the manner by which the President would have the peace guaranteed Other actions causing Capper concern included the President's appeal for a Democratic Congress in 1918 and the composition of the American peace commission in France Therefore, it was easier for opponents of the President to gain Capper's backing when it came time to vote on the Peace Treaty

Even before the peace conference got under way Harold T Chase, the editor of the *Capital*, took the stand that complete and absolute support of the national administration was neither expected nor required now that peace had come [6] Before much was known of the details of the treaty Capper wrote that it was his belief that "a

League of Nations is inevitable if the world is to be saved from anarchy " But he was also concerned because "what this nation has most to fear in the future is not war, but our swiftly increasing burden of taxation "[7] With honest and forthright candor Capper later wrote that he went "to the Senate with an open mind and with a friendly attitude toward the Peace Treaty and the League of Nations " But as time went on, he gravitated to the view that the original form of "the Peace Treaty was an unsatisfactory and inadequate one-sided pact."[8]

Time was of essence to the President's desires, both in Paris and in Washington The longer the delay at either the conference or in the Senate, the greater the possibility of defeat for President Wilson's plans Delay at Versailles had forced Wilson into compromise and the loss of treasured objectives Capper did not participate in the senatorial "Round Robin," used to weaken Wilson's position in Paris. A "strategy of strangulation" carried on in the Senate would deal an even more devastating blow to the President [9]

As the senatorial machinery slowly began to move, Capper, a mild and soft-spoken newcomer, was opposed to any delay in dealing with the treaty He was impatient about parliamentary maneuvers which slowed down action, and he was "sorry the debate has taken on this partisan tinge " In company with Taft and Will H Hays, chairman of the Republican National Committee, he felt "that the League should not be made a partisan question " In July it was his belief that it was "the duty of the Senate to ratify the treaty, including the League of Nations   . " And he further expressed an opinion that the ratifying resolution might contain some reservations, "but that the Treaty and Covenant will probably be ratified without amendment "[10]

Opposition to the peace treaty without reservation was slowly gaining strength in May and June, 1919 Capper was finding out from the "grass roots" that almost 85 per cent of those he polled did not favor "a League of Nations proposed by President Wilson without amendment "[11] When William Allen White wrote him in August that at least 60 "per cent of the Kansas people are against the League today," it merely confirmed his previous information [12] Responding also to pressures from Republican leadership in the Senate, Capper began to shift ground on the peace treaty to what he believed to be more consistent with views of the majority of his constituents

Wilson did not sense the change in public opinion this soon The forces within the Senate were lining up into three main groups, those who would accept the Treaty without change, the moderates or mild reservationists, and the irreconcilables, and the balance between these groups was growing more delicate with each passing day. Endeavoring to strengthen his position, Wilson conferred individually with fourteen Senators of reservationist leanings Only then did he realize the enormity of the task before him [13] Capper, as one of the fourteen, went to the White House on the afternoon of July 18 [14] The President seemed "greatly surprised at the opposition that had developed in America to the League of Nations Covenant . ." Capper reported that the President "did not ask me in set terms to support the treaty without change but his whole argument was designed to show he was very much opposed to any modification whatever in the terms of the treaty and the league covenant " By that time Capper believed that "the treaty could not be adopted without modification or reservations "[15]

Other Senators told the President much the same thing Senator James Watson, of Indiana, explained to Wilson that "there is just one way by which you can take the United States into the League of Nations " When reminded that it must be with the Lodge reservations, Wilson responded, "Never!" The issue, according to Wilson, must be taken to the people [16] In previous contests with Congress over domestic issues Wilson had won in this way Therefore, while the Foreign Relations Committee and the Senate debated, Wilson began a tour of twenty-three days, going as far as the West Coast, a tour abandoned only after his sudden illness A stubborn Wilson and an equally recalcitrant Lodge refused to provide any form of compromise for the peace treaty

The inflation and the increasing cost of living were as important to Capper as discussion over the peace treaty A Capper editorial in August, entitled "Back up the President," turned to be about inflation, not the treaty or league issue "For more than two years," Capper said, "I have been urging action along most of the lines suggested by the President in his address and I heartily welcome the entrance of the head of government into the fight "[17] While Capper was growing stronger in his opposition to Wilson's treaty, he could commend the President for other actions

By late October a shift in Capper's voting record can be detected Early in the month Capper had opposed some amendments favored by majority leader Lodge, but after the middle of the month he almost invariably voted the same way on the peace treaty as the Republican leadership An example is his vote on the Johnson amendment, designed to give the United States equality of voting with the British Empire in the proposed League of Nations Hiram Johnson, an irreconcilable from California, introduced his amendment on September 26, but it was not voted on for more than a month.

William Howard Taft, outstanding leader of the League of Nations to Enforce Peace, was concerned about the Johnson amendment, and on October 12 he wrote Capper a long, confidential, handwritten letter In it he said, "I hope that the reports that come from Washington that you are going to vote for the Johnson amendment are not true You and your papers have been such a tower of strength for the League that it will be a great disappointment to all of us who have felt grateful to you for your aid, and have rejoiced in your sledge hammer blows if by a vote of this kind you kill the League On your vote, probably, the issue will turn I'm not urging you to vote for the Treaty unchanged, for I know you have said you think there ought to be reservations, but I do plead with you not to vote for an amendment changing the text of the treaty and sending it back for a conference, or definitely taking us out of the League and sending us to seek a separate peace with Germany " Taft's solution to the dilemma were possible reservations to "keep the colonies out of the council and in the assembly " In closing he urged Capper, "Please don't take the responsibility—a heavy one—of beating the League by a vote on the Johnson amendment "[18]

The appeal from Taft had no influence on Capper's vote. Only a day or so after the letter arrived in Washington, Capper was supporting the Shantung amendments, which were defeated Then on October 29, he gave his vote for the Johnson amendment, which failed to pass by seven votes, with nineteen not voting Capper's vote had not been as crucial as Taft had predicted

Article X, identified by Wilson as "the heart of the Covenant" of the League of Nations, came to be a major stumbling block toward confirmation of the treaty In Article X, "Members of the League undertake to respect and preserve as against external aggression the territorial integrity and existing political independence of all members of the League " As the warm, sultry summer days of Washington gave way to crisp, bright days of early fall, Capper, along with many other reservationists, was sure that Article X could not stand intact He reported in mid-October that the "biggest thing in the Peace Treaty and the League of Nations discussion is the determination of the Senate that American boys may not be sent to Europe to settle boundary disputes and fight in every quarrel in which those nations may become embroiled That is the reason the Senate will not consent to the ratification of the treaty without reservations "[19] Tom McNeal recognized that "it is evident that with a few reservations the League of Nations compact will be ratified by the Senate " At the same time he thought only one reservation, "that the United States should have the unquestioned right to withdraw from the league on reasonable notice," was all that was necessary [20]

If the group of Senators identified as moderates on the League fight could have been divided into major and minor reservationists Capper would have been in the latter class He supported the Lodge reservations, but he would have been satisfied with less He continually voiced objection in his journals to the time-consuming tactics on the floor of the Senate, but there was nothing he could do to hasten parliamentary procedure Indicating his vexation, he wrote, "In the name of a more united United States, let's have done with saving Europe while letting America drift into industrial civil war and chaos We shall safeguard American principles and American honor in the Peace Treaty and League covenant "[21] When Senator Thomas P Gore, of Oklahoma, introduced an amendment to the league covenant, "providing that no nation, when not attacked, could go to war until the question of going to war had been submitted to the people and an advisory vote had been taken," Capper counted it as "one of the dramatic incidents in the Senate consideration of the Treaty of Peace " Only one-sixth of the Senators, including Capper, supported the Gore amendment [22] Capper, believing it to be "right in principle," was to return to this idea of a national war referendum on other occasions

On November 19, 1919, more than a year after the Armistice and with President Wilson in his White House bed recovering from a crippling paralytic stroke, the Senate took a vote on the treaty Lodge had control of a majority of the Senate, but he could not easily command the required two-thirds support needed for treaty ratification Twenty-four hours earlier Wilson had written Senator Gilbert M Hitchcock, Senate minority leader, that the true friends of the League of Nations should vote against the treaty as amended Thus, when the vote was taken, a quirk of fate found the Wilson supporters, led by Hitchcock, voting with the irreconcilables, who would not support any League organization, to bring about its overwhelming defeat Lodge blamed the President for what had happened, and he particularly called attention to the presidential letter directing loyal Democrats to "kill the Treaty rather than accept the reservations " William Howard Taft was more inclined to spread the blame between Lodge and Wilson, who "exalt their personal prestige and the saving of their ugly faces above the welfare of the country and the world "[23]

The explanation Capper gave for the Senate vote on the peace treaty was much like that of the Senate majority leader. Capper placed the responsibility for what happened on the President: "The Peace Treaty was finally rejected by two separate votes—the Democrats first voting against ratifying it with protective reservations and then voting for unreserved ratification " Capper had "not the slightest doubt that the Peace Treaty with the Lodge safeguarding reservations, would have been ratified by the Senate but for President Wilson's stubborn insistence on unconditional ratification." He further stated that the "Senate majority at no time sought to have the nation shirk its world responsibility It attempted nothing more than to keep our country out of the meshes of an entangling treaty while making sure it should be enabled to perform the full duty as one of the great powers It did not take from the covenant a single affirmative provision that actually makes for peace It simply attempted to reconcile the pact to the Constitution of the United States and to serve notice that any action under the league agreement must be subject to the limitations of the Constitution." Capper had voted for the treaty with reservations as his "mind and conscience dictated was right "[24]

During the next few months Capper reiterated his position that the action taken by the Senate on November 19 was the responsibility of the President But, at the same time, he held that Wilson "has it within his power to obtain ratification within 48 hours by consenting to reasonable reservations Americanizing the treaty "[25] While somewhat overlooking his position of a year earlier, he held that eighty Senators were always "favorable to the ratification of the treaty, [but] there never has been a majority favorable to ratification without reservation " He still felt that "the Peace Treaty's fate will rest, as it has all along, with Woodrow Wilson . ."[26]

Capper was not prepared for the "no compromise" position of the President After the March 19, 1920, vote on the treaty, which again ended in its defeat, Capper wrote an editorial entitled, "President Wilson Killed the Treaty " In simple language Capper told his readers that the "chief significance of the Senate's vote . is that it seals the fate of the Treaty for the present Congress . . Personally I voted for ratification—both March 19 and November 19—and until the last week or two before the final defeat I was hopeful enough changes would be effected among the Senators to enable the Senate to approve the Treaty with 14 Lodge reservations Personally I do not approve the stand of the irreconcilables, whether Republicans or Democrats I have sincerely favored ratification with safeguards and hoped all along to see it accomplished " Capper further noted the fact that "three times as many Democratic Senators voted for ratification on March 19 as voted that way November 19, tells the story of the disintegration of the President's party following " In a more generous analysis than he had previously given, Capper ended his editorial, "While all blame for the final defeat of ratification cannot be placed upon the President, yet, in the end, it was he, and not the little band of irreconcilables who defeated the Treaty "[27] Still later Capper wrote, "There were 267 roll calls on the Peace Treaty, including its numerous amendments and reservations, the Congressional Record shows I answered 263 of these calls and voted on every question of importance I refused to bind this country to a contract to send our young men to fight and die in defense of the territories of foreign governments "[28]

Naturally the Peace Treaty and the League of Nations became important issues of the national election of 1920 The American people had been aroused on the issue of the League, and Wilson hoped that the outcome of the balloting would be interpreted as a "solemn referendum," vindicating his avowed position But other issues helped to eliminate any clear-cut possibility of choice for the voter The election of Republican President Warren G Harding, a moderate and mild reservationist Senator on the League issue, was interpreted as a desire of the American people to stay outside the League Harding did not quarrel with this attitude, and he did nothing to revive interest in United States membership in the League of Nations Finally on October 18, 1921, a separate peace was made with Germany

Capper had voted for the Treaty of Versailles in 1920 with its amendments and against it without reservations Years later he was still of the opinion that the treaty making the United States a member of the League of Nations could have been ratified, "if just one or two things had been handled differently " The differences were not so much over the phrasing of the Covenant of the League as in the personalities of those who disagreed According to Capper, "the League treaty was a 'one-man' document It was negotiated by Woodrow Wilson alone 'He did not take along a member of the senate He did not consult with members of Congress at all ' " So the treaty failed, "Not because it was an evil thing, but because the good thing came by Woodrow Wilson's hand, because no senators were taken to the peace conference, the League was rejected   "[29]

Other analyses of why the League failed in 1919 and 1920 might provide a variety of reasons which differed from those of Capper The Kansas Senator, being fully in accord with the traditional Republican view, would naturally use a political explanation To some extent Capper's view was vindicated in the handling of the United Nations issue many years later No attempt was made to join together a plan for world organization with a treaty of peace into a "Siamese twin," which could not be separated Moreover, most of the objections voiced in the 1919 and 1920 debates were met in the United Nations Charter Few who had participated in the senatorial action on the League of Nations in 1920 would have the opportunity to act again on the entrance of the United States into a world organization Capper was one of the few, and his vote was cast for placing the United States in the United Nations

Chapter XIII

A Publisher's Shifting Fortunes

Capper's full devotion to his political career while he was Governor did not permit him to consider seriously any expansion in his publishing business When his years as Governor neared an end and World War I was over, Capper publications began to show increased activity. Capper's personal objection to their promoting the Capper name had greatly changed as a consequence of his career in politics For a decade beginning in 1919 there came many new developments which expanded various parts of the Capper business

Capper had prided himself on the personal management of his publishing house During his years as Governor of Kansas he was near at hand, although his contact with his business was irregular The break with his old position as a personal director was symbolized by an action that took place just before his train left for the East for the opening of Congress in May, 1919 With tears in his eyes Capper told Marco Morrow, his assistant publisher, "Here, you might need these," and handed Morrow his desk keys [1]

Plans were under way to produce papers and journals which would appeal to more people and would grow with the good times expected to follow the war But Capper was for some time adamant to changes in an enterprise which had been successful in the past After he had left the Governor's office and was on a Florida vacation with Mrs Capper, he had time to consider the implications of some of the changes in his business Reluctantly he wired Marco Morrow, "All right I surrender on Valley Farmer press proposition and I endorse your program for better papers . "[2]

One of the first of these changes was replacing the name of the *Missouri Valley Farmer* with *Capper's Farmer* [3] The issue of June, 1919, was the first under the new title The explanation for the change was similar to that for renaming the *Kansas Weekly Capital* some six years earlier The *Missouri Valley Farmer* had outgrown its name because its "circulation has not been confined to the valley of the Missouri River nor has the paper editorially limited itself to the peculiar farm problems of the Missouri Valley, hence it is apparent that we should not retain a name local in character In selecting a

135

new name we are happy in being permitted to identify the paper with the owner and publisher, a man who is a champion of the rights of the common people in general and the farmers in particular " The editors announced that they would "not handle any subject, agricultural, economical or political with gloved hands or in a hesitating manner " They would "always demand, always fight for—if necessary so to do—this fair deal for the farmers "[4]

Also in 1919 Capper purchased the *Kansas Farmer* and consolidated it with his *Farmers' Mail and Breeze,* with a new title, the *Kansas Farmer and Mail and Breeze* The transfer of that old-time Kansas farm paper, its printing plant, name, and good-will, was made to Capper on December 2, 1919 The *Kansas Farmer,* in announcing the sale, was generous in praise of the new owner and of expectations for the future Though reputedly a "deplorable scarcity" of print paper caused the sale of the publication, a deplorable lack of revenue-producing advertising matter on its pages is noticeable Actually, there was a paper shortage, but since the minimum press capacity for most publishers was sixteen pages, farm papers such as the *Kansas Farmer* were not reduced in size by governmental wartime restrictions [5] Circulation reached a high point of 63,071 in 1913 but by 1919 had declined to 20,728 [6]

The whole staff of the *Kansas Farmer* joined Capper's organization Those not used on the *Kansas Farmer and Mail and Breeze* were employed on other Capper publications The new, combined staff announced its intention to produce a larger, better paper with increased services The editors promised to pay special attention to the viewpoints of the various classes of readers and to keep the paper close to the "grass roots " A primary goal of the newly consolidated *Kansas Farmer and Mail and Breeze* was to champion economic justice, intelligent farming, and satisfactory living [7]

Thus the *Kansas Farmer and Mail and Breeze* became the only state farm paper in Kansas Through purchase and consolidation Capper had cleared the field of competition for his first paper, the *Mail* [8] Although some consolidations had been attained in states other than Kansas where papers of the Capper Farm Press operated, Capper papers in Nebraska, Missouri, and Oklahoma still had energetic competitors

Another development of 1919 was the construction of a four-story, seventy-five foot addition to the Capper Building The structure, first occupied in 1909, was too small to handle the growing needs of Capper Publications Offices for the business had been established in rented rooms at some distance away Inflationary prices hiked the cost of the new structure and equipment to $300,000, almost as much as Capper had paid for a larger building a decade earlier It was ready for occupancy in January, 1920 [9]

Visions of a long-time enormous demand for American farm goods and products created by the market activity during 1919 and the first half of 1920 caused the Capper organization to formulate plans to make use of the newly enlarged part of the Topeka building, to increase circulation, and to improve the reading matter and format of the various Capper publications [10] To facilitate this expansion Capper made use of the good-will and prestige of his name and papers among his subscribers In July, 1920, subscribers were offered the opportunity to invest in Capper Publications [11] A series of 7 per cent Gold Certificates, a kind of promissory notes backed by Capper's personal pledge, were issued for sales These certificates were in denominations of $100 and $500, with interest payable semiannually The lender had the privilege of withdrawing principal and accrued interest by giving thirty days' notice [12] Capper never failed to refund immediately money on demand for the certificates at face value, although he could have legally required notice.[13] Notes in later years bore lower interest rates By 1937 the aggregate amount of these unsecured demand notes, or Capper Certificates, was $3,952,400 [14]

This means of financing enabled Capper to do business without having to rely on banks [15] The selling of Capper Certificates was handled by mail When sufficient funds were on hand, notices offering the certificates for sale were dropped for as long as six to eight months from the columns of the various Capper papers While the average investment in the Certificates in 1935 was about $200, nine persons in 1939 had more than $15,000 investment each in Capper publication securities [16]

Money gained in this manner enabled Capper to buy the subscription list of *Field and Farm* in September, 1920 [17] This Denver, Colorado, publication, established in 1872, was one of the oldest farm journals in America [18] Within a short time the Capper formula for moving into another area was in operation, and *Field and Farm* was identified as the "Rocky Mountain Section" of the Capper Farm Press [19] Business and editorial offices were maintained in Denver, and the special editorial staff lived in Colorado, Wyoming, Utah, and New Mexico, the geographical area assigned to the new member of the Capper family However, the paper was printed in Topeka [20]

A precipitous decline in average market prices of farm products during the final quarter of 1920 caused Capper to become alarmed about expansionist plans in his business [21] Retrenchment was in order for the Rockies *Kansas Farmer and Mail and Breeze* was allowed to absorb the subscription list of *Field and Farm,* and the Denver paper was unceremoniously forgotten [22] This sudden decision was a hard blow to Capper, meaning, as it did, a forced reversal of his well-known policy of expansion, but he had become almost panic-stricken by the possibilities of a general depression One of his long-time employees remembered that Capper shed tears over this decision [23]

Retrenchment in Missouri resulted in the purchase of the Missouri Agricultural Publishing Company, and its paper, the *Journal of Agriculture,* for $86,000 [24] This large sum gave Capper a semi-monthly farm paper with the largest circulation in Missouri, a building and printing equipment in St Louis, and a state monopoly On February 1, 1921, the *Missouri Ruralist* became the only state farm paper in Missouri All of the mechanical work was done in St Louis, contrary to the usual practice found among members of the Capper Farm Press The business was conducted under the corporate name of the Missouri Agricultural Publishing Company [25]

When Capper cleared away all Missouri competition for the *Missouri Ruralist,* the Capper paper took the volume numbers of the *Journal of Agriculture* as its own Eminent Missouri farm papers were in its "family tree "[26]

Beginning on January 31, 1921, the daily Kansas City *Kansan* was published in Kansas City, Kansas, under Capper's auspices [27] Kansas City, Kansas, had found it difficult to support a daily newspaper because of the rivalry of the cross-town Kansas City *Star* and *Times* and other Missouri newspapers, and in 1921 the community had the dubious honor of being the largest city in the United States without a daily newspaper Previous publishers had gone "broke" when they tried to develop a paper which would do much more than carry the legal advertising of the city In hopes of promoting a community spirit, under the shadow of its neighboring Missouri metropolis, the local Chamber of Commerce sent representatives to Capper to persuade him to sponsor a paper After serious consideration Capper agreed to take over the name and good-will of the old *Kansan* if the Chamber would guarantee 15,000 subscribers and obtain pledges for $200,000 in advertising for the first year [28]

The president of the Kansas City Chamber of Commerce, William A Bailey, a former high-school principal and banker, with no experience in journalism, was employed by Capper as editor In spite of the guarantees and an expenditure of almost $350,000, the *Kansan* failed to show a profit for the first three years of its operation Kansas City, Missouri, firms refused to advertise in the *Kansan,* and $70,000 was lost during 1921 alone [29] Nevertheless, circulation grew to about the 20,000 mark, and the paper gained a position of influence in the community Capper had no desire to provide a formidable rival for the powerful *Star* and *Times,* and he made every effort to seem noncompetitive to them No attempt was made to sell the *Kansan* on the Missouri side of the border, and news featured on its pages dealt with the Kansas community rather than the entire metropolitan area The new daily across the border caused the *Star* and *Times* to carry more news about Kansas City, Kansas, rather than about the "West end," and a special edition was developed by these papers for the Kansas City, Kansas, reader [30]

The *Kansas Farmer* and the *Missouri Ruralist* had become state monopolies, but the *Oklahoma Farmer* and the *Nebraska Farm Journal* still had local, energetic state farm papers for competition Although this was a period of integration and although overtures for consolidation or sale were made in both states, those concerned could not reach agreement for several years [31]

An unexpected expansion in the Capper Farm Press was made on January 12, 1922, when Capper purchased controlling interest in the "Eastern trio" of farm papers, *Ohio Farmer, Michigan Farmer,* and *Pennsylvania Farmer* Morton J Lawrence, the major owner of these publications, moved to Washington after he retired, and he sold his 5,170 shares of stock in Lawrence Publishing Company to the Kansas publisher Capper paid $594,550 for the Lawrence stock, the account of the sale appearing under the date January 31, 1922 [32]

Lawrence had been active in agricultural journalism for almost fifty years, beginning with his purchase of the *Ohio Farmer* in 1872 He expanded to an "Eastern trio" of farm papers with the purchase of the *Michigan Farmer* in 1893 and the *Pennsylvania Farmer* in 1911 [33] He published his farm papers in a central plant in Cleveland, and his operation was similar in many ways to that of Capper publications Like Capper he had ideals of service for a definite territory "to make practical matter applicable to the wants of the readers of that locality and condense its influence, which is impractical in a paper of what is termed 'general circulation ' "[34] His policies of close contact with his subscribers, his support of the interests of agriculture, and his boast of absolute honesty in relations with both subscribers and advertisers closely parallel Capper's statements of policy Moreover, Lawrence spoke of his relationship with his employees much as Capper did, complimenting them as a "wonderful organization" composed of many "loyal helpers "[35]

Editorial employees of the Lawrence Publishing Company had fully expected to promote a company to purchase controlling stock if Lawrence had given them the opportunity As small stockholders in the company they were angry with both Lawrence and Capper because of the secrecy with which the transfer of the controlling stock was made To hold their allegiance, Capper agreed to purchase their stock at the price per share he had given Lawrence "at the expiration of one year, if they would remain with the company, giving faithful service during that time " Although the value of the stock fluctuated from time to time, renewals of these agreements were made almost automatically for many years [36]

In assuming control of the Lawrence Publishing Company, Capper promised to continue existing policies just as he had done with previous purchases [37] These three papers were the only Capper publications that ever had a sizable minority interest To some extent Capper's position with the "Eastern trio" was that of a business investor, rather than a functioning owner-and-publisher Although working in close harmony with other Capper farm papers, they were not immediately identified as members of the Capper Farm Press [38] It seemed important to Capper that subscribers to these Eastern

140

periodicals should not think their papers were coming out of Topeka [39]

Another expansion of the Capper papers was the extensive promotion of several journals designed for readers in the eastern United States *Capper's Weekly* began operation of an Eastern edition on January 6, 1923 [40] It was published in Washington, D C , in a plant Capper had bought *Capper's Weekly* defied being placed in the usual categories of newpapers, but there was no doubt the move to an Eastern edition was designed to enhance Capper's political career, for his aspirations had mounted as high as the Presidency The circulation for all editions of *Capper's Weekly* increased rapidly, but losses were great, and the Eastern edition ceased publication with the issue of June 6, 1925 [41] In its place, *Capper's Magazine,* a monthly, made its appearance the following month, only to suspend its operations January 1, 1927 [42]

Still interested in offering a journal that would appeal to the businessmen and businesswomen who wanted to keep informed on public matters, Capper took over the publication of *Public Affairs* in January, 1929 It was a short-article magazine, which presented the news in a factual, readable manner, and was printed in Topeka [43] In September, 1929, its name was changed to *Capper's Magazine,* and it came to an end in October, 1931 [44]

Before Capper took over the Lawrence Publishing Company he seemed to have no general plan for acquiring additional state farm papers While he had bought many farm papers, the original initiative for sales had come from someone other than Capper But in 1922 considerable time was spent investigating possible expansion The *Indiana Farmer's Guide* was one possibility, since its state name could easily be dropped and its circulation extended into Illinois to connect the western Capper papers with those in the East Later, the *Rural New Yorker,* the *Florida Farmer,* and other farm journals were offered to Capper, and he seriously considered the desirability of expansion Nonetheless, though tempted, after his purchase of controlling stock in the Lawrence Publishing Company he never again went into a new state to buy a farm paper [45]

As a matter of fact, when a state monopoly did not seem possible, he was inclined to withdraw On May 21, 1924, he sold the *Oklahoma Farmer* to the Oklahoma Publishing Company of Oklahoma City, publishers of the *Oklahoma Farmer-Stockman* [46] For two or three years efforts had been made to buy the *Oklahoma Farmer,* and the $85,000 paid for its name, good-will, and complete subscription lists was virtually Capper's asking price The last issue of the *Oklahoma Farmer* under the Capper regime appeared May 25, 1924. The relationship between the Oklahoma member of the Capper Farm Press and the *Oklahoma Farmer-Stockman* had never been good during the dozen years of Capper's ownership Capper was considered an interloper, an out-of-bounds intruder, and bitter competition had been the result [47]

On the same day that the transfer of the *Oklahoma Farmer* was completed, Samuel R McKelvie, owner of the *Nebraska Farmer,* was invited to Topeka to make an offer for the subscription list, name, and good-will of the *Nebraska Farm Journal.* The deal was quickly completed [48] Relations between the *Nebraska Farmer* and the *Nebraska Farm Journal* had been on a healthy competitive basis, but, once Capper decided to sell, little time was taken in negotiations The last issue of the Nebraska member of the Capper Farm Press appeared on June 15, 1924 The usual greetings were extended by the outgoing and incoming owners and editors

In keeping with the trend toward consolidation of state farm papers throughout the country a plan was worked out in 1928 to free Capper's Eastern papers of local competition This called for the consolidation of the two leading state farm papers in each of the states of Ohio, Michigan, and Pennsylvania The *Ohio Farmer* was consolidated with the *Ohio Stockman and Farmer,* formerly the *National Stockman and Farmer* The *Pennsylvania Farmer* consolidated with the Pennsylvania edition of the *National Stockman and Farmer,* and the *Michigan Farmer* with the *Michigan Business Farmer* [49] These consolidations brought together the Stockman-Farmer Publishing Company, headed by Thomas D Harman, the Rural Publishing Company, headed by George M Slocum, and the Lawrence Publishing Company, headed by Capper, into a new corporation with the name of Capper-Harman-Slocum, Incorporated [50] Capper maintained control of this new organization through the ownership of about 60 per cent of the stock [51]

Upon the organization of Capper-Harman-Slocum, Inc , the three members of the "Eastern trio" were published in their respective states The *Pennsylvania Farmer* was published in Pittsburgh, and editorial and business offices were moved to that city [52] The *Ohio Farmer* continued to be published in Cleveland, and the *Michigan Farmer* was printed in Detroit, where its editorial and business offices previously had been [53]

Closely related to his newspaper activity was Capper's entry into the field of radio broadcasting In 1922, he obtained a license to start WJAP, one of the nation's pioneer stations, indeed at the time of its operation the second oldest commercial station between the Mississippi River and the Pacific Coast [54] After two years of fighting for listeners and for parts, WJAP left the air In 1927 Capper sponsored the moving of WIBW, originally intended for Loganport, Indiana, to Topeka By September, 1928, he owned the controlling interest in the station, and in October, with complete control, he located WIBW on the roof of Topeka's tallest building The next year Capper's station became a link in the Columbia Broadcasting System, and it obtained a transfer to 580 kilocycles, one of the choicest spots on the radio dial There it shared time with station KSAC at Manhattan

By any measure the first two terms for Capper as United States Senator were a dozen years of building and expansion for the Capper business enterprises In 1919 he owned the Topeka *Daily Capital, Capper's Weekly, Household, Capper's Farmer,* and state farm papers in Kansas, Missouri, Nebraska, and Oklahoma Their combined circulation was just over two million copies with each issue By 1930 the major additions came in the "Eastern trio" of farm papers and the Kansas City *Kansan,* although *Capper's Magazine* was to have another year of life Circulation had grown to about 3,800,000 A small but enthusiastic group of listeners were "tuning in" on WIBW Subtractions from the Capper list were various Eastern editions of *Capper's Weekly,* the farm papers in Oklahoma and Nebraska, and the short-lived Colorado paper It was a dozen years of spirited and energetic activity for the various Capper publications Although they were generally prosperous, expenses of operating a large publishing house were growing faster than the main sources of income

Business activities over the country had generally been profitable in the 1920's Farmers, on the other hand, were largely a depressed part of the economy during the period, and this had some effect on agricultural journalism Following the stock market crash in late 1929, all forms of business activity began to grind to a slow, sickening halt Therefore, editorial policy and business activity of Capper Publications after 1930 had a different tone than in the rampaging twenties

During this same period of expansion of the Capper business, Arthur Capper was enjoying what were probably his most rewarding years in politics His party was in power in Washington, his counsel was listened to, and laws were passed bearing his name In the 1920's, Arthur Capper, United States Senator from Kansas, was well known throughout the whole land

Chapter XIV
The Farm Bloc and the Twenties

Before Arthur Capper left Kansas to be sworn in for the first time as a United States Senator he endeavored to sever one tie with his native state The Capper Mansion located at 1035 Topeka Boulevard was offered for sale at 60 per cent of its price of construction.[1] But there were no takers Instead the Capper home, which had been in use as the Governor's Mansion during Capper's four years as Governor, was to continue in the same role during the two terms of his successor, Henry J Allen Never again did Arthur and Florence Capper live in the home they had built some ten years earlier. Instead, the frequent trips of Capper back to Kansas found him rarely accompanied by his wife In Topeka Capper stayed in a hotel, usually the Jayhawker.

Allen was a prosperous Republican newspaper publisher like Capper In many ways the aggressive, outspoken Wichita newspaperman was the antithesis of his predecessor But Capper and Allen were in agreement on many things, and neither made any attempt to recall the biting Allen editorial, "The Human Vampire," written more than a dozen years earlier [2] Capper heartily endorsed the Kansas ratification of the national prohibition amendment early in Allen's administration, and he approved the Governor's inauguration statement, made only two months after war ended, that the German language must "be barred from elementary school " A natural parting of the ways came on the issue of compulsory military training, which Capper strongly opposed

Kansas was enjoying unparalleled prosperity in 1918 and early 1919, but there was already an uneasiness about growing inflation and declining prices for farm products To Capper these and other domestic issues would be as important as the question of United States' entry into a League of Nations

As a member of the newly dominant Republican majority in the Senate Capper was assigned to nine of the seventy-four committees at the first session of the sixty-sixth Congress He was chairman of the minor committee, Expenditures in the Department of Agriculture At the time, too, he began continuous service on the Agricul-

145

ture and Forestry Committee, the District of Columbia Committee, and the Committee of Claims Before his first term was half over he was chairman of the Committee on Claims, and early in his second term became an unofficial "mayor of Washington," with auto license number 12 in the role of chairman of the District of Columbia Committee He held that position for some seven or eight years and worked to beautify the Capital and to provide for its citizens, amid much acclaim from natives of the District of Columbia In his eighth year as Senator he became a member of the important Foreign Relations Committee

When he first arrived in the Senate Arthur Capper was assigned to a desk in the back row on the Republican side of the aisle A year and a half later his desk was in the fourth row, and a few months later he was regularly assigned to a second-row seat After almost eight years in the Senate he had sufficient seniority to give him a front-row position, which he preferred

Naturally, when he entered the United States Senate, Capper was one of the "low men" in the totem pole of senatorial seniority A year before he first came up for re-election he had already gained a position midway in the seniority scale Deaths, retirements, and defeat at the polls further enabled Capper's position of longevity to make him ninth in rank, with fifteen Senators senior to him when he began his fourteenth year of service in 1933

Usually Capper seemed little concerned about seniority privileges for a United States Senator His lowly rank in 1919 gave him one of the least desirable office suites on an inner court in the Senate Office Building As more favored offices became available through changes in Senate personnel, Capper had no interest in moving his office in spite of the pleading of his staff Though eventually additional Senate office space allowed him to expand his suite from three to four rooms, he ended his thirty years of service in the Senate in the rooms which he had occupied all those years

As an agricultural spokesman from a farming area Capper could be expected to speak out on behalf of agricultural interests His first speech in the Senate, made almost a half year after he took the oath of office, used as a theme the lack of recognition for agriculture Capper criticized the merchandising system for the rising cost of living, and statistics amply supported his position that the farmer was not receiving the benefits of higher food prices.[3] Never a dynamic speaker, Capper usually kept quiet in the Senate. His value to his party and to his constituents was in his organizing ability and in the strength of his publications, not as a manager of legislation on the Senate floor.

Often Capper was aware of "grass roots" thinking before it had been clearly stated, and he appeared to lead in changes in public attitude. One technique which he used to sample public opinion was to include a short list of questions in every letter that went out from his Washington office. Answers mailed back helped Capper to sense changes in the public pulse. In reality he was a follower of the dictates of the Kansas electorate, but his line of communications was so well established that a Capper position on public policy might be assumed before others had arrived at a formal stand. A Capper poll of opinion taken in late 1919 and early 1920 showed an overwhelming support for supervision of meat packers, return of the railroads to private ownership, a League of Nations with reservations, and opposition to universal military training.[4] Although Capper did not invariably follow the dictates of individual letters which came to him from Kansas voters, he was greatly influenced in his voting by his private opinion poll, and he persistently endeavored to determine the will of the people back home. To him this was the true role of a Congressman or Senator, and if he was steadfast on one question and wavering in his position on another it was due to his interpretation of public thinking on those questions.

When the post-war depression hit agriculture, American farmers entered a period of endless frustration and failure. The onslaught of economic forces upset the traditional, individualistic pattern of farm production and marketing, and farmers turned initially to self-help solutions. They drastically reduced their standards of living and gave greater stress to diversification and efficiency of production. With economic conditions worsening, farmers turned to agricultural co-operatives to find relief, but their efforts were often stalled by unsympathetic courts. Finally they turned to politics, where agricultural interests led in placing the government solidly in the business of farming.

Most Kansas farmers in the 1920's did not regard agriculture as an industry which was subject to existing economic laws. Prosperity for agriculture, they reasoned, would come if the farmer worked hard enough and produced more than he had ever produced before Few farmers paid any attention to marketing of agricultural commodities or to their consumption With many variables, such as climate and disease, affecting their production, the farmer was primarily concerned about producing a crop, not about marketing it Marketing of agricultural products was a strange and mysterious realm to the farmer, and he wanted no part of it It is little wonder that initial efforts to relieve agricultural depression in the 1920's came in other fields

In Congress the farm state Representatives and Senators first showed their combined strength in repealing the daylight-saving time law in spite of a veto of their action by President Wilson Senator Capper had received countless letters urging that the clock be put back on "God's time," and not on the time provided by "publicity-seeking politicians " The journals of the Capper Farm Press carried the controversy to their readers, and the farmer, who had to work by sun time anyway, was as concerned about the minor inconveniences of daylight-saving time as he was later about more fundamental questions of relief for depressed farm prices and market conditions

Perhaps success in repealing daylight-saving time showed the way toward other kinds of co-operation between Representatives and Senators from farming states The "Farm Bloc," as it was popularly called, came into being in May, 1921, following a meeting in the Washington offices of the American Farm Bureau Federation Senator W S Kenyon, of Iowa, who became the first "Farm Bloc" chairman, invited a group of Midwestern and Southern Senators to be present to discuss a definite plan of procedure to meet the economic needs of agriculture A dozen Senators and the chairman were present, along with advisers from the Department of Agriculture and the Farm Bureau Additional Senators from other farm states soon brought the total in the nonpartisan "Farm Bloc" to a figure fluctuating between twenty and thirty [5] In the House of Representatives a group of approximately one hundred farm-state Congressmen had a less formal organization [6]

The unexpectedness of the decline in farm-commodity prices brought violent protest from the farming areas Initially the Farm

Bloc concentrated on guiding the Emergency Tariff Bill through Congress, because of the belief that the bill would immediately provide relief for the crisis in agriculture When the prices of farm products continued to fall, a joint Congressional investigation was inaugurated to examine the whole farm problem Other minor statutes were passed in the 1921 session, when the Farm Bloc used its strength to prevent adjournment of the Congress One of these measures, the Capper-Tincher Grain Futures Act, sought to curtail "gambling in grain futures" through a highly restrictive tax Nine months later the Supreme Court invalidated the tax method of regulation in the law Consequently the Grain Futures Act of September 21, 1922, was passed with restriction based on the interstate commerce clause in the Constitution

In stepping up to the Senate from the position of Governor of Kansas Capper was attracting national attention, and he gained acquaintance with other nationally known personalities Friendship of long standing was established with men like Bernard M. Baruch, Thomas A Edison, and many others who were more active in governmental affairs [7] Baruch and Capper corresponded on many public issues, from profiteering to a workable farm program. Baruch, as a representative of big business, gave more than the usual recognition to the role of the farmer in America In 1923 he arranged a large dinner party in honor of Capper in New York City. Baruch had a dual purpose, to teach Easterners "that farm leaders were not horny-handed ignoramuses," and also to "allay the farm leaders' suspicions of the East " He believed his goal had been achieved when he heard the comments which came from this meeting.[8]

Although Capper was a member of the Grand Old Party, he was frequently critical of the Republican Presidents during the 1920's. National news media carried the Capper plea for legislation to "curb profiteering," and he seemed to become better news copy with each passing year [9] In fact, Capper was becoming so well known, especially in the area where his publications circulated, that the *Literary Digest* straw vote on Republican presidential candidates in 1920 ended shortly before the Republican National Convention with Capper as the leading write-in candidate He had almost twice as many write-in votes as General John Pershing but only about one-

149

tenth as many as the leading candidate in the poll, his good friend General Leonard Wood [10]

On occasion Capper was characterized as a "more advanced progressive than Governor Allen " But his advocacy of "a heavy retroactive tax on war profits" received only casual mention [11] The old farm bugaboo of high freight rates could not escape Capper's notice On the grounds that the railroads got "more for hauling farm products than the producers are paid for producing them" he held that freight rates were obviously too high [12]

Never a tool of the Executive, even though he might be of the same party, Capper always felt free to voice his criticisms In an analysis of the first six months of the Harding administration he declared that "the Administration [was] lacking in constructive spirit of progress " These remarks were interpreted by the New York *Times* as "a queer way of supporting one's friends," but this and similar comment by Capper was never made in the spirit of rancor [13]

Capper received additional national attention when he succeeded Senator Kenyon as the leader of the Farm Bloc after the latter was appointed as Judge of a United States Circuit Court Correctly, Capper was considered less able than Kenyon as a floor manager, but he was regarded as an experienced organizer who would likely hold the farm-state Senators together [14] He believed that the accomplishments of the Farm Bloc for the Congressional sessions in 1921 included the placing of an agricultural representative on the Federal Reserve Board of Governors, the revival of the War Finance Corporation to make loans to farmers and stock raisers, legalization of co-operative farmers' organizations, federal control of grain exchanges, and federal regulation of packers He was advocating, at the time, that the Farm Bloc push for intermediate credit facilities and for a law specifying the content of a fabric [15]

The fact that Capper could always express himself better in print than in spoken words gave some of his colleagues the impression that he was "a lion in Kansas and a lamb in Washington "[16] Others decided that Capper was not exactly " 'hard boiled,' but anybody who hopes to find him pliant where the farmer's interests are concerned is in for a shock "[17] But he was not always the docile and meek lamb in the national capital After President Harding presented his message to Congress in November, 1922, Capper found "nothing in the

President's message" he could "endorse except his statement that we must have legislation to relieve distress among the agricultural interests "[18] A short time later Capper teamed up with a few Farm Bloc Senators to lead a fight in opposition to a ship-subsidy bill strongly favored by Harding [19] Apparently the President considered such action an affront to the Republican leadership, for Capper was summoned to the White House for a conference Whether or not Capper agreed to relax his pressure on the administration is not now known, but it was obvious that the actions of the Farm Bloc were becoming "a disturbing factor in Republican politics "[20]

There were outspoken critics of the Capper leadership of the Farm Bloc A newspaper, influential in Kansas, contrasted the Capper as known in Kansas with the image created in Washington In Kansas he was pictured as "the champion of progressive, semi-radical measures " But in the "national capital, the Kansas senator is not regarded as a leader "[21] One member of the Farm Bloc was of the opinion that Capper "as President of the Farm Bloc" had betrayed the organization "It was either that," he wrote, "or he failed to grasp the situation "[22] To some of his senatorial colleagues Capper did not lead the Farm Bloc far enough, to others he was much too radical

Legislation bearing in its popular title the Capper name was almost completely confined to the decade of the 1920's and with one major exception was agricultural Briefly, this legislation was the Capper-Volstead Act of 1922 and of 1926 providing for co-operative marketing and producers' associations The first of these laws has been described as the "Magna Carta of Cooperative Marketing "[23] The Capper-Tincher Act dealt with grain futures and the Capper-Lenroot-Anderson Act made provision in 1923 for Intermediate Credit for farmers at a time when orderly marketing of farm products had virtually disappeared The Capper-Ketcham Act of 1928 made available federal funds to provide support for 4-H club agents A major non-agricultural law with a Capper name was the Capper-Crampton Act of 1930, which set the stage for the George Washington Memorial Parkway and a system of roads on both banks of the Potomac between the nation's capital and Mount Vernon [24] Many were the bills which Capper introduced in the Senate during the 1920's Some with his name in the popular title did not pass Most of those which successfully negotiated the large number of Congressional hurdles to be enacted into law were measures of a private nature, such as pensions for specified veterans or their kin or measures such as the granting of a captured German cannon to a Kansas community

To some farm leaders the agricultural laws obtained from Congress by mid-1923 would provide about "all the relief possible through legislation " Co-operative enterprises, along with individual farmer initiative, were looked upon as the future means of yielding the farmer increased income [25] But the advocates of further farm-relief measures were strongly supporting a farm-parity plan which was generally identified as the McNary-Haugen bill

The godfather of the McNary-Haugen bill was George N Peek, an official of a Moline, Illinois, agricultural implement company Peek recognized that his company could not sell a plow to a "busted customer," and with Hugh S Johnson, by December, 1921, he had prepared a parity plan of "equality for agriculture "[26] They sought to use the protective principle of the tariff in an amended form to "do for agriculture what it does for industry "[27] Late in 1923, Secretary Henry C Wallace of the Department of Agriculture came to the support of the Peek idea by having a legislative draft prepared incorporating a parity concept for agriculture After it was reworked, the sponsor of the Peek idea in the Senate was Charles L McNary of Oregon, and in the House Gilbert N Haugen of Iowa For five years, from 1923 until 1928, this McNary-Haugen bill in its several forms was attracting the attention of the American public No farm bill and perhaps no other piece of legislation at the time received so much notice in news channels

No doubt the Farm Bloc, following the resignation of Senator Kenyon, was weaker than it had been shortly after it was first organized The novelty of this bipartisan group had worn off by late 1923, and the area of agreement for such a diverse aggregation of Senators was indeed limited Capper continued in the role of leadership in the Farm Bloc, and he supported a program for the Congressional session, commencing in late 1923, which included the prohibition of tax-free bonds, the lowering of farm freight rates, and establishment of some corrective for the disparity of prices between farm products and other products [28] Capper held that the motto of the Farm Bloc was "if you help the farm the farm will take care of the Nation "[29] He also made one of the first "network" radio addresses on December 13, 1923, on the topic "Why the 'Farm Bloc' in Congress."

In 1924, when the McNary-Haugen bill and other farm-relief measures were being debated in Congress, Capper had high visions of a satisfactory solution to the farm problem To his Kansas readers he wrote, "The principles of the McNary-Haugen bill, which is to come to a vote within a few days, are economically sound I hope to see it pass The bill is nothing more than a workable plan for making the protective tariff effective in maintaining a fair domestic price level for crops of which we produce a normal surplus "[30] Capper was for the McNary-Haugen bill, but there were other farm-relief measures and many non-agricultural bills in Congress in which he was also interested Moreover, the year 1924 would be an election year in which he would be personally involved As an astute politician Capper wanted to keep his "fences mended," and he did not propose to back himself into a corner from which there would be no escape There was noticeable discontent in Kansas as the election neared Along with Senator Curtis of Kansas and many others, Capper had voted to override the Coolidge veto of the Soldiers' Adjusted Compensation Act, but he could still write of the President a week later that voters were gaining confidence in him [31] Another Coolidge veto, that of the McNary-Haugen bill, did not bring an attack from Capper directly on the President Instead he reported that "big special interests" were out to smash the Farm Bloc and that they had defeated the McNary-Haugen plan [32]

Capper's maverick tendencies and his independence from Republican leadership in Washington were causing criticism in Kansas Curtis, the Republican party whip in the Senate, was not condemned for voting to override a presidential veto, but Capper was—he was coming up for re-election Before the primary election in 1924, William Allen White, in an editorial, had said "Kansas on Trial, Not Capper," and he defended Capper's independent action White commended Capper for voting against the seating of Senator-elect Newberry and against other specified issues which were supported by the Republican majority in the Senate Commenting that "his courage is unpurchasable, and beyond the influence of big business or high society," White was strongly supporting his race for the Senate [33]

Capper's impressive victory in the 1924 election was gratifying to him To his readers he wrote, "If I were not proud of the tremendous testimonial given me at the polls by the people of Kansas, I should be less than human as well as lacking in appreciation and gratitude When on a previous occasion they voted me a majority of 162,000, that was thought to be a record But their indorsement on last Tuesday by a plurality of 275,000 of what I have been undertaking in the Senate, breaks all voting records west of the Mississippi and puts me under a heavy obligation indeed "[34] He usually defined his obligation as being not limited to those who had elected him but to all the people of Kansas

In a sense Capper weakened the chances of approval for the McNary-Haugen bill when he was asked by President Coolidge for advice on the appointment of a new Secretary of Agriculture to succeed Henry C Wallace, who had died on October 25, several weeks before the election In a speech given some ten years later Capper reported a conversation with Coolidge after Secretary Wallace's death Coolidge told Capper that he had seventy-nine applications and suggestions for Wallace's place Capper was asked, "Would it interest you at all?" When he responded negatively, the President said, "Well, there are two men that, as far as I can see now, would make pretty good Agricultural Secretaries, and they come from out in your country I have called you down here to find out what you think of them One of them is John Fields, now the President of the Farm Loan Bank at Wichita, and the other is Dr Jardine, President of the Agricultural College at Manhattan " Briefly Capper responded that "it is pretty hard   to pick between these two men, but if I was naming a man myself, I would probably name Jardine " Capper further reported that the next day President Coolidge sent the name of William M Jardine to the Senate as his appointment for Secretary of Agriculture [35] Jardine was an avowed opponent of the McNary-Haugen bill and its equalization tax feature [36] His view on this piece of farm-relief legislation carried far more weight with President Coolidge than did the position which Capper supported When Wallace was Secretary of Agriculture, the McNary-Haugen bill had a friend in the cabinet The elevation of Jardine to the position of Secretary of Agriculture created a further barrier to its enactment into law

Soon after the Cappers went to Washington in 1919 they established their home at 1100 Sixteenth Street, only a few blocks from the White House [37] Florence Capper had always enjoyed social activities, and in Topeka she circulated in a small and select group She had the Washington house partly remodeled and almost completely redecorated She enjoyed entertaining, and with her husband she took an active part in the social life of the national capital Her niece, Isabel Crawford, the daughter of her brother George, was invited to live with the Cappers for some time and was properly introduced to Washington society During her first few years in Washington Florence Capper became a close friend of Grace Coolidge, when Calvin Coolidge was serving as Vice President and presiding officer in the Senate This friendship continued when the Coolidges became occupants of the White House as a result of the unexpected death of President Harding

Kansas constituents' lack of knowledge about Capper's wife, due largely to her desire for anonymity, created a mystery which they sought to explain, although they had little information Capper's ardent prohibition stand was interpreted as evidence that his wife was an alcoholic in spite of the more obvious influence on his position by his father and mother during his formative years It was evident to those who knew Capper that he was devoted to his wife, but he also had an unusual interest in attractive women whom he met socially Even those who spoke kindly of Capper, who was then almost sixty years of age, said he was not too careful in all his social contacts More bluntly, others reported that he was a philanderer Capper more likely felt that he was complimenting beautiful and attractive ladies, of all ages, through his attention, and he did not recognize a social "error" in his actions

During Capper's first term in the Senate, Florence went with him on many vacation trips, but she did not usually return to Kansas with him During the early part of his second term Arthur and Florence Capper took a strenuous two-month trip in July and August, 1925, to Europe, where Capper spent much of his time studying European farm conditions The Cappers left New York on July 4 on the S S *Leviathan* During the voyage they were served at the Captain's table, along with Judge and Mrs Joseph Sabath and Commander and Mrs Leahy [38] In England they were briefly guests of David Lloyd George, the Speaker of the House of Commons, and they attended a garden party in Buckingham Palace which was given by King George and Queen Mary.[39] Capper also visited "several big publishing plants" and the birthplace of his father. News dispatches show that the Capper itinerary included France, Belgium, the Netherlands, Germany, Austria, Czechoslovakia, Yugoslavia, Switzerland, and Italy.[40] In each country Capper combined sightseeing and consultation with leading economists and statesmen.

Capper was greatly impressed by the opening session of the League of Nations at Geneva in 1925, which he attended in the company of Senators Thomas J. Walsh of Montana and Andrieus A. Jones of New Mexico. He reported that the League "is on the right track, . . . and is doing some good work with possibilities of accomplishing a good deal more." He also said that he had "not changed from the view" which he expressed on his vote on the League, and he thought "it inadvisable for the United States to join" at the present time.[41]

After about ten weeks out of the country the Cappers returned on the *Leviathan* and arrived back in Washington during the latter part of September. From there Arthur went immediately to Topeka, to be followed by Florence about a week later.[42] In Topeka, Capper rarely appeared in the news, but a speech of his was reported as complimentary of the United States' refusal "to recognize Soviet Russia."

He also expressed approval of the probable results from Colonel [Billy] Mitchell's attack on the weakness of the air force."[43] But Capper's expectations did not immediately materialize in Mitchell's case, because of the harsh treatment which Mitchell received from his superior officers. He praised Mitchell "as a courageous man, not afraid to speak as he thinks and undoubtedly on the right track."[44]

Florence Capper seemed to be thoroughly worn out from the European trip, and ample opportunity for rest did not restore her all too slim reservoir of energy. Early in 1926 she learned that she would require major surgery for which the chances of recovery were not good. An outstanding Baltimore surgeon performed the operation early in April at the Hospital for the Women of Maryland in Baltimore. Arthur was near her bedside, and he made frequent trips to Baltimore to be with her. Grace Coolidge was one of her daily correspondents and made at least one trip to visit her.[45] Three weeks after the operation her condition was considered unchanged, but physicians held "slight hope for recovery "[46] A few days later she was reported on the critical list, and "the Senator has been coming over from Washington daily "[47] Florence made several of her visitors promise not to tell Arthur the bad news, but he already knew and in her presence he sought to give every indication that she would recover. Florence Capper died on May 10, and her body was returned to Topeka Capper Publication offices and the city government and state government offices were closed during the funeral service, which was held in the Capper Mansion, with burial in the Topeka Cemetery [48] The Washington house at 1100 Sixteenth Street was closed, and Capper never went there again Henceforth, his Washington home would be the Mayflower Hotel, where he had a room with a small dressing room and bath

With his usual good taste William Allen White reminisced with rare imagery when he wrote

A third of a century ago more or less, a gay young crowd was butterflying around in Topeka Those were the good old-fashioned days when there were dances and parties and picnics and when young people paired off and "went together,"—no necking parties! They sat on front porches on cool summer evenings and sang a little and danced a little and came trooping down to Kansas avenue in surreys with fringed tops and basket phaetons behind good old family horses The whole carefree troop of them piled into an ice cream parlor and made merry riot The writer of these lines, as an outsider, used to see this group and sometimes was drawn a little way into the circle, but not far

The wedding celebration of Florence and Arthur was most delightful The young reporter rising in his profession surrounded by his fellow newspaper men and friends from all over the state was marrying a vivacious, charming girl, the leader of her circle, a most popular young woman, daughter of the former governor So the day sparkled with joy and the occasion was a rainbow of promise

Life has made the promise come true Florence Crawford and Arthur Capper have lived happily and usefully together all these years, partners, friends, lovers, with never a rift in their joy This week some of the same old friends looking over the peak of the hill of life into its sunset, gathered in Topeka to bid her goodbye and to give Arthur their handclasp, as they laid her away for her earthly rest

So a generation has passed, the bright, happy girl growing into a fine, strong, intelligent woman She had her work With her husband she rose to a place of leadership in the state, to one of the important positions in this nation and in the world They never became alien to their friends of that early day The simple loyal faith of their friends of that youthful circle which glowed around them and haloed them in their youth was with them as a benediction to the end of their journey together Nor did the simple love of their friends ever go That they held to the last How hard it is to realize that this girl's life has been lived and is over, that her work is done and her spirit gone to the next stage of experience We, who were young once, 30 years ago, who lived and laughed and loved in the gayety and joy of youth still in our heart know that the fire of youth is eternal—unquenchable To ourselves and to each other we have not changed and maybe not to God Himself But to others we are the older generation passing, a bit queer and old-fashioned and gradually becoming negligible Other youngsters go charging down the street full of the same exuberance, the same hopes, the same high visions and the same gay foibles which once were ours And so "the mourners go about the streets and the man to his lone home "[49]

Florence's death brought serious changes in Capper's life. Messages of condolence came to him from people in all walks of life The President and Mrs Coolidge were especially attentive to the bereaved Kansas Senator During the Christmas vacation from Congress after Florence's death Capper was a guest at the White House Later he told of this visit by saying that he had slept in the Abraham Lincoln bed "Will Rogers," he said, "was here last week and slept in this bed, in this room "[50]

The courteous attentions from the President and the First Lady were well received by the Kansas Senator However, when Coolidge again vetoed the McNary-Haugen bill early in 1927 Capper wrote, "In vetoing the farm-relief bill I believe the President has erred The distress of the farm industry persists, and we know why it persists Our agricultural depression is more than a farm problem. It is a national problem The McNary-Haugen bill may not have been 100 per cent perfect But neither was the first Constitution of the United States perfect   I believe it is the part of wisdom to bring the farmer's standard of living up to the general level, rather than to drag the rest of the country down,   Many economists unite with Vice President Dawes in declaring it practical   ."[51]

Some Middle Western farm leaders were sure that the reason Coolidge was continuing his opposition to the McNary-Haugen bill was his lack of knowledge about the area where farm relief was desperately needed They persuaded Coolidge to spend his 1927 summer vacation in the Black Hills of South Dakota Their strategy backfired when strong supporters of Coolidge commended him in his vacation retreat for his "courageous" vetoes [52]

In spite of his criticism of the presidential veto Capper was invited to spend part of the summer recess from Congress at the state game lodge where the President and Mrs Coolidge were vacationing in South Dakota [53] A vacation presidential office was set up in the high-school building in Rapid City, some thirty miles from the lodge, and Capper frequently made trips to and from Rapid City with the President Coolidge, who had a reputation for keeping his own counsel, enjoyed Capper's company, but he was never one to confide in the Kansas Senator Early in August, 1927, Capper issued a statement to news reporters, who were covering the Coolidge vacation, in which he "predicted the President's re-election   " But Coolidge had already made up his mind that on August 4 he would issue his famous statement, "I do not choose to run for President in Nineteen Twenty-eight " Reports stated that Capper "was quite as surprised as anyone The President has given not the slightest inkling of his decision . . ."[54]

Years later Capper liked to remember his connection with this widely known event The trip from the Summer "White House" that August morning in 1927 had been lacking in conversation Upon arrival at his temporary office the President went about his work At the regular news conference the reporters were told that an additional statement would be made at noon Capper recalled that he went into an inner office where the President dictated his brief statement to a secretary That was the first Capper had heard of it Shortly before the noon conference the required number of statements were typed and cut into strips for distribution When the reporters had all come into the office they were given the statement and they left hurriedly to file their stories [55]

Many Republicans in the 1920's considered Capper excellent presidential timber, and he had active support in the opinion polls taken in 1920 and 1924 With Coolidge out of the way in 1928 conservative and reactionary leaders in the Republican party, opposed to Capper, had some serious concern about his candidacy Considerable support was obtained to oppose him by backing Senator Charles Curtis of Kansas "as having all of the brains in the Western bloc

" Curtis' supporters were not necessarily sold on him either, but they reasoned that he could be easily dumped when Capper was stopped However, the Curtis publicity proved so good it was too much for them [56] Curtis was named as Hoover's vice-presidential candidate in 1928 and was elected

Senator George W Norris of Nebraska tempted Capper to "take a walk from his party" when the presidential line-up for the 1928 election was known Norris wrote that Hoover "is not right on the farm question and after the fight we have been making for several years for agriculture, and after the contest we have been waging to save the country from the domination of the power trust I cannot satisfy my conscience and get into the fight on behalf of the national ticket Neither can I understand how you can do this, but that, is, of course, entirely another matter If we are going to lie down every time and then come back again and try to elect these men who will undo what we are trying to accomplish I do not see where the end will be It seems to me we cannot crush our consciences and support somebody who we know in advance is opposed to the very vital things we have been fighting for for many years "[57] But Capper was more optimistic about success for farm legislation under Hoover and Curtis After all, they were both Western men, and in making up his mind Capper put much weight on that

Senator Arthur Capper served his state and nation in many ways during the 1920's, the most fruitful years of his senatorial career. He was almost constantly in demand as a speaker, and he soon recognized the value of radio in the life of a public official He was always willing to speak on behalf of prohibition, and he was positive that the prohibition experiment was proving successful In almost every session of Congress from the early 1920's he introduced legislation providing for uniform marriage and divorce laws He introduced bills to provide for full legal equality for men and women A forestry study carried out, in part, by the then new Senator Capper in 1919 became the basis for federal-state co-operation in examining and meeting national forestry problems Capper also had a role in developing a basic flood-control policy in the late twenties. He introduced numerous bills providing for "fair trading" practices, and some received nation-wide backing Legislation favoring the laboring man frequently won his support and he always approved of efforts to "take the profit out of war" or to help the veteran of past wars

One action on behalf of veterans which Capper shared with Senator Charles Curtis and with Senator Selden P Spencer of Missouri attracted considerable national attention During the closing months of World War I the 35th Division, made up largely of Kansas and Missouri boys, fought in the Meuse-Argonne offensive, and was withdrawn to regroup after five days of hard fighting In its march to the rear the division "looked more like a band of refugees than a military organization "[58] Before there was any opportunity for meals or for clean clothes Major Robert Gray Peck of the Inspector General's department arrived for an official inspection Peck critically examined the appearance and attitudes of the division and censured the division officers because of lost equipment and the lack of military precision which he found in many units Peck included in his report the statements that the "morale and spirit of the men in this division is excellent They are tired and dirty and need clean clothes, rest and recreation, but they all appear willing and eager to enter the fight again "[59] But his "insults" to division officers and his statement that most of the "organizations showed all the earmarks of National Guard units, which they are," obscured all else [60] Consequently when Peck's name came up for promotion in 1921, along with the names of 4,000 other officers, Capper, a member of the Military Affairs Committee, innocently inquired if Peck's name was on the list Faced with an impasse and the opposition of Curtis, Spencer, Capper, and others, President Harding withdrew the major's name [61] Eventually Peck became a lieutenant colonel in the regular Army, in spite of Capper's opposition, for the Senate in executive session confirmed the promotion in 1922 by a vote of 41 to 19, but Capper's action was admired by veterans back home and by all who were smarting under the insinuations that there was something of great value in regular Army units which National Guard or reserve outfits did not have [62]

After the defeat of the Versailles Treaty Capper paid more attention to foreign affairs He supported the World Court idea of President Harding, and later he strongly approved the purpose and idea of the Kellogg-Briand Peace Pact, begun as a bilateral agreement between the United States and France, and quickly expanded into a world-wide agreement "to renounce war as an instrument of national policy" The theme "outlawry of war" was frequently the basis for conversation and discussion in the late 1920's Various Senators, including Capper, introduced resolutions which they believed would commit the United States morally to the maintenance of peace [63] James T Shotwell and Nicholas Murray Butler lent a scholarly bearing to the "peace" talk, but some spokesmen in early 1928 criticized the Capper resolution and "other similar devices for the outlawry of war as largely gestures on paper containing inherent defects and objections of a meretricious and dangerous character "[64] Capper spoke to the Academy of Political Science in its November, 1928, meeting in New York City, and he objected to the "Paris Pact" on the grounds that it was "not positive enough," that it "did not provide sufficiently for the machinery of pacific settlement," and that the "treaty deprived nations of their sovereign rights "[65]

Early the next year Capper made concrete proposals to "put teeth" into the Paris Peace Pact, and the controversy over its acceptability gained a leading position among national news media [66] Capper suggested that the Peace Pact be strengthened by placing violating nations under a trade embargo The President, under this plan, had the "responsibility of determining whether a nation engaging in hostilities is an aggressor " When approval of Capper's suggestion came from Paris, London, and Geneva, opponents of the plan again criticized Capper by saying "that the Kansas Senator has lent himself to a secret and perverse scheme to bring the United States, after all, into the League of Nations "[67] President Coolidge, in his typical fashion, commented that "Capper's proposal goes a bit too far," and interest in the idea soon died down with the inauguration of the new administration and the development of higher priorities on other measures for foreign and domestic legislation [68] Later Capper felt his plan was vindicated by some of the neutrality legislation of the thirties

Throughout much of the 1920's Senator Capper was concerned about the handling of farm problems by the Republican leadership [69] When Hoover was elected President in 1928 Capper was optimistic about the success of a comprehensive program for farm relief He was still withholding major criticism after the new President had presented his first message to Congress However, he remarked

162

that he "had hoped the President would give us a detailed plan "[70] During the following month Capper was critical of an export debenture plan of indirect governmental subsidy for food products to be sold overseas He was, at the same time, laudatory of a real farm-relief program in a new "McNary Farm bill," and he had praise for the "leadership of President Hoover "[71] Almost a year later, after the stock market crash, Capper was still complimentary of the President in appraising his first year in office He held that it had been "a year of fact-finding, a year of work on data and blueprints, a year of foundation laying These are the marks of the engineering mind of President Hoover "[72] But he did not automatically endorse Hoover appointees Capper's refusal to confirm the appointment of a federal judge desired by Hoover created widespread interest in Kansas.[73]

Early in the Hoover administration Congress passed the Agricultural Marketing Act, in which much of the language was similar to that of the last McNary-Haugen bill Many supporters of the McNary-Haugen bill opposed this piece of agricultural legislation as inappropriate and ineffective, but Capper regarded it as "the most important legislation ever enacted   for agriculture " He wrote that it "is intended to do for agriculture what the Federal Reserve Act does for commerce, what the Transportation Act does for the railroads, what the protective tariff does for manufacturing and labor " He approved the elimination of the "debenture plan," and he had great "faith in Hoover " If the new law did not work, after a fair trial, Capper would favor then the "debenture or some other plan "[74] Thereafter, Capper cautioned that the Farm Board, created to administer the Agricultural Marketing Act, has a big job and it is "entitled to time and opportunity " In spite of the serious economic dislocation of commodity markets he asked for patience, and he expressed his confidence in the ability of the President and the Farm Board to help the farmer out of his difficulties [75]

During the early part of the Hoover administration Capper questioned the need for a higher protective tariff, especially if agriculture was to obtain no protection He frequently voiced his concern that the proposed tariff bill did "not bring the protection, as a whole, to which agriculture is entitled " His signed editorials in this period contained such headings as "Farm-Tariff Monstrosity,"

"Tariff Revolt Grows," and "Tariff Monstrosity an Economic Crime "[76] Eventually the Hawley-Smoot tariff bill was sufficiently changed for Capper to vote for "the tariff bill, as amended in the Senate," since he believed "that the measure as amended tends to restore the economic equality of agriculture with other basic industries "[77] A short time later he described the new law as the "best ever written for agriculture "[78] Capper was consistent in his thinking about tariffs, but he was not always in favor of protective rates He had voted for the emergency tariff legislation and the Fordney-McCumber Act of the early twenties, and he eventually supported the Hawley-Smoot bill His justification, in each case, was protection for agriculture which he believed these bills would provide Wherever a projected tariff law proposed increases in non-agricultural rates without comparable protection for the farmer, Capper opposed it, believing that he was supporting farm interests in his action

Capper's first two terms in the United States Senate were his most productive years in Congress He was a member of the majority party, and his party was also in control of the Executive departments of government It was a trying time for Capper because of the generally depressed condition of agriculture through the twenties, but he was able to convince most of his followers that he was always on the job and was doing the best he could for them So when he announced as a candidate for re-election in 1930, it was not surprising that he had no opposition in the primary His opponent in the general election was a farmer and former Democratic Governor of Kansas, Jonathan M Davis In spite of the economic hardships felt throughout the nation and the swing away from the party in power in 1930, Capper again polled a handsome majority, getting 61 1 per cent of the more than one-half million votes cast by Kansans

On occasion in 1930 Capper expressed optimism about the future, but more and more he was recognizing reality for what it was His signed editorials voiced this concern They had such titles as "The Farmer's Difficulties," "The Farmer and the Depression," and "We Face a Serious Emergency "[79] How serious the emergency might be was a question on everyone's mind as the influence of the depression was more deeply felt Before the stock market crash Capper had predicted some kind of collapse When it came, he wrote that the "expected has come to pass—the long overdue deflation of the stock

Key Capper personnel with the Senator, June, 1936. *Left to right:* Tom McNeal, Henry Blake, Marco Morrow, Charles Sessions, and Capper.

Courtesy of the Capper Foundation

Capper and his beloved *Capital*, in 1944. Among the pictures on the desk are those of Mrs. Capper, Thomas E. Dewey, and William Allen White.

Courtesy of the Capper Foundation

market " But Capper, no serious or original thinker on the issue of economic depressions, did not expect the grave consequences of actions on Wall Street and elsewhere to the economy of the entire nation His own business activities were severely damaged and the national government became more involved in economic affairs New forces were beginning to affect American life, and Capper was torn between his loyalty to his party and to his President and the desire for change He was often a reluctant witness to changes that were to occur after he took the oath of office as United States Senator in 1931 at the beginning of his third term in Congress, but he followed his rule to live each day as it comes

Chapter XV
The New Deal Years

In 1931, when Arthur Capper began his third term in the United States Senate, he was recognized for his vote-getting ability and for his "grass roots" interpretation of the American farmer. His active support of legislation favored by the people of Kansas and his denunciation of the evils of the commodity market and the stock market endeared him to his constituency. Always Capper sought to serve the "home folks," but his efforts during the twenties for farm legislation had never been more than partly satisfactory.

The impact of the depression shook Capper's faith in President Herbert Hoover, but he continued a somewhat independent backing of the leadership of the Republican party, while voting "with the Democratic-Insurgent Republican coalition" on several important measures [1] More responsive to the shifting sands of public opinion than the President, he particularly sought additional relief for distressed agriculture.

In Kansas, the selection of a Governor in 1930 overshadowed the senatorial races for the seats held by Capper and Henry J Allen, the latter having been named to the Senate after the election of Vice President Charles Curtis Younger men of similar background won the Democratic and Republican nominations for Governor, only to have the race complicated by the last-minute entrance of an Independent candidate, Dr John R Brinkley, "a nervous little man with a pink goatee, a radio station and physician's license that the State [medical] board won't recognize."[2] In making his appeal to the person in economic distress Brinkley employed his radio station in an extremely effective manner Although Brinkley did not become Governor, radio used for campaign purposes had reached a position of importance

To some the question, "Why was Arthur Capper taken and Henry Justin Allen left?" defied analysis [3] A primary reason for the outcome was due, no doubt, to the fact that Allen strongly supported the administration and was "Mr Hoover's spokesman" in Kansas He had defended and voted for confirmation of John J. Parker to the United States Supreme Court, while Capper had opposed confirmation because of the anti-Negro bias of the candidate [4] Allen wholeheartedly endorsed every part of the Hoover program, while Capper always seemed to have had reservations So the electorate, in venting their wrath on Hoover, replaced Allen with the Democratic candidate, George McGill, but at the same time they re-elected Capper to the six-year term Kansans also chose the Democratic candidate, Harry H Woodring, as Governor [5]

The depression greatly added to the work of the Congress and the national government The Congressional session ending in early 1931 had been hectic, and Capper reported that everyone "seemed to have a chip on his shoulder " It was a "cat and dog fight from start to finish " He agreed that Hoover was in for a "nerve-racking time" and that "criticism and abuse will continue " But the President, said Capper, was "entitled to a square deal" on his program [6]

Some of the activity of that legislative session was viewed favorably by Capper He had "not been as much impressed with the deadly menace of the Power Trust as . Senator Norris," but he "stood with him on Muscle Shoals "[7] On the other hand, when oil was not on the tariff list Capper reported that the omission had "started an insurrection that may junk the whole tariff policy "[8]

Many national journals and newspapers in the early thirties regarded the senior Senator of Kansas as a controversial figure Capper insisted that he was a progressive, and so he was to some extent But United States Senators with the recognized "progressive" label did not acknowledge his right to the designation Capper held that "the self-styled progressives are not, in reality, mere progressives, they are radicals " His role, he held, was that of a progressive, "but not a radical "[9]

Capper's name appeared as author of articles which received national coverage Generally he dealt with the serious condition faced by agriculture In a grave and earnest vein, he wrote for one magazine that the Kansas farmers "are puzzled, indignant, and discouraged The index of prices received by the producers is 80 per cent of the prewar levels, as compared with 123 per cent a year ago With some commodities, such as wheat, the markets have established new all-time lows Large amounts of unusually high quality wheat have been sold this year in Kansas for as little as 25 cents a bushel " The conviction was growing that something was "radically wrong with an economic system" where depressed prices were so severe and prolonged Realistically Capper recognized that "the Republican party gets considerable blame for the economic situation It has always taken the credit for the good times when it was in power, and now it" received just desserts for economic depression But the major complaint of the depression, according to Capper, "goes far deeper than merely questioning the superficial problems of party control" into the more complex question of the validity of the economic system [10]

Capper still supported Hoover, although the administration seldom followed his suggestions on agricultural matters When the President made plans for a "debt holiday" for German reparation payments, Capper was lavish in his praise He commended Hoover for revealing the "Navy League" as a lobbying group that "imposed on the public," rather than accepting its claim that it was merely a patriotic organization [11] Early in 1932 Capper noted that the "low point" of the depression had been "reached several weeks ago" and an upturn was now expected He was more closely identified as "a friend of the administration," and his expressions of support for the President became more abundant as the election neared [12] In radio addresses Capper pictured "President Hoover as having 'courage and backbone plus,' " and he regarded him as the " 'best bet' for the next four years of reconstruction" which should "not be turned over to new and inexperienced hands " Capper noted that had Hoover "failed us, had he weakened, it is not too much to say there would not be a bank open in America today "[13] He disagreed with Henry A Wallace on the effect and significance of Hoover's farm speech, and on the eve of the election Capper joined with other Republican leaders who spoke in a national radio broadcast on behalf of the candidacy of Hoover [14]

The presidential election of 1932 was a surprise to Capper only in the magnitude of the vote for Franklin D Roosevelt He first met Roosevelt when Josephus Daniels had introduced him to some of his staff in the Navy Department in 1919 On other occasions they were again introduced and when Roosevelt was Governor of New York an article he had written was published in *Capper's Magazine* Several weeks after the election Capper wrote a letter of congratulations to the President-elect, and a month later he received a reply in which Roosevelt expressed his "wholehearted desire to meet your offer of cooperation in the same spirit in which it is offered In matters of progressive principle, we are all, regardless of our political faith, commonly interested " Roosevelt continued, "I find myself in agreement with so many things that you mention in your letter that I am full of hope that we shall, not only after the new administration begins its work on March 4th, but during the Congress that is now in session, . enact a number of fundamentally important remedial measures to meet the serious national emergencies that confront us I think that this applies particularly to the relief of the farmer, and I note with satisfaction what you say on that subject "[15]

Herbert Hoover's last few months as President were a nightmare made worse by his inability to "work out a settlement" with the incoming President Capper did not criticize Roosevelt for that Instead he said the President-elect "has a perfect right to keep himself aloof from questions of policy until he is in a position to control those questions himself, in so far as they are within the control of the executive branch of the government "[16] William Allen White followed somewhat the same position as he expressed anxiety about the banks curtailing credit, and the insecure financial position White wanted Capper's help to reach Hoover, "through the cordon of his secretariat " He believed a "formula could be worked out that would revalue the dollar," and help save financial institutions [17]

Roosevelt's confident expectations for the future caused a growing feeling of optimism to prevail Capper responded by saying that "President-elect Roosevelt is pledged to a *new deal* Just what that means remains to be seen " In the same speech, in eulogy of former President Coolidge, Capper announced that "Calvin Coolidge probably was right when he declared it is not the job of the government to support the people, [but] it also seems to me it is the job of the government to insure the people the opportunity to support themselves by their labor "[18] Although he was loyal to the memory of Coolidge, the Kansas Senator was prepared to grant vast authority to the incoming President

But Capper was unwilling to give up the basic powers of Congress, and he increasingly used radio to report to his electorate After 1931 he made regular addresses by "delayed transcription" to Kansas listeners over WIBW and other stations Soon after the inauguration of Franklin D Roosevelt, Capper could report that things "are happening pretty fast these days, in the era of the New Deal " Candidly, he told how the President had asked for, and "Congress has granted, dictatorial powers over banking and currency and the federal budget.

and Congress has passed, a bill legalizing as I see it, the illegal sale of illegal beer, under the pretence of declaring intoxicating beer to be non-intoxicating " The Kansas Senator voted for the bills to balance the budget through various economy measures, but true to his long convictions he opposed the beer bill and the repeal of the Eighteenth Amendment [19]

Suggestions for agriculture met with Capper approval "It seems," he said, "that when President Roosevelt proposed a 'New Deal' for agriculture that he meant just exactly a New Deal And I believe that his proposed New Deal is intended to benefit agriculture, and have high hopes that it will benefit agriculture   In a way the Roosevelt plan for farm relief is a realization of actualities It faces some facts that only the farm organizations, farm leaders and some of us here who have been denominated 'the farm bloc' for the past ten or twelve years, have known to be the facts "[20]

Capper attributed the depression, beginning in 1929, to the fundamental role of agriculture in the national economy In 1933 he said that the "farm depression has existed for at least twelve years. The cumulative effect of those years of exchanging products every year at a loss, has destroyed the farmers' purchasing power When it finally disappeared, the wheels of industry stopped, business was paralyzed, credit evaporated, and the army of unemployed grew from one million to fourteen million men and women   Because when agriculture goes bankrupt, civilization of which agriculture is the base also inevitably goes bankrupt " Capper further remarked that "these are the facts, this is the situation, which justifies President Roosevelt in asking the broad, we might as well admit it, the dictatorial, powers to the secretary of agriculture to try to restore pre-war purchasing power to agriculture, in order that farmers and city dwellers both may return to prosperity thru the free exchange of farm products for manufactured commodities and for services " Because he felt that the presidential request was "justifiable in this critical situation in the public interest" Capper was willing to support it He realized that legislation "could have saved this situation ten years ago, even five years ago, by less drastic measures." But opponents of farm relief had "fought and defeated every one of the less drastic plans proposed Now they are going to have to take this one, it appears, and make the best of it "[21]

Capper sincerely believed that Representatives and Senators were obligated to respond to the wishes of the people they represented Because of this basic assumption Capper showered his support on measures requested by the administration He said, "Any time President Roosevelt asks for these broad powers on the ground the emergency demands them, I feel honor bound to grant him those powers " The people of Kansas had given their mandate to Roosevelt, and Capper would follow through [22] In a commendatory and humorous vein one Kansas editor wrote that if "a popular demand were voiced to reverse the law of gravitation and Arthur Capper were shown it was his duty to do so he would sponsor it It is a hundred to one shot he would at least have it amended "[23]

Capper was optimistic about the success of the measures passed during the hectic first hundred days of the New Deal He had faith in Henry A Wallace, Secretary of Agriculture, whom he pictured as "a high-class man, and the ablest agricultural economist we have in the West " He supported virtually every administration bill "because he believed the President had the leadership that the country needed "[24]

Following the short session of Congress which enacted many of the initial statutes for the New Deal, Capper spoke on a national Farm and Home Hour program He reported that the present Congress "was the best behaved Congress in the 14 years I have been in the Senate, tried harder to please the country and do something worth while   I have been urging cooperation for years We have been agreeing on the necessity for cooperation, for organization, if the individual farmer is to retain any measure of economic freedom
.   You may think I am unduly earnest in stressing this need for cooperation with President Roosevelt and Secretary Wallace, in carrying out this farm program to the best of our ability. I am very much in earnest I have been much worried, I might say almost frightened, at the steady downward course of agriculture in the last 12 years   This may be only a mediocre plan, but if it succeeds we get the benefits from it "[25]

A short time later an editorial analysis of Capper's activity in the special session of Congress, which had just concluded, reported that never "has he been busier or more useful than in this special session of Congress During three Republican Administrations he was kept on the jump all the time When the Democratic Administration came in, he thought there would be a little rest for him Instead, his mail increased and multiplied Kansas folks would write him Never has he had to work so hard Mr Roosevelt has been most friendly, has given 'his most courteous consideration' to all requests made by Mr Capper " Kansas had even been remembered with an administration-backed proposal for the Kiro dam, to be thrown across the Kaw a little west of Topeka [26] But most Kansans would have nothing to do with this flood reservoir extravaganza and it was never begun

Franklin D Roosevelt's assumption of the presidential office brought on many changes, and a major one was emphasis on the dynamic role of the federal government in the national economy "Few Presidents of the United States have aroused a deeper contemporaneous devotion, and none, by the political law of action and reaction, has provoked a deeper detestation "[27] Capper never regarded Roosevelt with either devotion or detestation, but because of the widespread support for the new President's program, the Kansas Senator was willing to respond to the call of the electorate

In evaluating the first year of the New Deal Capper wrote that he had "supported and voted for every one of the major relief proposals asked or advocated by President Roosevelt " So did most of his colleagues They considered it plainly their "duty to do so." Capper further indicated that during "the past year it seemed to me that the welfare of the people of the United States demanded, first of all, loyal support of the Roosevelt program It was the only program we had." The task of the Republican party, as he viewed it was, "first, to support every sound step of the Administration in its recovery drive, and support it wholeheartedly Second, to see that all legislation enacted provides a way for the return of constitutional government as soon as economic conditions permit "[28]

Plans for the 1934 election campaign resulted in the creation of a Republican Senatorial Campaign Committee and all of the Republican Senators were automatically members When a special "executive committee" was chosen to take active charge of the campaign, Capper was "passed over,   on the ground that he is disqualified

172

by his 'Democratic' utterances of late " Senator Peter Norbeck of South Dakota was the replacement for Capper on the executive committee The Kansas Senator learned of the change from a newspaper reporter [29]

That the small group of Republican Senators should seek vengeance upon one of their own number in their shelving of Capper evoked a humorous response from the New York *Times* These "keepers of the Republican joint" were considered "ill-advised " If Capper was guilty of "Democratic utterances," it was due to the fact, said the *Times*, that he was "a wholesale utterer of what he thinks the home folks in Kansas want to hear   Why should the Republican Tories pick on him?"[30]

William Allen White naturally supported Capper's position in Congress His Emporia *Gazette*, in a story based on an article in a Washington magazine, reported that Arthur Capper had a perfect record on legislative measures in favor of the "people against vested interests " Accordingly, Capper had been on the right side on the issues of open executive sessions, Muscle Shoals, drouth relief, wheat for the destitute, sales tax, the lame duck amendment, tax publicity, overland mail graft, the thirty-hour week, taxation of power companies, legalization of company unions, the taxing of tax-exempt securities, the remonetization of silver, a surtax increase, and "other measures along that line " Adapting some of Theodore Roosevelt's phrases, White's paper continued, "He speaks softly but he carries a big stick with an ungodly wallop for self-seeking interests when a vote is called in the senate "[31]

When Capper discussed the 1934 election for his radio audience he offered the opinion that while "the country is not entirely satisfied with what has been accomplished by the Roosevelt program to date, it has enough faith in the President's sincerity of purpose to go ahead with the program and give it further trial " The election in Kansas he interpreted as "not declaring for or against the New Deal as a whole Kansas simply placed the various phases of the New Deal on trial, and by its vote in the congressional election, delivered a mandate to its representatives in Congress to give the New Deal a fair trial "[32] The unusual drouth conditions in Kansas also caused Capper to feel that "much more had to be done to get us out of the depression "[33]

One analysis of major senatorial action in 1933, 1934, and 1935, shows that Capper voted like Senators Hayden, Bankhead, Wagner, Thomas, and Barkley—thus like leading Democratic Senators, and no other Republican voted as he did on all these major bills [34] He was a Republican "New Dealer" The principal Senate measures which had Capper support were the Federal Emergency Relief Act, the Agricultural Adjustment Act, the Tennessee Valley Authority, the National Industrial Recovery Act, the devaluation of the dollar, and the Securities Exchange Act He was one of five Republican Senators to support the Reciprocal Tariff Act passed in 1934, and he backed United States participation in the World Court, which lost in the Senate for want of a two-thirds vote Capper also voted for the Federal Relief Act of 1935, the Social Security Act, the National Labor Relations Act, the Public Utility Holding Company Act, and the Guffey-Snyder Act to regulate the bituminous coal industry [35]

Full Capper agreement with the Franklin D. Roosevelt administration lasted approximately two years Even during this span Capper asked for more time to consider important legislation "to justify it being called legislation instead of dictation"[36] After more than two years of Roosevelt leadership Capper announced that the " 'sublime confidence' felt in President Roosevelt and the New Deal even one year ago has been seriously impaired in the past six months" According to the Kansas Senator responsibility for this was due to "an apparent lack of leadership in the White House and in the Congress," and "confusion in the public mind," over the presidential tax program [37] Although he was in general agreement on levying "higher income taxes on large incomes," he opposed the general concept of deficit financing and "this spending spree in which the Federal Government is engaged" Still he had supported certain bills, knowing that they required large appropriations [38] The broad grant of authority given to the President for control of vast new expenditures was also a source of complaint [39]

The long hard session of Congress in 1935 caused Capper and others to suggest adjournment because activity of the session had "just become one fight after another"[40] Members of Congress were "fagged out," and they were becoming irritable [41] When the time came for a decision on adjournment, Capper voted to stay, and his action brought a commendation from the New York *Times* After noting that he was known "as a bold, good man," its editorial quoted some lines considered descriptive of the Kansas Senator.

> I'm a straight-spoken kind o' creetur
> Thet blurts right out wut's in his head,
> An' ef I've one pecooler feetur,
> Its a nose thet wunt be led [42]

Before the 1936 elections Capper could not agree with the administration proposal on repeal of the Eighteenth Amendment Because of his own experience and background he was fundamentally opposed to repeal Consequently he viewed the prospect with dismay. He suggested that the states "continue prohibition after repeal."[43] But his only source of satisfaction on the prohibition issue was the Kansas vote in the 1934 election, which made no change in its existing laws Counting on historical precedent, Capper concluded that "Kansas again is leading the war on statewide prohibition, as it did more than half a century ago "[44] Thereafter the Kansas Senator regularly introduced bills in each session of the Senate to bar liquor advertising from newspapers, from radio, from movies, from circulars mailed across state lines, and from all other communication media His voice was often raised on behalf of prohibition, and his presence at the special Congressional breakfasts of the International Reform Federation in Washington was an anticipated event for him

With equal strength Senator Capper opposed anything which he regarded as militarism He counted on the geographical and diplomatic isolation of the United States to keep the country out of war. Although he saw value in the Reciprocal Trading Agreements and in the Good Neighbor Policy toward Latin America, the suggested extension of these programs to Asia or to Europe brought his immediate opposition During the first Roosevelt administration Capper opposed practically all forms of military and naval developments because he considered them provocative of possible war. To Capper such military and naval expansion was the work of "enthusiastic jingoes" who were "urging that we should have the biggest army in the world, and also the biggest navy We are to compete with Great Britain, whose empire stretches over the seven seas, in the matter of a navy second to none And presumably we are to compete with Russia in building up an army second to none " Capper continued that the people of the United States "are a peaceful people We are a continental nation, as nearly self contained as any in the world We need only an army and a navy for defensive purposes And yet we find on hand a program calling apparently for a navy large enough to take five million men overseas in the next war "[45] Capper's own inclinations in the mid-1930's told him that war in which the United States would be involved was an impossible anachronism, and he was receptive to any program which would cut back military appropriations, instead of increasing them His own publications frequently carried his anti-war editorials He accepted the Nye Committee's interpretation of United States entrance into World War I He frequently lambasted the "war racketeer," and he sought support for Senate bills often backed by the American Legion to take the profit out of war with steeply graduated income and other taxes in wartime His response to the Nye Committee report was typical of Midwestern Senators and Congressmen He described war as "a cursed thing—the world's greatest foolishness," and he felt it was "an insult to the patriotism of America to say that one man's wealth is more sacred than another man's blood There is no reason," he reported in numerous speeches, "why we should be able to draft one man's life in a national emergency, and not another man's property "[46] A bill for a national referendum for a declaration of war found Capper support throughout the twenties and the thirties, but it never got much farther than the first time he had heard it discussed by Senator Gore immediately after World War I.[47]

By 1935 Kansans began to sense that Capper would be running for re-election again in 1936 He would be more than seventy-one years of age, but his strength among the Kansas voters seemed secure Conservative Republican discontent in Kansas with Capper's open-handed acceptance of much of the New Deal program was voiced by a Topeka attorney, Robert Stone Stone legalistically declared in a letter to a Topeka newspaper that "every vote and every official act of the senator's three years has been in support of policies to destroy the Constitution and the American standard of government His course has encouraged people to believe they should look to their government for support rather than assume individual responsibility to support the government "[48] The Stone blast particularly took issue with Capper's stand on the Agricultural Adjustment Act, Social Security legislation, and child labor laws, all of which were then being tested in federal courts Editorially the Topeka *Daily Capital* questioned Stone's motives and pointed out that it "is rather significant that he overlooked criticizing the Senator's vote in favor of the holding company bill That was the one vote of all votes cast by Senator Capper that displeased Stone the most and which no doubt was his real reason for writing the letter "[49] The public airing of Stone's opposition to Capper and the defense supplied by backers of the Senator brought numerous letters to Capper's Washington office indicating continued support [50]

Although his own re-election was important to him, Capper placed a paramount emphasis on the presidential race in which Governor Alfred M Landon was to take on the "champ " He gave his "Hearty Congratulations" to the Republican convention for nominating the Kansas Governor, partly because he had been one of the original Landon boosters [51] Capper had been on the Landon "bandwagon" even before the Kansas Governor had discarded his hesitancy to strive "after the first choice" in the Republican convention [52] The various Kansas Republican Congressmen, with Capper leading the way, helped others to board the Landon "special "[53] Politicians both experienced and inexperienced were able to build so much support for Landon that he was nominated on the first ballot at the Cleveland convention There were many likely candidates for the vice-presidential nomination Vandenberg was Landon's first choice, but he declined Styles Bridges could not be given the second place for fear that "Landon Bridges falling down!" would become a slogan, so Colonel Frank Knox, whom Landon recognized as a Theodore Roosevelt Republican, became the acceptable compromise

Senator Capper actively campaigned for the Landon-Knox ticket A formal notification of Landon's nomination was held in Topeka in late July Capper presided at a luncheon with two hundred guests and introduced the Republican candidate as the "next President "[54] To assembled voters, wherever he found them, Capper announced his support of Governor Landon "because as President he would retain the 'good things' and abolish the 'bad things' of the New Deal "[55]

At the Des Moines conference of Midwestern Governors in September the opposing candidates, Roosevelt and Landon, met in surroundings of "self-restraint" and "self-possession " As a result of this meeting Capper reportedly said, "Harmony dripped so steadily from every rafter   that I fully expected one of the candidates to withdraw "[56]

The Roosevelt landslide buried Landon even in Kansas, where the Republican candidate lost his own state by more than sixty-six thousand votes Capper, trailing Roosevelt by almost forty-five thousand votes, was able to eke out the narrowest margin of victory for any of his political battles when he defeated Omar B Ketchum, Topeka mayor, by slightly more than twenty-one thousand votes Kansas also put the Democratic candidate, Walter A Huxman, into the Governor's chair Clifford R Hope, Congressman from Southwest Kansas, congratulated Capper because he had "survived the storm in such good shape " Hope continued, "Considering the way things went, I feel that it is quite remarkable that any of us pulled through There was quite a campaign on the part of Democrats out here in the last week or ten days in the way of urging support of the straight Democratic ticket and it apparently had a lot of affect [*sic*] Your campaign for Alf Landon cost you a lot of votes I know, but I am sure that you don't have any regrets on that account. . . . I want you to know that I greatly appreciate your coming out to the Seventh District I know that your speeches did a lot of good . . ."[57]

Although he gained a great electoral victory in 1936, Franklin D. Roosevelt was unable to continue the momentum of New Deal legislation into his second administration Instead he was to face defeat "on one of his most important proposals, his failure to refashion the Democratic party along the line of his own preferences," and the Democratic tide began to recede [58]

Capper was lukewarm to the administration after the 1936 election An issue upon which almost all opponents of extreme Executive power could unite was the Roosevelt proposal to re-organize the Federal Judiciary, or as they expressed it, "pack the Supreme Court " Capper believed the "President's plan indefensible from the viewpoint of sound public policy" The "right way" was through an amendment to the Constitution, he said He had found himself "in agreement with the views of a minority of the Supreme Court on several important decisions in the past few years," but this did not mean that the judiciary should be "subservient to the White House "[59] According to Capper, "the real test of a soundness of the President's proposal would be found in how it would work in another administration, in another time, and with another program."[60] He further held that "President Roosevelt's remedy strikes me as being worse than the disease he seeks to cure."[61]

Although Roosevelt failed to get the law he wanted for reorganizing the federal judiciary, resignations in the Supreme Court enabled him to fill seven vacancies in the next four years The first of these Roosevelt appointees, Senator Hugo Black of Alabama, was confirmed by the Senate in its usual time-consuming manner, and Capper supported the nomination Later when disclosures of Black's connection with the Ku Klux Klan were made, Capper was asked to explain his vote He reported, "I am convinced in my own mind that I did the right thing under the circumstances in the light of the information before us   One reason why I voted to confirm Black was the vicious fight put up by powerful business and financial interests who were opposed to his confirmation " Capper believed in the honesty of the new judge However, the recent disclosures about the Klan would have made a difference, according to the Kansas Senator [62]

Throughout his life Arthur Capper was blessed with unusually good health Ordinarily he did not remember the last time he had been ill On April 2, 1937, after dinner at the Mayflower he became ill, and the hotel physician ordered his immediate removal to Emergency Hospital, where he was operated on for appendicitis [63] Even at the age of seventy-one years he made a swift recovery [64] Before long he was again on his feet, but the $1,000 bill for medical services somewhat appalled him He spoke to Senator Royal Copeland, of New York, who was himself a medical doctor, concerning the correctness of such charges Eventually he paid $750 in cash to the doctor performing the emergency appendectomy, who said that as a Republican he placed a high value on the life of a Republican Senator [65]

During the second Roosevelt Administration the emphasis was more on foreign relations than on the national scene Capper had strongly supported the domestic program of the New Deal, but his "isolationist proclivities" showed more closely on the surface from the mid-1930's on Earlier Capper had willingly accepted the Nye

Committee report, which credited American entry into World War I to the machinations of Wall Street bankers and American munitions-manufacturers He wrote that the "Nye committee has been rendering a most valuable public service in bringing to light the excessive profits of war and preparations for war that go to munitions makers, so-called merchants of death "[66] His strong support for putting "teeth" into the Kellogg-Briand Peace Pact in the late twenties reached partial fruition with the passage of the Neutrality Act of 1935 [67] He believed that war could be legislated out of existence, and his principal concern was that the neutrality laws were too lax and left loopholes too large to be ignored Initially he felt that private loans to belligerents were a dangerous invitation to our future participation in war He continually voiced an apprehension about our "drift toward war," and he proposed that neutrality laws be made more effective and that embargoes be imposed, and he was critical because "the Administration had evaded the spirit of the Neutrality Act while rendering lip service to the letter of the act "[68] By that time Capper and several other members of the Senate were identified as "ostrich-isolationists" and "peace-at-any-price pacifists "[69]

Because of his role on the Senate Foreign Relations Committee Senator Arthur Capper was aware of strong pressures in opposition to his isolationist position He corresponded with the United States Ambassador to Spain, who answered in a long, "Very Confidential" letter that "we alone among the Powers have not had a single incident, and we alone among them are conceded by both sides to have followed an honest policy of aloofness   That there is a conspiracy of the Fascist International to destroy Democracy in Europe and the world I have no doubt If it succeeds in Spain, then the next victim will be Czechoslovakia   I have not written with such frankness to anyone but Hull and the President "[70] To Capper the choice for the future was quite simple Peace had "its price the same as war," and it was worth a great effort [71] He did not believe war was inevitable, although he feared that the United States was being drawn into it In a radio interview sponsored by the National Council for Prevention of War he outlined a six-point peace policy He claimed no originality for his program, but he strongly urged its support to "keep us out of war " His plan was

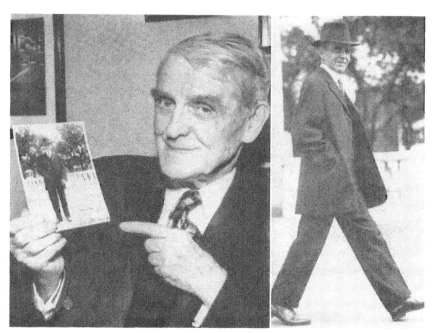

Capper in 1948 holding a photograph of himself similar to the one on the right, taken as he was entering the Capitol in 1919.

Courtesy of the Kansas State Historical Society

The Capper Foundation for Crippled Children, 3500 West Tenth Street, Topeka; the Foster Home on the left and the teaching, therapy, and administrative unit on the right.

Courtesy of the Capper Foundation

1 Keep out of the League of Nations and all alliances or understandings with other nations that would mean policing the world

2 Keep our ships at home, after giving our own people time to leave war zones

3 Keep our soldiers at home

4 Keep our dollars at home when invited to finance other nation's wars

5 Carry out the Neutrality Act

6 Pass a constitutional amendment giving the people the right to vote on participation in foreign wars [72]

Capper maintained that the wars in Spain and in the Orient were not "our affair" and that his peace views were held by many Americans and such organizations as the Veterans of Foreign Wars, not merely by those of "Quaker ancestry "[73] Foreign affairs, even Senator Capper observed, had become the most important problem before Congress in early 1938 Other issues important to him dealt with centralization of government administration and with legislation affecting the economy [74] Although he favored a navy so strong that it would be "positively unsafe" for any attack to be launched against the United States, he wanted it to be purely defensive [75] Proposals for naval expansion caused him to predict another armament race. He favored "trying to promote peace by peaceful means than by displaying force,   [rather than] bluffing the rest of the world with big navy threats, or by resorting to what might be termed power diplomacy "[76] Even after war broke out in Europe, with the invasion of Poland in 1939, Capper continued "emphatically against any change in the Neutrality Law," because he feared that "any relaxation of the stand embodied in that law will be a step toward war "[77] He defended the "arms ban," maintaining that when "we lift the arms embargo and start selling war supplies, it is almost equivalent to a declaration of war "[78] In fact, Capper asserted that we "can defend ourselves against imperialistic designs of any Old World nation with sufficient army, navy and air force " But, to him, the greatest danger was an inability to "solve some domestic problems, and get on the road to their solution right soon "[79]

In departing from his former approval of much of the New Deal Capper became disenchanted with the Reciprocal Trading agreements Persistently he brought up the issue of agricultural products which were imported and in competition with those produced in

Kansas and elsewhere He was critical of the most-favored-nation status arranged in most of these treaties, regarding it as giving "other nations something for nothing" Acting Secretary of State Sumner Welles accused the Kansas Senator of "discrepancies and false conclusions" because of such statements, some of which appeared in print In later years Capper opposed the various reciprocity treaties with Latin America and urged their repeal [80]

Senator Capper was disappointed when the first Agricultural Adjustment Act was invalidated by the Supreme Court, since he looked upon it as the "farmer's tariff," and a means of balancing economic inequalities between agriculture and other segments of the economy [81] He believed that "farmers wanted a permanent agricultural program which will be largely under their control," as a replacement for A A A He applauded the work of the soil conservation program, but he saw difficulty in the proposed "ever normal" granary plan for supporting farm prices [82] Initially Capper was in favor of the second A A A , but shortly before the 1938 elections he began to attack various "farm aid schemes," and the "centralization of authority in Washington," because he believed that farmers were "worse off now than five years ago " Some political observers viewed the changing Capper position as "a hint that he believes his State is going Republican this Fall, partly as a result of dissatisfaction "[83]

Capper's pronounced views on agriculture caused him again to state that agriculture was "fundamental to business as well as to all civilization Any disturbance of its function," he held, was "reflected adversely in the business world, even as any disruption in business depresses agriculture Neither can be deflected from its course without damage to the other "[84] Thus, when the listening posts in the Kansas "grass roots" detected general farm dissatisfaction during the recession of 1938, Senator Capper began to "back away" from the A A A program which he had formerly supported and defended He interpreted the general election of 1938 as a mandate "to revise radically the present National Farm Program "[85] Impelled by his desire to represent his constituency well Capper called on "Kansas farmers and farm organization representatives" to come to Topeka just before Christmas to engage in a "free-for-all conference" about replacements for "the weak points of the present program "[86] Although some farmers wrote that they could not afford to come and that those who would appear were the ones who already had their "snout in the trough," the turnout was far greater than was expected The meeting had to adjourn to a larger hall because of the overflow crowd of 700 persons, and the diversity of opinion among Kansas farmers quickly became apparent Virtually all of them "opposed production control from Washington," while wheat farmers often favored certain provisions of the current A A A program Others wanted no agricultural legislation, while some demand existed for restoration of the processing tax [87] Stenographic notes were taken of all prepared and impromptu speeches at the conference and Capper listened closely to the plea of the Kansas farmer A year later Capper held another farm forum in Topeka, and again he listened to "farm oratory" which lasted six hours From renewed nourishment at the "grass roots" he believed proposed farm legislation did not provide for "parity payments" and that farmers still believed in the idea of "tariff equality "[88] Government help for the farmer was still necessary, and Capper hoped that the solution for agricultural ills would "be not too long postponed "[89]

As the presidential year, 1940, approached, a seasoned campaigner in political battles such as Capper could expect many tugs and pulls from the political arena In October, 1939, Kansas Republican leaders asked him to be their "favorite son" at the 1940 national convention [90] A short time later he heard "from over the state . . that a solid Capper Delegation in 1940 Convention is very popular and will be of great value in doing this for the Republican party next year "[91] When the Republican National Convention convened at Philadelphia shortly after the fall of France, the eighteen votes of the Kansas delegates were cast for "favorite son" Capper on the first two ballots Thereafter, the Kansas delegates divided their vote among other candidates, only to consolidate their efforts again on the fifth ballot in casting their vote for Wendell L Willkie, who was officially nominated on the sixth ballot.

As usual, Capper supported the presidential candidate of his party Although he was sure that President Roosevelt would be the Democratic candidate again, he proclaimed his desire to do everything possible "to insure the election of Wendell Willkie "[92] On the eve of the election Capper wrote that "a vote for Willkie is a vote for peace unless war is unavoidable, a vote for Roosevelt is a vote for war at the earliest possible moment" According to Capper, similar alternatives were presented to the voter [93] After the third-term election of Franklin D Roosevelt, Capper saw "in the Willkie vote a twofold mandate—to keep the United States out of foreign wars, also a mandate to the President to work out an economic solution of our domestic problems that depends on something more than drafts upon the public treasury" [94]

For the next year each change in America's neutrality laws was viewed by Senator Capper as another step "down the Road to War" In using arguments to retain both the Johnson Act and the Neutrality Act without amendment, Capper cited as one example a letter written by the former Ambassador to Great Britain, Joseph P Kennedy, who wrote, in part, "our first obligation is to speed up defense with all our might" [95] Other national leaders whose statements were used to build up the Capper position were persons such as Dr Charles A Beard and Senators La Follette and Vandenberg, and Capper was liberal in praise of them [96] By March, 1941, he recognized that as "government policies, isolation and nonintervention are dead issues Today the foreign policies of the United States, the very life of the United States and the lives and fortune of the people of the United States are tied into the programs and policies of the British Empire in its fight against the Axis Powers" [97] Still he continued to oppose United States intervention and military participation, although he was aware of developments producing the "final steps toward a declaration of war" [98] Capper justified his opposition to repeal of neutrality legislation as prevention of an imperialistic, not a defensive war [99] Shortly before Pearl Harbor he prophetically wrote that he was "greatly alarmed over the situation with respect to Japan Japan's military machine seems to be spoiling for war They are making unreasonable demands which the United States cannot possibly grant—ought not to grant" [100]

Although he had expected an "all-out-war" for some time, Capper was not prepared for it when it came Few were He was in Topeka when Pearl Harbor was bombed His regular radio address that evening made no allusions to his previous isolationist position His support was then with "our President," and he believed "Kansas will support the President and the Government" [101] Immediately he left by rail for Washington, but he arrived too late to vote on the war declaration, for which he announced his approval Just as in the case of World War I, Capper opposed anything which he interpreted as pushing the United States into war, but when the issue was no longer in doubt, he wholeheartedly supported the national effort

Through his many years in Washington Arthur Capper, Senator from Kansas, had a large following, which did not seem strange to those who knew him One Kansas newspaperman who was a partisan backer of Capper's senatorial colleague from Kansas in the late 1930's found that the latter was "crude, cross and at times downright discourteous " On the other hand, while he had been prejudiced against Capper, he later wrote, "It was astounding to me to find anyone in Washington so kindly of disposition and one who would go to any length" to help someone who meant nothing to him [102]

Capper gained a reputation of always having time to show Kansas visitors around the Capitol He entertained many of them with luncheons in the Senate restaurant, and he willingly intervened when they were in trouble with District of Columbia traffic officials His human side was further shown when he was stopped one evening by a traffic officer for speeding between the Senate Office Building and his hotel His explanation to the officer, who recognized him as a member of the Senate because of his license number, was that he was in a hurry to get home to hear "Amos and Andy "

Washingtonians knew Capper as a party-goer par excellence. Evelyn Walsh McLean, Mrs Eleanor (Cissie) Patterson, and Perle Mesta frequently invited him to their famous parties Capper was noted for dropping "in at half a dozen teas, receptions, cocktail parties and dinners between the time the senate recesses in the late afternoon and bedtime "[103] At the time of their annual state party in 1939, Kansans in the national capital danced the "Capper Canter" to honor the state's "genial senior Senator "[104] Capper was also asked to crown "Miss Secretary, 1939" in proper ceremonies in Washington, and he frequently was named as a member of a senatorial committee to greet officially important guests of the nation

Early in 1939 a serious controversy broke out in Washington, D C , because Marian Anderson, noted Negro singer, was denied permission by the Daughters of the American Revolution to use their Constitution Hall Mrs Eleanor Roosevelt and a group of people, including Senator Arthur Capper, sponsored the Easter Concert of

185

Miss Anderson from the steps of the Lincoln Memorial Later Capper proudly showed the "Marian Anderson" autograph on his program [105]

In looking back over the decade before United States entrance into World War II, Arthur Capper saw many changes During the closing years of Hoover's administration he supported the President but he was constantly rebuffed in his desires for remedial agricultural legislation During the days of the early New Deal his voting record was closely identified with many important New Deal laws Later he issued his own "declaration of independence" from Roosevelt-backed legislation, he voted to override the veto of the Soldier Bonus bill, he supported the Soil Conservation Act, and thereafter on most major bills before World War II, he was anti-administration Only on the National Housing Act and the wheat crop insurance bill did he satisfy backers of the New Deal Capper's vote was cast in opposition to the administration viewpoint on the amendment to give control of relief to the states, the proposal to enlarge the Supreme Court, the bill to authorize the President to reorganize the executive department, the naval expansion bill of 1938, the Fair Labor Standards Act, the bill to extend the service term of drafted men, and the first Lend-Lease Bill.[106]

At the same time significant changes were occurring in the United States and in the world Private enterprises were responding in various ways to new pressures of the time Capper's own business organization was adjusting to the demands for economy of operation and to the more competitive position of the 1930's Although most of the decisions for his business were made by others, Arthur Capper, the owner and publisher, was still consulted on all major policy changes for Capper Publications

Chapter XVI
Capper Publications, Incorporated

The stock market crash in 1929 and the depression of the early thirties, following as they did a decade of serious economic dislocation in agriculture, enlarged economic disaster for Capper Publications Before 1930 the development of the Capper enterprises was accompanied by a large number of changes in the publications After 1930 the days of innovation with new publications were over for Capper, although he did engage in new activity in the field of radio Formerly his business had been one of relative prosperity, but the hard times of the thirties forced the Capper business to "tighten its belt" and to adopt extreme economizing measures in order to survive

The most profitable farm publication in the Capper syndicate was *Capper's Farmer*, and except for one or two years it earned excellent profits However, *Household* was generally a loser, and its retention was assured for a while only because of the prestige value of its large circulation *Capper's Weekly* was not much better The state farm papers contributed either small profits or small losses during the thirties, while large profits, as well as sizable expenses, were the general rule for radio station WIBW The daily papers in Topeka and Kansas City closely reflected economic conditions, and sometimes supplied a respectable return on the investment [1]

General poor business conditions led to numerous blanket salary cuts for the staffs of Capper-Harman-Slocum and of Capper Publications between October, 1930, and March, 1933 [2] Even during the early years of World War II, revenue dropped so low that 10 per cent wage cuts were necessary for all employees receiving more than fifty dollars a week [3] Capper removed himself from the payroll during the depths of the depression to enable his business to meet its load of debt, he took no dividends from his stock ownership, and for many years his income was primarily his senatorial salary [4]

A variety of choices faced the executives of Capper Publications in their effort to improve the position of the Capper journals A strong new editorial program might be developed to attract greater reader response and new circulation From such a development

187

might come increased advertising revenues Circulation, if considered too expensive, might be intentionally reduced Economies might be exploited in the various business and printing operations Or combinations might be developed between various Capper publications and their competitors in order to eliminate costly duplication As a matter of fact, all of the foregoing expedients were considered, and most of them were used in varying degrees in helping Capper Publications to adjust to a more rigorous economic climate

The first of these developments occurred in the evolution of a new editorial program for *Capper's Farmer* After 1923, editor Ray Yarnell sought to present agricultural prospects optimistically, and he showed in his *Capper's Farmer* editorials his fundamental belief in the dignity and worth of agriculture Reader response was considered creditable, but the staff of the monthly farm paper were searching for a way more completely to serve their readers They pioneered in developing terse, pointed reporting in the agricultural press, and they told *what*, with less interpretation, letting the farmer draw his own conclusions [5]

This drift toward shorter articles written in journalistic style began after World War I Growing competition among radio stations, daily newspapers, and extension divisions for the farmer's attention caused editors to emphasize short articles, attractive presentation, and "catchy phrases "

In the late 1920's *Capper's Farmer* began a series, almost by accident, which laid a heavy emphasis on "methodizing agriculture," and the reader response which it created belatedly led the journal's editors to realize the importance of this type of presentation This series began with the publication of an article on a new method of raising chicks, in the October 24, 1925, issue of *Kansas Farmer* The commercial hatchery business was undeveloped at the time, and only about 55 per cent of baby chicks survived in farm brooder houses County Agent J A Hendriks sought to reduce such losses by finding out how chicks could be raised as if they were with their natural mothers A basic procedure was worked out, and after three years of testing in Chase and Anderson counties in Kansas, an account of the method was printed and distributed free to some 3,000 poultry-keepers who promised that they would not reveal the method to their neighbors Hendriks was primarily interested in recognition, and he insisted on promises of secrecy as the best means of arousing interest in his method, in reality not original with him

Further articles about the Hendriks method of raising baby chicks were published in *Kansas Farmer* before the story was first published in *Capper's Farmer* in January, 1927 Case histories and pictures illustrating the method were included, and readers were told to write directly to the county agent for free information Within a short time subscribers from all over the Middle West sent in 20,000 requests for copies of his booklet on chick-raising, necessitating the employment of several girls to mail out the booklets [6] The big demand caused further copies to be made available through the Poultry Editor of *Capper's Farmer* During the course of the next fifteen years this offer was kept alive, and approximately 300,000 booklets were distributed through *Capper's Farmer* [7]

Although the response was encouraging, the meaning of "methodizing agriculture" was not yet fully understood by the editors of *Capper's Farmer* They were confronted with a problem of finding other farming techniques to publicize, a search in which competing journals were also engaged As the impact of the Hendriks method was making itself felt, *Successful Farming*, the principal competitor of *Capper's Farmer,* published an article on raising turkeys, using a step-by-step procedure for better description [8] *Capper's Farmer* found it advisable to obtain the story, and in January, 1928, the article, "Why Hatch 4 Turkeys to Raise 1?" was published, with the claim that it would "do for turkey raisers what the Hendriks method did for chicken growers " A booklet describing the new method was made available at a cost of two two-cent stamps to cover postage and mailing charges [9] Within a month after the first turkey story some 26,000 copies of the booklet had been mailed, and in all *Capper's Farmer* distributed almost 200,000 booklets describing the turkey-production method [10]

"Methodizing agriculture," through the use of simple, step-by-step methods, prompted reader response far greater than anything formerly used, and editors of *Capper's Farmer* consciously began a search for such procedures During the next fifteen years some twenty different techniques of "methodizing agriculture" appeared on the pages of *Capper's Farmer* In one twelve-month period the editorial department reported receiving more than 450,000 letters from subscribers, a total more than half of the circulation figure of the time.[11]

The enthusiasm for "methodizing agriculture" which Editor Yarnell created in his magazine sometimes led to exaggerated claims or to the adoption of unwise methods Yarnell suggested that the Agricultural Adjustment Administration support a method of testing cows by mail as a means of culling dairy herds, but he failed to get its co-operation [12] At times the publicizing of "methodizing agriculture" emphasized trivial details and diverted attention from the person or agency which had originated the practice being discussed Such was probably the case for the Hendriks method and for other techniques described by *Capper's Farmer* [13] Nevertheless, the vigorous campaign for "methodizing agriculture" was beneficial to many farmer readers, and one of the competitive farm magazines was apparently altering its "editorial policy to conform more closely to that of *Capper's Farmer* "[14]

Campaigns of a similar nature were carried on in the various Capper state farm papers "Power farming" promotion began even before 1920, with the presentation of publicity favoring tractor power on the farm Closely related to this compaign was the encouragement of "power homemaking," especially during the period when rural electrical lines come into extensive use In time the major criteria determining whether an article should appear in a Capper farm paper were its value in showing how to accomplish some particular agricultural goal If it showed how to reduce labor, costs, or time, how to increase yields, or how to translate savings and earnings into a more satisfactory farm life there was a place for it [15]

With the growth of the Capper Farm Press and of its influence there was a related disappearance of the early fear which farmers had of the "book-farmer" representatives from agricultural extension agencies Farm papers more and more came to respect the capabilities of agricultural specialists and the results that could be obtained by following their suggestions [16] Generally the editors of farm papers were followers rather than leaders, but they were proud of occasional instances in which they endorsed new practices ahead of confirmation from experiment stations For instance, Capper Publications advocated the use of hybrid corn before the agricultural experiment station in Kansas had given its approval [17] This one example is frequently cited to contrast the difference between bulletins put out by experiment stations and the work of agricultural journals, or, more specifically, to contrast developments in "pure science" and in "practical science." Dr George H Shull first proposed a method of producing hybrid corn in 1909, but it took men like Henry A Wallace, of Iowa, and Dr D F Jones of the Connecticut Experiment Station to popularize Shull's experiments [18]

The various means of providing reader interest in the journals and farm papers of Capper Publications helped to ease the task of the circulation department Between 1930 and 1948 the combined circulation figures of the various Capper publications increased from approximately 3,800,000 to almost 4,500,000 Attractive editorial format should bring larger rewards in circulation, and an enlarged circulation should justify greater advertising revenues But such was not always the case Advertisers could resist increased advertising rates, and sometimes they did This happened in 1938 during the midst of a short, sharp recession Cost of production was increasing for paper and labor, and because of social security, unemployment insurance, and other taxes [19] Advertising rates could not be increased to make up the difference, since revenues from that source were already declining [20] Strict economies were imposed, some wages were cut, and as a way out of the impasse subscription rates were increased on some of the publications Capper had considered the possibility of actually reducing circulation as a means of reducing expense, but his executives advised strongly against this in view of the prestige of a large circulation [21]

Another means of providing initial economies in the business was to have several of the papers published by a commercial printer rather than obtaining newer printing equipment During the late thirties business conditions did not justify the purchase of newer presses, and after World War II such equipment, much more expensive than formerly, was delivered to purchasers some two years to forty months after orders were placed Even if new presses had been available there was no space within the Capper Building for them [22] Moreover, large advertisers were demanding color illustrations, and Capper Publications lacked equipment to handle such orders [23] Before 1947 Capper always resisted suggestions that printing of any of his publications be moved away from Topeka, on the grounds that this would reduce mail leaving through the Topeka Post Office and that it would reduce local job opportunities But the alternative was to build a new plant outside the congested area of downtown Topeka to house new equipment, and such a program was considered too costly So additional demands for office space were met with the purchase of the Redden Building at 912 Kansas Avenue on September 3, 1946, for $80,000 It was soon occupied by the Capper Printing Company and some of the editorial and advertising offices [24] A solution to the printing problem was made in 1947 through a contract with the Dearing Company of Louisville, Kentucky, to print and mail *Household* [25] A few years later *Capper's Farmer* was also printed and mailed by the Louisville establishment [26]

While all of the Capper state farm papers had a position of virtual state monopoly by 1928, most of the other Capper publications had vigorous competitors An easing of the expense budget for the Topeka *Daily Capital* came with the creation of the Topeka Newspaper Printing Company in 1941 Contrary to a nation-wide tendency which favored evening newspapers, the *Capital*, as a morning paper, had consistently held first place in circulation and advertising linage in Topeka Almost always competitive in their dealings, the *Capital* and the Topeka *State Journal*, published by Frank P Mac-Lennan, had maintained fairly peaceful relations With the depression, the disappearance of newspaper profits, and the death of MacLennan in 1933, the nature of this rivalry began to change. In 1935 the *Journal* was purchased by Henry J Allen and his associates, who set out to capture a larger share of a shrinking income from Topeka newspaper advertising Capper soon received reports that Allen was price-cutting and that he violated time-honored custom in acquiring exclusive contracts for advertising from some of the department stores [27] Suggestions were even made to buy out Allen's partners so that Capper could take over the *Journal* [28] Allen appealed to Capper in an endeavor to acquaint him with discriminatory practices which *Capital* salesmen were using [29] Capper wanted to avoid "a program of cut-throat competition similar to that which has prevailed in Wichita," and he soon discovered that the situation was not all that he expected Consequently, he offered to meet Allen "half way, or more than half way, in discussion or adjusting misunderstandings which may arise as to matters of policy"[30] Capper asked

Allen to let the newspapers live together "side by side," and relations between the *Capital* and the *Journal* finally improved But prospects for profitable handling of more than one daily newspaper in Topeka appeared dim, although both newspapers were able to raise their profits from circulation Fear of recession seemed ever on the minds of the executives and editors of Capper Publications [31]

When Oscar S Stauffer acquired the Topeka *State Journal* early in 1939, an opportunity to make changes in the city's newspaper field seemed to present itself Negotiations were soon begun about the advisability of some sort of consolidation It was soon recognized that Topeka did not have sufficient business to maintain two vigorous daily newspapers except in above-average times Capper had initial doubts about the advisability of combination, on the grounds that "eliminating competition usually reduced the volume of business "[32] Much study was made of possible means of consolidating the two daily newspapers, an important question being the political consequences of such a move Capper was advised that the two papers should be autonomous and that they should be as independent of each other editorially as possible, without having the public say, "Capper is straddling the fence He blows hot and he blows cold "[33]

Finally, on July 31, 1941, the business, advertising, circulation and mechanical departments of the *Capital* and the *Journal* were combined to form the Topeka Newspaper Printing Company, Incorporated [34] Editorially the newspapers continued their competition, but in other ways they were consolidated with a considerable saving [35] Capper held two-thirds of the stock in the new company and was responsible for two-thirds of the directors of the new board Profits or losses were to be shared in the same proportion

In the meantime, the parent company for all of the Capper newspapers and journals, Capper Publications, was long overdue for a change Capper was always proud of the personal direction of the company, delighted with his "Capper family," and reluctant to change his relationship with them In order to expand his business after 1920 he sold promissory notes which he identified as Capper Certificates When the Securities and Exchange Commission was created, however, Capper's methods of financing became of interest to this federal agency [36] The S E C claimed jurisdiction over Capper Certificates because Capper Publications was doing an interstate business The federal agency had no legal complaint about Capper's method of financing, but it ruled that the Capper Certificates would have to be issued under the same regulations applied to all securities subject to federal regulation Therefore, Capper found that it would be necessary to incorporate his business [37]

After almost two years of planning and preparation the Capper business received its charter as a Kansas corporation on October 29, 1937 [38] The business was given an estimated value of $8,500,000, and one hundred thousand shares of common stock of a par value of ten dollars each were issued Capper retained all but 114 shares, which were distributed to 114 individuals, most of them his employees [39]

The Capper Printing Company was chartered at the same time Equal ownership in this corporation was shared by Arthur Capper, his sister Mary, and his sister-in-law, Mrs. George M Crawford [40]

A related activity was the radio station of Capper Publications, WIBW, operated as a farm station for a farming state On February 4, 1934, studios and business offices of the station were moved to the Capper residence at 1035 Topeka Avenue, and in December, 1934, daytime power of the station was increased to 5,000 watts [41] In its new location WIBW grew and prospered, and after World War II a sister station, WIBW-FM, was operated for a short time [42] The small number of FM radios in Topeka and the lack of opportunity to gain increased advertising caused the station to close Previous efforts to induce Capper to buy a local Topeka station to handle local advertising had failed because of the attitude of the Federal Communications Commission toward "duopoly," or having one owner for two radio stations in a community [43]

However, the Federal Communications Commission did not so strongly oppose single ownership of two radio stations in different communities On November 12, 1935, Capper Publications purchased radio station WLBF of Kansas City The following year it was assigned call letters KCKN, and it was organized as the KCKN Broadcasting Company, closely affiliated with the Kansas City *Kansan* [44]

Other developments, in the interest of economy of operation, resulted in the transfer of the mechanical work of the *Missouri Ruralist* to the Topeka plant on January 1, 1933, and the consolidation of the mechanical operations of Capper-Harman-Slocum at Cleveland in 1941 The business of the *Missouri Ruralist* was operated under the ownership of the Missouri Agricultural Publishing Company after Capper had purchased the *Journal of Agriculture* in 1921 [45] The move to print the *Missouri Ruralist* in Topeka left Capper with the building and equipment of the St Louis plant, which continued in use until it was sold on October 5, 1944, for $40,000 [46] The move taken by Capper-Harman-Slocum in 1941 brought into one location the press rooms, composing rooms, mailing rooms, accounting departments, and other mechanical operations for *Ohio Farmer, Pennsylvania Farmer,* and *Michigan Farmer* Skeleton forces were able to carry on the editorial responsibilities of the Pennsylvania and Michigan papers, and their editorial offices were moved outside the large cities, either to the state capital or to the location of the state agricultural college [47]

Many of the laws passed by Congress in the 1930's and supported by Senator Capper resulted in complications for his business enterprises The long arm of the federal government was reaching out to touch many businesses in the land through such laws as the Social Security Act, the National Labor Relations Act, and of course, the Securities and Exchange Commission Act Social Security legislation caused Capper Publications to hire additional clerical help to handle records required by the federal government The influence of the Securities and Exchange Commission has been discussed The National Labor Relations Act gave additional powers to labor groups, which made them harder to deal with, according to management

Labor relations for Capper Publications became increasingly complex after 1935 [48] Printers employed by Capper enterprises were unionized almost from the time Capper became a publisher After World War II almost all of the other workers in the mechanical operations of the business belonged to labor unions Through it all there was never a strike at Capper Publications [49] But at times, management granted what seemed exorbitant demands of union labor Some of the unions with few workers in the publishing plant gave the most trouble One such difficulty was settled only after Capper Publications "laid off" four non-union Negro sack handlers in the mailing room when a labor union claimed jurisdiction over their jobs [50] Such disputes never went beyond the discussion stage Compromises were made by both sides, and the most serious troubles were settled by arbitration [51] During Capper's senatorial years his labor record was generally approved until the mid-1940's, when he supported Taft-Hartley legislation On sixteen test votes the C I O found him right on only five, and this affected the labor relations of his business [52]

The freedom which Capper had given his editors continued in the period after 1930 The operation and content of the *Missouri Ruralist* and the *Kansas Farmer* were similar in many ways, although each was designed especially for the area it served John F Case and Tom McNeal, long-time editors of these publicatitons, had special talents, and so their work was traded back and forth, with some of McNeal's articles appearing in the Missouri paper and some of Case's in the *Kansas Farmer* The *Ohio Farmer, Michigan Farmer,* and *Pennsylvania Farmer* operated as distinctly different papers There, as elsewhere in the Capper chain, editors were scarcely conscious of anyone above them administratively [53] On many occasions one of the eastern trio of editors was reported to be taking great delight in opposing political measures supported by Capper Capper's main goal with these papers was to keep each in "tune with the state" where it was circulated, and the editors of the "Eastern trio," like other Capper editors, had virtual independence in their editorial program [54]

By the time Capper's business was incorporated in 1937, some of the editors and executives who had been with him for many years were beginning to pass off the scene The associates of an earlier day were being replaced by younger, more vigorous men who helped make the fundamental decisions of the first fifteen years of Capper Publications, Incorporated Two of these younger executives were Henry S Blake and Philip Zach Both had entered the business in the years immediately following World War I Blake had come to Capper Publications in 1920 as director of circulation, a position which had been occupied by at least five different men in the previous dozen years [55] In 1928 Blake became business manager, and in 1937 he advanced to general manager, besides being a member of the board of directors Blake was becoming exceedingly valuable to his employer through his lengthy informative letters to Senator Capper while Capper was in Washington His intensive activity on behalf of the business erupted into bitter feeling with Marco Morrow, wit-

196

nessed in many encounters by men in leading positions in Capper Publications Tom McNeal wrote Capper that something had to be done, "either get rid of both or get rid of one," since the "quarrel between the two can not be reconciled "[56] As a result of friction among important leaders in his business, Capper got Morrow to retire in 1941 at the age of seventy-two, and Blake took over as vice president of the corporation

Philip Zach's long service for Capper Publications, which began in 1919, was primarily in the advertising end of the business outside of the main offices in Topeka For many years he was the eastern manager for Capper Publications, with headquarters in New York City His abilities were recognized in 1937 when he was named as one of the first directors of the Capper corporation, the only one with an address outside Topeka With Morrow's retirement in 1941 he became Director of Advertising, but he continued personally to handle the advertising accounts of the New York office [57] Other editors, secretaries, executives, and foremen in the mechanical departments were important to the Capper business in the period after 1930, but to name one would require naming all

Advertising for Capper Publications, as was true of almost all publishers of periodicals, was an immensely important part of the business Expectations that circulation charges would pay a considerable share of the costs of the business were often realized, but advertising revenues enabled the business to function and to grow As a publisher, Capper was frequently asked to speak before advertising and business groups His theme often dealt with the value of advertising to business and the consumer alike He believed that "no phase of business is more greatly misunderstood than is advertising," and he sought to enlighten his hearers [58] To those who maintained that advertising was costly Capper would answer that "a dollar spent in one department of business which saves a dollar and one cent in another department is not an expense but an economy "[59]

Advertising standards in most publications had greatly improved by 1930 Capper felt that advertising men had acquired a finer appreciation of their responsibilities He reported that the spirit of service was stronger, that standards were higher, and that periodicals were printing cleaner columns, and he favored government support for such developments through a truth-in-advertising bill [60]

197

Capper's early goal of obtaining enough advertising to fill half the space of every issue of his periodicals was not fully realized for most of them during the poor business years of the 1920's and 1930's During World War II the necessity of producing a tighter paper resulted in considerable improvement in business conditions and in enlargement of the proportion of each publication devoted to advertising The farm publications, by that time, were using 60 per cent of their pages for advertising and 40 per cent for editorial matter An even greater proportion of the daily newspapers was devoted to advertising

Because Capper Publications was located near the geographical center of the nation, the business maintained advertising offices in New York, Detroit, Cleveland, Chicago, and eventually San Francisco Although Capper did not originate this approach to big advertising contracts, he frequently maintained an advertising staff that was much larger than those of his major competitors To acquaint city-bred advertisers with the Middle West the Capper Publications sponsored train-and-automobile tours for advertisers to the farms and small-town homes for direct contact with the people who read Capper periodicals Guided tours by railroad companies and American real estate companies were commonplace in earlier days, but Capper felt that he was pioneering in using the idea in the advertising field [61]

Advertising standards for all the Capper publications were virtually identical after 1920 Advertisements of cancer cures had been taboo for many years, and patent-medicine advertisements became less popular as medical standards increased [62] All liquor and beer advertising was refused after 1905, and Capper saw "no good reason for departing from that policy" after the Eighteenth Amendment was repealed or after the Topeka *Daily Capital* became a part of the Topeka Newspaper Printing Company [63] Although oleomargarine advertisements were acceptable in *Household* and in some of the other non-farm periodicals, they did not appear in the Capper farm journals Such material was recognized as antagonistic to "nearly every farmer who milks cows "[64]

Capper's operation of many publications both helped and hindered him in obtaining advertising The very size and number of periodicals made the maintenance of national advertising branches somewhat more economical Nonetheless, Capper soon learned that it was unwise to concentrate and formalize operations rigidly Since few publishers were spread over such a wide field, there was little to guide Capper Publications in obtaining national advertising Through experience Capper learned that less advertising was sold if his agents solicited accounts for all papers in his chain instead of concentrating on a smaller number Consequently Capper advertising men were divided into four groups to sell advertising space in the Capper media Constantly Capper advertising men had to assure advertisers that there was no duplication among Capper Publications and that the area of claimed circulation was not overconcentrated.[65]

Assurance for such claims was provided for Capper advertising men by intensive research carried on by Capper's advertising department in Topeka In 1919 a separate research department was established for Capper Publications, but it was soon integrated with the advertising department because Capper doubted the value of the independent organization [66] Factual data, gained from analysis of Census records, the Audit Bureau of Circulation reports, and the circulation coverage of various Capper publications, were presented to prospective advertisers, to show them the advantage in using Capper's periodicals

For advertising purposes there were various publications such as the *Capper Bulletin,* operating before World War I, *Rural Trade,* published in the mid-twenties, and the *Better-Times Chronicle,* published irregularly in the early thirties by six Capper farm papers and four other farm journals None of these specialized publications had a general circulation All of them were mailed primarily to advertisers at no subscription cost

As a result of a growing need for additional information on the effectiveness of Capper Publications in reaching the consumer a new central Research Department was organized in 1946 The personnel assigned to this department increased rapidly in numbers and were ever on the alert to justify the existence of their role by directing all of their research to the sale of advertising in Capper periodicals Because of the nature of the Capper journals, this department stressed the importance of the small-town and rural market National advertising agencies operated in an urban industrial environment, and they were frequently unaware of the changes taking place in rural America Capper's Research Department saw their duty as fighting inertia in national advertising which "wrongly" pictured the farmer as largely self-sufficient or at least responsive to appeals directed to mass markets [67] Instead Capper and his staff described the readers of Capper publications as a quality market

Because of membership in the Agricultural Publishers Association, the individual members of the Capper Farm Press also cooperated in the Continuing Study of Farm Publications, carried on by the Advertising Research Foundation [68] Between 1946 and the end of 1950, fourteen farm publications, including *Ohio Farmer*, *Kansas Farmer*, and *Capper's Farmer*, were surveyed to provide data on who read farm publications and what they read [69] The study was designed to help advertisers and advertising agencies make more effective use of the farm publications Such data supplied highly useful information to advertisers, but the cost was high The two years of experimental research for perfecting the sampling techniques had cost more than $40,000 [70] Some farm publications resigned from the association rather than pay the increased assessment for the continuing study, so that the project was abandoned after four years of operation [71]

Capper consistently maintained that the most important part of his business was the "Capper family " Most of the senior members of the staff by 1930 had worked for Capper for many years and had gained a position as a Capper "Old Timer" because of twenty-five or more years of work for the business Following World War II these veterans in the business numbered several hundred, with many others on "retired" status Capper took "greater pride .   that so many   choose to stay with us than   the mere size of the publications " He expressed his gratitude to this group for their "loyalty to the interests of the business" and again and again he told them "how rich I am in your friendship "[72]

Capper's business enterprise was exceedingly important to him, but so was his position in the United States Senate By 1941, when Capper was seventy-six years of age, he was no longer able to handle his own affairs so efficiently as he had in the past At the same time the cares and worries and time-consuming tasks associated with the role of a United States Senator were increasing with the entrance of the country into World War II In the face of these new responsibilities, the senior United States Senator from Kansas quickly made the statement "As for myself, I am dedicated to the cause of my country in war—now that war has come—just as completely, and wholeheartedly and patriotically as I held myself dedicated to the cause of peace as long as there was the slightest hope that we might remain at peace "[73]

Chapter XVII

Senator Capper and the Forties

The year before the Japanese attack on Pearl Harbor was a trying year for Senator Arthur Capper He had a premonition that war would soon come, but he continually wrote, spoke, and acted on behalf of groups whose purpose was to keep the United States out of war [1] His consistent opposition to military preparedness or to anything he considered a jeopardy to American neutrality earned for him the title of "a leading isolationist" and the "most effective isolationist," because of his gentle manner Capper had voted against the Lend-Lease bill, then when it passed he supported the multi-billion dollar appropriation to implement it because it was law, "by a Congressional majority "[2] Capper's support for isolationist groups, always freely given, was unpopular to those who opposed any pacifist scheme, and it was criticized by his good friend William Allen White, who was formerly the chairman of the Committee to Defend America by Aiding the Allies White told Capper that "there has been a turn in the tide in the last two or three months and I am afraid it is running away from your theory "[3] A short time later contemporary observers noticed a "quiet shift" in Capper's position toward support of President Roosevelt's policy concerning the war in Europe, which to some was an indication that the "general opinion" or the "American consensus" was also changing [4]

The impact of war was soon felt in Washington and on the Congress Before the end of 1941, Capper could write that the "past week or two has meant a lot of hard work for out [our] office Washington is now a booming war town and it seems to make more work for the Senators "[5] In a nation-wide network broadcast Capper acknowledged that he had been one "who opposed with every legitimate means United States intervention in this war " But a "new-found unity of purpose," fortified by the Christmas week strategy meetings in Washington, attended by representatives of thirty-three nations, would assure "all-out defeat of the Axis powers ."[6]

The year 1942 was another election year for Capper Correspondence picked up between Capper and William Allen White and other Kansans who might offer advice about the approaching election

White wrote Capper that he did not believe "that your isolationist record would seriously hurt you . I think they agreed with you until the fall before Pearl Harbor, then there was a fairly swift shift Of course, Pearl Harbor did the business But I think that you are not seriously in danger for anything that happened before December 7 "[7] Capper became aware through his "more than 500 letters daily from Kansans" that the folks at home were in an "ugly state of mind" about the low pay for servicemen while labor was striking for higher pay and stopping production of war supplies [8]

As a direct result of this correspondence and their long-time friendship, William Allen White wrote a laudatory article which was widely reprinted in the press serving Kansas and was placed in the *Congressional Record* [9] White rated Capper as one of Kansas' five great senators, along with Jim Lane, Preston Plumb, John J. Ingalls, and Edmund Ross But he also said he was "more than a Senator He is an influence He is a sort of incarnate institutionalized voice of the farm and the small town, a quiet, gentle voice, arising from a Quaker's kindly heart, but a brave voice that has never been hushed by fear nor raised by ambition " White added that Capper "has represented Kansas well and has stood always for the farmer and the small businessman, the union man free from his racketeering labor leaders He fights the Quaker fight with dogged pertinacity and unflagging zeal As a Quaker he made an isolationist record It was his religion But of his 24 years in the Senate that record covered less than two years The day Pearl Harbor fell, Capper forgot the past "[10]

Most Republican leaders in Kansas also were aware of latent Capper strength in spite of his seventy-seven years and pre-Pearl Harbor record Governor Payne Ratner considered entering the race for the Senate, but his sampling of sentiment throughout the state caused him to "look for something else "[11] In the primary Capper did have an opponent, who entered the race even though aware that Kansas' senior Senator had "built up personal friendships in various groups which are an asset but few Kansas statesmen have ever possessed "[12]

On the whole, winning in the primary election was easy But Capper was disturbed when the first news of the big expansion of the North American Aviation Fairfax Bomber plant in Kansas City,

Kansas, was announced by Missouri Senator Harry S Truman [13] Capper spent only a short time in Kansas before the primary, because of the demands on his time in Washington, probably, too, his managers were no longer confident that his personal appearance would arouse voter support But only a few days after the primary, "when Tom McNeal died, Capper dropped everything he had on hands in the senate and came home to attend the funeral services " Such loyalty and devotion to an old friend attracted widespread favorable comment [14]

With reason he took the general-election race more seriously Former Senator George McGill was Capper's principal opponent, and there seemed to be a concerted effort in nationally published magazines and in other media to unseat the "indestructible Arthur Capper," still identified as "a war-stoppered isolationist "[15] By innuendo the Kansas senator was accused of being a collaborator with the enemy and compared to the Copperheads of the Civil War because of his attacks on the President [16] A sensational article described Capper as a "living contradiction of every known rule of political success," who has occupied the "strangest and most puzzling political roosts " He had "his ability to change with the public on every issue, [and] it could be said that Capper represents the essence of the theory of Democracy " But the article insisted that "it isn't leadership and it isn't statesmanship "[17]

Capper had long been a "lone wolf" in Kansas Republican politics, and an important adviser cautioned the Senator that "we have got to be careful in this campaign, and 'play' with the State Committee We cannot get in the attitude of running our own campaign We must cooperate with them to the limit If we don't they will get sore and tell us to go and run our own campaign, and pay no attention to us "[18] In the month before the election word was received that it "looks like a walk away in Kansas this year The Democrats are not creating very much of a hullabaloo "[19] But at the same time Capper was informed that he would not get the usual endorsement from organized labor Since both Capper and his opponent were recognized as friends of labor, labor leaders could not choose between them in the election [20]

Capper's margin of victory in his fifth election to the United States Senate was almost four times what it had been six years earlier [21] Soon after the election he expressed "to the people of Kansas generally and individually, [his]   appreciation of the magnificent vote of confidence   " He resolved "in the coming months and years" to "devote every energy and ability" to represent "the best people on earth, the people of my native state of Kansas "[22]

A great portion of a Senator's time during the early forties was taken up with duties directly connected with the war effort He spent much of his legislative activity on a special committee on Small Business, which resulted in legislation favorable to such enterprises during wartime He also helped some constituents establish their priority for scarce commodities and helped others in relations to various government-connected activities He sent condolences to families of Kansas war casualties, a gesture that was not always well received

Inspired by the war but almost completely separate from his other senatorial activities was correspondence which passed between the President and the Kansas Senator in June, 1943 President Roosevelt wrote Capper that "I received in the mail this morning a letter from a man in Kansas, referring to an editorial or statement in the Topeka Daily Capital of Thursday, May 20, 1943 What shall I tell my correspondent?"[23] Since he had not read the article involved, critical of a press ban on the Hot Springs international food conference, Capper obtained a copy, and in reply he wrote "I am sorry it was printed, particularly that paragraph which compared you with Hitler I believe you know me well enough to know I never would have used such language or made such a comparison, and I was somewhat shocked that any one on my paper should have done so   I would be less than honest with you, Mr President, if I did not add that I also regretted the course of action taken in regard to press relations   In every way possible, I want to help win this war I apologize for the intemperate language used in the one paragraph printed in my paper, and again state that of course I would never accuse you of having the same intentions as Hitler I also express again my opposition to any steps that might in time lead to a government-controlled press "[24] The President could not let the issue die at that point, and he replied at length saying, "I am sure that you, as a newspaper owner, feel just as I do—that one cannot believe all one reads in the press After all, the purpose of the presence of the press at Hot Springs was to obtain news Most decidedly they should not have been there for the purpose of creating trouble and controversy and yet, that is exactly what certain newspaper owners . . . ordered their people to do " The sole restriction on the press, he explained, was that they "be not allowed in the hotel where the delegates were living, except at certain appointed hours That is what the tempest in the teapot was about My dear Arthur, there is a difference between news on the one hand and gossip and the recording of discussion on the other . . I think the press is doing itself great harm as a purveyor of false news but after all that is the funeral of the press "[25] The Kansas Senator and the President could not agree particularly on the meaning of freedom of the press, but they could honestly present their views to each other

Much of the news in the first full year of World War II had been disheartening By 1943 the strength and resources of the United States were beginning to make themselves felt on all military fronts To fulfill the demand for increased taxes supplying the sinew and strength for American military might Beardsley Ruml, chairman of the New York Federal Reserve Bank, suggested that some kind of pay-as-you-go arrangement for handling income taxes be devised Capper, along with Representative Frank Carlson of Kansas, introduced resolutions for early enactment of such a program in their respective houses of Congress [26] When the presidential budget was presented to Congress a similar plan of paying income taxes was urged [27] However, the Treasury soon supported a modified version of the Capper-Carlson proposal, which delayed immediate enactment of any change in paying income taxes [28] Eventually a pay-as-you-go or withholding tax bill was passed with a general increased rate, and it had some similarity to the earlier Ruml-Capper-Carlson proposal

By mid-1943, in spite of the major attention devoted to happenings on the war fronts, Capper was beginning to think about the presidential election of 1944 In correspondence with Alfred M Landon he opposed the suggestion that the name of the Republican party be changed, and he sensed that there was "quite a trend toward Dewey" as the nominee for 1944 [29] But in late 1943 Capper announced his support for either General Dwight Eisenhower or General Douglas MacArthur as the Republican presidential candidate in 1944 [30] However, by the time Republicans nominated Thomas E Dewey, the Kansas Senator had boarded the Dewey bandwagon [31]

Capper was receiving innumerable letters from Kansas lamenting wartime restrictions, the blanket powers granted to the President, and post-war planning, designing the place of the United States in the unknown world of the future He was therefore happy at the prospect for adjournment of Congress in mid-1943 so that he could attend his annual birthday party and "get back to Topeka for a visit with God's people "[32] In seven weeks of intensive visitation Capper immersed himself in Kansas attitudes, which he sought to represent in his seat in the Senate [33] The climax for this visit home was a farm forum on August 31, in which Capper asked Kansas farmers to tell the Congressional delegation "what Congress ought to do " Out of the four-hour welter of discussion he found general opposition to extravagant government expenditures, and to confusion due to controls exercised by the federal government, but Kansas farmers expected Congress to do "everything necessary to win the war "[34]

Late in 1943 and early 1944 the Finney bond scandal, which had rocked the fledgling Landon administration some ten years earlier, was reopened when Ronald Finney made plans to seek a parole William Allen White, a close friend of the Finney family, who had always felt that the younger Finney was a victim of unusual circumstances, sought aid from Capper and others Although sick and besieged with several days of hiccoughs, White wrote that Finney had already served "the longest consecutive sentence . . by any man now in a state or federal prison for a crime such as defalcation, embezzlement, or forgery "[35] Capper responded willingly to the White call for assistance by writing him that "I feel I owe you more than any other man in Kansas and will always welcome a chance to help on anything in which you are interested "[36] Although he had no direct personal interest in the Finney matter, Capper wrote a confidential letter to the editor of the Topeka *Daily Capital* telling of White's concern [37] Later, when William Allen White was no longer able to handle his correspondence, his son William L continued to support Finney's cause and shortly before the death of the Emporia editor on January 29, 1944, the Governor was persuaded to recommend a parole [38]

Capper's long years in the Senate were paying off in seniority on important committees Also he was recognized as a "pioneer in the canned political broadcasting business," because of his long-time use of the Congressional recording studio [39] The *Pictorial Directory of the War Congress* in 1944 featured his picture on the cover The important positions held by the senior Senators, many at least seventy years of age, caused widespread comment and criticism of a system which placed such heavy responsibilities for the future on the shoulders of aged men [40] Later Capper remarked, when asked whether he favored an age limit for Senators, that he would set one at a hundred years of age, but this "statement is subject to amendment when I reach the age of 99 " More realistically, he noted that a "lot depends on the person   If a man at 69 is no longer able to eat grains and meats, probably he should be put out on grass "[41] The subject of old men in Congress was also discussed by the man who had seniority of service in the Senate, Senator Kenneth McKellar of Tennessee, who lauded Capper, then the oldest member, as "one of the finest and most honorable men" he had ever known and a noble and efficient member of Congress [42]

According to the *Congressional Quarterly,* Senator Capper had one of the best records of answering roll calls and attending committee meetings, in spite of his age He was described as a "middle-of-the-road conservative" on the basis of his votes [43] Conscientiously he sought ever to present the view of his constituents, and on rare occasions when he could not vote he readily announced his position A close friend and employee recorded the inner struggle involved in Capper's decisions "And the Senator—well, he does so much want every one on every side of every question to think well of him and highly of his judgment Sometimes I think he is not a tight-rope walker, he is a slack-wire performer as well How he keeps from taking one tumble after another is one of the mysteries, if not one of the facts of life "[44]

Through the 1940's Capper continued to build his autographed picture collection, and he maintained widespread interest in the people he met from all walks of life The stories which he told often dealt with the great and the near-great whom he had met in his role as Senator from Kansas Outstanding in his memory were the visits he had with Winston Churchill and with Mme. Chiang Kai-shek [45]

208

In the first shock of the knowledge of the death of President Franklin D Roosevelt he told of their first meeting during the days immediately following World War I, and a newer star on the horizon, President Harry S Truman, also became the subject of Capper's stories When Truman first went to the Senate in 1935 Capper was one of the first to congratulate the freshman Missouri Senator, who remarked, "You know, my mother is one of your great admirers, she quotes you to me every little while   She takes Capper's Weekly, and sometimes I think it a good thing she doesn't vote in Kansas "[46]

An important event to Capper, as well as to the social and political circles of Washington, was the celebration of his eightieth birthday on July 14, 1945 The day began with participation in a radio broadcast over NBC, "Coffee with Congress," and between intermittent callers and presentations of cakes, loaded with eighty candles, Capper was honored with a luncheon, and a party in the evening given by Mrs Evelyn Walsh McLean for seventy-five wounded servicemen from a nearby convalescent hospital [47] Stories of the birthday anniversary were printed in newspapers from coast-to-coast, and comments such as "cagey type and hard to corner" and "intensely democratic He always speaks to all pretty women he meets, whether he knows them or not," were used to describe the eighty-year-old Capper [48]

Whenever Capper made a speech on the floor of the Senate it was a rare and unexciting experience However, he strayed from his usual practice of presenting only brief remarks by strongly urging the acceptance of the United Nations Charter [49] Capper said that in "the years immediately ahead it will be the task of the United States, Britain, and Russia to cooperate to keep the peace of the world through the mechanism of this Charter If these three nations can work together, the charter will succeed If they cannot, or do not— well, the attempt is worth trying Not to make the attempt would be criminal " Capper recalled that he "was a member of the Senate in 1919 and 1920 when the League of Nations Covenant failed of ratification, finally by a vote of 49 for to 35 against—the necessary two-thirds majority not being attained   It has been most interesting to compare the differences between the two instruments and the differences in procedure by which they were formulated and brought to the Senate for action " He further stated, "I voted for ratification of the League of Nations Covenant on March 19, 1920, with the reservations I did so with a clear conscience at the time, and have no apologies to make now "[50]

In the year following World War II Capper became pessimistic about the strife existing between management and labor Although he reluctantly arrived at the conclusion, he felt that "Congress will have to regulate labor as well as finance and industry "[51] He seemed to fear increasing strength for organized labor, and he felt that the little "industries are the ones that are going to take a beating" under the existing conditions Because of these remarks and his post-war voting record labor leaders came to identify him as a member of the opposition rather than as a friend of labor In his remaining years in the Senate he supported restrictive legislation generally opposed by organized labor [52]

Postwar politics attributed the confusing economic problems of high prices, black markets, strikes, and the housing shortage to the party in power Because of this and other reasons the Republicans gained control of Congress in the 1946 election for the first time since the advent of the New Deal, and provided Capper with an opportunity he had not had for many years As the ranking minority member of five Senate committees in the latter part of the seventy-ninth Congress he had excellent possibilities for obtaining a chairmanship in the incoming eightieth Congress Immediately following the election Capper indicated his preference for the chairmanship of the Committee on Agriculture and Forestry of which he had been a member for twenty-eight years [53] Senator Arthur Vandenberg, of Michigan, wrote Capper asking assistance in becoming chairman of the Senate Foreign Relations Committee, and the Kansas Senator agreed to defer to him, because of his own desire for the position on Agriculture [54] News stories reported that Capper was "insistent" on the Agricultural post and in fact he was eager to get it Supposedly, "one of the Republicans, braver than the rest, brought up the point that Capper was hard of hearing and that he would have trouble following hearings before the important farm committee If only Capper would wear a hearing aid, the Republican said Capper heard him and snapped 'You get me one and I'll wear it ' "[55]

Capper defended his right to the position as chairman of the Committee on Agriculture and Forestry, and when the Congress was organized early in 1947 he was officially given that place, the companion committee in the House being headed by another Kansan, Representative Clifford Hope [56] Because of Capper's age and his confidence in Representative Hope, an impression existed outside Congress that Hope handled much of the guidance of both the Senate and the House committee The Kansas Senator was also returned to the Foreign Relations and the District of Columbia Committees

The program for agriculture was one of the critical problems facing solution by Congress in the transition from war to peace Plans were made under Capper's chairmanship to develop a long-range program [57] A prudent and deliberate study and discussion of agriculture's problems were considered essential to make sure "that the economic disaster that overtook farmers in the thirties" not be repeated, that soil be conserved, and that the government should provide adequate protection for the family farm While a score or so of minor agricultural measures were passed in the first session, meeting in 1947, Capper looked to the second session to produce an extension of support prices for certain basic agricultural commodities [58] But his expectations were not fully realized In spite of the modified parity program and other farm legislation Capper believed that "the farmer and the Farm Belt are to be made the 'goats' for the inflation and the high prices that result from the inflationary policies the federal government has been following for the past decade and more "[59] Repercussions from this feeling may have been felt at the polls in 1948, because farm-based opposition is usually given credit for Dewey's defeat.

During his last year in the Senate more interest was stirred by Capper's announcement on October 31, 1947, that he would seek renomination for the position he had held so long, than anything else he did [60] Even before the Capper announcement former Governor Andrew Schoeppel appeared as a likely candidate, and another prospect, receiving considerable mention, was Milton Eisenhower, then president of Kansas State College (later, University) at Manhattan The leadership of the "Grand Old Party" in Kansas was in turmoil Although he was "not very happy about Capper running for the United States Senate again either," Alfred M Landon observed that "no one can defeat Capper," and he was ready to support

211

him, especially if his opponent was Schoeppel [61] Furthermore, Landon "expected most of the active party organization to be against Capper It always has been, but he has always got thousands of votes that the politicians don't even know where to find "[62] In his correspondence, Landon pictured the Capper-Schoeppel race as an ideological struggle between a man who could not "be attacked on his record" and one who had "too many bad spots in his record " The primary objection to Capper was his eighty-two years, in fact it would be eighty-three by the time of the election, and word was generally spread throughout Kansas not only that the senior Senator from Kansas was deaf but also that his mind was slipping in a pathetic way and that he "may not live till next November "[63] In private correspondence with another old-time Capper supporter, Landon wrote, "Our situation is very similar I didn't encourage him to run but told him I would do everything I could to help elect him "[64]

Through the early months of 1948 disquieting statements made in Kansas concerning his candidacy were heard by Capper Most significant to him was the strong opposition coming from William L White, son of his old friend on the Emporia *Gazette*, and Roy Roberts, editor of the Kansas City *Star* White expressed opposition to the aged Capper, who he said was in the race solely at the insistence of Landon, for whom the Emporian had developed an intense dislike [65] And Roberts, though his cordiality had been indicated in 1940 when he wrote Capper, "You know there is nothing I wouldn't do for you at any time," sought to eliminate the aged Senator from the race [66] Capper prepared a statement for distribution on May 6, which said, "All this pressure has been so great that I have finally concluded it would be unwise for me at my age to continue in the Senate," but it was never released to the press [67] Instead he sent a long letter to White thanking him "for the kind words, but your editorial contains two misstatements of facts   In the first place, I did not became a candidate for the United States Senate at the behest of any one person I did so after talking and corresponding with many of my friends all over the state, in all walks of life and in every line of business and of practically every political belief Surely my record of service and my wide experience with the people of Kansas entitle me to go to the people for advice in this manner   Above all, let me assure you the decision to be candidate this year was mine and mine alone The responsibility of my decision is on me solely and on no one else Now, as always, I acknowledge no master but the people of Kansas—my home and my beloved state "[68]

Kansans were commenting in the state press about the forthcoming race The Wellington *Daily News* began a story about efforts to sidetrack Capper, "All the evidence points to dirty work at the crossroads, mates!"[69] And many were sending their views directly to the Senator In spite of the general opposition the feeling still existed that Capper could "put this thing over" if he made "a prodigious effort," but it would be a "terrific struggle" to win Further expectations pointed to a cost in excess of fifty thousand dollars for the primary election alone,[70] a figure many times the cost of three previous primary races for Capper [71] Additional correspondence mentioning difficulties to be encountered finally tipped the scales so that Capper reconsidered and announced his withdrawal as a senatorial candidate on June 6, 1948, after first notifying a group of his leading backers [72]

A taste of the kind of criticism that would have faced him through the campaign, by critics using tactics which he never employed personally, was printed in leading newspapers early in June, but Capper's decision was already made [73] Press comments about the proposed retirement were commendatory and favorable [74] But later Capper's reasons for retirement were taken out of context, and he was reputed to have said that "he will not be a candidate for re-election because he would rather retire than become involved in the plan of national Republican bosses to double-cross the farmers "[75]

As long as he had plans for the distant future Capper seemed to be in excellent health for a man of his age But when he took himself out of the race for the Senate his Washington staff began to notice his health decline On June 19, 1948, he was sent to Bethesda Naval Hospital, where he remained for six days because of "exhaustion and a mild respiratory trouble "[76] Some eight weeks later he was back in the hospital for a short time "for treatment of a severe cold "[77]

Capper had experienced exciting and important changes in the nation's capital during the 1940's He had participated in momentous decisions and he had viewed significant events But he was never above dealing with little things, and he actively sought legislation requested by his constituents [78] During the fall and winter of 1948 he was increasingly honored with commendations by many national organizations, in special ceremonies in Washington, and citizen groups in the District of Columbia were equally complimentary.[79] With a feeling of nostalgia he prepared his last transcribed record from Washington for presentation, January 3, 1949, on his radio station, WIBW On January 12, he boarded the train to return home to Topeka and an end to his public career, an end to thirty-four years in high state and national office As usual Capper rode the Pullman Only on one occasion had he taken a roomette to or from Washington It was never again for him because he "was in there all alone, and everyone else in that car was shut off by himself" On his ride into private life Capper still maintained his interest in people, what they thought, and what they believed, and his particular trait was responsible for developments, begun much earlier, which offered promise that the Capper name would remain alive, long after the man was gone

Chapter XVIII

Capper and Kansas

William Allen White did not exaggerate when he referred to Arthur Capper as a Kansas institution Many natives of the area subscribed to four or five publications, such as a daily newspaper, a weekly newspaper, a farm weekly, a women's magazine, and a farm monthly, all originating in the Capper establishment. More than likely these same persons also listened to the Capper radio station and had faith in Arthur Capper, "the Farmer's Friend "[1] The seven political victories Capper achieved in gaining the positions of Governor of Kansas and United States Senator caused it to be repeated that voting for Capper was "just like chawin' tobaccar—it's got to be a habit." His longevity in major public office was exceeded by few

When Senator-turned-private-citizen Capper went home to Topeka early in January, 1949, he was moving out of the limelight which he had enjoyed for many years But there were still activities to take up his attention By almost any measure Capper Publications and its subsidiaries had shown immense growth The ten publications in 1949 included *Household,* which circulated nationally, *Capper's Farmer,* with distribution primarily in fifteen Midwestern states, and *Capper's Weekly,* which was concentrated in the plains and neighboring areas The state farm papers were *Kansas Farmer, Missouri Ruralist, Ohio Farmer, Michigan Farmer,* and *Pennsylvania Farmer,* and the Topeka *Daily Capital* and the Kansas City *Kansan* rounded out the Capper list Their combined circulation was about four and a half million, a far cry from the days of the North Topeka *Mail,* when Capper proudly circulated little more than a thousand copies with each issue [2] The Capper Printing Company was by itself a fair-sized business, and the radio stations, WIBW and KCKN, possessed an extensive audience in northeast Kansas The number of employees by that time was almost twelve hundred The gross revenues had shown a mighty increase, although expenses sometimes placed the outcome of a year's work on the debit side of the ledger.

In no case had Capper started a new publication Someone else had provided the impetus for all of his ten publications of the late forties, and he initiated the purchase only of his first paper Some of

215

his papers had never had a change of name or a combination with another journal This was true of the Topeka *Daily Capital* or the Kansas City *Kansan* But *Household* had been *Push*, acquired in 1903 *Capper's Farmer* had been the *Missouri Valley Farmer*, with the change in name in 1919 *Capper's Weekly* had begun life as the *Kansas Weekly Capital* until its new name was adopted in 1913 In the 1920's its eastern edition was sometimes called *Capper's Magazine*, and at least one combination was made With few exceptions the newspaper heritage of Capper's state farm papers was much more complex *Kansas Farmer*, alone, was the product of sixteen or seventeen combinations, seven of which Capper was involved in [3] The *Missouri Ruralist* had a background almost as complicated Capper made no combination on the *Nebraska Farm Journal*, there were three which he engineered for *Oklahoma Farmer*, and at least two each for the members of the "Eastern trio" in which he owned majority control In addition, he obtained at least two other papers which did not enter directly into combination, and *Poultry Culture*, published for a time Analysis shows that at different times there were twenty-eight different journals personally under Capper control or combination, of which ten survived the publisher

Few people have the opportunity to be on the spot when the history of a nation is being made Because of his long occupation of high office, the mild-mannered, slender, and soft-voiced Arthur Capper came to know and to observe the great and the near great, and to participate in many historic events at both the state and national level Because of his unprepossessing nature he was almost never the center of attention, although he did have a knack for placing himself on the near sidelines Frequently his conversation sparkled with little intimate references to well-known public figures He liked to recall homely illustrations of the restrained behavior of President Coolidge He also told how Will Rogers "landed in my office" on his last visit to Washington The Kansas Senator invited Rogers to a luncheon in the Senate restaurant, and several other members of the Senate joined the party Midway through the meal, the ebullient and effusive Senator Huey Long entered the room After "Share-the-Wealth" Huey was invited to share the Capper meal, he accepted and monopolized the conversation The luncheon was the subject of Will Rogers' last radio broadcast, for two weeks later he was the victim of a plane crash in Alaska Huey Long was assassinated sixty days later in Louisiana [4]

Capper and Prime Minister Winston Churchill were together at a luncheon in Washington in 1947 One person was seated between them, but it proved ' no bar to their conversation" which was about "you guessed it!—wheat "[5] Capper liked to tell about the "history-making pens" he had received from various Presidents after they had formally signed important legislation His stories, especially in his old age, frequently dealt with happenings of his youth, such as the time he shot off a firecracker in church, his arrival in Topeka, his transfer to the editorial offices from the mechanical operations of the newspaper, his visit to the frontier in southwest Kansas, and his experiences on the metropolitan New York *Tribune* One story he delighted in telling, chuckling all the while, was his experiences with a suckling pig that one of his constituents had sent him in the late 1920's, when he was living at the Mayflower in Washington After keeping it in the hotel refrigerator for a few days, the manager, on a Thanksgiving morning, said they would need the space, then Capper cheerfully put the pig into a box, placed the box in his car trunk, and set out to give it to friends The first three families he had in mind were out of town, and he thought of Secretary of Agriculture William M Jardine But no, the Jardines did not have an oven large enough to roast a pig in, so they politely refused In desperation Capper concluded that he had to get rid of the pig before he went back to the hotel He recalled a secluded nook in Rock Creek Park, and he decided it was a good place to drop the box with the pig No one would see him, but he became less sure of his plan as he came nearer to the park The box was about right to hold a baby Suppose someone saw him hide it under a bush All kinds of things might be thought of, to his embarrassment But he resolved to carry out his plan The place was deserted, with no one in sight He took the box from his car and threw it into some bushes, and he returned home, his heart pounding Later in telling the story, he concluded, "I never felt so like a criminal in all my life "[6]

Capper's interest in the game of golf provided the basis for another story He had long been an avid golf fan and a member of golf clubs in Topeka and the national capital He regularly played every Sunday and on other occasions when time would permit He was an acknowledged Quaker, although a self-confessed backslider who rarely attended meetings On one occasion, Mrs Herbert Hoover, also a member of the Society of Friends, invited Capper to attend church with her on the following Sunday Capper told the President's wife he would be happy to—if it were raining Several Sundays went by before it rained in the morning Senator Capper then showed up at the White House to go to church with the President and Mrs Hoover

Capper was rightly considered a man of wealth, but usually the monetary value of his possessions was overestimated, and he maintained that he was no millionaire [7] His only real estate was that of his home and his business He owned no stocks or bonds and on occasion returned such property to the person who had given it to him [8] The prospectus for financing various Capper Publications' operations stated that it "is worthy of note that from the inception of his publishing business Arthur Capper has not engaged in any outside ventures He has withdrawn no monies for outside investments All profits have been ploughed back into the business " In 1951 his income from his business was $3,600 as president of Capper-Harman-Slocum, $15,000 as president of Capper Publications, $250 for rent on his house, and no dividends on his stock The medical expenses of his last illness took most of the year's income, and he had left over more than sixty thousand dollars in checking accounts in three banks His ownership of Capper Publications was the basis of his wealth

Because of the general impression that he was a man of great wealth Capper received requests for contributions in almost every mail He did donate sizable sums to the Kansas 4-H Club Ranch and to the William Allen White Foundation, and generally he contributed to other worth-while projects Much of these contributions came from his personal income, not from his business [9] After the disastrous 1951 flood he sent a check to the Florence Public Library to purchase children's books, in honor of his wife, Florence, for whom the town had been named In the 1920's he began the practice of starting a ten-dollar savings account for the newly born children of employees, and he regularly kept it up until his death A further drain on his financial resources was payment of annual dues for at least eighteen lodges and clubs, for five lodge insurance companies,

218

and for a multitude of other organizations Through the years his dues amounted to hundreds of dollars annually, and when he was called on to address fraternal groups he would often begin with the story that he had overheard one member ask the treasurer who that man was over there The treasurer replied, "He doesn't come very often but, thank God, he pays his dues "

Capper's early training in thrift caused him to be careful with his money He lived modestly, especially after his wife died Although he had earlier owned bigger cars, his last two automobiles were a 1934 Chevrolet sedan and a 1946 Plymouth He was also a light eater, not very regular in his eating habits, and his favorite recipe was one for cornbread [10] His wardrobe was not as extensive as might be expected of a person in his official position Descriptions of his appearance frequently emphasized his loosely fitted suits and his "poorly knotted-tie encircled [by] a high stiff collar "[11]

Partly because of the prestige of his public positions Arthur Capper was asked on many occasions to serve as a board member or a sponsor of a national organization He greatly relished his association with the National Committee on Boys' and Girls' Club Work, the National Council of Boy Scouts of America, the Board of Incorporators of the Red Cross, the National Association for the Advancement of Colored People, and similar organizations He allowed many groups to use his name, and most of the time he was proud of these associations, but sometimes this generosity gave him trouble During World War II he accepted an invitation to sponsor the celebration of the tenth anniversary of United States relations with the Soviet Union These sponsors were then identified with the National Council of American-Soviet Friendship, Inc , which was exposed by the New York *World-Telegram* in 1946 as a subversive group Capper along with "a dozen leading sponsors" withdrew from the Council Several years later the organization was also listed by the Attorney General as subversive In 1950 Capper heard that he was still included as a sponsor by the National Council of American-Soviet Friendship, Inc , and he again asked them to "drop my name from your membership list and remove my name from your letterheads "[12] In 1945 Capper agreed to serve as a sponsor of the American League for a Free Palestine, Inc , and his name was placed on the official stationery of the League The Palestine Emergency Fund, without his knowledge, also included him as a national sponsor [13]

Throughout his long political career, Capper received a diversity of support that was truly amazing It was a gross exaggeration to illustrate the nature of his support as William L White did in late 1951 White wrote that "the 1924 election was turbulent, with bitter fights over the leftist LaFollette revolt and also the Ku Klux Klan, in which many candidates became disastrously involved, some against their will But Arthur Capper, with the endorsement of the labor unions, the Knights of Columbus, Bnai Brith and the Ku Klux Klan, came through with a thundering majority "[14] Capper did have organized labor's support in most elections, he frequently received endorsement from members of the Catholic clergy as well as from Protestant ministers, veterans' groups and Negro organizations backed him, and the common people of the small towns and the farm areas gave him widespread support Actually B'nai B'rith was almost nonexistent in Kansas, and the Ku Klux Klan was a passing phenomenon which lacked the strength attributed to it and soon fell into disrepute

Some attempts to explain the hold Capper had on Kansas people have identified him as an enigma or a freak For those who wanted a simple explanation there was no solution, Capper was not that easily explained The fact that he was meek and never fought back was not easily interpreted, nor was his ability to survive precipitous changes in political opinion His folksy, modest, and self-effacing manner was accepted by most of his supporters, and no attempt was made to analyze it The fact that diametrically opposite sources of information would identify Capper as the "meekest, stubbornest man in the world" and "solicited the least by professional lobbyists" illustrated the complexity of the man [15]

Capper's own interpretation of his role was that he should serve as a mirror of the attitudes and interests of the people he represented There were certain things in the "Capper lexicon" that were always right "the American woman, the American farmer, the American prohibitionist, and America's colored people And the record will bear out that he has never been squeamish—never minced words about it "[16] The groups named were those to which Kansans were committed, although the prohibition law was repealed in the late forties, when Capper still believed that Kansas would return to prohibition

Certainly there was no *one* thing which caused Capper to be well received by the Kansas voters in seven elections or to remain one of the best-known Kansans of the state's first century There was his success as a businessman, his capacity for detail, his mastery of his trade There was his marriage to the scion of Kansas "royalty," and his acceptance in the most refined social circles There was his early untiring work in the lower echelons of his political party, and the wide acquaintance he built up throughout the state There was his deserved reputation as a fighter against trusts and other interests, on behalf of the farmer and the common people There was his ability to get divergent groups to work together, to administer the government of the state There was his support of youth activities, especially his work on behalf of the handicapped There was his aggressive encouragement of "moral" legislation, his basic belief that the masses were "good" and that a composite of all opinion would be in the best interests of the nation There were his economic attitudes, his feeling that government's role in the economy was limited, but at the same time, interventionist in a way to preserve opportunity for the "little man " There was his charity for a political adversary, his meekness in face of partisan attack, and his willingness to champion the "underdog " Finally, there was his boundless energy that wore out his office staff and outdistanced men half his age, his desire to serve and to help, his longing for approval from his fellow men These were the things that made Arthur Capper tick His goals were quite simple and were never far removed from the present, but his manner of procedure was increasingly complicated by the multiplicity of his roles as publisher of newspapers and farm magazines, politician, and farm leader

Although not inclined to discuss his innermost thoughts and no philosopher, Arthur Capper did rely on a set of dicta, some of which were the product of his Quaker rearing Some evidence of his practical bent is found in a "House Book" he prepared for his six hundred employees around 1910 [17] His expressed desire was to have his business "known throughout the business world as an institution ruled by highest motives and in full sympathy with the present-day spirit of honest, useful service in business The Golden Rule stands

pre-eminent as the world's greatest business maxim "[18] His only instructions "to the news department" were "for a strict adherence to
truth, the utmost fairness "[19] He stressed courtesy, and he supported moderation and even concession no matter how "unreasonable the demands of a subscriber or an advertiser may seem "[20] Correspondents judged a business "by the little things as well as by the
more important matters," and he asked that every "letter received in
his office, in any department, should have an immediate reply "[21]
He expected visitors to come to see his business, and he wanted them
to have "a most cordial welcome "[22] A few years later, many of these
maxims were formalized as "mottoes," some of which were posted
around the Capper plant [23] He also avoided lawsuits, preferring to
settle disputes out of court, even at great loss His office procedures,
worked out for private enterprise, stood him in good stead when he
served as Governor and United States Senator He always had a
knack of stirring up business on a Saturday afternoon, or getting out
long letters a little before closing time He used his time efficiently,
often recording with a stub of a pencil things he must do or items for
speeches on little cards, two by three inches

Until he was elected Senator, Capper had standing orders that
news about his own activities must be severely limited in his own
publications His picture was almost never published in his own
papers, and Mrs Capper had a kind of anonymity which she preferred Probably no Kansas Governor had been so little featured in
the Topeka *Daily Capital* as when Capper occupied that post However, by 1919, things began to change Advertising salesmen for
Capper Publications were aware that their prospects had never seen
Capper, although they had seen "Pierce, Meredith, Wallace, Cyrus
Curtis and others Very few of them know very much about Capper
as a man, and most of what they think they do know is based upon
what some other representative has told them, and they have the idea
that we are putting out a bunch of cats and dogs matter, duplicating
editorial matter in the different sections, using the scissors at every
opportunity, and making a special play for mail order business " So a
campaign was mapped out to use pictures of Capper more frequently, and in order to help sell advertising, to show the publisher's interests in the political field [24] Thereafter, stories about Capper and
the use of his picture became more frequent in the news columns of

his publications After thirty years of such a policy, observers pointed out that if "the Capper brain trust had a guide book, it would probably say (1) Please the farmer, (2) help the farmer get along, (3) keep it simple, (4) keep it clean, (5) make nobody mad, (6) report what the Senator does and says and print his picture as often as decently possible "[25]

By the time he had reached his eighties, Capper was repeatedly asked to tell his philosophy of life Such statements as, "I try to live each day so that I like to live with myself," and "Live and let live— and lift a little more than your share," received widespread circulation He also reported that he started his career by "breaking larger goals down into smaller ones "[26] In a commencement address he stated that in "my own collection of great Americans I carry three as The Great Ones One of them, by the way, is a woman The Three are, George Washington, who gave us liberty, Abraham Lincoln, who preserved and extended liberty, and Miss Susan B Anthony, who fought gallantly all her life, and finally successfully to bring liberty to women To my mind, there are the Three Great Ones in American history " He further warned his audience that the "first steps toward depriving the individual of his liberty are taken when he is cajoled, or purchased or coerced into the position where he depends upon his government, instead of upon himself, to take care of his needs and provide for his wants "[27] Of course, many of the speeches, editorials, and articles which were presented in the name of Arthur Capper were "ghosted" by a member of his staff Almost always he carefully went over the prepared material with a stubby pencil and altered it in his own handwriting, to include the names of people, or to clarify a statement That he had an excellent style of writing was undisputed among his editors, for sometimes he did turn in a "story written out in long-hand, and even the most meticulous copyreader could not improve upon it He was the master of putting facts into readable news stories in the fewest possible words "[28]

In the closing years of his life Capper received numerous citations for his accomplishments as publisher, officeholder, and citizen [29] Though he was actively interested in his business, his long immersion in politics had seen control of business decisions pass to other hands [30] Most of his time was spent in visiting with old friends, in correspondence, in preparation of his memoirs, and in talking with friendly people whom he met in various gatherings in Topeka, in Washington, and elsewhere [31] By 1950 he was celebrating his eighty-fifth birthday anniversary, and although he had no apparent illness, the years were beginning to tell He was hard of hearing and frail Finally, after an attack of pneumonia, it became harder for him to walk the short block between his office and his hotel apartment He began to lose interest in eating, and his weight, already low, declined. Floods during the summer of 1951 renewed his interest in his surroundings, and he visited every flood-ravaged community within a short driving distance of Topeka [32] Then in December, he caught a cold which developed into pneumonia Round-the-clock nursing care was given to him in his Jayhawker Hotel room "He was particularly thoughtful for the comfort of those   who remained by his side day and night," but his strength slowly ebbed away [33] Arthur Capper died December 19, 1951, at the age of eighty-six years Tributes of many persons, from bootblack to President, flowed into Topeka from all parts of the nation President Harry S Truman wired that "an era in the history of the old Midwest came to a close with the passing of Senator Capper "[34] Numerous messages of sympathy and editorials about Capper appeared in many newspapers [35] His body was permitted to lie in state in the Kansas Statehouse, the third to be so honored The national flag on the Statehouse grounds was at half-mast until after the funeral [36]

Within a week, Capper's fifteen-page will was filed in the Shawnee County Probate Court The major bequest was $250,000 for the Capper Foundation for Crippled Children, and provision was made for perpetuation of Capper Publications, Inc, under the same managers who had operated the company for many years Fourteen other Topeka charities were specifically mentioned in the will, and bequests were made for the few Capper relatives Most of the remainder of the estate was given to Capper's surviving sister, Mrs Edith Capper Eustice, and to certain legatees still in his employ or that of Capper Publications [37] Capper's plan of leaving stock to employees was influenced by the example of the employee-owned Kansas City Star Company, and the manner in which he transferred stock was similar to a plan used by the Milwaukee *Journal* [38] Capper did not stipulate that stockholders in Capper Publications, Inc, must dispose of their stock upon retirement from the business, but the new owners made private arrangements limiting ownership to persons active in the business [39]

Thus, under the presidency of Henry S Blake, long-time vice president, leading stockholder, and executor of the Capper estate, Capper Publications entered a new era The business continued to show growth during these years Total circulation for the ten Capper publications mounted to more than five million, and WIBW-TV was developed and began operations on a daily schedule [40] Capper was no longer around to serve as a balance wheel for his business enterprise, and internal disharmony, never apparent before on the surface, displayed two contending groups seeking to dominate the life of the business Such friction and the large size of the Capper operations delayed the settlement of the Capper estate, still incomplete when Blake suddenly died in March, 1956 [41] Formerly the probate judge had ruled that the Capper Foundation bequest could be 25,000 shares in Capper Publications, Inc , stock But after Blake's death a new petition, representing some of the stockholders, asked that the former ruling be set aside and that the bequest be handled with cash rather than stock [42] Litigation over the disposition of the stock in Capper Publications, Inc , ceased in mid-September, 1956, with the announcement that Stauffer Publications, Inc , had paid $2,498,675 for all of the stock in the corporation [43] Approval of the sale of the radio and television properties by the Federal Communications Commission delayed the formal transfer of ownership until February 1, 1957 Since the purchaser assumed obligations in outstanding Capper Certificates, subscriptions, and similar liabilities of about four and a half million dollars, the total transaction involved an amount of approximately seven million dollars [44]

The trend of the 1950's, of curtailing production of the publications of general appeal with sizable circulation, finally caught up with *Household* and *Capper's Farmer* [45] *Household* was sold to Curtis Publications, and it came to an end with the November, 1958, issue [46] *Capper's Farmer* was discontinued with the issue of April, 1960 [47] Even the Capper Printing Company suspended operations in mid-1959, after an earlier sale to a Chicago firm [48] However, Stauffer Publications, Inc , new owners of Capper Publications, Inc , made plans to build a still greater newspaper and magazine publishing empire A new plant was projected in 1960, outside the crowded downtown area of Topeka to handle the growing business The same year saw the addition of three new farm publications—*Indiana Farmer, Kentucky Farmer,* and *Tennessee Farmer*—to the organization [49] Early in 1961 the eight state farm papers, including the five Capper had owned for so long, were sold by Stauffer Publications [50]

In the estimation of Arthur Capper, the Capper Fund for Crippled Children, begun at Christmas-time in 1920, was of far greater value than all the other worthy sponsored projects and promotional activities of his business Because of the dispersal of business assets associated with Capper, the program which he began for crippled children seems destined as the major agency to recall the Capper name to later residents of Kansas and the nation Capper had long co-operated with other Topeka businessmen in delivering Christmas packages to the homes of many of the poor of Topeka Con Van Natta, composing-room foreman, was usually in charge of arrangements for Capper Publications' part in this yearly activity After making his deliveries, he always reported to Capper on the reception of the packages Generally he would mention the plight of the crippled children into whose homes he had gone In his report after the visits in 1920, Van Natta described the retrogression of some of these child cripples Stirred by the stories, Capper immediately gave Van Natta the responsibility of arranging "terms with the best equipped hospitals," obtaining the "services of the most skillful surgeons," and with Capper money and influence behind him to begin the immediate care of these children [51]

In the beginning Capper provided all the money for their care Surgeons made little or no charge for their work, but the financial burden of the other services for the handicapped grew. Civic organizations in Topeka were solicited, and the various Capper newspapers and journals publicized the Capper Fund and asked aid from their readers In 1925, at the suggestion of a mother of six children, contributions of ten cents for each member of the family were flowing into the Capper Fund from many sources Actually the "thin dime" campaign was not a great financial aid in the early days, but it helped to spread support for the work [52] Con Van Natta furnished stories of the work of the Fund to Capper periodicals, especially during the Christmas season The "highly specialized orthopedic services" undertaken, or the improvement of a spinal-curvature victim of infantile paralysis, was described [53] Still a large share of the expense of caring for the handicapped was a personal liability willingly assumed by Senator Capper The work of the Capper Fund grew under the guidance of Con Van Natta, and, by the time of his death in 1934, widespread knowledge of its operations existed throughout the Middle West [54]

On September 26, 1934, the Capper Foundation for Crippled Children was incorporated as a "purely charitable" organization to continue the work begun many years earlier by the Capper Fund [55] The new foundation had initial assets of $32,820 and the goodwill of almost all who heard about it Already known as a "pioneer in crippled children work," Capper urged widespread support on their behalf [56] When the Kansas Crippled Children's Temporary Commission was created in 1929, followed by the Kansas Crippled Children's Commission on July 1, 1931, the state officially recognized a need that Capper had seen years earlier Because the state agency received its support from state and federal tax revenues, whereas the Capper Fund, and later the Capper Foundation, was privately supported, there was no need for duplication of effort, there was more than enough for each to do By 1935 Capper could proudly proclaim the support of "contributors [who] have helped us to make more than a thousand little folks whole "[57] An increasing number of crippled children were cared for in later years, and expenses grew upon entry into the field of spastic paralysis [58]

In 1947 when the Topeka Orphans' Home was discontinued, the assets of the home, including a brick building, were given to the Capper Foundation, and the first Comprehensive Rehabilitation Program in the area was established Prior to that time the Capper Foundation had cared for children, primarily through hospitalization, and occasionally some children were sent to experts in Chicago, New York, or Rochester, Minnesota But with the newly available building, a rehabilitation center was established as a convalescent home for crippled children [59] In its first year of operations in the old Topeka Orphans' Home about a hundred children were provided for, and a staff of eight, some on a part-time basis, were employed.[60]

With the vast expansion of its assets occasioned by the sale of its Capper Publications stock, the directors of the Capper Foundation for Crippled Children purchased a four-acre tract in west Topeka and developed plans for a new and enlarged program [61] A modern, well-equipped building was dedicated in April, 1959 Funds for the new structure were provided by the Arthur Capper bequest and a federal grant through the Hospital Survey and Construction Act [62] Because the academic department was fully accredited, schooling from kindergarten through high school was provided, in addition to the specialized services in physical, occupational, speech, and recreational therapy In 1960 a clinical training program in the therapy sections and a program for pre-schoolers were added to the services of the Foundation During the year 128 children, 54 on a full-day schedule, were aided by the Foundation About 50 additional children received financial and hospital assistance without coming to the Foundation [63]

Annual expenses for the Capper Foundation for Crippled Children in the first years of full-time operations averaged slightly more than one hundred thousand dollars About 60 per cent of this money came from contributions—from the Capper Foundation Holiday Seal Campaign, polio chapters, and various individuals and groups Income from the Capper endowment provided about one-fourth of the annual operating expenses, parent repayment about 2 per cent, although sometimes as much as 5 per cent, and the rest came from wills and bequests made to the Foundation [64]

By mid-1961 a twenty-room air-conditioned boarding home was completed west of the main Capper Foundation building for housing forty-five out-of-city children who were receiving therapy and other services These capital improvements were financed by the Foster Humane Society of Topeka, the Arthur Capper endowment, and matching federal funds [65]

Developments of the Capper Foundation for Crippled Children could hardly have been visualized when the Capper Fund for Crippled Children came into existence in 1920 or when the Foundation was incorporated in 1934 As Kansas entered her second century, Arthur Capper, one of her heroes in the first hundred years, will be remembered in this, his main memorial

There were several significant posthumous memorials for Arthur Capper other than the Capper Foundation In 1954 a new west-side school in Topeka was named the Capper Junior High School [66] As soon as it was possible, within the rules, Capper was named to the Kansas Newspaper Hall of Fame [67] Also in 1954, an announcement was made in the nation's capital that the first major slum clearance project carried out by the National Capital Housing Authority would result in a new group of buildings in a seven-block area in Southeast Washington, near the Capitol, which would have the name Arthur Capper Dwellings [68] Capper had helped sponsor the legislation which created the Authority When he had first gone to the Senate he was ambitious to serve on the Foreign Relations committee, but he was assigned to the Committee on the District of Columbia instead He soon discovered that the people of the District "were really his 'foreign relations' "[69]

The eulogies presented at the time of his death show typical attitudes descriptive of Arthur Capper To some he "was the epitome of the sturdy Midwest farmer—a conservative in many ways and a progressive in many more "[70] He coupled "native ability with missionary zeal" to serve as "the spokesman for the American farmer" in Congress [71] Statements that he "had no political machine and he never caused a vocal row in party meetings," that "he was never narrowly partisan and he seemed to have a genius for being sturdily loyal to his party and to his farm constituents without stirring bitterness anywhere," provided a commentary on his political behavior [72] Another said he "was no mossback He was receptive to new ideas and he preached and practiced the philosophy or doctrine of helpfulness his name was a synonym for big-hearted philanthropy "[73] Capper's "remarkable capacity for hard work," his "thousands of favors for people not of the 'influence peddling' variety," and the fact that he "never talked down to the people nor sought to bring them to a common level" gave indication that he believed the "American people are a wonderful people "[74]

Yet some wrote that in spite of Capper's success, by "no yardstick could he be called great," while others were willing to accord him the title of "statesman "[75] Capper had conceded years earlier that a statesman was a dead politician, but there were indications that he was aware of his place in history and that he had early aspirations to be recognized as a statesman [76] No doubt the failure broadly to grant the title of statesman to the Kansas Senator was due partly to his expert ability to discover the ebb and flow of Kansas opinion and to

229

shift with the tide His ability accurately to express "the will and sentiments of the average citizen of Kansas" while "never leading" and always following faithfully was criticized as a failure to perform his "full functions" as a publisher, a Governor, and a Senator [77]

It would be difficult to visualize the development of Kansas during its first century without a man such as Arthur Capper He was born in the days of the state's infancy, he grew to manhood and became acquainted with all of her Governors, and in the process married the daughter of the third He had corresponded with John Greenleaf Whittier, and he had second-hand reports of Frémont's expeditions through pre-territorial Kansas His father told him of personal contacts with John Brown As a newspaperman he had been an overnight guest in the home of John J Ingalls on several occasions, and he showed justifiable pride in the "advancement of Kansas, which in his youth was a land of sod houses and dugouts, of lariats and six-shooters" He had personal memories of hatchet-swinging Carry Nation, as "a fine woman and absolutely fearless" in her goal to drive out the saloon He had played a part in the development of the state with his publications "In a day when Kansans were still planting crops by phases of the moon, being gypped by professional rainmakers and were stringing impailed [sic] snakes on their backs along the barbed-wire fences to break the droughts, he was entering their homes through his publications to give them scientific information about how to make dairying, farming, stock raising and fruit-growing pay "[78] Later as the first native-born Governor of Kansas and as United States Senator for thirty consecutive years he made an indelible impression on the state's history Observers have noted that the Jayhawker state, at the turn of the century, was scornfully looked upon as the place where whiskers grew as long as the grass was high, and it was considered the main habitat of the crank, the agitator, the cyclone, and the grasshopper Capper, and many others, sought to change that impression, and in a large measure they succeeded The fact that the slogan for the Kansas Centennial year, "Midway, U S A ," had more than a geographical connotation, was due, in large measure, to the development of attitudes in Kansas during years of Capper's political leadership Yes, "Capper and Kansas" have become synonymous terms [79]

Bibliographical Note

The most important source of information about Arthur Capper is the Capper papers in the Archives of the Kansas State Historical Society in Topeka These materials, partly in manuscript, fill almost forty file drawers and are primarily the correspondence, speeches, and office records of a long-time political figure Most of the files cover the 1930's and 1940's, although considerable source material is found for earlier years Cramped office and filing space of more than thirty years ago forced the disposal and destruction of many of the file materials of the 1920's, an irreparable loss to the more complete reconstruction of that interesting period in Capper's life Some of the Capper "diaries" are little more than appointment schedules, but the journals of Florence Crawford and Arthur Capper, covering about eight months in 1891 and 1892, supply contemporary information on a period for which almost no material was previously available

The Agricultural Bloc, published by Harcourt, Brace and Company in 1922, is the only book in which Arthur Capper is listed as the author There are also pamphlets and instruction handbooks for the Capper staff which were prepared by Capper Numerous regional and national magazines, several books, and many newspapers contain articles attributed to him Prior to World War I, most of these articles, as well as his signed editorials in his own publications, were his own work, and they show a vigorous, precise, and terse use of the English language For the next fifteen years or so published materials, reputedly the work of Capper, were prepared under his close supervision, by Marco Morrow, Clif Stratton, or some other member of his staff By the 1930's his views were so well known to his staff that many items were prepared for Capper's signature with a minimum of instruction, although he always carefully reworked speeches and editorials to meet his own personal desires Many of the Capper publications contained these signed editorials as a regular feature While they were not the complete product of his own pen, they give expression to the publisher's view on many public and private matters, and they provide a running commentary on changing positions over the years.

During his many years as a publisher more than 450 volumes of different newspapers and magazines were prepared under Capper's guidance The North Topeka *Mail,* and its successors, the *Mail and Breeze* and the *Kansas Farmer,* accounted for fifty-eight of these volumes Through a combination of the Kansas State Historical Library and the morgue of Capper Publications (now Stauffer Publications) in Topeka, and the United States Department of Agriculture Library and the Library of Congress in Washington, D C , all of the Capper Publications are avail-

231

able Very little material not found in Topeka exists in any of the governmental libraries and archives in Washington

Additional original sources were located in other manuscript collections, particularly the Landon papers, at the Kansas State Historical Library Two master's theses, "The Public Career of Arthur Capper Prior to his Senatorial Service," by Byron M Crowley, and "The Senatorial Career of Arthur Capper," by Jesse P Jewell, both done at Kansas State College of Pittsburg, provided some information not available elsewhere

Another important source of information for this biography has been interviews with persons having some connection with the topic Following an interview with Arthur Capper on April 7, 1950, there have been more than fifty other interviews with active and retired Capper employees, as well as with persons never directly connected with the Capper enterprise A fourteen-page bibliography, listing most of these interviews, and the most complete listing of Capper materials, outside the notes of this book, is available in Homer E Socolofsky, "The Capper Farm Press," University Microfilm (Mic A54-3462), pages 325-38

Notes

I

1 Herbert's mother died at childbirth at the age of thirty-nine His father lived until sixty-seven, dying from a fall from a roof of a house where workmen under his direction were preparing downspouts Years later Capper wrote that his grandfather Thomas was also a Methodist minister

2 Letter from Herbert Capper to George Mitcheson, Aug 1, 1853

3 Letter from Herbert Capper to George Mitcheson, May 9, 1854

4 Letter from Herbert Capper to George Mitcheson, Nov 27, 1854

5 One source, *Kansas Historical Collections*, VII, 238, credits McGrew with the ownership of one slave This seems unlikely, considering McGrew's Iowa residence and later reputation as a strong free-state man According to William Mitchell, *Linn County, Kansas A History*, 248, Lewis Campbell, the man in question, was a fugitive slave who lived for some time at the Simon B McGrews

6 Mitchell, 354

7 The first forty acres for which patent was received was the NW¼ of SW¼, sec 4, T 20S, R 19E, purchased from Daniel Harman on Oct 2, 1858, for $100 The W½ SE¼ and NE¼ of SE¼, sec 5, T 20S, R 19E, 120 acres, was obtained with military land warrant no 55479 The remaining 40 acres of the same quarter-section was obtained with pre-emption certificate 1377, both patented Dec 20, 1863 The other 40 acres, SW¼ of SW¼, sec 4, T 20S, R 19E, was obtained from brother Alfred Capper on Nov 10, 1862 W F Osbourn purchased the entire 240 acres for $1,200 on June 1, 1868, and it later was a part of the Mongo Young farm

8 Letter from Herbert Capper to George Mitcheson, Oct 11, 1861

9 *Ibid*

10 Letter from Herbert Capper to George Mitcheson, Nov 27, 1854

11 Letter from Herbert Capper to George Mitcheson, April 10, no year

12 Letter from Herbert Capper to George Mitcheson, April 15, 1862

13 Letter from Herbert Capper to George Mitcheson, Oct 11, 1861

14 Letter from Herbert Capper to George Mitcheson, Dec 25, 1861

15 Garnett *Republican-Plaindealer,* April 2, 1897

16 Letter from Herbert Capper to George Mitcheson, Oct 11, 1862

17 Letters from Herbert Capper to George Mitcheson, Oct 11, 1861, and Nov 18, 1862

18 William S Mitchell, *Linn County, Kansas A History,* 353-4

19 Typed material in the Capper file, n d

20 *Ibid*, Mitchell (see note 18) Simon B McGrew was a giant of a man, six feet three and one-half inches tall, and possessed great physical strength He did surveying work with John Brown and bought Brown's surveying compass when Brown left Kansas

21 Typed material in the Capper file, n d

22 The federal land office was returned from Mapleton to Humboldt the previous year

23 Letter from Herbert Capper to George Mitcheson, Nov 18, 1862

24 Signed document, issued June 8, 1914, by Office of Kansas State Militia

25 Garnett *Journal,* Dec 20, 1884

26 Records of the Register of Deeds, Anderson County, Garnett

II

1 Notes in Arthur Capper file, n d

2 Copy of letter from Arthur Capper to Betty Ann Archer, Jan 26, 1942

3 Letter from Isabella Capper to Arthur Capper, Feb 13, *c* 1885

4 *Household,* Jan , 1925

5 Copy of letter from Arthur Capper to Garland R Farmer, July 5, 1939

6 Letter from Simon B McGrew to Arthur Capper, Feb 2, 1876 The McGrews had lived in Iowa a dozen years by 1876 and family visits were rare

7 Harry Johnson, *A History of Anderson County, Kansas*, 14, 179 L F Busenbark had opened Garnett's first stove and tin shop at the northeast corner of Seventh and Pine in 1860

8 Deed records for Anderson County Capper paid $3 per acre for the school land This was the legal minimum and the usual price at which the common school lands of Kansas were sold

9 Manuscript federal census returns for Anderson County, Kansas, 1870 The proportion of property, not real estate, increased greatly over the census figures of five years earlier

10 Henrietta Elma Mann, "A Brief Historical Sketch of the Settlements of Elk County," Master's thesis, Kansas State College of Pittsburg, 1940, 52-6

11 "Corporation Charters," II 530, and A 4, Archives, Kansas State Historical Library The chartered company's name change was made Aug 3 and filed Aug 6, 1872

12 Garnett *Plaindealer*, Sept 16, 1870 The letter carried a date of four days earlier The first issue of the *Howard County Ledger*, Feb 23, 1871, indicated that "Mr Kirby built a store house, now occupied by H Capper, with tin and hardware "

13 *Howard County Ledger* (Longton, Kansas), Feb 23, 1871

14 Copy of letter from Arthur Capper to Mary Anderson, July 2, 1948

15 Address by Arthur Capper at Tom Thompson dinner, Oct 17, 1931, at Howard, Kansas

16 Receipt in Capper file The subscription cost $60 and the Cappers received a sewing machine in addition to the newspaper

17 Copy of letter from Herbert Capper to Horace Greeley, "18th 9th Mo 1871," and reply from Greeley

18 Notes in Capper file

19 Mary Audrey Neeland, "History of Elk County, Kansas," Master's thesis, Wichita University, 1933, 23 In 1875 Elk and Chautauqua counties were organized from Howard County

20 Copy of letter from Arthur Capper to J Howard Rusco, July 27, 1946 This was before the days of William Rockhill Nelson

21 *American Young Folks* (Topeka, Kansas), July, 1878, 107

22 Topeka *State Journal*, June 28, 1924, as reported in Byron M Crowley, "The Public Career of Arthur Capper Prior to his Senatorial Service," Master's thesis, Kansas State College of Pittsburg, 1938, 2

23 William E Connelley, *Kansas and Kansans*, IV, 1973, Crowley, 2

24 *Arthur Capper's Candidacy for Governor*, Capper for Governor Club, 1914, as reprinted from Garnett *Review*

25 *American Young Folks* was a monthly periodical, sometimes described as an auxiliary young people's publication of the Topeka *Daily Capital* "Aunt Mary" was Mrs J K Hudson The Boonville *Weekly Advertiser*, Nov 3, 1911, reported that when Capper was employed at the *Journal* he "succeeded in getting dismissed the first day" because he "pied the form" but he got his job back because there was no other "boy in the village who would take it "

26 A journal kept by Arthur Capper, Nov 23, 1891, indicates an acquaintance with the Jamesburg, New Jersey, area nine years earlier

27 Copy of letter from Emma W Middleton to Brook Haines, Jan 13, 1944

28 Copy of a letter from Arthur Capper to Mrs Elizabeth D York, Nov 17, 1938 The manuscript census taken by the State of Kansas on March 1, 1885, shows that the entire Capper family had come from New Jersey to Kansas, and that all of the children were born in Kansas

29 Garnett *Journal*, Dec 6 and 20, 1884

30 *Ibid*, April 12, 1884, letter from Isabella Capper to Arthur Capper, Feb 13, c 1885

31 *Republican-Plaindealer* (Garnett, Kansas), April 2, 1897
32 The St Louis, Kansas and Arizona was later part of the Missouri Pacific system The Leavenworth, Lawrence and Galveston railroad had arrived in Garnett in March, 1870, and had built on south This road later became a part of the Santa Fe system
33 "Anderson County, Deed Record," XXX 450 This transaction, costing $5,000, gave Capper half interest with L K Kirk, in two areas at the corner of Oak and Fifth, a main intersection in downtown Garnett
34 *Anderson County Republican,* Aug 31, 1883
35 Harry Johnson, *A History of Anderson County, Kansas,* 61
36 Frank W Blackmar, *Kansas A Cyclopedia of State History,* III, part I, 65 Garnett school records for this period no longer exist
37 Garnett *Journal,* April 5, 1884
38 *Ibid ,* Nov 1, 1884
39 The other graduates were Ethel V Hearst, Anna Williams, Debbie J Douthett, Emma E Vaughan, Annettie A Paxton, Madora A Everline, Esmah Woodcock, and Stella Haughey This group comprised Garnett's third class of high-school graduates
40 *Republican-Plaindealer,* June 6, 1884
41 Notes in the Capper file
42 Notes in the Capper file
43 Garnett *Journal,* June 7, 1884
44 Zula Bennington Green, "As Peggy of the Flint Hills Sees It," Topeka *Daily Capital,* July 14, 1944, Boonville (Missouri) *Weekly Advertiser,* Nov 3, 1911, interview with F D Farrell, July 10, 1951, and June 11, 1952 At least three times Capper told Dr Farrell, the former president of Kansas State University, the story of his settling in Topeka
45 Topeka *Daily Capital,* Feb 28, 1909, and July 16, 1939, *Capper's Weekly,* Dec 29, 1951, interview with F D Farrell, July 10, 1951
46 *Anderson County Republican,* June 13, 1884, Garnett *Journal,* June 14, 1884, *Republican-Plaindealer,* June 13, 1884

III

1 The dailies were the *Capital, State Journal, Commonwealth,* and the *Critic* The latter was published from March 5 to June 23 The weeklies were the *Kansas Weekly Capital, North Topeka Mail, Weekly State Journal, Commonwealth, Saturday Evening Lance, Tribune-Recorder, Times,* and a German language weekly, the *Kansas Telegraph*
2 *History of Typographical Union, #121* He may have been an apprentice member of the union, but the *Capital* did not have a union shop until 1886 Capper did pay dues to the Knights of Labor on Oct 4, 1886, and perhaps at other times
3 William G Clugston, *Rascals in Democracy,* 227 "Jointists" was a Kansas term for keepers of liquor joints or saloons Martin, a Democrat, was successful in spite of overwhelming Republican strength
4 Topeka *Daily Capital,* Oct 9, 12, and 22, 1884 In 1884 the *Capital* was spoken of as an organ of the Kansas State Temperance Union
5 Capper was most fortunate in the move because of the linotype developments of the late 1880's which would greatly change the printing trade Notes in the Capper file and in Clugston, 223, report that there was a $15 difference in weekly pay, a situation hardly likely considering the going wage for printers in 1884-85
6 Garnett *Journal,* and *Republican-Plaindealer,* also located in Garnett, for late Nov and Dec , 1884 According to the *Journal,* Herbert Capper stood for "righteousness of personal rights and personal opinions as expressed by every American citizen," while his opponent supported the idea that "all principle is incorporated in *party*"
7 Topeka *Daily Capital,* June 9, 1885
8 *Ibid ,* Feb 28, 1909
9 *Jewell County Record* (Mankato, Kansas), Dec 27, 1951

10 Clugston, 230

11 Capper Diary, Jan 10, 1886, to Dec, 1887

12 Abstract records at Columbian Title and Trust Company, Topeka, Kansas One example of a Capper real-estate activity was the purchase of two lots on Jackson Street for $7,500 on March 11, 1886, and the sale of this property a month later for $7,700 However, the mortgage on the property, assumed by Capper, was not released until 13½ years later

13 *Republican-Plaindealer,* April 1, 1887 The report, made by E A Edwards, indicated that former Garnett residents, Dr W S Lindsay, Arthur Capper, and Harry Sparks, had gained by the speculation

14 The *Capital* began a Monday morning edition when all the "big" battles of the war seemingly were fought on Sunday, but even later there were no regular Monday editions for many years

15 One of them, according to a diary entry, was a copy of Eugene F Ware's poems

16 Capper Diary, July 11, 1886, and Jan 21, 1887

17 The reporters who were pictured with Capper were "McCabe, Wright, Colver, McIntosh, Thornton, Holliday, Clark, Ewing " See Capper Diary, Sept 23, 1886, Oct 3, 1886, and Jan 4, 1887

18 Capper Diary, Feb 3, 1886

19 *Ibid,* July 5, 1886

20 Topeka *Daily Capital,* July 22, 1886, *ibid,* July 31, 1927 Capper had forgotten his activities on his twenty-first birthday when asked some forty years later

21 *Ibid,* July 29, 1886 Volume I, number 1, of the *Little Sand-Pounder,* "devoted to the science of pounding sand in a rat hole," made its appearance at Abilene on Aug 14, 1886

22 Topeka *Daily Capital,* Oct 26 and 27, 1886

23 Garnett *Journal,* Sept 3, 1887

24 Capper Diary, May 20 and Nov 29, 1886

25 Lawrence *Daily Journal,* Aug 30, 1887, Garnett *Journal,* Sept 3, 1887

26 Capper Diary, a letter from T W Johnston, Jr, to Arthur Capper, June 26, 1889, complimented Capper on the general merit of his work as the representative of the *Star* in Topeka Capper had resigned in a previous letter to Johnston

27 Capper Diary Capper's income shows $45 for Nov, 1887, from these outside sources

28 Baker, sometimes identified as the "Horace Greeley of Kansas," came to Kansas in 1860 and in 1863 to Topeka, where he purchased part ownership in the *Kansas State Record* When the *Record* consolidated with the *Commonwealth* in 1871, he sold out and went to Texas, only to return in 1875, when he became editor and proprietor of the *Commonwealth,* a position held until consolidation in 1888 with the *Capital*

29 Capper Diary

30 *Ibid,* Sept 25 and Oct 2, 1886

31 Capper Diary, *Republican-Plaindealer,* Sept 3, 1886

32 Charles C Howes, *This Place Called Kansas,* 55-65

33 C C Isely, "Senator Capper Once Almost Became Hugoton Editor," Wichita *Eagle,* March 2, 1945 Isely's article was based on Capper's reminiscence to Isely and other citizens of Wichita Capper usually said he took a "bus" from Hartland to Hugoton Another version of Capper's first trip to southwest Kansas is found in the Oct 28, 1911, issue of the Topeka *State Journal*

34 *Hugo Herald* (Hugoton, Kansas), March 16, 1887

35 Isely, cited in note 33 This story reminds one of the descriptive painting of the Montana frontier by Charles Russell, "In without Knocking"

36 Hugoton *Hermes,* Aug 12, 1887 Charles M Davis was the editor and publisher

37 Byron Monroe Crowley, 7

38 *Ibid* Jay E House was the reporter

39 Stock certificates held in the vault of the Capper Building Attached to the last ten shares of this stock, all from J K Hudson, was a promissory note for $3,000

"payable in one year from July 2nd 1890 bearing 8 per cent interest " "Corporation Charters, Secretary of State, State of Kansas," XL, 229, located in the Archives of Kansas State Historical Society Capper was one of six directors in a charter filed June 6, 1890

40 Additional shares held in the vault in the Capper Building

41 Letter from John J Ingalls to Arthur Capper, July 24, 1890 Joseph L Bristow was treasurer of the Kansas Republican League about the same time Capper served as secretary

42 Letter from Benjamin Harrison to Arthur Capper, Feb 16, 1887 Harrison was the successful Republican candidate for President in 1888

43 Copy of letter from Arthur Capper to Dr George Major, June 26, 1948

44 Reminiscence of Bob Maxwell, March 28, 1949, in Capper file

IV

1 For example, Victor Murdock left Wichita for the Chicago *Inter-Ocean* in June, 1892, and returned a year and a half later to become managing editor of the Wichita *Eagle*

2 Topeka *Capital* as reported in the Garnett *Eagle*, June 26, 1891 The Garnett *Journal* on July 3, 1891, printed a similar story

3 Journal kept by Arthur Capper, June 19, 1891 See Homer E Socolofsky, "A Kansas Romance of the Gay Nineties," *Midwest Quarterly*, III 1 (autumn, 1961), 81-93

4 Garnett *Journal*, June 12, 1891

5 Journal kept by Arthur Capper, June 20, 1891 Capper's parents returned to Garnett by late June or early July, according to the Garnett *Journal*, July 3, 1891

6 *Ibid*

7 *Ibid*, June 22 and 25, 1891

8 *Republican-Plaindealer* (Garnett, Kansas), July 10, 1891 This article also contained a clipping attributed to the *Journalist* of New York, telling of Capper's trip to the East

9 Talmage's tabernacle was closed on Capper's first trip to Brooklyn Journal kept by Arthur Capper, June 28, 1891 A letter from M W Hudson, wife of Major J K Hudson, to Capper on July 15, 1891, reported from Mrs Crawford that they hear that Capper was "feeling a little more at home recently "

10 Journal kept by Arthur Capper, June 27 to July 10, 1891 Newspaper offices visited included the *Sun*, the *Mail and Express*, the *Tribune*, the *Wall Street Journal*, the *Journalist*, the *Irish World*, and the *Tablet*

11 Letter from M W Hudson to Capper, Aug 3, 1891

12 Journal kept by Florence Crawford, June 19 to July 11, 1891

13 *Ibid*, July 15, 1891

14 *Ibid*, July 6, for example, and Oct 16, 1891

15 *Ibid*, July 12, 1891

16 *Ibid*, July 18, 1891

17 *Ibid*

18 Journal kept by Arthur Capper, July 10, 1891

19 *Ibid*, July 18, 1891

20 Journal kept by Florence Crawford, Aug 8, 1891

21 Journal kept by Arthur Capper, Aug 8, 1891

22 Journal kept by Florence Crawford, Aug 10 through Aug 26, 1891

23 Journal kept by Arthur Capper, Aug 11 to Sept 9, 1891

24 *Ibid*, Sept 12, 1891

25 Journal kept by Florence Crawford, Sept 13, 1891

26 Journal kept by Arthur Capper, Sept 20, 1891

27 Journal kept by Florence Crawford, Sept 14 and 15, 1891

28 *Ibid*, Sept 20, 1891

29 Journal kept by Arthur Capper, Sept 21 to Nov 21, 1891

30 *Ibid*, Nov 26, 1891

31 *Ibid*, Nov 27 through Dec 4, 1891 While in Boston Capper spent a day with Professor Marsh at Harvard and attended services at the South Congregational Church, where he heard Edward Everett Hale

32 Topeka *Daily Capital*, Dec 5, 1891 Five of the seven Kansas Congressmen and one Senator in that session were Alliance men

33 Topeka *Daily Capital*, Jan 29, 1892

34 Journal kept by Arthur Capper, Dec 1, 1891

35 *Ibid*, Dec 7, 1891

36 *Ibid*, Dec 9, 1891

37 *Ibid*, Dec 17, 1891 Senator Plumb, former Kansas newspaperman, was Capper's main source of news

38 *Ibid*, Dec 19, 1891

39 *Ibid*, Dec 20, 1891 He recorded that "Dick Lindsay was at the other end of the line" Topeka *Daily Capital*, Dec 20, 1891 The story of Plumb's death covered the entire first page of the *Capital* Capper, according to his 1886 diary, had interviewed Senator Plumb as early as Nov 19, 1886

40 Journal kept by Arthur Capper, Dec 22, 1891

41 *Ibid*, Dec 28, 1891, and Jan 2, 1892

42 *Ibid*, Jan 1, 1892

43 Journal kept by Florence Crawford, Jan 13, 1892

44 *Ibid*, Jan 14, 1892

45 *Ibid*, Feb 19, 1892

46 Journal kept by Arthur Capper, Jan 31 through Feb 19, 1892

47 *Ibid*, Feb 23, 1892

48 Topeka *Daily Capital*, Feb 14, 1892

49 *Ibid*, Feb 14 and 19, 1892 The Fort Scott *Monitor* in acknowledging their use of the *Capital* specials reported "Capper is evidently on to things in Washington in great shape and gets there like Eli"

50 Journal kept by Arthur Capper, Feb 26, 1892

51 *Ibid*

52 *Ibid*

53 Topeka *Daily Capital*, April 19, 1892, for example

54 *Ibid*, April 3, 1892

55 *Ibid*

56 *Ibid*

57 *Ibid*, April 8, 1892

58 *Ibid*

59 *Ibid*, May 15, 1892

60 Edwin H Funston, incumbent Second District Congressman, was seated when Congress convened, but his election was investigated and he resigned Aug 2, 1894, to be replaced by a Populist

61 Topeka *Daily Capital*, May 1, 4, and 8, 1892 See also the Kansas City *Star*, May 5, 1892, and the Topeka *State Journal*, May 5, 1892

62 Kansas City *Star*, May 4, 1892

63 Kansas City *Star*, May 7, 1892

64 *The Lance* (Topeka, Kansas), Dec 3, 1892 Capper wrote "The Passing of Stover and Hovey," in *Agora*, July, 1892 It was a justification, citing established precedent, for the failure of the Republican State Convention to renominate State Treasurer Stover and State Auditor Hovey

65 The Crawford residence, located at the northwest corner of Fifth and Harrison, is now occupied by the Jewish congregation of Beth Sholom

66 *The Lance* (Topeka, Kansas), Dec 3, 1892

67 Topeka *State Journal*, Dec 2, 1892 Wedding presents ranged from a "handsome Hambletonian riding horse" and "Fifty dollars in gold" from Governor Crawford, to pictures, lamps, silver, cut glass, and clocks

68 Notebook kept by Florence Crawford Capper of her marriage to Arthur Capper
It contained an invitation to the wedding, a list of guests and of the wedding presents
and of the guests at the reception held after the honeymoon

69 *The Annals of Kansas,* I, 148 Taken from the Kansas City *Star*

70 *Ibid ,* 158 The Bank Commissioner used these figures, however, to justify the
ability of the banks to weather "the storm so well "

71 Capper speech at E H Crosby dinner, *c* 1930

72 A photostat of the three-page contract in Capper's handwriting on the Topeka
Mail stationery is in the Capper file Payment of $200 sealed the bargain, and $1,600
was to be paid at the time of transfer of the property An additional $500 was to be
paid in ninety days, and advertising and job work, to the value of $200, was due the
seller

73 Capper speech at E H Crosby dinner

74 The Topeka *Mail,* Sept 22, 1893 Capper later reported the *Mail* had about
1,000 subscribers when he took over See the Topeka *Mail and Breeze,* May 22, 1896

75 Interview with Marco Morrow, June 16, 1952 Capper always expressed such
sentiments with pride

76 Topeka *Daily Capital,* Aug 25, 1929

V

1 Lester F Kimmel, "Kansas Newspapers—Twentieth Century" in John D
Bright, ed , *Kansas, The First Century,* II, 381

2 Nyle H Miller, "Kansas Newspapers to 1900," in John D Bright, *ibid ,* I, 531
This total is supposedly greater than that found in any other state

3 Frank Luther Mott, *American Journalism,* revised edition, New York, 1950, 275

4 Topeka *Mail,* Sept 29, 1893

5 *Ibid*

6 Capper speech at E H Crosby dinner

7 Topeka *Mail,* Oct 6, 1893

8 *Ibid ,* Oct 13, 1893, and Jan 5, 1894

9 Elizabeth N Barr, "The Populist Uprising," in William E Connelley, *Kansas
and Kansans,* II, 1117

10 Topeka *Mail,* Dec 28, 1894

11 J L King, "Arthur Capper,' *Kansas Newspaper World,* July, 1894

12 Interview with Marco Morrow, Aug 1, 1952

13 Interview with F D Farrell, July 10, 1951

14 Copy of letter to William Allen White from Arthur Capper, Sept 3, 1941
Capper told White that he had paid $500 to Harry Frost for the *Saturday Lance*

15 Clipping from the *Brown County World,* n d , in Biographical Scrapbook C,
Vol I, Kansas State Historical Library The consolidation was made Sept 5, 1895
McNeal was generally considered unaggressive in gaining advertising support

16 Topeka *Mail,* Sept 6, 1895

17 Topeka *Mail* and *Kansas Breeze,* Nov 29, 1895

18 *Capper's Weekly,* Aug 15, 1942, from a radio address of Arthur Capper over
WIBW, Aug , 1942

19 Topeka *Mail* and *Kansas Breeze,* Sept 13, 1895

20 Interview with T A McNeal, March 26, 1938, in Byron M Crowley, "The
Public Career of Arthur Capper Prior to His Senatorial Service," Master's thesis,
Kansas State College of Pittsburg, Pittsburg, Kansas, 1938, 8

21 Interview with Marco Morrow, June 16, 1952

22 Topeka *Mail* and *Kansas Breeze,* Oct 11, 1895, and Jan 3, 1896 The guest
editors were such persons as General A L Williams, Eugene F Ware, and Captain
Joseph G Waters The use of the Rev Charles M Sheldon, as an editor for a few
issues, anticipated his famous week on the *Capital* by almost five years

23 This issue celebrated the 25th birthday anniversary of the founding of the North Topeka *Times,* a predecessor of the *Mail*

24 Topeka *Daily Capital,* Aug 25, 1929

25 Topeka *Mail* and *Kansas Breeze,* May 22, 1896 The linotype, a Mergenthaler Duplex Typesetting machine, reputedly was the first to be used for a weekly journal "in the great region west of the Missouri river "

26 *Ibid,* copy of letter from John J Ingalls to Arthur Capper, Jan 19, 1900 During the Curtis campaign of 1900, John J Ingalls wrote Capper that the Atchison *Globe* would provide Curtis with "good notices next to reading matter at reasonable advertising rates," but it "wouldn't do to send an office boy, nor take Marshall's band along "

27 Biographical Scrapbook, C, Vol I, Kansas State Historical Library, clipping from Kansas City *Journal,* Aug, 1896, and *Brown County World,* c 1898 Since Capper was secretary of the Kansas Day Club from 1893 to 1897 and was president in 1898, he was well known in legislative circles

28 Topeka *State Journal,* Dec 18, 1902

29 Kansans first voted for their State Printer in the general election in 1906 Jay E House in the Dec 17, 1922, Philadelphia *Public Ledger* told of Capper's two political reverses when trying for the State Printer position In attacking the "appointive" State Printer Capper indicated that the "take" of the office was $25,000 per year

30 Clipping dated Aug 22, 1896, with no indicated source in Biographical Scrapbook, C, Vol I, Kansas State Historical Library

31 Clif Stratton, "Famous Kansas Artist Coming Home for Visit in October to be Honored by Press Club," Topeka *Daily Capital,* Sept 25, 1949

32 *Ibid,* Kansas Magazine, Aug, 1911, 22

33 Topeka *Daily Capital,* July 16, 1939 This was apparently Capper's way of providing extra income for his immediate relatives Perhaps his closest relatives were given this opportunity of extra income so that he would feel no obligation of sharing his ownership of the publishing enterprise It was not his general practice to bring relatives of administrative personnel into the business

34 Topeka *Mail and Breeze,* Aug 3, and Oct 26, 1900, *Kings and Queens of the Range,* June 15, 1899, declared that Capper was one of the "brightest young journalists in the State of Kansas" with the "largest circulation of any newspaper in the Sunflower State "

35 Topeka *Mail and Breeze,* Aug 3, 1900

36 Copy of letter to William Allen White from Arthur Capper, Sept 3, 1941

37 Kansas State Historical Society, *History of Kansas Newspapers,* Kansas State Printing Plant, Topeka, 1916, 143, 291 The *Missouri Valley Farmer* began publication Jan 4, 1893, was moved to Kansas City, Missouri, in 1898 and from there went to Capper in Topeka Much of its early life before 1900 was as an agricultural weekly, Stephen Conrad Stuntz, compiler, and Emara B Hawks, editor, "List of the Agricultural periodicals of the United States and Canada published during the Century July 1810 to July 1910," Misc Publication, No 398, United States Department of Agriculture, Government Printing Office, Washington, 1910, 104 This citation lists 1892 as the date of the establishment of the *Missouri Valley Farmer,* whereas page 8 of *Missouri Valley Farmer,* Aug, 1910, as well as many other issues, stated "est 1891 " Capper employees had the general impression that the *Missouri Valley Farmer* was in run-down condition at the time of the sale

38 A study of farm papers of this period shows use of similar types of advertisements

39 There appears to be no reason for the delay in putting the Capper name on the masthead of the magazine

40 Topeka *Mail and Kansas Breeze,* Nov 15, 1895, "First Things," MS in Capper file The time when J R Mulvane took over operations of the *Capital* is listed here as Nov 9, 1895 This change, for a brief time, severed Capper's direct contact with the *Capital,* since he no longer was on the board of directors

41 Topeka *Daily Capital,* Feb 28, 1909 The new directors were Fred O Popenoe, Chas L Holman, Dell Keizer, Harold T Chase, Richard L Thomas, and Col A S Johnson J K Hudson was again listed as editor Keizer was his son-in-law

42 *Ibid ,* May 13 to 19, 1900

43 These contracts, dated March 23 and May 10, 1901, for the purchase of the *Capital* were in the vault of Capper Publications, Inc , for many years, interview with Rod Runyan, then Assistant to the President, Capper Publications, Inc , April 7, 1953 Chase, as editor, Thomas as business manager and bookkeeper, and Robey, on the staff in the circulation department, were all employees of the *Capital* Since each purchase of a newspaper or a journal was an individual matter, this procedure set no precedent for future Capper purchases of newspapers

44 "First Things", notes in the Capper file indicate that Capper bought R L Thomas' 75 shares on Aug 10, 1904, and on Dec 30, 1904, he purchased the 125 shares owned by Chase and the 48 shares owned by Robey

45 *Push,* Sept , 1902 Place of publication was at 501-5 Jackson Street, Topeka, which was the office of the *Mail and Breeze* Transfer of ownership probably came with Volume I, number 8 (April, 1903), the first issue which did not have a Reid cartoon on the cover and a named editor on the masthead Presumably little money changed hands with the transfer, as Capper was responsible for future subscriptions, interview with Marco Morrow, June 16, 1952 Morrow, not then on Capper's staff, had published a *Push* at Springfield, Ohio, in 1895, apparently known to Capper, since he had advertised in it

46 Interview with Marco Morrow, June 16, 1952

47 *Household* carried the volume number and issue number of the preceding journal

48 Copy of letter from Edwin C Madden, Third Assistant Postmaster General, to Postmaster, Topeka, March 17, 1904

49 See *Missouri Valley Farmer,* Aug , 1900, and subsequent issues Here again there appears no reason for the delay in acknowledging the position of the publisher on the masthead

50 Interview with Marco Morrow, Aug 1, 1952

51 For example, the Topeka *Mail and Kansas Breeze,* Sept 5, 1902

52 Interview with Marco Morrow, Aug 1, 1952 Morrow, who was in the agricultural advertising business in 1905, did not hear of the change in the *Mail and Breeze* until he went to Salina, Kansas, on a business trip, letter from N M Sheffield, special advertising, to Arthur Capper, Nov 27, 1905 Sheffield's agency had served as Capper's Chicago agent until late 1905 The six months' notice by Capper to sever relations was not well received Subsequent bills issued by Sheffield caused Capper to write "Convinces me more strongly than ever that only way is to handle business ourselves "

VI

1 Another combination, The Orange Judd Weeklies, included *American Agriculturist, New England Homestead,* and *Orange Judd Farmer,* and later *Northwest Farmstead* and *Southern Farming* were added

2 *Farmers' Advocate* was operated for a few years by men who had worked for Capper

3 Interviews with Marco Morrow, Nov 28, 1952, and April 7, 1953

4 *Ibid ,* Nov 28, 1952

5 *Agricultural Advertising,* April, 1906, 379, other publications used in this campaign included *Profitable Advertising, National Printer-Journalist, Advertisers Magazine, The Western Monthly,* and *Judicious Advertising and Advertising Experience*

6 *Printers' Ink,* June 10, 1908, front cover

7 Denison (Texas) *Herald,* Jan 11, 1909

8 Initial contacts to fill these positions were made in Chicago when Capper served as a delegate to the Republican National Convention "First Things" says Morrow began his work with Capper on Aug 16, 1908

9 *Poultry Culture*, May, 1909, interviews with Marco Morrow, Nov 28, 1952, and April 7, 1953

10 Interviews with Marco Morrow, Nov 28, 1952, and April 7, 1953

11 *Annals of Kansas*, I, 457

12 Topeka *Daily Capital*, Feb 28, 1909

13 Copy of letter to J H Slavely from Arthur Capper, Feb 23, 1911

14 Capper employees elsewhere brought the total to more than 500

15 Notes in Capper's handwriting, on the occasion of opening the new building

16 Topeka *Daily Capital*, Feb 28, 1909 This edition with 136 pages in nine sections had the most pages per copy of any issue of the *Capital* to that time The total paper requirement for this issue was about twenty-one tons

17 Interview with Marco Morrow, Aug 1, 1952

18 Interview with Marco Morrow, April 7, 1953, copy of letter from Arthur Capper to William Allen White, Sept 3, 1941

19 Winifred Gregory, ed , *Union List of Serials*, 2nd edition, 2246, 2848 Publications such as the *Helpful Hen* and *Western Poultry Review* had been absorbed by *Poultry Culture* Initially this journal was the official magazine of the Kansas State Poultry Association

20 "First Things", interview with Leland Schenck, April 7, 1953 Victor O Hobbs of Trenton, Missouri, bought only the subscription list and the name, *Poultry Culture*, and moved it to Kansas City, Missouri

21 Letter from W T Laing to Arthur Capper, July 15, 1908

22 Copy of letter from Arthur Capper to N A Strohm, Aug 3, 1909

23 N W Ayer and Sons, *Directory of Newspapers and Periodicals, 1911*, 552, *Capper Bulletin*, Feb , 1917 The 1916 yearbook of the Nebraska State Board of Agriculture gave the *Farm Journal* indirect recognition by using its articles for twenty-two of fifty pages reprinted from four Nebraska farm papers

24 See *Nebraska Farmer*, June issues of 1924 and earlier, *The Twentieth Century Farmer*, published by the Omaha *Bee*, suspended operations in 1918, interview with Marco Morrow, April 7, 1953 Competition in Nebraska was regarded as healthy and this promotion policy as shrewd and legitimate even by members of Capper Publications

25 Letter from W E Hurlbut to Col Ed R Dorsey, June 4, 1910

26 The initial price placed on the *Ruralist* was $10,000, which included accrued advertising accounts The earliest letter of congratulations in Capper's first issue was dated June 23, 1910, from President H J Waters, of Kansas State Agricultural College, and former dean of the College of Agriculture, University of Missouri

27 *Missouri Ruralist*, Sept 17, 1910

28 No information was published in various newspaper directories about the circulation of *Breeder's Special*, which was presumably small Nor is there available information on the cost of this paper to Capper T W Morse, one of the owners of *Breeder's Special*, was the new editor

29 The contract and bill of sale transferring *Oklahoma Farmer* to M L Crowther and accepted by Arthur Capper was in the vault at the Capper Building

30 *Oklahoma Farmer*, May 1, 1912 Sale price of the *State Farmer* is not known

31 *Oklahoma Farmer*, Nov 23, 1915, letter from C E Carpenter to Arthur Capper, Dec 8, 1915, in the vault at the Capper Building for many years Capper paid for "equipment, etc purchased in connection with the Oklahoma Farm Journal " Hence the price of $24,000

32 *Oklahoma Farmer*, Nov 23, 1915

33 Letter from Charles W Bryan to Arthur Capper, Oct 26, 1915 The contract allowed Bryan to provide subscribers with the *Missouri Valley Farmer* and keep the money collected at 12½ cents per subscription until the total amount was reached

34 Advertising was the major source of income on farm papers, and Capper had reason to believe that subscription departments never made money on the first subscription

35 According to a letter from J E Griest to W W Rhodes, Nov 18, 1915, *American Homestead* subscribers were given a choice of either *Missouri Valley Farmer* or *Nebraska Farm Journal* to complete their subscriptions

36 *Capper's Weekly,* Sept 6, 1913 Capper associates had the opinion that Capper was not responsible for the name change, although he agreed to it

VII

1 "Copeland County" referred to the Copeland Hotel, located near the Capitol, where railroad lobbyists maintained large suites of rooms while the legislature was in session

2 Copy of letter from Arthur Capper to J H Slavely, Feb 23, 1911

3 Interview with Marco Morrow, June 16, 1952

4 Letter from H C Sticher to Arthur Capper, Sept 28, 1906 Sticher was writing because of an article in the Manhattan *Republic* which told of the offer made to Capper On April 4, 1910, J R Mulvane of the Bank of Topeka wrote Capper, "We must insist on your cutting your old Capital note down " From such contacts Capper became more suspicious of outside influences

5 Interview with Marco Morrow, April 7, 1953

6 See letter from Frederick Funston to Arthur Capper, Nov 3, 1910

7 Interview with Rod Runyan, June 18, 1952

8 Interview with Marco Morrow, June 17, 1953

9 These developments were the sensational exposure by muckrakers of evil advertising in national magazines, the publication in 1911 of the model statute by *Printers' Ink,* the postal act of Aug 24, 1912, requiring labeling of advertising, and the formation of the Audit Bureau of Circulations in 1913

10 Scrapbook, "Progressive Party Clippings and Pamphlets," Kansas State Historical Library, pp 15-16, clipping from Kansas City *Journal,* n d , c 1912 It is interesting to note that Allen served as governor of Kansas during the two terms immediately following Capper's four years and that he occupied the Capper house rather than the state-supplied Governor's Mansion

11 The *Evening* (Ottawa, Kansas) *Herald,* Oct 10, 1905 Long after Allen and Capper were close political associates this editorial was used in attacks on Capper's reputation

12 Wichita *Beacon,* Oct 2, 1912, according to Marco Morrow (interview, Nov 5, 1953) Capper and Allen were ordinarily good friends, but in 1914 were opposition candidates for Governor

13 Letter from D R Anthony, Jr, to Arthur Capper, Aug 30, 1909

14 J R Burton, "who was going to do terrible things if the Capital was not run just as he wanted it," had written Capper his most insolent letter

15 Copy of letter from Arthur Capper to D R Anthony, Jr, Sept 1, 1909

16 Letter from D R Anthony, Jr, to Arthur Capper, Sept 4, 1909

17 "Republican Party Clippings," Vol 9, part II, in Kansas State Historical Library The writer was Albert T Reid in the Leavenworth *Post*

18 Interview with Marco Morrow, Nov 5, 1953

19 See Topeka *Daily Capital,* Jan 2, 1900, and later

20 Letter from E E Critchfield to Arthur Capper, Jan 11, 1907 International Harvester was the company canceling the advertising The farm editor, Henry Hatch, was the author of the condemned material He wrote that the Congressional investigations into the machinery trust would do little good because "sharp corporation lawyers could find technical points in a barrel of sauer kraut if they tried "

21 *Ibid*

22 MS "My Story about Arthur Capper," by John Francis Case
23 Interviews with Marco Morrow and Ray Yarnell, June 16, 1952
24 *The Capper House Book,* 7
25 Topeka *State Journal,* Dec 20, 1951
26 *Ibid ,* Topeka *Daily Capital,* Jan 5, 1936 From 1915 to 1919 House served as mayor of Topeka, after which he went to work in Philadelphia for the *Public Ledger* and the New York *Evening Post*
27 Copy of letter from Arthur Capper to S B Farwell, March 18, 1918 For more complete discussion see Homer E Socolofsky, "The Capper Farm Press," University Microfilms, 1954, Chapter IV
28 *Farmers' Mail and Breeze,* July 13, 1912 The same view was expressed at a dinner complimenting Harold T Chase on his many years of service to the *Capital*
29 *Industrialist,* April 10, 1909, from "Fourth Annual Reunion Bulletin of the Topeka Daily Capital Folks," Jan 1, 1909
30 Manuscript prepared by Clif Stratton, based on a Capper speech to employees, *c* 1943
31 *Ibid*
32 Letter from Joseph L Bristow to Arthur Capper, March 26, 1909
33 *Ibid ,* April 2, 1909
34 Topeka *State Journal,* March 4, 1909 The commission was signed on March 9 for the four-year term ending April 1, 1913
35 *Ibid ,* March 5 and 6, 1909
36 Letters from E H Madison to Arthur Capper, Dec 24, 1910, and from William Allen White to Arthur Capper, Jan 19, 1911
37 Letter from E H Madison to Arthur Capper, Dec 24, 1910
38 Copy of letter from Arthur Capper to Charles Curtis, May 13, 1909
39 Copy of letter from Arthur Capper to Will Beck, Feb 18, 1911
40 Detroit *Free Press,* June 22, 1919

VIII

1 Clugston, 238-9 Apparently Capper had written Joseph L Bristow in 1909 that he was no more fitted to be Secretary of Agriculture than to be a Methodist bishop, because Bristow replied on April 2, 1909, "I would really rather risk you as a member of the cabinet than as a Methodist bishop I wouldn't recommend you for a Methodist bishop, but I would be glad to exert all the influence I may be able to accumulate to get you in the cabinet "
2 Interview with Marco Morrow, April 7, 1953
3 Letter from William Allen White to Arthur Capper, April 19, 1911
4 Copy of letter from Arthur Capper to W T Beck, June 28, 1911
5 Letter from J L Bristow to Arthur Capper, July 5, 1911, letter from William Allen White to Arthur Capper, July 14, 1911
6 Letter from J L Bristow to Arthur Capper, July 5, 1911
7 *Ibid*
8 Letter from William Allen White to Arthur Capper, July 14, 1911
9 *Capper Bulletin,* Aug , 1911
10 *Saturday Evening Post,* Aug 12, 1911, 19, *Collier's,* July 8, 1911, 8
11 Topeka *State Journal,* May 4, 1911 Capper was designated as "A Harmony Candidate" in *Kansas Magazine,* Aug , 1911, 71-2
12 Roosevelt received 278 of the 350 delegates votes up for "grabs" in presidential primaries
13 Kansas City *Journal,* Feb 4, 1912
14 *Addresses and Messages by Arthur Capper,* Capper Printing Co , 301-2
15 Bright, *Kansas The First Century,* II, 45
16 Many newspaper clippings, sources identified in Biographical Scrapbook, C, Kansas State Historical Library

17 Since both Ryan and Capper were native-born Kansans, the Kansas City *Journal*, May 5, 1912, reported that "Republicans Will Name 'Native Son,'" for the first time in the state's history Stubbs gained the senatorial nomination because he carried the most districts, not because he got the most votes

18 Atchison *Globe*, April 11, 1914 Jay E House gave these descriptions

19 Copy of letter from Arthur Capper to J H Slavely, Feb 23, 1911

20 Topeka *State Journal*, Nov 1, 1912

21 Democratic campaign literature, 1912, in Kansas State Historical Library Henry J Allen's editorial, "A Human Vampire," was also in the political pamphlet

22 Topeka *Daily Capital*, Sept 27, 1912

23 *Farmers' Mail and Breeze*, July 20, and Oct 26, 1912 Whether Capper's losses because of this position were offset by new support from "T R" supporters is problematical In view of the Kansas political scene, it appears likely that his position cost him the election

24 See *Kansas Farmer*, Sept 21 to Nov 2, 1912

25 *Ibid*, Oct 26, 1912

26 Capper's circular "A Malicious Attack," was also mailed to all retail dealers in the state Available in the Kansas State Historical Library According to the Kansas City *Journal*, Oct 30, 1912, the Kansas City *Star*, "concluding that Capper is only nine-tenths Progressive, has come out for Hodges "

27 Circular, "Hodges Member of the Lumber Trust," Kansas State Historical Library

28 *Kansas Farmer*, Oct 19, and Nov 2, 1912 No Taft advertisements were carried in Capper's Kansas publications, although he did allow such advertising in *Missouri Ruralist* and in the *Nebraska Farm Journal*

29 Wichita *Eagle*, Nov 7 to 13, 1912 The election was on Nov 2, 1912

30 *Ibid*, Nov 15, 1912

31 General election ballot of Kansas, 1912

32 *Reports of Cases Argued and Determined in the Supreme Court of the State of Kansas*, LXXXVIII, 387

33 *Ibid*, 389

34 *Ibid*, 387-8

35 *Ibid*, 403-5

36 *Eighteenth Biennial Report of the Secretary of State of the State of Kansas, 1911-'12*, Topeka *Daily Capital*, Dec 1, 1912 Socialist candidate George W Kleihege received 24,760 votes, and 70 votes were cast for a scattering of candidates

37 *General Statutes of Kansas, 1909*, 716

38 Topeka *Daily Capital*, Dec 11, 1912

39 "Why I shall not enter a contest though undoubtedly elected governor, a statement to my friends," Topeka, Allied Printing, 1912

40 *Ibid*

41 Louis H Bean, *How to Predict Elections*, New York, 1948, 68 Bean maintained that Wilson would have received half the "T R" vote

42 Letter from D O McCray to Arthur Capper, Dec 27, 1912

43 One such letter from Eugene C Pulliam of the Atchison *Champion*, to Arthur Capper, Jan 9, 1913, indicates that Pulliam would handle the publicity for Capper and Anthony in the First Congressional District and that he would immediately receive $250 from both the Topeka *Daily Capital* and the Leavenworth *Times* If Atchison County was carried for both Capper and Anthony the amount would be doubled

44 "Gaddin' About," *Miami Republican* (Paola, Kansas), Dec 28, 1951

45 "Bull Moose Clippings," Vol I, Kansas State Historical Library, Topeka *Daily Capital*, Dec 5, 1912 In a letter to Capper on Dec 7, 1912, Joseph L Bristow told of planned club organizations to precede a new party organization However, his plan failed to materialize

46 Topeka *State Journal*, May 13, 1913, and Sept 18, 1914

47 *Ibid*, Sept 19, 1914

48 Topeka *State Journal*, Jan 8, 1914

49 Byron Monroe Crowley, "The Public Career of Arthur Capper Prior to his Senatorial Service," Kansas State College of Pittsburg, Master's thesis, 1938, 29

50 Topeka *State Journal*, Jan 21, 1914

51 *Capper's Weekly*, Feb 14, 1914 For more discussion on the change to *Capper's Weekly* see Homer E Socolofsky, "The Evolution of a Home Grown Product, Capper Publications," *Kansas Historical Quarterly*, XXIV (1958), 157

52 Topeka *State Journal*, Feb 25, 1914

53 *Nineteenth Biennial Report of the Secretary of State of Kansas, 1913-'14* Bristow narrowly went down in defeat as Curtis captured the Republican senatorial contest The Kansas City *Star*, Aug 9, 1914, held that "Kansas standpatters were in control again—only the old Copeland Hotel and the free pass missing"

54 Topeka *Daily Capital*, June 28, July 1 and 5, 1914 Topeka *State Journal*, Sept 19, 1914 Hodges explained that almost half of these "new" positions were local fire chiefs making fire reports for which they were paid small fees

55 *Addresses and Messages of Arthur Capper*, 319

56 Kansas Democratic campaign literature, 1914, Kansas State Historical Library

57 Interview with Marco Morrow, Nov 28, 1952

58 Topeka *State Journal*, July 8, 1914

59 Topeka *Daily Capital*, July 22, 1914

60 Hodges carried 19 counties in 1914 and 40 in 1912, Allen carried the two most populous counties and received a total vote of 84,000, while J B Billard, the independent who led in one county, and the Prohibition and Socialist candidates trailed the field

61 Extract from speeches used in 1916 campaign, found in small red notebook in Capper file

62 Walter Johnson, ed, *Selected Letters of William Allen White, 1899-1943*, 156

63 Atchison *Globe*, Nov 10, 1914

IX

1 Address of Arthur Capper to Harvey County Republicans' Banquet at Newton, Nov 20, 1914, in *Addresses and Messages by Arthur Capper Twenty-second Governor of Kansas*, Capper Printing Company, n d, 309-312

2 First Inaugural Address of Governor Capper, Jan 11, 1915

3 Interview with Marco Morrow, June 16, 1952

4 *Farmers' Mail and Breeze*, Nov 28, 1914

5 *Proceedings of the House of Representatives of the State of Kansas, 1915*, 483-4, *Proceedings of the Senate of the State of Kansas, 1915*, 387-8

6 *State of Kansas, Session Laws, 1915*, 21, 27, 46, 52, 53, 64-5

7 *State of Kansas, Session Laws, 1915*, Cecil Howes, "Arthur Capper," in Connelley, *Kansas and Kansans*, II, 865-7

8 *Farmers' Mail and Breeze*, Sept 11, 1915, from Labor Day speech at Columbus

9 *Ibid*, July 17, 1915

10 *Ibid*, Aug, 1915

11 Letter from E E Brewster to Arthur Capper, Jan 4, 1915 Even before his inauguration Capper had been advised of "awful conditions down there" Governor's file, 1915, Archives, Kansas State Historical Library

12 See page 129

13 *Annals of Kansas*, II, 127

14 Copy of letter by registered mail from Arthur Capper to Jeremiah D Botkin, Sept 16, 1915

15 *Annals of Kansas*, II, 127

16 *Miami Republican* (Paola, Kansas), Dec 28, 1951

17 Red notebook used by Arthur Capper in 1916 campaign

18 Capper file

19 Capper received an honorary degree of Doctor of Laws from Campbell College, June 2, 1915

20 Arthur Capper Diary and appointment schedule, 1915, Capper file

21 *Annals of Kansas,* II, 116 Four hundred Kansans served as delegates to this conference which urged disarmament, Edgar Langsdorf, "The World War I Period," in Bright, *Kansas The First Century,* 11, 51 Capper was elected president and Tom McNeal secretary of the organization created by the conference

22 *Farmers' Mail and Breeze,* July 3, 1915

23 Telegrams and letter from Henry Ford to Capper, Nov 24 and 27, 1915

24 Telegram from Louis P Lochner to Capper, Nov 29, 1915

25 Keith Sward, *The Legend of Henry Ford,* 88

26 Langsdorf, 52

27 Letter from Oswald Garrison Villard to Arthur Capper, Jan 31, 1916

28 *Addresses and Messages by Arthur Capper,* 7

29 Capper file

30 George P Morehouse, "Kansas as a State of Extremes in Its Attitude during the World War," *Kansas Historical Collections,* XV, 27

31 Speech by Arthur Capper at Axtell, July 20, 1916

32 Crowley, 33 The Kansas City newspapers used the bond-burning scene as a springboard to condemn the small appropriations made by the 1915 legislature

33 Red notebook used by Arthur Capper during 1916 campaign

34 The Democratic candidate in 1916 was W C Lansdon, and the Socialist and Prohibition parties also had candidates for governor Not until 1928 did a Kansas gubernatorial candidate receive more votes than Capper did in 1916 Capper had almost 80,000 more votes than did Hughes, the Republican candidate for President

35 *Addresses and Messages by Arthur Capper,* 213-23

36 New York *Times,* Feb 24, 1917

37 The Letter from Leo Nusbaum to Arthur Capper, Sept 28, 1917

38 "The Road Program of Kansas," a leaflet, n d , c 1918

39 Interview with Marco Morrow, Aug 1, 1952

40 "The Road Program of Kansas "

41 *Proceedings of the House of Representatives of the State of Kansas, 1917,* 645-6, 745, 862, 863-4

42 *Annals of Kansas,* II, 160

43 Letter from William H Taft to Arthur Capper, Jan 1, 1917

44 Pittsburg *Weekly Headlight,* Nov 10, 1916, in Jesse Paul Jewell, "The Senatorial Career of Arthur Capper from 1919 through 1946," Master's thesis, Kansas State College of Pittsburg, 1946, 12

45 New York *Times,* Jan 6, 1917

46 *Annals of Kansas,* II, 165

47 New York *Times,* Feb 4, 1917

48 *Ibid ,* March 24, 1917

49 *Ibid ,* March 27, 1917

50 *Annals of Kansas,* II, 169

51 *Addresses and Messages by Arthur Capper,* v

52 Statements claiming that the Kansas State Council of Defense was the model on which "the National Council of Defense, with its branches in all the states, was later patterned," seem to confuse cause and effect relationships See *Addresses and Messages by Arthur Capper,* v, Pittsburgh *Gazette Times,* Oct 30, 1919

53 *Annals of Kansas,* II, 169-70

54 *Addresses and Messages of Arthur Capper,* v ff

55 Arthur Capper, "The West is all Right," *Leslie's Illustrated Weekly,* July 5, 1917, 16, 31

247

56 Copy of letter from Arthur Capper to Woodrow Wilson, Aug 8, 1917

57 Copy of letter from Arthur Capper to Newton D Baker, Sept 24, 1917

58 Copies of letters in the Capper Governor files, Archives, Kansas State Historical Library Herbert Hoover, Food Administrator, opposed injecting the prohibition issue into wartime food legislation, because it added to already existing problems See New York *Times,* May 27, 1917

59 New York *Times,* Aug 18 and 21, 1917

60 *Annals of Kansas,* II, 192

61 Letter from Frank S Larabee to Charles Sessions, Nov 3, 1917, copy of letter from Arthur Capper to Larabee, Nov 12, 1917

62 New York *Times,* Aug 5, 1918

63 In a letter to Gen Wood, Dec 19, 1917, Capper proclaimed Wood an honorary citizen of Kansas

64 Correspondence in Governor Capper file, Nov and Dec, 1917, with Major General C C Ballou, Topeka *Daily Capital,* Oct 13, 1918, letter from Woodrow Wilson to Arthur Capper, July 2, 1917

65 *Addresses and Messages by Arthur Capper,* 2-161

66 For example, copy of letter from Arthur Capper to Col Hoisington, Oct 22, 1917, Governor Capper file, Archives, Kansas State Historical Library

67 Slacker File in Governor Capper records, Archives, Kansas State Historical Library

68 H C Peterson and Gilbert C Fite, *Opponents of War, 1917-1918,* 297-8

69 Letters from Arthur Capper to Frank Strong and the Rev William Herrman, Nov 15, 1918 German was not immediately reinstated with the Armistice

70 An early statement to this effect is recorded in the March 30, 1913, Topeka *Daily Capital*

71 Peterson and Fite, *Opponents of War, 1917-1918*

72 Theodore Saloutos and John D Hicks, *Agricultural Discontent in the Middle West, 1900-1939,* 189

73 Letter from J L Cross to Arthur Capper, Feb 27, 1918

74 Copy of letter from Arthur Capper to Cross, March 4, 1918

75 Letters to Arthur Capper from M L Amos, March 23, 1918, T A Case, March 12, 1918, and Henry Nottorf, March 20, 1918

76 Copy of letter from Arthur Capper to M Stensaas, May 6, 1918

77 Copy of letters from Arthur Capper to P E Zimmerman, March 30, 1918, Elmer T Peterson, April 27, 1918, Maurice McAuliffe, May 4, 1918, letters from Peterson to Capper, April 25, 1918, and Zimmerman to Capper, April 19, 1918 Governor Capper file, Archives, Kansas State Historical Library

78 Manhattan *Nationalist,* May 9, 1918, reported that Arthur Capper had placed his "OK on Non-Partisan League", Saloutos and Hicks, 189 This book holds that "the League did not consider entering the state elections until 1920, but it did indicate its preference for Governor Arthur Capper for the United States Senate " Capper was a senatorial candidate in 1918 and did not ask for or accept League support

79 Interview with Clif Stratton, Aug 4, 1952

80 Copy of letter from Arthur Capper to Louis Kopelin, Dec 4, 1917

81 Copy of letter from Arthur Capper to Louis Kopelin, Dec 12, 1917

82 *Annals of Kansas,* II, 217

83 James M Harvey was governor during 1869-1873, and he was elected to an unexpired term in Feb, 1874

84 *Literary Digest,* July 26, 1919, 64

85 Letter from Henry J Allen to Arthur Capper, Oct 5, 1918

86 Topeka *Daily Capital,* April 18, 1918, *Twenty-first Biennial Report of the Secretary of State, 1917-'18,* 54-7, 73 The vote in Wallace County was 266 for Stubbs and 254 for Capper

87 "The Light of Experience," Democratic campaign literature of 1918, Kansas State Historical Library

88 *Twenty-first Biennial Report of the Secretary of State, 1917-'18*
89 One explanation for the great majority achieved by Republican candidates in Kansas in 1918 was resentment built up by the "Administration's treatment of General Wood, commanding at Camp Funston " See *Outlook,* Nov 20, 1918, 433
90 From address by Arthur Capper at Assaria, Nov 28, 1918

X

1 *The Capper House Book,* 3
2 *Ibid ,* 11
3 Interviews with Capper employees and people who know how the Capper organization operated vouch for this statement Specific sources in print include William E Connelley, *Kansas and Kansans,* IV, 1972-4, Manhattan *Tribune-News,* Aug 26, 1948, "Life Story of Arthur Capper," Capper for Governor Club, 1911, campaign literature in Kansas State Historical Library, and many of the newspaper eulogies at the time of Capper's death
4 Harold T Chase had worked for the *Capital* more than ten years when Capper bought it
5 Albert Nelson Marquis, ed , *Who's Who in America,* XIX, 1936-7, 1677, Topeka *Daily Capital,* Aug 8 and 9, 1942, *History of Kansas Newspapers,* 57
6 In his book *When Kansas Was Young,* 80-2, McNeal stated that the previous editor, attired in molasses and sand burs, had been run out of town on a pole Tar and feathers were unavailable
7 Capper was Statehouse reporter for the *Capital* during these years
8 *History of Kansas Newspapers,* 57 One of McNeal's appointments while he was mayor was that of Jerry Simpson to the post of city marshal This was the first public position of "Sockless" Jerry Simpson, of Congressional fame
9 *Ibid*
10 Interview with Marco Morrow, June 16, 1952 During most of McNeal's active life with Capper Publications he worked primarily with the *Mail and Breeze* and its successors
11 Topeka *Daily Capital,* Aug 9, 1942, *Capper's Weekly,* Aug 15, 1942, from a radio address by Capper over WIBW, Aug 9, 1942
12 Interview with Marco Morrow, Nov 28, 1952
13 *Twenty-third Biennial Report of the Secretary of State, 1921-'22,* 32-3
14 Topeka *Daily Capital,* Aug 8 and 9, 1942 The date of McNeal's death was Aug 7, 1942
15 *Who's Who in America,* XIII, 1924-5, 698, Topeka *Daily Capital,* June 23, 1935, Topeka *State Journal,* June 23, 1935, *History of Kansas Newspapers,* 132-3 Chase was "the editor" when J K Hudson retired in 1900
16 Topeka *Daily Capital,* June 23, 1935, Topeka *State Journal,* June 23, 1935
17 Chase died June 22, 1935
18 Topeka *Daily Capital,* Feb 8 and 9, 1936
19 Interview with Marco Morrow, Nov 28, 1952
20 *Ibid ,* Topeka *Daily Capital,* Feb 8, 1936
21 *The Capper House Book,* 17
22 *Who's Who in the Midwest, 1949,* 900
23 Interview with Dean Frank Luther Mott, July 17, 1952
24 Editorial by R G Clugston in Topeka *Daily Capital,* March 2, 1959
25 Marco Morrow, "Why I Like Topeka," Topeka *Daily Capital,* Feb 16, 1954
26 Interview with Marco Morrow, Nov 28, 1952
27 *Who's Who in the Midwest, 1949,* 900 Morrow survived eighteen years after his retirement in 1941, dying on Feb 28, 1959
28 Topeka *Daily Capital,* Dec 26, 1942, *Who's Who in America,* XIX, 2189
29 McNeal also served as Hoch's private secretary for six months

30 Sessions was a successful Republican candidate in 1912, whereas Capper had lost the gubernatorial race by twenty-nine votes See pp 132-3

31 Topeka *Daily Capital*, Dec 27, 1942

32 Interview with Marco Morrow, Nov 28, 1952 Sessions died Dec 25, 1942

33 Topeka *Daily Capital*, July 29, 1943 Kittell died in 1943 at the age of sixty-two years

34 Case's editorial office was located at Kansas City until 1915, then near Whitesville, at Wright City, at Kirksville, at Ironton, and back to Wright City

35 *Who's Who in America*, XXVII, 409 At various times Case was president of the Missouri State Board of Agriculture, director of the Missouri State Fair, president of the State Plant Board, member of the Missouri Conservation Commission, and member of the Board of Visitors of the University of Missouri

36 *The Capper Bulletin*, Feb, 1916, 5 The margin of Fields' defeat in 1914 was about 5,000 votes

37 *Who Was Who in America*, I, 396 Fields died in 1934

38 Interview with Marco Morrow, Nov 28, 1952

39 *Ibid*, Topeka *Daily Capital*, April 2, 1939 Mary May died in Evanston, Illinois, on April 1, 1939

40 Topeka *Daily Capital*, April 9, 1929 Griest died April 8, 1929

41 Julius T Willard, *History of the Kansas State College of Agriculture and Applied Science*, 211, the *Capper Bulletin*, June, 1913, 6

42 Interview with Marco Morrow, Nov 28, 1952

43 *Who's Who among North American Authors, 1929-30*, IV, 294

44 Topeka *Daily Capital*, May 8 and 9, 1937

45 A L Shultz, "Capper Strength in Knowledge of Voter Sentiment," Topeka *State Journal*, Dec 22, 1951 Wright's death came May 7, 1937

46 Topeka *Daily Capital*, March 8, 1934 Van Natta died March 7, 1934

47 Interview with Robert Maxwell in Capper file, March 28, 1949

48 Topeka *Daily Capital*, June 7, 1955 Maxwell died at the age of eighty-nine years on June 6, 1955 Maxwell, as a charter member of the Topeka Pressman's Union, took part in its fiftieth anniversary celebration in 1946

XI

1 Florence Crawford Capper, *Poems*, n p, n d This little booklet, containing fourteen poems, takes babies as the theme of half of them Capper's feelings about children can be recognized as a constant concern throughout his life

2 *Giving Boys and Girls a Greater Vision of Farm Life*, booklet, n p, n d, c 1919, 15

3 *Mail and Breeze*, May 10, 1901 Youths joined the Golden Rule Club by filling out a coupon in which they pledged to protect song birds and other useful birds, to practice temperance in all things, and to observe the Golden Rule A five-cent fee took care of expenses Claimed membership by 1911 was 15,000, and there were some 5,000 to 8,000 former members over twenty-one years of age In 1914 the organization was identified as the Golden Rule Bird Club, with a membership reputed to be 12,000 boys and girls See Margaret Hill McCarter, "Arthur Capper as an employee and public-spirited citizen," campaign material used in 1914, in the Kansas State Historical Library

4 Margaret Hill McCarter reported that the membership of this group was said to be 3,000 in 1914 and that in six years 150,000 packets of seeds had been distributed

5 Topeka *Daily Capital*, July 15, 1939

6 Atchison *Globe*, Dec 20, 1951

7 Topeka *Daily Capital*, July 14, 1944, July 15, 1945, *Farmers' Mail and Breeze*, July 12, 1919, *Missouri Pacific Lines Magazine*, Aug, 1919, 17, New York *Times*, Sept 4, 1929

8 *Farmers' Mail and Breeze*, Jan 12, March 30, and May 11, 1907

9 *Ibid*, April 2, 1910 The new name was the result of a contest and was reportedly the suggestion of more than half of the enrolled members of the organization Initially the contest was open to youths under twenty-one years of age and prizes were offered for the best ear of corn they raised First prize was $100, second prize a $20 gold watch, and third was a Webster's Unabridged Dictionary Ten prizes were offered in 1910, ranging from $50 to a year's subscription to the *American Boy* Membership was free to boys whose families were paid-in-advance *Mail and Breeze* subscribers

10 *Farmers' Mail and Breeze*, April 9, 1910, and March 11, 1911

11 *Ibid*, March 16, 1912 In 1912, $300 in cash prizes were divided among boys in Missouri, Kansas, and Nebraska, with a $25 silver cup going to the boy living outside those states who had the best ear of corn grown that season, *Oklahoma Farmer*, April 5, 1912 This paper was purchased by Capper on March 30, 1912, and the Capper Boys' Corn Club was organized almost immediately, with total prizes for the first season amounting to $50 Thereafter prize money in each state totaled $100 each year By 1913 the membership in the corn clubs was said to be approximately 5,000

12 *Oklahoma Farmer*, March 10, 1915 While there was a Capper farm club in Oklahoma, prizes were given for successful competition with other youth in the state agricultural youth program

13 *Nebraska Farm Journal*, March 15, 1918 These contests were sponsored by the state's extension service

14 *Missouri Ruralist*, May 5, 1917

15 *Farmers' Mail and Breeze*, April 1, 1911, and Feb 15, 1913 A Young People's Farm League had been organized March 25, 1911, to bring all the Capper farm clubs together into one big organization to "promote temperance, protect useful birds and prevent cruelty to dumb animals "

16 *Oklahoma Farmer*, June 1, 1912

17 *Farmers' Mail and Breeze*, Feb 15, 1913 Prizes were $25, $15, and $10

18 *Ibid*, June 20, 1914

19 *Ibid*, Dec 21, 1912, Feb 28 and June 27, 1914, and Nov 6, 1915

20 *Ibid*, Nov 6, 1915, *The Capper Clubs*, pamphlet, n d, n p, c 1928, Sabetha *Star*, Dec 13, 1917, *American Magazine*, Nov, 1917, 54, *Advertising Age*, Dec 20, 1951

21 *Farmers' Mail and Breeze*, Nov 6, 1915 The age limit for this club was twelve to eighteen years

22 E T Meredith, of *Successful Farming*, had a similar program for youth in club work in Iowa See Lester Sylvan Ivins and A E Winship, *Fifty Famous Farmers*, 395-6

23 Copy of letter from John F Case to Mary Musson, n d, c 1943

24 Sabetha *Star*, Dec 13, 1917

25 *Giving Boys and Girls a Greater Vision of Farm Life*, booklet, n p, n d, c 1919

26 *Ibid*, *Farmers' Mail and Breeze*, May 12, 1917

27 *Kansas Farmer*, March 27, 1920, interview with E H Whitman, May 18, 1953 Whitman was one of the early club managers and was still an employee on Capper Publications in 1953, interview with Raymond H Gilkeson, Nov 5, 1953

28 Copy of letter from John F Case to Mary Musson, n d, c 1943

29 *The Capper Clubs*, pamphlet, n p, n d, c 1928

30 *Ibid*

31 *Kansas Farmer*, Dec 22 and 29, 1928 An interesting sidelight concerns the use of a swastika symbol as part of the design associated with the Capper Clubs See issues of May 25, 1929, and April 12, 1930 There was no reason for this other than the need for a small symbol or design and the availability of the swastika from American Indian lore

32 Interview with J M Parks, May 18, 1953 Parks was the manager of the Capper clubs from 1928 until about 1938, *Kansas Farmer*, July 16, 1927, and April 11, 1936 Some of the new departments available in 1936 included four for sewing projects and projects for dairy calves and bees, *Marshall County* (Marysville) *News*, Feb 22, 1929 Livestock projects in the 4-H program did not require the use of a purebred animal

Since this was a requirement in the Capper clubs a purebred animal might be used as a project in both 4-H and a Capper club

33 *Kansas Farmer*, April 11, 1936 This was one of the last lengthy articles on the Capper clubs Coupons for enrolling in the organization were published and a picture in the Sept 25, 1937, issue contained the caption, "more than 350 boys and girls gathered at the Capper Pavilion at the Kansas Free Fair " However, no more than 120 people, some of whom were adults, were in the picture The April 22, 1939, issue was the first for many years that did not list the Capper Clubs in its masthead, copy of letter from Capper to the Board of Directors, Capper Publications, Inc , March 3, 1938 The cost of the club during the previous year was assessed at $2,558, including salary allowance of the club manager and clerical work, interview with Raymond H Gilkeson, Nov 5, 1953

34 Notes in the Capper file, *Yearbook of Agriculture, 1928,* 110

35 *Kansas Farmer*, March 2, 1935, Oct 20, 1945 May 18, 1946, and Jan 18, 1947 Other large gifts for Rock Springs Ranch included $25,000 from the Sears, Roebuck Foundation, and fifteen Palomino horses from the Palomino Association

36 *Ibid ,* Jan 18, 1947, letter from Gertrude L Warren to *Kansas Farmer,* n d This honor, given in 1947, was supplemented in late 1948 by a plaque which was also a gift of the Kansas 4-H Clubs

37 Letter from Rod Runyan to author, March 9, 1954

38 *Master Farmers of America,* a pamphlet published by the Standard Farm Papers, 1928, 43, F D Farrell, *Kansas Rural Institutions, VII, Kansas Master Farmers,* Kansas Agricultural Experiment Station, Circular 274, June, 1951, 2 There had been earlier recognition for excellence in farming when the College of Agriculture of the University of Wisconsin established the Wisconsin Hall of Fame for Agriculturists in 1909, and Utah State College awarded its first honorary degree of Master Farmer in 1915

39 *Master Farmers of America,* 5-43, Clifford V Gregory, "The Master Farmer Movement," *Agricultural History,* X, Jan , 1936, 47-58 *Ohio Farmer* editors had been planning a "Standard Farmer Award" but had not been able to put it into practice

40 Farrell, 3-4, 8 During the first five years of the Master Farmer program in Kansas, there were 1,671 eligible nominees named and only 45 selected for the award

41 Gregory, 50

42 *Kansas Farmer,* Feb 11, 1939, memo from Florence McKinney to author, Feb 22, 1954 About seventy Master Homemakers were named in Kansas between 1939 and 1954

43 *Kansas Farmer,* March 6, 1954, memo from Dick Mann to author, n d , c Feb , 1954

44 *Wallaces' Farmer,* April 18, 1953 Iowa, Pennsylvania, and a few other states also had Master Farmer awards in the 1950's Other groups such as the Junior Chambers of Commerce were recognizing certain farm families

45 *Ohio Farmer,* Nov 7, 1936

46 *Ibid , Missouri Ruralist,* Aug 1, 1926

47 *Kansas Farmer,* Oct 8, 1927 County champions entered the state contest without an entry fee, with the winner and runner-up receiving a free trip to the national contest and other prizes

48 *Ohio Farmer,* Nov 18, 1939, Nov 16, 1940, Nov 15, 1941, letter from Marco Morrow/to Arthur Capper, April 1, 1941

49 *Ohio Farmer,* Nov 21, 1936, and Jan 3, 1948 This was the largest recorded attendance for a National Corn Husking Contest

50 *Ohio Farmer,* July 16 and 30, 1927, *Kansas Farmer,* July 30, 1927

51 *Kansas Farmer,* Oct 15, 1927 The cost of the two-week "Seeing the East" special promoted by *Kansas Farmer* was $177 80, but this did not include meals and extra sightseeing expenses, *Capper's Farmer,* Feb , 1931 A forty-one day, ten-thousand-mile tour of six European countries promoted by *Capper's Farmer* in 1931 had a basic cost of less than $500

52 Topeka *Daily Capital,* Nov 13, 1929, *Scientific Monthly,* Aug , 1931, 192 The members of the first committee to select the recipient of the award were F D Farrell, president of Kansas State Agricultural College, John H Finley, editor of the New York *Times,* Carl R Gray, president of Union Pacific, James T Jardine, director of the Oregon Agricultural Experiment Station, Frank O Lowden, former Governor of Illinois and owner of Sinsissippi Farms, Oregon, Illinois, H A Morgan, president of the University of Tennessee, and Walter T Swingle, plant physiologist and agricultural explorer for the United States Department of Agriculture During the second year of operation, Alexander Legge, president of International Harvester Company, replaced Lowden Dr Farrell was chairman, and F B Nichols, managing editor of the Capper Farm Press, acted as the committee's secretary

53 Interview with F D Farrell, July 10, 1951, Topeka *Daily Capital,* Nov 13, 1929

54 *Kansas Farmer,* June 21, 1930, *Ohio Farmer,* June 28, July 5, 1930, *Capper's Farmer,* Aug , 1930, *Capper's Magazine,* Dec , 1930, 34

55 N S B Gras, *A History of Agriculture,* 2nd edition, 1940, 329, 336, *Encyclopedia Americana,* 1950, III, 4

56 *Scientific Monthly,* Aug , 1931, 192, *Kansas Farmer,* June 20, 1931, *American Men of Science,* 8th edition, 1184 Dr Howard had just celebrated his seventy-fourth birthday when the Capper award was announced

57 Interview with F D Farrell, Dec 19, 1953, correspondence between officials of Capper Publications, Inc , and the estate of Dr Marion Dorset, Jan 10 to July 17, 1946

58 *Wallaces' Farmer,* July 2, 1926

59 *Kansas Farmer,* Feb 12, 1927, *Capper's Farmer,* Aug , 1927, *Missouri Ruralist,* Oct 15, 1927 This plan began early in 1928 within the "Eastern trio" of Capper farm papers /

60 *Kansas Farmer,* Feb 12, 1927 Signs were made available upon payment of ten cents for mailing charges

61 Interview with J M Parks, May 18, 1953

62 *Ohio Farmer,* Sept 22, 1928

63 *Kansas Farmer,* Jan 14, 1939, interview with J M Parks, May 18, 1953

64 *Kansas Farmer,* Jan 14, 1939 Part of this immense cost was returned in the small fee charged for the service and its value in helping to sell subscriptions

65 *Ibid ,* Jan 2, 1943

66 Total rewards by 1943 mounted to $135,219 75, paid for the convictions and sentencing of 6,220 thieves During the next seven years there were only 187 additional cases where rewards were paid by the protective service

67 "Corporation Charter Book," Secretary of State of Kansas, CXXX, 138, in the Archives of the Kansas State Historical Library The Capper Credit Union was chartered June 3, 1931, as "not for profit" so that it could "act as a thrift agency in accepting money of its members in payments for shares and to make loans to said members "

XII

1 Topeka *Daily Capital,* Nov 16, 1918

2 Copy of letter from Arthur Capper to Henry Cabot Lodge, Dec 4, 1918

3 Chautauqua Address by Arthur Capper at Sterling, July 25, 1919

4 William Allen White, *Woodrow Wilson The Man, His Times, and His Task,* 413, 420

5 *Addresses and Messages by Arthur Capper,* 155-7 The dates on these messages were Oct 7 and 13, 1918

6 Letter from Henry E Thayer to Arthur Capper, Dec 5, 1918 This letter was critical of the recent *Capital* editorials

7 *Farmers' Mail and Breeze,* March 1, 1919

8 *Ibid ,* Nov 29, 1919

9 John A Garraty, *Henry Cabot Lodge,* 352
10 *Farmers' Mail and Breeze,* July 5, 1919
11 Capper file
12 Walter Johnson, ed , *Selected Letters of William Allen White, 1899-1943,* 200
White still advised Capper to vote for the League of Nations
13 Roger Burlingame and Alden Stevens, *Victory without Peace,* 254-5
14 Letter from Woodrow Wilson to Arthur Capper, July 16, 1919
15 *Farmers' Mail and Breeze,* Aug 2, 1919 Ever aware of his public, Capper wrote
of Wilson, "Never in our time has any President been so punctillious [*sic*] in regard to
his dress "
16 Burlingame and Stevens, 255-6
17 *Farmers' Mail and Breeze,* Aug 16, 1919 For this show of approval Joseph
Tumulty sent the President's expression of gratitude to Capper
18 Letter from William H Taft to Arthur Capper, Oct 12, 1919 The letter was
endorsed "Personal & confidential "
19 *Farmers' Mail and Breeze,* Oct 18, 1919
20 *Ibid ,* Oct 25, 1919
21 *Ibid ,* Nov 8, 1919
22 *Congressional Record,* 66 Cong , 1st Sess , LVIII, Part 8, 8013
23 Garraty, 379
24 *Farmers' Mail and Breeze,* Nov 29, 1919
25 *Kansas Farmer and Mail and Breeze,* Dec 20, 1919
26 *Ibid ,* Jan 24, 1920
27 *Ibid ,* April 3, 1920
28 *Ibid ,* July 31, 1920
29 Dayton (Ohio) *News,* Aug 2, 1945

XIII

1 Interview with Marco Morrow, June 16, 1952
2 Telegram from Arthur Capper to Marco Morrow, Feb 22, 1919
3 "First Things " The change was made on April 21 For a more complete story
of these developments see Homer E Socolofsky, "The Development of the Capper Farm
Press," *Agricultural History,* XXXI, No 4 34-43.
4 *Capper's Farmer,* June, 1919
5 Interview with Marco Morrow, Nov 28, 1953
6 N W Ayer and Sons, *Directory of Newspapers and Periodicals,* for 1914, 339,
for 1920, 351
7 *Kansas Farmer and Mail and Breeze,* Dec 13, 1919
8 Consolidation was the order of the day in agricultural journalism, with a great
drop in the numbers of farm periodicals in the 1920's Competition still existed with
such papers as the *Weekly Kansas City Star,* later called the *Weekly Star Farmer,* but
there was no state farm competition
9 This structure was located just east of the older building The Kansas-based
operations of Capper Publications are discussed in Homer E Socolofsky, "The Evolution
of a Home Grown Product, Capper Publications," *Kansas Historical Quarterly,* XXIV,
No 2 151-67
10 Copy of letter from Arthur Capper to Ralph W Mitchell, Jan 3, 1919
11 *Kansas Farmer and Mail and Breeze,* July 31, 1920 According to "First Things,"
the first Gold Certificate was sold July 12, 1920, Capper issued a prospectus "Seven
Per Cent and Safety," for these first Gold Certificates
12 *Ibid ,* July 31, Aug 14 and 28, Sept 25, 1920 A program of financing a farm
publication through appeals to subscribers had been used by *Orange Judd Farmer,* of
Chicago, after its building had been gutted by fire early in 1907, *Orange Judd Farmer,*
Feb 2 and June 22, 1907, Jan 11 and 18, 1908

13 Interview with Rod Runyan, Sept 4, 1953

14 From the prospectus of Capper Publications, Inc, which was sent to the Securities and Exchange Commission, c 1952, 8

15 He had no particular objection to bank loans, he felt he had more freedom in this method of financing

16 Copy of letter from Arthur Capper to John J Burns, General Counsel, Securities and Exchange Commission, Feb 7, 1935, letter from E C Nash to Arthur Capper, Feb 9, 1939 Seven of these nine investors had Kansas addresses One had an investment of $55,000 The average investment for this group was more than $26,000 Some concern was expressed by Capper's financial advisers about these large investors that they might all require liquidation of their holdings at the same time

17 *Field and Farm,* Sept 25, 1920, Ayer, 1918, 110, 1229 The circulation of this paper was in second rank for farm papers in Colorado

18 Letter from Marco Morrow to Agencies and Advertisers, Oct 22, 1920 National Archives, Agricultural and General Services Section, Washington, D C

19 *Field and Farm,* Oct 5, 1920

20 *Ibid,* Sept 25, 1920, *Western Farm Life,* Nov 1, 1920, letter from Marco Morrow to Agencies and Advertisers, Oct 22, 1920

21 Interviews with Marco Morrow, June 16, Aug 1, 1952, and April 7, 1953

22 *Union List of Serials,* 1010

23 Interviews with Marco Morrow, June 16, Aug 1, 1952, and April 7, 1953 The last issue of *Field and Farm* was Dec 5, 1920

24 "First Things"

25 Letter from Marco Morrow to A I Foard of the *Journal of Agriculture* staff, Jan 17, 1921, *Missouri Ruralist,* Feb 1 and 15, 1921

26 *Union List of Serials,* 729, 1435, Stephen Conrad Stuntz, 32, 60, 62, 88, 94, 101, 103, 156, 157 Other important members of the "family tree" were the *Farmer's Advertiser,* the *Valley Farmer,* the *Planter and Stockman,* the *St Louis Midland Farmer,* and *Colman's Rural World*

27 "First Things"

28 Elbert B Macy, "Former Educators among Kansas Editors and Publishers," Master's thesis, Kansas State University, 1939, 54-7

29 *Ibid,* 55, 57, interview with Marco Morrow, June 16, 1952 The business was arranged so that Capper expected a 6 per cent profit on his investment

30 Interview with Marco Morrow, June 16, 1952

31 *Ibid,* letter from Charles Sweet to author, May 13, 1953 The mailing list of *The Commoner,* the newspaper of Charles and William Jennings Bryan, was taken over by Capper in 1923 See New York *Times,* June 18, 1923

32 The "Eastern trio" of farm papers announced the change in ownership with their issues of Jan 28, 1922, Topeka *State Journal,* Jan 31, 1922 Additional material about this sale is found in the Topeka *Daily Capital,* Aug 25, 1929, and July 16, 1939, and in the prospectus of Capper Publications, Inc, which was sent to the SEC

33 *Ohio Farmer,* Jan 5, 1918 Lawrence had also published the *Practical Farmer* for a few years

34 *Ibid*

35 *Ibid*

36 Interview with Marco Morrow, June 16, 1952, letter from Marco Morrow to Arthur Capper, March 28, 1939

37 *Michigan Farmer,* Jan 28, 1922, *Pennsylvania Farmer,* Jan 28, 1922

38 *Ohio Farmer,* Aug 23, 1924 Many changes in advertising connections were required before this change was recognized

39 Interview with Marco Morrow, Nov 28, 1952 This apparent reversal of an earlier practice of having all or almost all of the farm papers printed in Topeka was due to the psychological advantage which an in-state farm paper had over one published outside the state, as well as to the buildings and equipment owned by the Lawrence Publishing Company

40 "First Things"

41 Interview with Marco Morrow, April 7, 1953, Ayer, 1923, 377, Ayer, 1924, 386, Ayer, 1925, 394, "First Things"

42 "First Things"

43 Topeka *Daily Capital*, Aug 25, 1929 This magazine had been published from Washington, D C, for eleven years

44 "First Things", interview with Marco Morrow, April 7, 1953

45 "First Things" One of the most recent letters was the offer of *Better Farms* of Buffalo, New York Letter from Roy F Bailey to Arthur Capper, Nov 5, 1949

46 The contract of sale of the *Oklahoma Farmer*, May 21, 1924, written in longhand on stationery of the New Willard Hotel, Washington, D C, was on file in the vault at the Capper Building

47 Interview with Marco Morrow, June 16, 1952

48 *Ibid* The price paid was presumably about the same as that paid for the *Oklahoma Farmer*

49 *Ohio Farmer*, Sept 22, 1928, *Michigan Farmer*, Sept 22, 1928, *Union List of Serials*, 1733, 2078, 2173 The date of merger was Sept 15, 1928, however, stock in the newly formed company was issued Aug 23, 1928, "First Things", Topeka *Daily Capital*, Aug 25, 1929, and July 16, 1939

50 *Ohio Farmer*, Sept 22, 1928 The Stockman-Farmer Publishing Company had been located at Pittsburgh, Pennsylvania The home office of the Rural Publishing Company was Detroit, Michigan

51 Interview with Rod Runyan, July 10, 1952 Capper selected 60 per cent of the directors of the corporation, and Harman and Slocum interests had the remaining seats, Topeka *Daily Capital*, July 16, 1939 As in many of his other mergers and consolidations Capper continued to employ the editors of the papers which he merged with his own

52 Topeka *Daily Capital*, July 16, 1939, Ayer, 1929, 952

53 Ayer, 1929, 492, 830

54 Topeka *Daily Capital*, June 7, 1953

XIV

1 Letter from Arthur Capper to E H Crosby, Nov 14, 1918 The price was set at $45,000

2 See p 65

3 *Capper's Weekly*, Oct 25, 1919

4 Questions with summary of results in Capper file

5 Arthur Capper, *The Agricultural Bloc*, 10-12

6 James H Shideler, *Farm Crisis, 1919-1923*, 156

7 Letter from Bernard M Baruch to Arthur Capper, Jan 3, 1920, letter from Thos A Edison to Arthur Capper, Dec 1, 1924

8 Margaret L Coit, *Mr Baruch*, 386-91

9 New York *Times*, Jan 25, 1920

10 *Ibid*, June 6, 1920

11 *Ibid*, May 9, 1920

12 *Ibid*, May 8, 1921

13 *Ibid*, Sept 2, 1921

14 *Ibid*, Feb 12 and 17, 1922

15 *Ibid*, Oct 15, 1922

16 Letter from Peter Norbeck to B B Haugen, July 11, 1922, quoted in Shideler, 165

17 Topeka *Daily Capital*, April 3, 1922, as reprinted from the New York *Evening Post*

18 New York *Times*, Nov 22, 1922

19 *Ibid*, Nov 26, 1922

20 *Ibid*, Dec 2, 1922, John D Hicks, *Republican Ascendancy, 1921-1933*, 54 Hicks pointed out that members of the Bloc insisted on limiting business favors from government and on priority for agricultural matters

21 Kansas City *Star*, March 25, 1923

22 Letter from Peter Norbeck to S W Clark, Jan 29, 1924 Copy in Western Historical Manuscripts Collection, University of Missouri

23 Saloutos and Hicks, 288

24 Notes in the Capper file, Washington *Star*, Aug 6, 1939

25 Shideler, 249

26 Gilbert C Fite, *George N Peek and the Fight for Farm Parity*, 38

27 *Ibid*, 39

28 *Kansas Farmer*, Nov 10, 1923

29 *Ibid*, Dec 22, 1923

30 *Ibid*, May 24, 1924

31 *Ibid*, May 24 and 31, 1924, generally Capper and Coolidge were on the best of terms In a letter to Capper, Dec 13, 1923, Coolidge responded to a Capper inquiry about "twenty or more colored soldiers imprisoned at the Federal Penitentiary at Leavenworth for participation in riots at Houston, Texas, some years ago "

32 *Ibid*, June 28, 1924

33 *Ibid*, June 14, 1924, according to a letter from N C Keiser to W C Hays, June 11, 1924, copy in Capper file, the "ringleaders of the movement [against Capper] are former Lieut Gov Troutman of Topeka, and former Congressman C F Scott of Iola, and Chester I Long, former Senator of Wichita "

34 *Capper's Weekly*, Nov 15, 1924 Capper received an impressive 70 1 per cent of the total vote in 1924

35 Copy of a Capper speech, "Naming Secretaries of Agriculture," *c* 1930's Jardine's appointment was confirmed by the Senate on Feb 19, 1925, letter from William M Jardine to Arthur Capper, Feb 18, 1925, expressing "grateful appreciation" for Capper's endorsement

36 Fite, 116

37 *Official Congressional Directory*, Dec, 1919, through Dec, 1925 The occupant of that address in later years was a business and commercial college, Benjamin Franklin University

38 Engraved invitation from Captain Herbert Hartley in Capper file

39 New York *Times*, July 26, 1925, Topeka *Daily Capital*, July 16, 1925, Kansas City *Star*, July 20, 1925 Six thousand guests, including about one hundred Americans, attended the garden party, letters from Arthur Capper to J E Griest, July 17, 1925, and reply Aug 3, 1925 Capper had copies of his publications sent to Lloyd George

40 New York *Times*, Nov 8, 1925, Topeka *Daily Capital*, Aug 8 to Sept 10, 1925, the passport is in the Capper file

41 Topeka *Daily Capital*, Sept 8, 1925

42 *Ibid*, Sept 28, 1925

43 *Ibid*, Oct 15, 1925

44 New York *Times*, Nov 4, 1925

45 Woman's Kansas Day Club, "Sketches of the First Ladies of Kansas," MSS, 1959

46 New York *Times*, April 29, 1926

47 *Ibid*, May 4, 1926

48 Topeka *Daily Capital*, May 10, 1926, Kansas City *Journal-Post*, May 10, 1926, New York *Times*, May 13, 1926

49 Emporia *Gazette*, May 14, 1926

50 Story in Capper file

51 *Kansas Farmer*, March 5, 1927

52 Fite, 186-7

53 Letter from Calvin Coolidge to Arthur Capper, July 18, 1927 Coolidge wrote,

"I hope you can pay us a visit during the summer We are pleasantly situated here in the Black Hills and want you to come and see us and get cool"

54 New York *Herald Tribune,* Aug 3, 1927, letter from Everett Sanders to Arthur Capper, Dec 1, 1938, with enclosed manuscript

55 Story in Capper file According to William Allen White in *A Puritan in Babylon,* 357, Mrs Coolidge reported that Capper was not with the President when Coolidge announced his decision not to run in 1928 The New York *Herald Tribune,* Aug 3, 1927, on the other hand, stated that Capper ' went in with the newspapermen at the appointed hour" Sanders said that Capper 'only saw the President tell them that the line formed on the left and saw him hand" each reporter a slip of paper

56 Norfolk *Virginian-Pilot,* Jan 9, 1952

57 Letter from G W Norris to Arthur Capper, Aug 2, 1928

58 Wilford Riegle, "Peck's Bad Boys," *Kansas Historical Quarterly,* XXIII, 79

59 New York *Times,* March 2, 1922

60 Riegle, 79

61 New York *Times,* June 11 and 17, 1921

62 Riegle, 79 Peck served only seven months in the new rank before he resigned from the service

63 New York *Times,* Jan 4, 1928 According to a letter to Arthur Capper from Joseph P Chamberlain of Columbia University, Aug 27, 1928, Capper had a share "in arousing sentiment in the United States, out of which has grown the treaty "

64 New York *Times,* Jan 8 and 22, 1928

65 *Ibid ,* Nov 24, 1928

66 *Ibid ,* Feb 11, 1929 ff

67 *Ibid ,* Feb 12, 1929

68 *Ibid ,* Feb 11, 12, July 28, and Aug 1, 1929

69 Arthur Capper, "The Push behind Farm Relief," *The Independent,* Oct 29, 1927

70 New York *Times,* April 17, 1929

71 *Ibid ,* May 5, 1929

72 *Ibid ,* March 4, 1930

73 Letter from Victor Murdock to Arthur Capper, May 12, 1930 Murdock commended Capper s position taken in "the reactionary atmosphere of Washington," and reported that "Kansas is in some kind of ferment which I can tell you sense although you are so far away " Capper's action in opposing Judge John J Parker as Associate Justice of the Supreme Court was due to the Judge's anti-labor and anti-Negro reputation According to the Kansas City *Times,* May 6, 1930, Capper's vote was "An Echo of Civil War "

74 *Kansas Farmer,* June 22, 1929

75 *Ibid ,* Jan 4, March 1, Aug 30, and Oct 11, 1930

76 *Ibid ,* July 6, Sept 21, and Nov 2, 1929

77 *Ibid ,* April 5, 1930, New York *Times,* July 8, 1930 The *Times* story identified Capper as one "who voted with the Democratic-Insurgent Republican coalition on several occasions in the recent tariff struggle "

78 *Kansas Farmer,* June 21, 1930

79 *Ibid ,* Aug 30, Oct 11, and Dec 27, 1930

XV

1 New York *Times,* July 8, 1930

2 *Ibid ,* Nov 8, 1930

3 *Ibid*

4 Parker's failure in getting Senate approval is also credited to his circuit court defense of the "yellow dog" contract

5 Frank Haucke was the Republican candidate for Governor

6 *Kansas Farmer,* March 28, 1931
7 *Ibid,* March 7, 1931
8 *Ibid,* March 28, 1931
9 Topeka *State Journal,* Dec 28, 1931
10 Arthur Capper, "What Kansas Farmers Think," *Review of Reviews,* Sept, 1931, 53-4, Hicks, *Republican Ascendancy,* 237-8, other Capper articles appeared in such publications as the New York *Times,* as well as in his own journals On one occasion Capper reported that he had just received his "semi-annual calling down from the Chicago Journal of Commerce"
11 New York *Times,* June 21 and Nov 9, 1931
12 Examples can be found in the New York *Times,* Jan 17 and 29, June 15, Sept 11 and 27, 1932
13 *Ibid,* Sept 27, 1932
14 *Ibid,* Oct 6 and Nov 8, 1932 Capper spoke from the radio station of his friend Henry Field, who was the unsuccessful Republican candidate for the Senate from Iowa
15 Letter from Franklin D Roosevelt to Arthur Capper, Dec 22, 1932 Capper's letter to Roosevelt was written Nov 26, 1932
16 Speech by Arthur Capper, Jan 3, 1933, over the Columbia Broadcasting System
17 Letter from William Allen White to Arthur Capper, Jan 3, 1933
18 Speech of Arthur Capper over WIBW, Jan 10, 1933
19 Radio address by Arthur Capper, March 21, 1933, *Congressional Quarterly,* I, 176-8
20 Radio address by Arthur Capper, March 21, 1933
21 *Ibid*
22 *Ibid*
23 Sabetha *Herald,* Aug 9, 1933
24 New York *Times,* June 20, 1933
25 Radio Address by Arthur Capper over the N B C Farm and Home Hour, June 29, 1933
26 New York *Times,* Aug 4, 1933
27 Dexter Perkins, *The New Age of Franklin Roosevelt, 1932-45,* 6
28 New York *Times,* March 4, 1934
29 *Ibid,* Feb 20, 1934, Kansas City *Times,* Feb 24, 1934
30 New York *Times,* Feb 26, 1934
31 Emporia *Gazette,* Aug 30, 1934
32 Radio address by Arthur Capper over WIBW, Nov 7, 1934
33 *Capper's Weekly,* Jan 5, 1935, from radio address given by Capper over WIBW, Dec 23, 1934
34 *Congressional Quarterly,* I, 176-8 These were items 21 to 33 in the *Congressional Quarterly* listing of principal Senate votes from 1919 to 1944 Senator Hayden was from Arizona, Bankhead from Alabama, Wagner from New York, Thomas from Oklahoma, and Barkley from Kentucky
35 *Ibid*
36 New York *Times,* Jan 24, 1934
37 *Ibid,* July 1, 1935
38 *Ibid,* July 1 and 15, 1935
39 *Capper's Weekly,* Feb 2, 1935
40 Radio address by Arthur Capper over WIBW, May 23, 1935
41 New York *Times,* July 26, 1935 Senators Norris and Capper predicted that Congress could not adjourn before Sept 1, nevertheless, Capper joined Senator Royal Copeland in urging immediate adjournment
42 *Ibid,* Aug 2, 1935
43 *Ibid,* Sept 10, 1933
44 Radio address by Arthur Capper over WIBW, Nov 7, 1934
45 Radio address by Arthur Capper over WIBW, May 23, 1935

46 Undated manuscript of a speech used by Arthur Capper in the 1930's His anti-war editorials were generally used in *Capper's Weekly,* but *Kansas Farmer, Capper's Farmer,* and his other farm journals also had such editorials

47 See p 131 An example of Capper support for this issue can be found in his extension of remarks of July 25, 1935, in the *Congressional Record*

48 Topeka *State Journal,* Aug 19, 1935, New York *Times,* Aug 20, 1935

49 Topeka *Daily Capital,* Aug 20, 1935

50 At least nine letters in the Capper file deal with the Stone "issue," and promises were made for continued support for the Senator

51 Donald R McCoy, "Alfred M Landon and the Presidential Campaign of 1936," *Mid-America,* Oct , 1960, 201

52 *Ibid ,* 199, in an editorial Aug 31, 1935, the New York *Times* sarcastically reported that Capper wanted to be President Capper was then seventy years of age

53 McCoy, 201

54 New York *Times,* July 24, 1936

55 *Ibid ,* July 29, Oct 18, 1936

56 Arthur M Schlesinger, Jr , *The Politics of Upheaval,* 610

57 Letter from Clifford R Hope to Arthur Capper, Nov 5, 1936 Kansas Congressional seats went to five Republicans and two Democrats

58 Perkins, 58

59 New York *Times,* Feb 10, 1937 Senator Harry S Truman, in the same article, favored "rehabilitation of the Federal courts," but he doubted the "constitutionality" of the proposal

60 *Ibid ,* Feb 26, 1937

61 *Kansas Farmer,* Feb 27, 1937

62 Copy of letter from Arthur Capper to Joe E Denham, Sept 24, 1937

63 New York *Times,* April 3, 1937

64 *Ibid ,* April 4, 1937

65 Notes in Capper file

66 *Capper's Weekly,* April 13, 1935

67 Jewell, 21

68 New York *Times,* Dec 1, 1937

69 *Ibid ,* Nov 18, 1937

70 Letter from Claude G Bowers to Arthur Capper, Sept 29, 1937

71 *Capper's Weekly,* Oct 9, 1937, from a radio address over WIBW on Oct 3, 1937

72 *Ibid ,* Dec 11, 1937

73 *Ibid ,* Dec 25, 1937

74 New York *Times,* Jan 3, 1938 The space given Capper's views by the *Times* is amazing

75 *Ibid*

76 *Ibid ,* March 14, 1938

77 *Ibid ,* Sept 20, 1939

78 *Ibid ,* Sept 30 and Oct 17, 1939

79 *Capper's Weekly,* Dec 9, 1939, New York *Times,* Dec 4, 1939

80 New York *Times,* Nov 10, 1937

81 *Kansas Farmer,* Nov 9, 1935, *Capper's Weekly,* Jan 11 and 18, 1936

82 New York *Times,* Nov 16, 1937

83 *Ibid ,* Oct 30, 1938

84 *Kansas Farmer,* Jan 4, 1938

85 *Ibid ,* Nov 19, 1938

86 *Ibid ,* Dec 17, 1938

87 New York *Times,* Dec 25, 1938

88 *Ibid ,* Dec 21 and 31, 1939, *Kansas Farmer,* Dec 30, 1939

89 *Capper's Weekly,* Dec 30, 1939, from a radio address by Arthur Capper over WIBW, Dec 24, 1939

90 Telegram from J N Dolley to Arthur Capper, Oct 8, 1939
91 Letter from J N Dolley to Arthur Capper, Oct 17, 1939
92 *Capper's Weekly,* July 6, 1940
93 *Ibid ,* Nov 2, 1940
94 *Ibid ,* Nov 16, 1940
95 *Ibid ,* Dec 28, 1940
96 *Ibid ,* Feb 15 and March 8, 1941
97 *Ibid ,* March 29, 1941
98 *Ibid ,* Nov 1, 1941
99 *Ibid ,* Nov 15, 1941
100 *Ibid ,* Dec 6, 1941
101 *Ibid ,* Dec 13, 1941
102 Hays *News,* Aug 26, 1937
103 Kansas City *Star,* Oct 29, 1939
104 Washington *Times-Herald,* Feb 4, 1939
105 The concert was at 5 00 P M on April 9, 1939
106 *Congressional Quarterly,* I, 172-5

XVI

1 Financial records in Capper file, notes of annual meeting of stockholders of Capper Publications, Incorporated, March 10, 1941
2 "First Things", copy of letter from Arthur Capper to George H Slocum, May 8, 1941
3 "First Things " Wages were cut between Oct , 1930, and March, 1933, on various Capper enterprises Because of 10 per cent cuts, given four times, a $35 per week employee in the Advertising Department would have seen his pay drop to almost $23 per week between May, 1932, and Feb , 1933 Blanket cuts were given three times in that period
4 Letters from Henry S Blake to Capper, May 5, 1944, and March 27, 1947 When the business was making money during World War II, the War Production Board refused to permit Capper to accept a salary for his role as president of his business because he had received none when the war began
5 Letter from F E Charles, associate editor of the *Furrow,* to the author, Dec 30, 1953
6 *Capper's Farmer,* April, 1927
7 *Objective Journalism in Action,* 9, interview with Ray Yarnell, Aug 4, 1952
8 *Successful Farming,* March, 1927
9 *Capper's Farmer,* Jan , 1928
10 *Objective Journalism in Action,* 11, interview with Ray Yarnell, Aug 4, 1952
11 *Capper's Farmer,* June, 1937, and Aug , 1939, memo to the Board of Directors of Capper Publications, Inc , from Ray Yarnell, n d , c Feb , 1941 There were methods for getting better prices for lambs, for growing 100-bushel-per-acre corn, for raising more potatoes per acre, for pasture farming, for making profits at low prices, for a new system of farming, for rubber-tired tractors and farm implements, for farm-family partnerships, for deferred feeding, for brome instead of alfalfa, for new land management, for the safety method of farming dry-land wheat, for a new sorghum-planting method, for grass silage, for subsistence irrigation, for control of noxious weeds, for sodding native grasses, and many others
12 Letter from Ray Yarnell to Chester Davis, March 27, 1934, National Archives, in a letter from A H Lauterback, Chief, Dairy Section, United States Department of Agriculture, to Ray Yarnell, June 26, 1934, copy in National Archives, the response was unenthusiastic, since the program had been tried before without major success
13 Interview with Loyal F Payne, Dec 17, 1953, interview with C W McCampbell, Dec 17, 1953

14 Memo to the Board of Directors of Capper Publications, Inc , from Ray Yarnell, n d , *c* Feb , 1941

15 Interview with Raymond H Gilkeson, Nov 5, 1953 "How to" was emphasized rather than "You farmers should do this '

16 *Ibid* This idea was found among farm papers in all of the Capper states, as well as among farmers in general, verified in interviews with C W McCampbell, Dec 17, 1953, and with F D Farrell, Dec 19, 1953 The fact that the younger editors were generally graduates of the Middle Western agricultural colleges and that Capper had an interest in such schools may have encouraged closer relations between the Capper farm papers and the agricultural colleges

17 Interview with Raymond H Gilkeson, Nov 5, 1953, *Kansas Farmer,* Jan 29, 1938, interview with Charles C Howes, Oct 21, 1952

18 Interview with Marco Morrow, Nov 5, 1953, *Collier's Encyclopedia,* VI, 17, *Encyclopedia Americana,* VII, 700, *Who's Who in America,* XXVII, 2213 Shull was awarded a gold medal in 1940 by the DeKalb Agricultural Association, as the inventor of hybrid corn

19 Letter from Charles Sessions to Arthur Capper, March 17, 1938

20 Copy of letter from Arthur Capper to Ray Yarnell, April 9, 1938

21 Memo from Henry S Blake to Arthur Capper, July 17, 1937

22 Letter from Henry S Blake to Arthur Capper, May 9, 1947

23 Copy of letter from Arthur Capper to Henry S Blake, May 12, 1947

24 "First Things " Remodeling expenses were around $12,000, and occupancy occurred early in 1947

25 "First Things " The type was set in Topeka and shipped to the Louisville plant The first issue of *Household* from Louisville was Nov , 1947

26 The first issue of *Capper's Farmer* from Louisville was Feb , 1953

27 Memo from Henry S Blake to Arthur Capper, July 17, 1937, letters from Henry S Blake to Arthur Capper, July 22, 1937, and Jan 12, 1938

28 Letter from Henry S Blake to Arthur Capper, July 26, 1937

29 Letter from Henry J Allen to Arthur Capper, Jan 10, 1938

30 Copy of letters from Arthur Capper to Marco Morrow and Henry S Blake, Jan 11, 1938, and to Henry J Allen, Jan 15, 1938, letters from Marco Morrow to Arthur Capper, Jan 13, 1938, and from Henry S Blake to Arthur Capper, Jan 19, 1938

31 This fear was frequently expressed in letters to and from Capper for the years 1937 through 1941

32 Letter from Henry S Blake to Arthur Capper, Jan 27, 1940, copy of letter from Arthur Capper to Henry S Blake, Jan 29, 1940, letters from Oscar S Stauffer to Arthur Capper, Feb 1 and May 18, 1940

33 Letter from Marco Morrow to Arthur Capper, March 22, 1940, letter from James A McClure to Arthur Capper, Feb 14, 1940

34 Topeka *Daily Capital,* Aug 1, 1941, Topeka *State Journal,* Aug 1, 1941

35 *Editor and Publisher,* Aug 2, 1941, *Printers' Ink,* Aug 8, 1941 The plan of consolidation was similar to one used by the Nashville Printing Co , in Tennessee The *Journal* moved its offices into the Capper Building

36 Copy of letter from Arthur Capper to John F Burns, General Counsel, Securities and Exchange Commission, Feb 7, 1935

37 Copy of letter from Arthur Capper to Mary Capper, Dec 23, 1936 If Capper were to die while there were outstanding Capper Certificates, each individual holder of a certificate would be obligated to present an individual claim for his money If the business were incorporated there would be no change in certificate procedure due to the death of the owner A first mortgage on the property eventually provided security for the Capper certificates See the brochure, "The Story of Capper Publications, Inc ," n d , *c* 1937

38 "Amendments and Miscellaneous Charters," A-44, Secretary of State Records in the Archives of the Kansas State Historical Library, 432-6

39 In addition to Capper the board of directors of Capper Publications, Inc, included Morrow, Blake, Sessions, and Philip Zach, the manager of Capper's New York advertising office

40 "Amendments and Miscellaneous Charters," A-44, Secretary of State Records in the Archives of the Kansas State Historical Library, 432-6 Henry S Blake and Marshall Crawford, son of Mrs George M Crawford and Capper's nephew, were each given one share of Capper Printing Company stock This qualified them as members of its board of directors Capper also owned the Wichita Engraving Plant, which was sold to Midcontinent for $25,000 on April 16, 1937

41 The report in the Topeka *Daily Capital*, June 7, 1953, uses the February date for the move, whereas "First Things" says that the move was made in April, 1934

42 Chart, n d , with letter from Henry S Blake to Arthur Capper, Sept 9, 1941

43 The FM equipment was given to Kansas State University, where it was used as a low-powered, student-operated, community station for Manhattan, copy of letter from Arthur Capper to Henry S Blake, March 1, 1940, *Printers' Ink*, Aug 1, 1941, 56 The Kaw Valley Broadcasting Company was incorporated for this purpose, but it remained inactive because of the adverse decision

44 According to "First Things," the purchase option was signed on Dec 26, 1934, and extended three times, letter from Ellis Atteberry to Rod Runyan, Dec 10, 1943 WLBF began operation on Nov 1, 1925, from Kansas City, Missouri, using a frequency of 1430 kilocycles and a power of 25 watts Power was gradually increased, but the company went bankrupt in 1928 and was taken out of receivership in 1930, when it was incorporated Call letters KCKN were assigned on Nov 26, 1936 Power was raised to 250 watts on Sept 18, 1939, and a new frequency of 1340 was assigned on March 31, 1941

45 See p 138

46 "First Things", the Missouri Agricultural Publishing Company did job printing, printed colored Sunday comic supplements, and carried on a general printing business The sale price in 1944 was considerably below the purchase price, but Capper was able to dispose of an enterprise which had been losing money for years Moreover, tax laws in 1944 enabled the loss to be written off The Missouri Agricultural Publishing Company was dissolved on Oct 2, 1945, by Judge Emory H Wright in the Circuit Court of Jackson County, Missouri See Case No 505024

47 Letters from Neff Laing to Executive Committee of Capper-Harman-Slocum, Inc , Jan 4 and June 13, 1941 The move of *Pennsylvania Farmer* from Pittsburgh to Harrisburg was a product of the expiration of a lease on its building with orders to vacate This move seemed to affect *Michigan Farmer*, which soon moved its editorial office to East Lansing, letter from Ruth Forbes to Arthur Capper, Feb 26, 1947 The number of C-H-S employees in 1947 was 113, of which 84 were located in and near Cleveland

48 Letters from Henry S Blake to Arthur Capper, Feb 10, 1940, and March 26, 1947, and from Leland Schenck to Arthur Capper, March 28, 1940

49 *Kansas Labor Weekly*, July 18, 1940, Topeka *Daily Capital*, July 16, 1939, interview with Rod Runyan, Sept 4, 1953

50 Letters from Leland Schenck to Arthur Capper, March 28, 1940, and from Henry S Blake to Arthur Capper, Feb 18, 1940

51 Interview with Rod Runyan, Sept 4, 1953

52 Letter from W C Keiser to Arthur Capper, July 7, 1947, Topeka *Daily Capital*, July 25, 1948

53 Interview with F D Farrell, Dec 19, 1953 One of the *Michigan Farmer* editors made this statement to Dr Farrell in 1949

54 Interview with Marco Morrow, Nov 5, 1953 Morrow reported that Editor E S Bayard of the *Pennsylvania Farmer* frequently criticized Capper's political position in his Pennsylvania paper

55 *Kansas Business Magazine*, March, 1949, 12, interview with Leland Schenck, May 18, 1953 Blake had previously worked on circulation departments for the Des

Moines *Register-Tribune*, the Houston *Post*, the Winnepeg *Tribune*, the St Louis *Star*, the St Paul *Pioneer Press and Dispatch*, and the Kansas City *Journal*

56 Copy of letter from T A McNeal to Arthur Capper, Feb 10, 1938

57 Copy of letter from Arthur Capper to Philip Zach, Feb 4, 1944 This letter offered congratulations for twenty-five years of service with Capper Publications

58 Notes of Capper's speeches to advertising clubs, particularly in the 1920's

59 *Ibid* To this end Capper cited the example of the two million dollars spent by Henry Ford in newspaper advertising to announce his new automobile models in 1924 Ford reduced the selling price at the same time

60 Notes of a speech delivered by Arthur Capper at the Commodore Hotel, New York City, Feb 17, 1926 The first truth-in-advertising bill introduced by Capper was in 1933, but the legislation was based on the model *Printers' Ink* statute which had long been law in many states

61 Interview with Charles Sweet, July 15, 1953

62 Inter-office memo from C C Clark to Marco Morrow, Oct 27, 1930

63 Copy of letter from Arthur Capper to Allen B Russell, The Potts-Turnbull Co, Kansas City, Missouri, May 4, 1939

64 Letters from Neff Laing to Capper, Dec 15, 1947, from Henry S Blake to Capper, Dec 17, 1947, and copy of letter from Arthur Capper to Neff Laing, Dec 30, 1947

65 Interview with Leland Schenck, July 23, 1953

66 Interview with Marco Morrow, Aug 1, 1952

67 Interview with Victor Hawkins, July 10, 1952

68 The Advertising Research Foundation was sponsored jointly by the Association of National Advertisers and American Association of Advertising Agencies The Agricultural Publishers Association defrayed all costs of the continuing study

69 *Summary Bulletin, the Continuing Study of Farm Publications*, Bulletin No 2, April, 1951

70 *The Continuing Study of Farm Publications, Study Number Eight, Kansas Farmer, Issue of October 2, 1948*, Advertising Research Foundation, New York, 1949, 6

71 Interview with Charles Sweet, July 15, 1953

72 Example from a copy of a letter from Arthur Capper to Mrs Clara Chute, Nov 24, 1933, *Kansas Labor Weekly*, Aug 31, 1944, Topeka *Daily Capital*, Dec 20, 1953 By the end of 1953 there were 326 active and retired employees with "Old Timer" pins

73 *Capper's Weekly*, Dec 20, 1941, *Capper's Farmer*, Feb , 1942

XVII

1 Capper was either a member or in correspondence with such groups as the War Referendum Council, the Keep America out of War Congress, the World Peace ways, Inc, the Public Action Committee, the National Council for Prevention of War, the Women's International League for Peace and Freedom, the George Washington League, and the America First Committee

2 Brooklyn *Citizen*, April 12, 1941, New York *Times*, Dec 20, 1951

3 Letter from William Allen White to Arthur Capper, Sept 6, 1941

4 Baltimore *Sun*, Sept 16, 1941, Washington *Post*, Sept 19, 1941 In Jan , 1941, Capper expressed the opinion that Willkie, who was supporting the Roosevelt program, had given the Republicans a "raw deal," by his failure to oppose every presidential action But by October Capper was pleased with the naval seizure of a German radio station in Greenland

5 Copy of letter from Arthur Capper to Henry S Blake, Dec 31, 1941

6 "The United Nation," a speech of Arthur Capper, broadcast over NBC, Dec 29, 1941

7 Letter from William Allen White to Arthur Capper, Feb 4, 1942

8 Copy of letter from Arthur Capper to William Allen White, March 12, 1942

9 *Congressional Record,* 77 Cong , 2 Session, April 27, 1942, Kansas City *Star,* April 22, 1942

10 Emporia *Gazette,* April 23, 1942

11 Letter from Milt Tabor to Arthur Capper, May 18, 1942

12 Copy of letter from A Q Miller to John W Allison, May 14, 1942

13 Copy of letter from Arthur Capper to Col Robert A Ginsburgh, July 2, 1942, and reply, July 3, 1942

14 Great Bend *Tribune,* Aug 17, 1942, from the Newton *Kansan-Republican*

15 Walter Davenport, "Hot Seats," *Colliers,* Sept 19, 1942, 51

16 Rex Stout, ed , *The Illustrious Dunderheads,* A A Knopf, New York, 1942, 152-3, and preface

17 Edwin V Burkholder, " 'Pig Club' Capper from Kansas," *Pic,* Nov 10, 1942, 16-17 A marginal notation on the copy of this article in the Capper file says, "A pack of lies written by a political crook circulated in Kansas just before election The voters answered it by giving Capper a larger majority " Some articles appeared in the metropolitan press recognizing Capper's uncanny ability to sense what people thought See Washington *Times-Herald,* Sept 2, 1942

18 Letter from Charles H Sessions to Arthur Capper, Sept 25, 1942

19 Letter from Alfred M Landon to Arthur Capper, Oct 7, 1942 In a letter of Oct 23, Landon predicted a hundred thousand majority for Capper and about sixty thousand for the Republican gubernatorial candidate

20 Letter from William Green to Arthur Capper, Oct 22, 1942

21 Capper received 284,059 of slightly less than a half million votes His plurality was 83,622, compared with his narrow margin of 21,188 votes in 1936, when a strong Democratic tide was running in Kansas

22 *Capper's Weekly,* Nov 14, 1942

23 Letter from Franklin D Roosevelt to Arthur Capper, June 5, 1943

24 Copy of letter from Arthur Capper to Franklin D Roosevelt, June 11, 1943

25 Letter from Franklin D Roosevelt to Arthur Capper, June 16, 1943

26 New York *Times,* Jan 8, 1943

27 Topeka *Daily Capital,* Jan 12, 1943

28 *Ibid ,* Jan 15, 1943, *Capper's Weekly,* Feb 6, and March 20, 1943

29 Copy of letter from Alfred M Landon to Arthur Capper, May 10, 1943, and letter from Capper to Landon, June 18, 1943, Landon collection

30 New York *Times,* Sept 11, 1943

31 *Capper's Weekly,* July 8, 1944

32 Letter from Arthur Capper to Alfred M Landon, June 25, 1943, Landon collection

33 Topeka *Daily Capital,* Aug 30, 1943

34 *Ibid ,* Sept 1, 1943

35 Letter from William Allen White to Arthur Capper, Dec 3, 1943

36 Copy of letter from Arthur Capper to William Allen White, Dec 7, 1943

37 Copy of letter from Arthur Capper to Milt Tabor, Dec 8, 1943

38 Letters from William L White to Arthur Capper, Dec 29, 1943, and Jan 10, 1944, and copies of letters from Arthur Capper to William L White, Jan 5 and 12, 1944 The Board of Penal Institutions granted the parole in 1945 In 1949 the Kansas Governor gave Finney a conditional pardon which became a citizenship pardon later that same year Finney died in late 1961

39 New York *Times,* Dec 12, 1943

40 *Fortune,* May, 1945, 153-6

41 Copy of letter from Arthur Capper to Bert Andrews, Dec 9, 1946

42 *Congressional Record,* Sept 20, 1944 Capper later had considerable correspondence with the Bureau of Vital Statistics in which he sought information about the seven men older than he who had served in the United States Senate

43 *Congressional Quarterly*, I, 12

44 Letter from Clif Stratton to Henry S Blake, Jan 9, 1944

45 Official visitors to the Senate also included King Albert of the Belgians, the King and Queen of Great Britain, and leading public officials from Europe and from many Latin American countries

46 *Capper's Weekly*, April 28, 1945 This conversation was verified by former President Harry S Truman in a letter to the author, Feb 8, 1956, however, he doubted whether his mother would ever vote for a Republican

47 Copy of letter from Julia McKee to Mrs Edith Eustice, July 17, 1945 Capper was unable to return to Topeka for his thirty-eighth annual picnic

48 San Francisco *Examiner*, July 15, 1945, Washington *Post*, April 12, 1945, New York *Times*, July 15, 1945, Kansas City *Star*, July 15, 1945

49 New York *Times*, July 27, 1945

50 *Congressional Record*, 79 Cong , 1 Sess , 8086-7, *Capper's Weekly*, July 21, 1945, speech by Arthur Capper over WIBW, July 15, 1945, although Capper made frequent short remarks in the Senate, an extended statement, not usual or typical, made on March 3, 1947, commended William Randolph Hearst for his sixtieth anniversary as a newspaper publisher

51 New York *Times*, Jan 21, 1946

52 *Congressional Record*, 79 Cong , 2 Sess , Extension of Remarks, June 5, 1946, letter from W C Keiser, Vice president of the Brotherhood of Locomotive Firemen and Enginemen, to Arthur Capper, July 7, 1947, in a copy of a letter from Brook Haines to George H E Smith, Jan 28, 1946, Capper's major legislative activities, as listed by Capper's executive secretary, included District of Columbia housing bills, a measure to sanction the Kansas-Colorado compact on division of the waters of the Arkansas River, and an amendment to exclude the Tuttle Creek Dam project from the flood control authorization

53 Telegram from Arthur Capper to Brook Haines, Nov 6, 1946, New York *Times*, Nov 7 and 10, 1946

54 Letters from Arthur Vandenberg to Arthur Capper, Nov 8 and 19, 1946, and copy of letter from Arthur Capper to Arthur Vandenbeg, Nov 11, 1946

55 Chicago *Sun*, Dec 16, 1946, Washington *Post*, June 8, 1948 Capper reputedly had eight different hearing aids, but he did not like to wear even one and sometimes he would turn it off during committee meetings

56 Copy of letters from Arthur Capper to Wallace H White, Nov 19, 1946, and to Harland J Bushfield, Nov 21, 1946, New York *Times*, Nov 19, 1946, and Jan 1 and 3, 1947

57 *Capper's Farmer*, June and Aug , 1947

58 *Capper's Weekly*, Aug 9, 1947

59 *Ibid* , Sept 11, 1948

60 New York *Times*, Nov 1, 1947 His reason for returning to the Senate was to allow the "mid-continent area" to retain the "chairmanship of the Senate Committee on Agriculture" In a letter from Henry S Blake to Arthur Capper, May 17, 1947, Blake wrote, "Landon will run if you do not run and if you want him to run "

61 Copy of letters from Alfred M Landon to Dr George E Burket, Aug 4, to C H Smith, Oct 29, and letter from J Arthur Hamlett to Landon, Nov 6, 1947, Landon collection

62 Copy of letter from Alfred M Landon to C H Smith, Dec 1, 1947, Landon collection

63 Correspondence with Landon in late 1947 and early 1948, Landon collection

64 Letter from J N (Polly) Tincher to Alfred M Landon, Dec 2, and copy of reply from Landon to Tincher, Dec 5, 1947, Landon collection

65 *Capper's Weekly*, May 22, 1948

66 Letter from Roy Roberts to Arthur Capper, July 8, 1940

67 Copy of statement in the Capper file
68 Copy of letter from Arthur Capper to William L White, May 8, 1948
69 Wellington *Daily News*, May 12, 1948
70 Letter from Henry S Blake to Arthur Capper, June 1, 1948
71 1930—$707, 1936—$657 50, 1942—$155 50
72 The persons given advance information by telegram were Justice William A Smith, Alfred M Landon, Mrs Frank W Boyd, J N Tincher, Payne Ratner, Harry Darby, Marcellus Murdock, Willard Mayberry, George Austin Brown, W L Cunningham, John McCuish, Don Little, and Fred White, Topeka *Daily Capital*, June 7, 1948
73 Letters from Henry S Blake to Arthur Capper, June 7 and 8, 1948 Milton Eisenhower decided to stay out of the race because of the limited time until the primary
74 Examples include Topeka *State Journal*, June 7, 1948, Hartford (Conn) *Times*, June 8, 1948, Washington *Star*, June 10, 1948, and *Editor and Publisher*, July 17, 1948, 13
75 Duncan (Oklahoma) *Eagle*, Oct [no day], 1948
76 New York *Times*, June 21 and 26, 1948
77 *Ibid ,* Aug 16, 1948
78 His proposals for legislation included setting aside the period between Thanksgiving and Christmas to emphasize Bible reading, provision for postal cancellations marked "Observe Sunday," support of a medal to be given Scout Executive James E West, and provision for a memorial postage stamp honoring William Allen White Only in the last was he successful
79 Honors were also awarded to him in New York and other eastern cities

XVIII

1 George E Shankle, *American Nicknames Their Origin and Significance*, New York, 1937, 93 Apparently this nickname was first used in *The Washington Post Magazine*, March 4, 1923, New York *Times*, Dec 20, 1951
2 Socolofsky, *Kansas Historical Quarterly*, XXIV, 165
3 *Kansas Farmer* was started in Topeka in 1863 By the time Capper purchased it in 1919, *Farmers' Advocate* had been added, bringing into the combination the *Advocate and News*, the *Kansas News*, the Topeka *Tribune*, and the *Alliance Tribune* The North Topeka *Mail*, *Capper's* original publication, had been earlier combined with the North Topeka *Times*, which had in its background the *Kaw Valley Chief* and perhaps the *Daily Topeka Argus* Additions Capper personally made were the *Richland Argosy*, the *Kansas Breeze*, the *Sunflower*, the *Saturday Lance*, and the *Richland Observer* In addition his *Mail and Breeze* became the *Farmers' Mail and Breeze* in 1906 After purchase of *Kansas Farmer*, the *Field and Farm* was added, so that Capper personally accounted for seven of the combinations found in this one publication The *Missouri Ruralist* had in its background papers such as the *Breeder's Special* and the *Journal of Agriculture* which Capper had personally added
4 When this story was retold, the names of other persons at the luncheon sometimes changed, but the basic story remained
5 *Life,* April 14, 1947
6 Kansas City *Star*, Jan 6, 1952, interview with Mrs Henry S Blake, Sept 8, 1960 A variant of this story ended with Capper's giving the pig to a porter in the hotel, who had no way to get it home, so Capper paid his taxi fare
7 Chicago *Tribune*, June 9, 1935
8 Prior to World War I, Capper did own some real estate not connected with his business or his home, but he had long ago disposed of such property Copy of letter from Rod Runyan to J C Compton, May 9, 1947

9 A separation of his private and public business found him carefully avoiding the use of a franked envelope in his private correspondence

10 Topeka *Daily Capital,* March 21, 1948, and Dec 30, 1954, Kansas City *Star,* Jan 9, 1955, interview with Julia McKee, Sept 8, 1960

11 Chicago *Tribune,* June 9, 1935

12 Copy of telegram from Arthur Capper to Corliss Lamont, Sept 20, 1943, New York *World-Telegram,* Nov 14, 1946, Washington *Post,* June 30, 1948, copy of letter from Arthur Capper to the National Chairman, National Council of American-Soviet Friendship, Inc, June 29, 1950

13 Copy of letter from Arthur Capper to the Better Business Bureau, March, 1946, and reply, June 11, 1947

14 Emporia *Gazette,* Dec 24, 1951

15 Frank S Mead, "He Plays the Game Straight," *Christian Herald,* May, 1948, reprinted in *Kansas Farmer,* June 5, 1948, *National Weekly Social Justice,* April 22, 1940 The last publication was founded in 1936 by Father Charles E Coughlin

16 Radio address by Jack Warren Ostrode over KTOP, Jan 23, 1949

17 *The Capper House Book A Statement of the Policies and Aims of the Capper Publications,* Arthur Capper, Topeka, n d

18 *Ibid*, 5

19 *Ibid*, 8

20 *Ibid*, 11-12

21 *Ibid*, 13

22 *Ibid*, 14

23 *Current Opinion,* July, 1919, 21-2

24 Office Memo from Ray H Haun to Marco Morrow, Dec 1, 1919

25 Manhattan *Tribune-News,* Aug 26, 1948, portions of this story were taken from the *Editor and Publisher,* July 17, 1948, 13

26 Copy of letter from Arthur Capper to Melvin L Hayes, June 9, 1949

27 Commencement address by Arthur Capper at Lincoln Memorial University, Harrogate, Tennessee, June, 1946

28 Milton Tabor, "Topeka Roundup," Topeka *Daily Capital,* Dec [no day], 1951

29 Included were honors given by the National Council of Farmer Cooperatives, the American Forestry Association, the American Farm Bureau Federation, the National Capital Housing Authority, the Kansas 4-H Clubs, the Society of Natives of the District of Columbia, the City of New York, the Missouri Farmers' Association, the Washington Junior Chamber of Commerce, the Council against Intolerance, the Kansas State Board of Agriculture, the American Planning and Civic Association, the Topeka Chamber of Commerce, the Topeka Hospital Council, the Topeka Aerie of the Fraternal Order of Eagles, the International Reform Federation, the Kansas Cooperative Council, and the National Safety Council Honorary degrees had earlier been awarded to Capper from Washburn University of Topeka, Campbell College of Holton, Kansas, and Lincoln Memorial University of Harrogate, Tennessee Recognition was also accorded to him by numerous other fraternal, veteran, labor, religious, political, and business groups

30 Interview with Arthur Capper, April 7, 1950

31 Interview with Julia McKee, April 7, 1950 Very little was ever accomplished on the memoirs

32 Interview with Clif Stratton, Aug 4, 1952, *Capper's Weekly,* Dec 29, 1951

33 Copy of letter from Julia McKee to Mr and Mrs William A Souders, Dec 28, 1951

34 *Capper's Weekly,* Dec 29, 1951

35 Topeka *Daily Capital,* Dec 21, 1951 Capper was buried beside his wife Florence in the Topeka Cemetery

36 *Ibid*, Jan 6, 1952 Fred Brinkerhoff pointed out a coincidence that Senator Preston B Plumb had died almost sixty years to the day earlier and that his casket

also was opened in the Statehouse Capper had been in Washington when Plumb died and had written most of the stories which appeared in Kansas about his death

37 The original will was ten years old, having been executed in Washington on March 19, 1941, and all efforts by Capper's attorneys to revise it had failed About fifteen of the twenty-nine employees identified in the will qualified for their bequests

38 Interview with Rod Runyan, April 7, 1953

39 Topeka *Daily Capital*, April 24, 1956

40 Circulation figures from various editions of *Ayer's Newspaper Directory*, Topeka *Daily Capital*, June 7 and Nov 11, 1953 The television station construction permit was obtained in June, 1953, and regular operations began in November of the same year

41 Topeka *Daily Capital*, March 10, 1956 Phil Zach became the new president

42 The reason for this request was the belief that the trustees of Blake's estate, who were also directors of the Capper Foundation, were in a position whereby they could control a majority of the publishing company's stock

43 Topeka *Daily Capital*, Sept 16, 1956, and Feb 2, 1957

44 *Editor and Publisher*, Sept 22, 1956, 9, Nov 17, 1956, 42, and Dec 22, 1956

45 Kansas City *Star*, Jan 14, 1957

46 *Household*, Nov , 1958

47 Manhattan *Mercury*, March 4, 1960 Subscription commitments were handled by a variety of farm publications

48 Topeka *Daily Capital*, July 21, 1959 Stauffer Publications had sold the Capper Printing Company on Feb 6, 1959

49 *Ibid* , May 8, 1960, Kansas City *Star*, Jan 27, 1957 There were eleven daily newspapers in Stauffer Publications at the time it acquired Capper Publications They were the Arkansas City *Daily Traveler*, the Topeka *State Journal*, the Pittsburg *Headlight and Sun*, the Maryville (Missouri) *Daily Forum*, the Shawnee (Oklahoma) *News-Star*, the Grand Island (Nebraska) *Independent*, the Newton *Kansan*, the York (Nebraska) *News-Times*, the Independence (Missouri) *Examiner*, the Nevada (Missouri) *Daily Mail*, and the Santa Maria (California) *Times* Three radio stations, KSOK at Arkansas City, KSEK at Pittsburg, and KGFF at Shawnee, Oklahoma, were also owned and operated by the corporation, *Editor and Publisher*, Nov 17, 1956 Stauffer Publications, Inc , showed assets and surplus of more than three and a half million dollars, without Capper Publications, which was identified by W L White as "a dead horse of fantastic proportions" so the entire enterprise easily revolved in the area of high finance See *Time*, Oct 1, 1956

50 Topeka *Daily Capital*, Sept 16, 1960, *Kansas Farmer*, March 4, 1961

51 *The Capper Foundation for Crippled Children*, pamphlet, 3-4, interview with Constance Van Natta, daughter of Con Van Natta, July 9, 1952 At first Miss Van Natta, a victim of a severe case of polio at the age of four and a half years, resented being the inspiration for the Capper Fund Later she was pleased with that role Her father did not promote her handicap so that she could become Capper's first beneficiary, for he proudly paid his own bills, but because of her he was more concerned with similar handicaps in other children

52 *Kansas Farmer*, Dec 1, 1928 Receipts from the campaign in 1925 were 5,000 dimes, in 1926, 10,000 dimes, and in 1927, 12,500 dimes

53 *Ibid* , Dec 11, 1926, Oct 6 and Dec 1, 1928

54 Interview with J M Parks, May 18, 1953

55 "Corporation Charter Book," Secretary of State of Kansas, in the Archives of the Kansas State Historical Library, CXXXII, 251 Doris Schenck served as secretary of the foundation until 1941

56 New York *Herald-Tribune*, Sept 27, 1931, speech by Arthur Capper over WMAL, Washington, May 18, 1933, *The Crippled Child*, Jan , 1934, speech by Arthur Capper over WJSV, March 30, 1934, the *Commercial Journal*, Oct , 1934 Capper strongly supported the work of the Shriners and of the International Society for Crippled Children

57 Speech by Arthur Capper at Belleville, Sept 25, 1935

58 Interview with Constance Van Natta, July 9, 1952

59 Interview with J M Parks, May 18, 1953

60 Letters from Ruth McKinnis, the director of the Foundation Capper File Expenses in 1947 had averaged $120 28 per child

61 *The New Capper Foundation Rehabilitation Center,* brochure, n d , c 1959

62 Topeka *Daily Capital,* April 26, 1959 The late Leland H Schenck, former Capper executive, became the president of Capper Foundation Sale of Capper Foundation stock to Stauffer brought $624,668 75

63 Interview with Frank McGrath, executive secretary, Capper Foundation for Crippled Children, Nov 1, 1960

64 *Ibid*

65 "History & Development," information released by the Capper Foundation for Crippled Children According to the corporation charter of the Foster Humane Society, filed Nov 23, 1896, "Corporation Charter Book," Secretary of State of Kansas, in Archives of the Kansas State Historical Library, XLV, 26-7, Arthur Capper was one of the original directors and he was one of eight witnesses, subscribing to the charter, who appeared before the notary public

66 Topeka *Daily Capital,* May 4, 1954 The original structure costing $700,000 was enlarged the following year with a $532,000 addition See Topeka *State Journal,* July 14, 1955, and Topeka *Daily Capital,* Nov 17, 1955

67 Topeka *Daily Capital,* Oct 3, 1954, the *Kansas Publisher,* Nov , 1954, featured the selection of the Hall of Fame with a cover picture of Arthur Capper

68 Washington *Star,* Oct 6, 1954, Washington *Post and Times Herald,* Oct 7, 1954, Topeka *Daily Capital,* Oct 6, 1954, and Oct 7, 1956 The project bounded by 2nd, 7th, and M streets, and Virginia Avenue, in the old Navy Yard neighborhood, would provide low-rent accommodations for 612 families, and some provision would be made for elderly couples and families with physically handicapped members Total cost of the 80 one-bedroom, 419 two-bedroom, 17 three-bedroom apartments, and the 96 two-story houses was $6,759,000

69 Washington *Star,* Dec 23, 1951, other memorials included a new daylily, "The Senator Arthur Capper," and the creation of the Capper Memorial Museum Association to restore and organize the Capper birthplace in Garnett See Topeka *Daily Capital,* May 11, July 14, 1956, Wichita *Eagle,* Nov 3, 1955, *Capper's Weekly,* March 13, 1956, Garnett *Review,* April 30, 1956, Garnett *Anderson Countian,* Aug 9, 1956 The charter of the Capper Memorial Association, Aug 4, 1955, allowed it to purchase the small house where Capper was born Capper Publications had put up money and a loan to get the Memorial Association functioning

70 Roanoke (Virginia) *World News,* Dec 24, 1951

71 Ada (Oklahoma) *News,* Dec [no day], 1951, Pittsburg *Headlight,* Dec [no day], 1951

72 Pittsburg *Headlight,* Dec [no day], 1951, Worcester (Massachusetts) *Telegram,* Dec 21, 1951

73 Winston-Salem (North Carolina) *Journal,* Dec 26, 1951

74 Dodge City *Globe,* Dec 21, 1951, Atchison *Daily Globe,* Dec 21, 1951, Monroe (Wisconsin) *Evening Times,* Dec 21, 1951, Garnett *Review,* Nov 16, 1948

75 Pittsburgh (Pennsylvania) *Post-Gazette,* Dec 29, 1951

76 Arthur Capper, "Moral Re-Armament," *Vital Speeches,* VI, 215-16, Jan 15, 1940 Initially delivered as a radio address on Dec 3, 1939

77 Joplin (Missouri) *Globe,* Dec 21, 1951, Springfield (Ohio) *News,* Jan 16, 1952

78 Jacob Simpson Payton, "Capper of Kansas," *Christian Advocate,* Nov 22, 1945 Also published in the *Christian-Evangelist,* Nov 21, 1945

79 See Emporia *Times,* July 19, 1945

Index

Abbott, Lyman, 31
Abolition, 2, 3, 4
Addresses and Messages by Arthur Capper, Twenty second Governor of Kansas, 244n*14*, 246n*55*, 247n*28, 35, 51, 52, 54,* 248n*65*
Advertising and postal restrictions, 50, for Capper publications, 55-7, political influence on, 64, compared with editorial policy, 64, and editorial policy, 69, competition in 1930's, 192, standards by 1930, 197, Research Foundation, 200, mentioned, 191
Agora, 50
Agricultural Adjustment Act declared unconstitutional, 182, 174, 176, 183
Agricultural Adjustment Administration, 190
Agricultural Advertising, 57
Agricultural Marketing Act, 163
Agricultural periodicals, 53
Agricultural problems after World War II, 211
Agricultural Publishers Association, 200
Agriculture and Forestry Committee, 146, 210
Alabama, 179
Alaska, 217
Aldrich, Nelson W , 73
Allen, Henry J and "The Human Vampire," 65, and State Printer, 65, later view of Capper, 66, Governor-elect, 105, mentioned, 83, 145, 150, 166, 192, 243n*10, 12,* 245n*21,* 248n*85*
Allison, William B , 35
Alvey, C P , 10
American Academy of Political Science, 162
American Agricultural Editors' Association, 111
American Farm Bureau Federation, 148
American Homestead, 61
American League for a Free Palestine, Inc , 219-20
American Press Association, 30
American Red Cross, 101, 219
American Woman Suffrage meeting, Topeka, 23-4
American Young Folks, 13-4
"Amos and Andy," 185
Anderson, John A , 23
Anderson, Marian, 185-6
Anderson County, Kansas, 2, 3, 4, 9, 25, 188
Anderson County Republican, 16
Ann Arbor, Michigan, 30
Anthony, Daniel R , Jr , 66-8, 77, 243n*13, 15, 16*
Anthony, Susan B , 24, 223
Anti-Crime Association, 124

Anti-slavery *See* Abolition
Anti-war editorials, 176
Appanoose County, Iowa, 2
Appeal to Reason, 103
Arkansas City *Traveler,* 39
Arthur Capper Dwellings, 229
Article X of League Covenant, 130-1
Atchison, Topeka and Santa Fe Railway, 19, 25
Audit Bureau of Circulation, 199
Austria, 156
Axis Powers, 184

Babcock, Stephen M , 123
Bailey, William A , 139
Baker, F P , 24, 236n*28*
Baker, Newton D , 248n*57*
Ball, Frank, 57
Baltimore, Maryland, 156
Bank of Topeka, 49
Bankhead, William B , 174
Barkley, Alben W , 174
Baruch, Bernard M , 149, 256n7
Bates County, Missouri, 3
Beard, Charles A , 184
Beck, M M , 26
Beck, Will T , 26, 73, 75-6, 244n*39*
Belgium relief aid from Kansas to, in 1915, 93, 95, mentioned, 156
Benjamin Franklin University, 257n*37*
Bethany College, Topeka, 28
Bethesda Naval Hospital, 213
Better Times Chronicle, 199
Bismarck Grove, 23
Black, Hugo, 179
Black Hills of South Dakota, 159
Blaine, James G , 20, 34
Blake, Henry S , 196-7, 225, 262n*21-32 passim*
Bleeding Kansas, 8
B'nai B'rith, 220
"Bone Dry" prohibition law, 96
"Boss-busting," 63, 69
Boston, 29, 33, 34
Boston *Globe,* 24
Botkin, Jeremiah D , 91, 246n*14*
Bourbon County, Kansas, 3, 5
Bowers, Arthur, 32
Bowers, Claude G , 180, 260n*70*
Boys' and Girls' Corn Raising Contest, 116
Breeder's Special, 60
Bridges, Styles, 177
Brinkerhoff, Fred, 268n*36*
Brinkley, John R , 166
Bristow, Joseph L , 63, 68, 72, 75, 83, 100, 104, 237n*41,* 244n*32, 1,* 245n*45*
British Empire, 184
Brooklyn, 31
Brooks, Phillips, 34
Brown, John, 2, 230, 233n*20*

Bryan, Charles W , 61, 242n*33*, 255n*31*
Bryan, William Jennings, 43, 61, 255n*31*
Bufford, Jeff, 2
"Bull Moose," 79, 81
Burton, J R , 47, 243n*14*
Bushfield, Harland J , 266n*56*
Business conditions in 1930's, 187
Butler, Nicholas Murray, 162

California, 14
California Fruit Growers' Exchange, 122
Camp Doniphan, 100
Camp Funston, 100
Campbell, Lewis, 233n*5*
Campbell College, Holton, 247n*19*
Canada, 121
Capital Publishing Company sold to Capper and others, 50, cost, 50, directors, 241n*41*
Capper, Alfred (uncle of Arthur C), 4, 233n*7*
Capper, Arthur birth, 1, birthplace, 7-8, birthplace restoration, 8, unnamed on 1865 census, 9, childhood in Longton, 11, early vocational interests, 12, childhood escapades, 12-13, early philosophy, 13, selling Kansas City *Times,* 13, and toy printing press, 13, first real newspaper job, 13, earliest published letters, 13-14, work in post office, 16, activities in high school, 16, scholastic record, 16, high-school commencement, 16, valedictory address, 17, favorite poem, 17, plans after high-school graduation, 17, search for work, 18, delayed by mumps, 18, to Topeka *Daily Capital* in 1884, 18, as compositor, 19, no formal membership in union, 19, becomes journalist, 20, first news story for *Capital,* 20, as telegraph and city editor, 20, personal diary, 21, early income, 21, speculation in real estate, 21, activities in Topeka, 22, early companions, 22, uses Pittman shorthand, 22, on twenty-first birthday, 23, first vote (straight Republican), 23, editor of *Capital,* 24, other opportunities, 24, correspondent for out-of-town papers, 24, interviews Mrs Julia Ward Howe, 24, health, 24-5, an early vacation, 25, on southwest Kansas frontier, 25-6, becomes director of Topeka Capital Company, 26, increasing reputation, 26, early loyalty to Republican party, 27, minor political party positions, 27, autograph collection, 27, social activity, 27, physical appearance, 27, bicycle, 27, 35, engagement to Florence Crawford, 28, a Congressional reporter, 29, diary, 29-30, comments on Florence, 30, in Detroit, 30, at Niagara Falls, 30, comments on Toronto, Canada, 30, first assignment on New York *Tribune,* 32, sends engagement ring to Florence, 32, yacht race story in *Tribune,* 32, on Schnorer Club excursion, 33, interviews Benjamin Harrison, 33, witnesses test of Sims-Edison torpedo, 33, to Nantucket, 33, to Gettysburg with Tammany regiment, 34, misses William McKinley, 34, in Washington as correspondent, 34-39, introduced to Washington society, 36, slight illness, 36, article on Jerry Simpson, 37, completes journal, 38, leaves Washington, 39, marriage to Florence Crawford, 40, honeymoon, 40, at home at Crawford mansion, 40, purchases first newspaper, 41, changes on paper, 42, described by J L King, 44, early alignment with Republican party, 44, gains control of *Mail and Breeze,* 45, other newspapers offered to him, 45, support in 1896 from Republican Flambeau Club, 47, rise in Republican party offices, 47, early backing for Curtis weakened, 47, purchases *Missouri Valley Farmer,* 48, takes over *Push,* 50, offered majority control of *Capital,* 50, and minority stockholders, 50, publications of 1906, 52, as political insurgent and progressive, 53, liberal classification in politics, 53, work procedure, 54, "open door" policy as publisher, 54, "method" of command, 55, launches nationwide advertising campaign, 55, intuition on business policy, 55, major role in early business activities, 56, plans for expansion, 57, haphazard procedure in adding newspapers, 59, political views of early 1900's, 63, and State Printer, 63, gives credit for establishing reputation in Kansas, 63, early political philosophy, 64, refusal to sell *Capital,* 64, called a "human vampire," 65, reply to Anthony's charges, 66-7, defense of Dodd Gaston, 70, experiences with first cars, 71-2, suggested as Secretary of Agriculture, 72, first public position, regent of K S A C , 72, 73, new political role, 73, candidate for Governor of Kansas, 74-86, announcement of candidacy for Governor, 76, backs T R for President in 1912, 76, 78, campaign procedure, 79, accused of betraying Republican party, 79, method to contest election in 1912, 80-81, indecision after 1912 election, 82, speeches, 83, elected Governor, 85-86, as Governor of Kansas, 87-105, first Inaugural Address, 87, mail from constituents, 88, view on constructive legislation, 88, his "open door" policy, 88, business policy while Governor, 88, evaluation of first legislation, 89-90, handling of first legislature, 90-91, letter-writers seek advice from Governor, 91, attitude toward spoils

system, 92, appointment of official delegates, 92, as chairman of Kansas committee to aid war-devastated Belgium, 93, as Kansas chairman of League of Nations to Enforce Peace, 93, 127, opposes preparedness, 93, 94, introduces President Wilson in Topeka, 94, view on Presidents, 94, again candidate for Governor, 95, Second inaugural address as Governor, 95, 96, legislative accomplishments of second term, 96, use of Governor's veto, 97, proclamation for Peace Sunday, 98, fundamentally a pacifist, 98, likened to Copperheads of Civil War, 98, Loyalty Day proclaimed for April 6, 1917, 98, "about-face" after war was declared, 99, helps organize Kansas for World War I, 99, proposes a draft of capital during wartime, 100, topics of war speeches, 100, announced goals of Kansas during war, 100, at Camp Doniphan, 100, at Camp Funston, 100, receives complaints of disloyalty of Kansans, 101, personal contributions during World War I, 101, and Non-Partisan League, 102-3, announces candidacy for U S Senator, 104, campaign attitude, 104, vacation trip with Mrs Capper, 105, dual role of politician and publisher, 106, and Republican party, 112, and "grass roots" sentiment, 113, 147, early charitable activities, 113, his longtime private secretary, 114, recognition of children, 115, interest in children analyzed, 115, Boy Scouts, 116, Y M C A, 116, gives Thanksgiving dinner to all newsboys, 116, support for 4-H, 119-20, member of National Committee on Boys' and Girls' Club Work, 120, elected U S Senator, 126, statement after 1918 election, 126, partisan feeling and World War I, 127, letters to Wilson, 127, Kansas chairman of League of Nations to Enforce Peace, 127, early attitude on League of Nations, 128, not in senatorial "Round Robin," 128, and reservations on treaty, 128, 129, 131, endorses some Wilson stands, 129, visits President Wilson, 129, other issues of 1919 special session, 129, shift on treaty, 130, letter from Taft, 130, and Gore amendment, 131, and United Nations, 134, 209, and vote on Versailles Treaty, 132-3, analysis of vote on Versailles Treaty, 134, departure for Senate, 135, purchases Lawrence Publishing Company, 139-40, political aspirations in 1920's, 141, first radio station, WJAP, 143, uses own home while Governor 145, agreement and disagreement with Henry J Allen, 145, committee assignments in Senate, 145-6, seniority in

Senate, 146, unofficial "mayor of Washington," 146, farm spokesman in Senate, 146-7, responsibility as Senator, 147, at Baruch dinner, 149, partisanship in 1920's, 149, write-in candidate for President in *Literary Digest* poll, 149, criticized, 150, becomes chairman of Farm Bloc, 150, 151, compared to Henry J Allen, 150, early "network" radio address, 153, maverick tendencies, 153, re-elected in 1924, 154, turns down position as Secretary of Agriculture, 154, on McNary-Haugen bill, 154, social traits in Washington, 155, early and later residence in Washington, 155, 157, vacation with Florence in Europe, 155-6, speeches in Topeka, 156, guest at White House, 158, to Black Hills with Coolidges, 159, as presidential possibility, 159, senatorial career of 1920's, 160, on Military Affairs Committee, 161, on Paris Peace Pact, 162, on Agricultural Marketing Act, 163, support for tariff, 164, productive period in Senate, 164, expects economic collapse, 164-5, and party loyalty, 165, feeling toward Hoover, 166, his political strength, 166-7, as author, 167, and progressive label, 167, supports Hoover in 1932, 168, first introduced to F D R, 168, on election of F D R, 169, use of radio transcriptions, 169, eulogy for Coolidge, 169, other views on depression, 170, describes "first 100 days," 171, on Farm and Home Hour, 171, criticized as too New-Dealish, 172-3, interprets election of 1934, 173, agreement with early New Deal, 174, vote compared to that of leading Democratic Senators, 174, and prohibition, 175, and foreign policy of early thirties, 175, and national referendum on a declaration of war, 176, on "packing" the Supreme Court, 178, isolationism, 175-6, 180, 181, role in Landon race, 177-8, appendicitis, 179, and six-point peace program, 180-1, turns against New Deal and Reciprocal Trading Agreements, 181, opposes naval expansion, 181, convenes farm conference in Topeka, 182, and political position in 1938, 182, on invalidation of AAA by Supreme Court, 182, "favorite son" in 1940, 183, usual support for Republican party, 183, interprets vote for Willkie, 184, pre-Pearl Harbor alarm, 184, in Topeka when Pearl Harbor is bombed, 184, described by critic, 185, as party-goer, 185, unable to vote on declaration of World War II, 185, and Marian Anderson concert, 185-6, removes himself from business payroll, 187, opposes publishing papers outside Capper plant, 191, opposes "cut-throat competition," 192, and labor legislation, 195-6, and editorial freedom, 196, and advertising, 197, goals of advertising, 198, advertising policy, 198-9, view on his business and employees, 200, as "a leading isolationist," 202, 204, "quiet shift" in support of F D R 's policy on war, 202, no personal campaign in 1942, 204, lacked usual labor support in 1942, 204, victory statement in 1942, 205, on press ban at Hot Springs Conference, 205, and withholding tax, 206, no personal interest in Finney matter, 207, is host at another farm conference, 207, receives complaints on wartime restrictions, 207, autographed picture collection, 208, rated by close friend, 208, rated in *Congressional Quarterly*, 208, seniority in Senate, 208, comments on age limit for Senators, 208, eightieth birthday, 209, radio "network" broadcast over NBC, 209, approves United Nations Charter, 209, compares charters of United Nations and League of Nations, 209, chairman, Committee on Agriculture and Forestry, 210, labor attitudes after World War II, 210, hearing problems, 210, potential candidate for Senate in 1948, 211, opposition developing in 1948, 212, withdraws from senatorial race, 212-3, health in old age, 213, retirement, 213-4, commendations, 214, political offices summarized, 215, not a beginner of new publications, 215, a Kansas institution, 215, participates in many historic events, 216, reminiscences, 216-8, and golf, 217, his own feeling of wealth, 218, fraternal groups, 218, appetite, 219, board member of national organizations, 219, modest living conditions, 219, interprets his role as Senator, 220, diversity of political support, 220, explanation of political success, 221, business maxims, 222, change in publicizing own activities, 222-3, speeches and editorial writing, 223, own estimate of greatest Americans, 223, retirement, 223, death and funeral, 224, will, 224-5, pioneer in helping crippled children, 227, posthumous memorials, 228-9, summary of life, 230, author of *The Agricultural Bloc*, 231, membership in Knights of Labor, 235n2, secretary of Kansas Republican League, 237n41, Kansas Day Club, secretary and president, 240n27, people first told of withdrawal from Senate race, 267n72, proposals for legislation, 267n78, honors, 268n29, interview with, 268n30

Capper, Benjamin (brother of Arthur C), 9, 16, 24

Capper, Bessie (sister of Arthur C), 9, 16

Capper, Edith (sister of Arthur C), 9 *See also* Mrs Edith Capper Eustice

Capper, Elizabeth (grandmother of Arthur C), 1, 233n1

Capper, Florence (Mrs Arthur C) and Capper's first car, 71, view on Capper's political activity, 74, illness and death, 156-8, *Poems*, 250n1, 46, 50, 115, 145, 155

Capper, Herbert (father of Arthur C) arrival, in Anderson County, 2, abolition sentiments, 2, 3, tinner, 2, 4, 6, 11, first homestead, 4, prohibition, 4, citizenship, 4, politics, 4, Union support, 4, marriage to Isabella McGrew, 4-5, resided in Mapleton, 5, in Home Guard, 6, real estate activity, 6-8, 10, 12, 16, considered well-to-do, 9, enumeration in 1865 census, 9, principles, 9, physically not strong, 9, post-Civil War, 10, enumeration in 1870 census, 10, move from Garnett, 10, locating in Elk Rapids (Longton), 11, respects Horace Greeley, 12, move from Longton, 12, moves family to New Jersey, 14, frequent change of residence, 14, ill health, 14-5, political views, 20, moves family to Lawrence, 24, returns family to Garnett, 24, 1, 30, 233n2, *3, 4, 8-14, 16, 23,* 235n6

Capper, Isabella (mother of Arthur C), 1, 5, 9, 10, 30, 233n3, 234n30

Capper, Mary (sister of Arthur C), 1

Capper, Mary May (known as May—sister of Arthur C), 9, 16, 48, 55, 112, 194, 250n39, 262n37

Capper, Thomas (grandfather of Arthur C), 1, 233n1

Capper Award for Distinguished Service to American Agriculture selection committee, 253n52, 122-3

Capper birthday party, 115-6

Capper brain trust's guide book, 223

Capper Building construction and occupancy, 57-8, description, 58, 72, 137, 191, 236n39

Capper Bulletin, 76, 199, 244n9

Capper canter, 185

Capper Certificates, 137, 193, 225

Capper-Crampton Act, 151

Capper Credit Union, 124, 253n67

Capper editorial freedom, 69-70, 196

Capper employees, 106

Capper "family," 58, 106, 111, 112, 193, 200

Capper farm papers sold, 226

Capper Farm Press growth and pattern, 59, early expansion outside Kansas, 59-61, and Master Farmer movement, 120, promotion, 123, 62, 107, 109, 121, 136, 138, 139, 140, 142, 148, 190, 200

Capper Foundation for Crippled Children, 224, 225, 227-8, 269n42, *51*

Capper Foundation Holiday Seal Campaign, 228
Capper Fund for Crippled Children, 226
Capper gold medal, 123 See also Capper Award
Capper-Harmon-Slocum, Incorporated, 142, 187, 195, 218
Capper heirs, 224
Capper "House Book," 221
Capper Junior High School, Topeka, 228
Capper-Ketchum Act, 120, 151
Capper-Lenroot-Anderson Act, 151
"Capper Lexicon"—things always right, 220
Capper Mansion, 72, 94, 145, 157, 194
Capper Memorial Museum Association, 270n69
Capper "old-timers," 112-4, 200
Capper papers, 231
Capper Printing Company replacement for Mail Printing House, 62, board of directors, 263n40, 113, 192, 194, 215, 225
Capper Publications offices, 54, double-entry bookkeeping first used, 55, advertising, 55-7, 78, 104, 197, 198, recapitulation in 1914, 62, editorial freedom, 69-70, employee relations, 106, development when incorporated, 114, first youth contests, 115, gifts and scholarships, 120, 124-5, long-range plans, 137, 141, expansion, 1919-1930, 143, retrenchment in depression, 138, payroll cuts, 187, economizing measures of 1930's, 187, alternatives for improvements, 187, circulation, 1930-1948, 191, labor relations, 195, train and automobile tours, 198, summary in 1949, 215-6, signed editorials, 231, board of directors when incorporated, 264n39, and Stauffer Publications, 269n49, 109, 110, 111, 135, 157, 186-201
Capper Publications, Inc, 194, 197, 218, 224, 225
Capper-Tincher Grain Futures Act, 149, 151
Capper-Volstead Act of 1922 and 1926, 151
Capper Youth Clubs 115-120, Boys' and Girls' Poultry Contest, 117, Boys', Corn Club, 116, Capper Boys' Corn Club, 116, Capper Boys' Swine Club, 117, Capper Boys' Baby Beef Club, 117, Capper Boys' Colt Show, 117, Capper Girls' Tomato Club, 117, Capper Pig Club, 117, Capper Poultry Club, 118, initial membership, loans, prizes, "pep trophies," motivation, 117-8, Capper Calf Club, 118, summary, 118-9, replaced by 4-H, 119, Young People's Farm League, 251n15
Capper's advertising research department, 199-200
Capper's eastern farm papers, 142

Capper's Farmer changed from Missouri Valley Farmer, 135, 143, 187, 188, 189-190, 192, 200, 215, 216, 225
Capper's Magazine, 141, 143, 168, 216
Capper's National Protective Service, 124
Capper's Weekly new name for Kansas Weekly Capital, 61-2, 83, eastern edition, 141, 62, 109, 111, 143, 187, 215, 216
Carleton, M A, 123
Carlson, Frank, 206
Case, John Francis, 111, 196, 244n22, 250n34, 251n23, 28
Chase, Harold T, 35, 50, 63, 69, 108, 127, 241n41, 244n28, 249n4, 15
Chase County, Kansas, 188
Cherokee Strip, 39
Chiang Kai-shek, Mme, 208
Chicago, 30, 76, 198, 225, 227
Chicago World's Fair, 43
Churchill, Winston, 208, 217
Cincinnati, Iowa, 1, 4
Cincinnatus, Kansas, 25
Civil War, 1, 8
Clark, George, 68
Clay Center, Kansas, 23
Cleveland, Grover, 20, 34, 92, 94
Cleveland, Ohio, 140, 143, 177, 195, 198
Clover, Ben, 38-9
Collier's, 76, 244n10
Colorado, 27, 138
Columbia Broadcasting System, 143
Committee on Claims, 146
Committee to Defend America by Aiding the Allies, 202
Commoner, 61, 255n31
Congress of Industrial Organization, 196
Congressional Quarterly, 208
Congressional Record, 203
Connecticut Agricultural Experiment Station, 191
Conservatory of Music in Boston, 28
Continuing Study of Farm Publications, 200
Coolidge, Calvin, 153, 154, 155, 158, 159, 162, 169, 216, 257n31, 53
Coolidge, Grace, 155, 156, 158, 258n55
Copeland, Royal, 179, 259n41
"Copeland County Politics," 63, 243n1
Corn, hybrid, 190-1
"Corn Shucking" contest, 121
Coughlin, Charles E, 268n15
Council Grove, 113
Country Gentleman, 54
County-seat war, 25
Crawford, Florence birth in Topeka and early training, 28, musical accomplishments, 28, engagement to Arthur Capper, 28, diary, 29-30, receives engagement ring from Arthur, 32, at Nantucket Island, 32-3, completes journal, 36-7, to Washington, 38, marriage, 40, 29, 31, 36, 71, 157, 218 See also Florence Capper

Crawford, George Marshall (brother of Florence C), 28, 33, 34, 48, 155
Crawford, Mrs George M , 194
Crawford, Isabel, 155
Crawford, Samuel J (father of Florence C) signed school-land patents bought by Herbert Capper, 10, 28, 33, 35, 37, 41
Crawford, Mrs Samuel J (mother of Florence C), 28, 29, 32, 38
Crawford Building, 48
Crawford-Capper wedding, 40, 238n67
Crawford Mansion, 40, 238n65
Crosby, E H , 239n71, 73, 6, 256n1
Crosby Brothers, 43
Crowley, Byron M , 232, 234n22, 236n37
Crowther, M L , 60
Curtis, Charles, 23, 47, 73, 75, 94, 153, 159-60, 161, 166, 240n26, 244n38
Curtis, Cyrus, 222
Curtis Publications, 225
Czechoslovakia, 156, 180

Daniels, Josephus, 168
Daughters of the American Revolution, 185
Davies, Gomer, 26
Davis, David, 27
Davis, Jonathan M , 164
Davis County, Iowa, 1
Dawes, Charles G , 158
"Daylight saving" issue, 148
Dearing Company, 192
Democratic party, 77, 78-9, 84, 90
Democratic campaign against Capper in 1918, 104
Democratic-Insurgent Republican coalition, 166, 258n77
Denver, Colorado, 137, 138
Denver *Tribune,* 24
Depressions of 1893, 40-1, after World War I, 138, 147, for Kansas agriculture, 167-8, of 1929, 164-5
Des Moines conference of Midwestern Governors, 177
Detroit, Michigan, 30, 143, 198
Dewey, Thomas E , 206, 207
Dillon, Charles J , 112, 113
Disloyalty charges of World War I, sent to Governor Capper, 101
District of Columbia Committee, 146, 211, 214, 229
Dolley, Joe N , 74, 78
Dorset, Marion, 123
Dorsey, Ed R , 60
Draft capital in wartime, 100
Drakesville, Iowa, 1

"Eastern trio" of farm papers, 139-140, 142, 143, 196, 216
Edison, Thomas A , 149, 256n7
Editorial policy compared with advertising, 64, and business activities, 69, in Topeka *Daily Capital,* 69
Eighteenth Amendment, 100, 175
Eisenhower, Dwight D , 206
Eisenhower, Milton S , 211, 267n73
Election contest in Kansas, 80-1
Elections of 1912, outcome, 79-81, party column ballot, 80, 246n60
of 1914 issues, 84, proposal for debate, 85, 246n60
of 1916 results in Kansas, 95, interpreted, 95
of 1918, 105, 126
of 1920, 133-4
of 1924, 154
of 1930, 164
of 1934 interpreted by Capper, 173
of 1936, 178, 265n21
of 1942, 202-4
of 1946, 210
Elk Rapids, Kansas (Longton), 11
Ellis, Kansas, 112
Emergency Tariff Bill of 1921, 149
Emporia, Kansas, 28
Emporia *Gazette,* 173, 212
Eustice, A L , 112
Eustice, Mrs Edith Capper, 224

Fair Labor Standards Act, 186
Faneuil Hall, 34
Farm and Fireside, 54
Farm Bloc, 145, 148-154
Farm conference in Topeka, 182-3, 207
Farm co-operatives, 151, 152
Farm Journal, 54
Farm Loan Bank of Wichita, 154
Farmers' Advocate, 54
Farmers' Alliance, 26-7, 35, 38, 43
Farmers' Mail and Breeze Boys' and Girls' Corn Raising Contest, 116, consolidated with *Kansas Farmer,* 136 *See also Mail and Breeze*
Farmers' National Committee on War Finance Capper as chairman, 100
Farmer's Wife, 121
Farrell, Francis D , 235n44, 239n13, 262n16, 263n53
Federal Communications Commission, 194, 225
Federal Emergency Relief Act, 174
Federal Farm Board, 163
Federal Intermediate Credit Bank of Wichita, 112
Federal Land Bank of Wichita, 112
Federal Relief Act, 174
Federal Reserve Bank of Kansas City, 102
Federal Reserve Bank of New York City, 206
Finney, Ronald, 207, 265n38
Field, Henry, 259n14
Field and Farm, 137-8
Fields, John, 61, 111, 112, 154, 250n36
Florence Public Library, 218

Florida, 135
Florida Farmer, 141
Flying Farmers' organizations, 124
Ford, Henry, 93, 247n23, 264n59
Fordney-McCumber tariff, 164
Foreign Relations Committee, 129, 146, 180, 210, 229
Ft Scott, Kansas, 25
Foster Humane Society of Topeka, 228
Foster's Crossing, Ohio, 109
Four-H Clubs, supported by Capper, 119, 151
France, 156
Freedom for Capper editors, 69-70, 196
Frémont, John C, 4, 230
Funston, Edwin H, 238n60
Funston, Frederick, 97, 243n6

Galva, Kansas, 14
Galveston, Texas, 40
Garden City, Kansas, 93
Garnett, Kansas, 1, 3, 5-6, 9, 10, 13, 14, 15, 16, 18, 19, 22, 24, 30, 270n69
Garnett *Eagle,* 29
Garnett High School third graduating class, 235n39, 17
Garnett *Journal,* 13
Garnett Opera House, 17, 25
Garnett *Plaindealer,* 11, 15
Garnett *Republican-Plaindealer,* 21
Gaston, Dodd *See* Jay E House
Geneva, 156, 162
George V of England, 156
George, David Lloyd, 156, 257n39
George Washington Memorial Parkway, 151
Georgia, 14
German reparation question, 168
Germany, 98, 156
Gettysburg, 34
Gilkeson, Raymond H, 252n33, 262n15, 17
Girard, Kansas, 103
Good Neighbor Policy, 175
Good Roads Association, 97
"Good Roads Day," 91
Gore, Thomas P, 116, 131, 176-7
Gougar, Mrs Helen, 24
Governor of Kansas, 90
Grain Futures Act of 1922, 149
Grant, U S, 12
Grant County, Kansas, 25
"Grass roots," 113, 128, 136, 147, 166, 183
Greeley, Horace hero for Herbert Capper, 12, 234n17
Green, William, 265n20
Greenback party, 26
Griest, John E, 112, 113
Guffey-Snyder Act, 174
Guthrie, Oklahoma, 60

Haddonfield, New Jersey, 14
Hale, Edward Everett, 238n31

Harding, Warren G, 134, 150-1, 155, 161
Harman, Thomas D, 142
Harris, J P, 2
Harrison, Benjamin, 27, 33, 35, 94, 237n42
Hartland, Kansas, 25
Harvard, 108
Harvey, James M, 248n83
Haucke, Frank, 258n5
Haugen, Gilbert N, 152
Hawley-Smoot tariff, 164
Hayden, Carl, 174
Hays, Will H, 128
Hearst, William Randolph, 266n50
Hendriks, J A, 188, 189
Hendricks method of chick raising, 188-9
Heslet, Jim, 23
Hicks, Phil, 25
Highland Park, 26, 49
Hitchcock, Gilbert M, 132
Hitler, Adolph, 205
Hoch, Edward W, 107, 111, 249n29
Hodges, George H, 77, 79, 80-1, 84-6, 90, 91, 93
Holland, James C, 57
Hoover, Herbert, 160, 162-3, 166, 167, 168, 169, 186, 218, 248n58
Hoover, Mrs Herbert, 218
Hoover debt holiday, 168
Hope, Clifford R, 178, 211, 260n57
"Horace Greeley of Kansas," 236n28
Hospital for the Women of Maryland, 156
Hospital Survey and Construction Act, 228
Hot Springs International Food Conference, 205-6
House, Jay E, 70-1, 236n38, 245n18
Household new name for *Push,* 51, early advertising policy, 51, 52, 54, 62, 65, 78, 109, 124, 143, 187, 192, 198, 215, 216, 225
Howard, Leland O, 123
Howard County, Kansas, 11
Howard County Ledger, 11
Howe, Mrs Julia Ward, 24
Hudson, J K, 20, 26, 35, 36, 49, 54, 236n39, 241n41, 249n15
Hudson, Mrs J K (Mary W, "Aunt Mary" of *American Young Folks*), 13-4, 31, 234n25, 237n9, 11
Hughes, Charles Evans, 127, 247n34
Hugoton, Kansas, 25
Hugoton *Hermes,* 26
Hull, Cordell, 180
"Human Vampire," 65, 145
Huxman, Walter A, 178

Iler, G W, 6
Illinois, 120, 141
Independence (Kansas) Progressive Club, 82
Indiana, 120
Indiana Farmer, 226
Indiana Farmer's Guide, 141

Indian Territory, 9, 52
Industrial Workers of the World (I W W), 103
Ingalls, John J, 27, 203, 230, 237n41, 240n26
In His Steps, by Charles M Sheldon, 49
Insurgent, 53, 63
International Copyright law, 32
International Farm Youth Exchange, 124
International Reform Federation, 175
Intolerance of wartime, 101
Iowa, 1, 2, 4, 5, 53, 64, 111, 148, 152
Isolationism, 175-6, 179, 264n1
Italy, 156

Jackson, Fred, 83
Jamesburg, New Jersey, 234n26
Japan, 184
Jardine, William M, 154, 217, 257n35
Jayhawker Hotel, 145, 224
Jayhawker state, 230
Jefferson County, Ohio, 5
Jewell, Jesse P, 232
Johnson, Charles, 116
Johnson, Hiram, 130
Johnson, Hugh S, 152
Johnson, Mabel, 31
Johnson, Madge, 31
Johnson Act, 184
Johnston, William Agnew, 80
Jones, Andrieus A, 156
Jones, D F, 191
Journal of Agriculture, 138, 195
Journalism in Kansas, 42
Juvenile Flower Club, 115

Kansas state census of 1865, 9, change in journalism, 42, politics of 1890's, 43-4, direct primary, 63, reform legislation, 63, primary elections in 1912, 77, election contest, 80-1, Senate in 1912, 81, woman suffrage, 84, 85, political lineup and legislation of legislature in 1915, 89, role of Governor, 92, Loyalty Day—April 6, 1917, 98, and conscription, 99, Republican senatorial candidates of 1918, 104, politics, 112, 23, 52, 62, 116, 136, 143, 159, 161, 167, 230
Kansas Breeze, 45, 107
Kansas Capital description, 51, renamed *Capper's Weekly,* 61-2, 83, 49, 52, 54, 135, 216
Kansas City *Journal,* 110, 245n26
Kansas City *Kansan,* 138-9, 143, 194, 215, 216
Kansas City, Kansas, 139, 187, 194, 203-4
Kansas City, Kansas, Chamber of Commerce, 139
Kansas City, Missouri, 60, 139
Kansas City *Star* erroneous report of Crawford-Capper marriage, 40, 24, 113, 138, 139, 212, 245n26
Kansas City Star Company, 224

Kansas City *Times,* 13, 110, 138, 139
Kansas Crippled Children's Commission, 227
Kansas Day Club, meeting in 1914, 82, 240n27
Kansas Extension Service, 121
Kansas Farm Bureau, 103
Kansas Farmer background, 54, consolidated with *Mail and Breeze,* 136, absorbs *Field and Farm,* 138, 27, 78, 82, 120, 121, 122, 123, 139, 188, 196, 200, 215, 216, 231, 267n3
Kansas Farmer and Mail and Breeze, 136
Kansas Farmer Company, printed *Mail and Breeze,* 46
Kansas Farmer Protective Service, 123
Kansas Farmers Union, 103
Kansas 4-H Club Camp, Rock Springs Ranch, 120, 218
Kansas Magazine, 50, 244n11
Kansas National Forest Reserve, 93
Kansas Newspaper Hall of Fame, 229
Kansas Republican League, 27, 237n41
Kansas Secretary of State, 111
Kansas State Agricultural College, 72, 73, 111, 113, 116, 154
Kansas State Board of Administration, 97
Kansas State College, 211
Kansas State Council of Defense, 99, 102
Kansas State Highway Commission, 96
Kansas State Historical Society, 231
Kansas State Militia, 6
Kansas State Penitentiary, 91
Kansas State Printer and Kansas politics, 46-7, 63, 73, 240n29
Kansas State University, 263n43
Kansas Supreme Court, 80
Kaw Valley Broadcasting Company, 263n43
KCKN Broadcasting Company, 194
Kellogg-Briand Peace Pact, 161-2, 180
Kennedy, Joseph P, 184
Kentucky Farmer, 226
Kenyon, W S, 148, 150
Ketchum, Omar B, 178
Kirk, L K, 24
Kiro dam proposal, 172
Kittell, A G, 111
Knights of Columbus, 220
Knights of Labor, 235n2
Knox, Frank, 177
Kopelin, Louis, 103, 104
Ku Klux Klan, 179, 220

Labette County, Kansas, 113
Labor and Capper, 204, management problems, 210
La Follette ("LaFollette"), Robert, 75, 103, 184
Laing, W T, 59
Lamont, Corliss, 268n12
Landon, Alfred M, 177, 178, 206, 207, 211-2, 260n51, 265n19, 266n61-4
Lane, James H, 9, 203

Lansdon, W C , 247n*34*
Lawrence, Morton J , 139
Lawrence, Kansas, 18, 23, 24, 63
Lawrence Publishing Company, 139-40, 141, 142, 255n*39*
League of Nations and partisan feeling, 128, issue, 129, and other issues, 145, in Geneva, 156
League of Nations to Enforce Peace, 93, 95, 97, 127
Leavenworth, Kansas, 19, 77, 109
Leavenworth *Standard*, 109
"Legislative War" of 1893, 40
Leland, Cy, 68
Lend-Lease Bill, 186, 202
Liberty Bonds of World War I, 101
Library of Congress, 231
Lincoln, Abraham, 1, 4, 158, 223
Lincoln Memorial, 186
Lincoln Memorial University, Harrogate, Tennessee, 268n*27, 29*
Lincoln, Nebraska, 61
Lindsay, Dick, 31, 238n*39*
Lindsay, Sam, 16, 22
Linn County, Kansas, 2, 5, 25
Literary Digest straw vote in 1920, 149, 248n*84*
Lockwood, Mrs Belva, 24
Lodge, Henry Cabot, 126, 129, 130, 132, 253n*2*
Lodge reservations, 129
Logan, John A , 23
Loganport, Indiana, 143
London, 162
Long, Chester I , 257n*33*
Long, Huey, 216-7
Longshore, E W , 21
Longshore, Joe, 74
Longton, Kansas lost election to be county seat, 12, 11, 14
Longton, Staffordshire, England, 1
Louisiana, 217
Louisville, Kentucky, 192
Loyalty Day in Kansas, April 6, 1917, 98

MacArthur, Douglas, 206
McCarter, Margaret Hill, 250n*3, 4*
McCray, D O , 74, 81-2
McGill, George, 167, 204
McGarth, Frank, 270n*63*
McGrew, Abner (uncle of Arthur Capper), 22
McGrew, Isabella (Mrs Herbert Capper) marriage to Herbert Capper, 4-5
McGrew, the Rev Samuel B (great-uncle of Arthur Capper), 2, 5
McGrew, Simon B (grandfather of Arthur Capper) the "Fighting Quaker," 5, free-state sympathy, 5 reminiscences of Arthur's early childhood, 10, 2, 233n*5, 20*, 234n*6*
McGrew, Ura Marsh (grandmother of Arthur Capper), 5

McKee, Julia, 268n*10, 31*
McKellar, Kenneth, 208
McKelvie, Samuel R , 142
McKinley, William, 34, 94
McKinney, Florence, 252n*42*
McLaughlin, Drew, 82
McLean, Evelyn Walsh, 185, 209
MacLennan, Frank P , 192
McNary, Charles L , 152
McNary-Haugen bill Coolidge veto, 153, 152, 158, 163
McNeal, Thomas A and *Kansas Breeze,* 45, as editor of *Mail and Breeze,* 46, 106-8, involvement in Republican party politics, 107, 50, 66, 67, 102, 131, 196, 197, 204, 239n*20*, 247n*21*, 249n*6, 8, 10, 29*, 264n*56*
Madden, Edwin C , 241n*48*
Madison, Edmond H , 63, 72-3, 244n*36*
Madison Square Garden, 34
"Magna Carta of Cooperative Marketing," 151
Mail and Breeze printed in Kansas Farmer printing plant, 46, "Quarter Centennial Illustrated Edition," 46, moved into Crawford Building, 48, circulation growth, 48, partisan expression, 51, takes on role of agricultural journal, 51, area of circulation in 1904, 51-2, becomes *Farmers' Mail and Breeze,* 52, 53, competition, 54, and controversial material, 68, 46, 48, 63, 79, 107, 109, 112, 113, 115, 231
"Mail and Breeze Golden Rule Club," 115
Mail-order journals, 65
Mail Printing House, 48, 112
Mann, Dick, 252n*43*
Mann, Henrietta Elma, 234n*10*
Mapleton, Kansas, 5
Marion County, Ohio, 107
Martin, John, 20
Maryland, 5
Master Farmer promoted by Capper Farm Press, 120, method of selection, 120-1, and Master Farm Homemaker, 121
Master Homemaker, 121
Maxwell, Robert, 112, 114, 237n*44*, 250n*47*
Mayflower Hotel, Washington, D C , 157, 179
Medicine Lodge, Kansas, 107
Medicine Lodge *Cresset,* 107
Meredith, Edward T , 222
Mesta, Perle, 185
"Methodizing agriculture," 189-91
Miami, Florida, 105
Michigan, 195
Michigan Business Farmer, 142
Michigan Farmer, 120, 139, 142, 143, 195, 196, 215
Miller, A Q , 265n*12*
Milwaukee *Journal,* 224

Minnesota, 111, 122
Missouri, 52, 59, 60, 61, 62, 111, 116, 136, 144, 161
Missouri Agricultural Publishing Company, 138, 195, 263n46
Missouri Republican, 24
Missouri Ruralist, 60, 111, 116, 117, 120, 121, 138, 139, 194-5, 196, 215, 216
Missouri Valley Farmer purchased by Arthur Capper, 48, advertising standards and growth, 49, changed to *Capper's Farmer*, 135, 52, 53, 54, 61, 62, 65, 109, 216
Mitchell, William L (Billy), 156
Mitcheson, George, 232n2-4, 8-14, 16, 17, 23
Moline, Illinois, 152
Montana, 156
Montgomery, F C, 45
Montgomery County, Kansas, 82
Morrow, Marco employed by Capper, 57, as assistant publisher, 74, 110, on Capper Publications advertising, 78, background, 109, as "ghost writer" for Capper, 110, 135, 196-7, 231, 239n75, 12, 241n45, 46, 50, 3, 242n8, 9, 10, 17, 18, 243n3, 5, 8, 12, 18, 244n23, 2, 246n57, 3, 247n39, 249n10, 12, 19, 26, 250n32, 38, 42, 254n1, 2, 5, 255n21, 23, 29, 30, 36, 39, 256n41, 44, 47, 262n18, 263n54, 264n66
Mott, Frank Luther, 249n23
Mound City, Kansas, 2, 5
Mt Vernon, Ohio, 114
Mulvane, David W, 47, 49
Mulvane, John R, 47, 49, 240n40, 243n4
Murdock, Marcellus, 26
Murdock, Victor, 26, 63, 76, 82, 83, 237n1, 258n73

Nantucket Island, 29, 32
Nation, Carry, 230
National Association for the Advancement of Colored People, 219
National Capital Housing Authority, 229
National Committee on Boys' and Girls' Club Work, 120, 219
National Corn Husking Contest, 121-2
National Council of American-Soviet Friendship, Inc, 219
National Council of the Boy Scouts of America, 116, 219
National Council for Prevention of War, 180
National Industrial Recovery Act, 174
National Labor Relations Act, 174, 195
National Security League, 93
National Stockman and Farmer, 142
National Teachers' Convention, Topeka, 23
Navy League, 168
Nebraska, 52, 59, 62, 111, 116, 136, 143, 160

Nebraska Farmer, 60, 139, 142
Nebraska Farm Journal, 59-61, 111, 116, 117, 142, 216
Neeland, Mary Audrey, 234n19
Nelson, William Rockhill, 234n20
Netherlands, 156
Neutrality, 93, 180, 181, 184
Newberry, Truman H, 153
New Deal, 169, 170, 171, 173, 177, 178, 181, 186
New Haven Connecticut, 33
New Jersey, 14, 29, 34
New Mexico, 138, 156
New Orleans, Louisiana, 14
New Willard Hotel, Washington, D C, 256n46
New York City, 29, 30, 32, 33, 34, 111, 149, 162, 197, 198, 227
New York *Independent*, 12
New York *Irish World*, 237n10
New York *Journalist*, 237n10
New York *Mail and Express*, 237n10
New York Press Club, 30
New York *Sun*, 237n10
New York *Tablet*, 237n10
New York *Times*, 150, 173, 174
New York *Tribune*, 32, 34, 35, 217, 237n10
New York *World-Telegram*, 219
Niagara Falls, 30
Nichols, Arthur Lon, 108
Non-Partisan League in Kansas, 102, 103, 248n78
Norbeck, Peter, 173, 256n16, 257n22
Norris, George W, 160, 167, 258n57, 259n41
North American Aviation Fairfax Bomber Plant, Kansas City, Kansas, 203
North Carolina, 14
North Dakota, 103
North Topeka, Kansas, 19
North Topeka *Mail* See Topeka *Mail*
Nye Committee report, 176, 179-80

Ohio, 85, 94
Ohio Farmer, 120, 122, 139, 142, 143, 195, 196, 200, 215
Ohio Stockman and Farmer, 142
Oklahoma, 52, 60, 61, 62, 111, 116, 136, 143
Oklahoma City, Oklahoma, 111, 141-2
Oklahoma Farmer, 60-1, 111, 117, 139, 141, 216
Oklahoma Farmer-Stockman, 142
Oklahoma Farm Journal, 61
Oklahoma Publishing Company, 141
Oklahoma State Farmer, 61
Olathe, Kansas, 77
Omaha Bee, 109
Oregon, 152
Osage County Chronicle, 113
Ottawa, 2, 9, 18, 31, 65

Pacifism, 97-8
Palestine Emergency Fund, 220
Panama-Pacific Exposition, 92
Pancoast, John L , 25
Paola, Kansas, 82
Paris, 162
Paris Peace Pact, 161-2
Parker, John J , 166, 258n73, 4
Parks, J M , 251n32
Parsons, Kansas, 36
Patterson, Eleanor (Cissie), 185
Pawnee County, Kansas, 112
Peace and Equity League, 94
Peace Ship Oscar II, 93
Pearl Harbor bombing, 202-3
Peck, Robert Gray, 161
Peek, George N , 152
Peffer, William, 27
Pennsylvania, 111, 112, 195
Pennsylvania Farmer, 120, 139, 142, 143, 195, 196, 215
Pennsylvania State College, 111
People's party, 26, 35, 39, 43, 91
Perkins, Bishop W , 36
Pershing, John, 149
Philadelphia, Pennsylvania, 1, 183
Pictorial Directory of the War Congress, 208
Pierce, James, 64, 222
Pierce Publications, 53
Pittsburgh, Pennsylvania, 143
Plumb, Preston B , 35, 203, 238n37, 39, 268n36
Poem, "Work Wins" gift to Arthur Capper from his father, 17
Poland, 181
Political gossip of 1914, 83
Populists *See* People's party
Postmaster of Topeka, 111
Poultry Culture, 59, 62, 216
Powell, G Harold, 122
"Power farming," 190
Prairie Farmer, 120
Price, Sterling, 6
Printers' Ink advertising campaign in, 56, 78
Progressive party, 77, 83, 87
Progressive reform, reaction to, 73
Progressive Republicans, 53, 63, 76, 167
Prohibition in Kansas, 19-20, 96, party, 91, during wartime, 100, 175, 198, 220-1
Public Affairs, 141
Public Utility Holding Company Act, 174
Push taken over by Arthur Capper, 50, 216

Quakers, 3, 5, 6, 10, 14, 181, 203, 218, 221
Quay, Matthew S , mentioned, 35

Radio "network" broadcast, 153, 168
Radio station KCKN, 194, 215, KSAC, 143, WIBW, 143, 169, 187, 194, 214, 215, WIBW-FM, 194, WJAP, 143, WLBF, 194
Railroads and Kansas government, 63
Rapid City, South Dakota, 159
Ratner, Payne, 203
Reciprocal Tariff Act of 1934, 174
Reciprocal Trading Agreements, 175, 181
Red Cross during World War I, 101, Board of Incorporators, 219
Redden Building, 192
Reid, Albert T , 47-8, 50, 51, 68, 243n17
Reid, James L , 122
Republican Flambeau Club, 47
Republican League of New York City, 30
Republican National Committee, 128
Republican newspaper publisher, 145
Republican party national convention in 1912, 76, national convention of 1916, 112, national convention of 1920, 149-50, national convention of 1936, 177, national convention of 1940, 183, stand-patters, 63, progressive or insurgent wing, 53, 63, tactics in 1912, 79, senatorial primary in 1918, 104, control of Congress in 1919, 126, members in League of Nations to Enforce Peace, 127, control of Congress after 1946 election, 210, 23, 27, 39, 43, 73, 76, 82-3, 112, 166, 168, 177, 182, 206
Republican Party League, 78-9
Republican presidential candidates in 1920, 149
Republican progressives, 53, 63
Republican Senatorial Campaign Committee, 172
Republic County, Kansas, 23
Richland *Argosy*, 45
Richland *Observer*, 45
Roberts, Roy, 212, 266n66
Robey, W B , 50
Robinson, J B , 16
Robinson, John, 27
Rochester, Minnesota, 227
Rock Springs Ranch *See* Kansas 4-H Club Camp
Rogers, Will, 158, 216-7
Roosevelt, Eleanor, 185
Roosevelt, Franklin D , 168-9, 170-2, 178, 179-80, 183-4, 186, 202, 205-6, 209, 259n15, 265n23, 24, 25
Roosevelt, Theodore, 63, 76, 78, 87, 94, 173
Root, Elihu, 127
Root, Frank, 41, 52
Ross, Edmund, 203
Ruml, Beardsley, 206
Ruralist, 60
Rural New Yorker, 141
Rural Publishing Company, 142
Rural Trade, 199
Runyan, Rod, 241n43, 243n7, 255n13, 256n51, 263n49, 51
Ryan, Frank J , 77, 245n17

Sabath, Joseph, 155
Sage, Mrs Russell, 34
St John, John P , 20
St Louis, Missouri, 15, 138, 195
St Louis, Kansas and Arizona Railroad, 15
St Louis *Post-Dispatch*, 24
St Louis *Republican*, 74
Salem, Iowa, 5
Salina *Journal*, 113
San Francisco, California, 198
Santa Fe Railway *See* Atchison, Topeka and Santa Fe Railway
Saturday Evening Post, 76, 244n10
Saturday Lance, 45
Saturday Night Club, 107
Schenck, Doris, 269n55
Schenck, Leland, 242n20, 263n55, 264n65
Schnorer Club excursion, 33
Schoeppel, Andrew, 211, 212
Scott, Charles F , 104, 257n33
Scott, Will, 18
Secret Service, 101
Securities and Exchange Commission Act, 174, 193, 195
Sedalia, Missouri, 60
Senatorial candidates, Kansas Republican primary in 1918, 104
Senatorial "Round Robin," 128
Sessions, Charles, 80, 110, 111, 248n61, 250n30, 32
Shawnee Building and Loan, 41
Shawnee County, Kansas, 27
Shawnee County Probate Court, 224
Sheldon, Charles M , 49, 239n22
Sherman, John, mentioned, 35
Shotwell, James T , 162
Shull, George H , 191
Simpson, Jeremiah, 37, 38-9, 249n8
Sims-Edison torpedo, 33
"Slacker File," maintained by Governor Capper during war, 101
Slocum, George M , 142
Smith, Peter, 41
Snow Hall, University of Kansas, 24
Socialist party, 103-4
Social Security Act, 174, 176-7, 195
Society of Friends *See* Quakers
Soldiers' Adjusted Compensation bill of 1924, 153
Souders, William H , 114, 268n33
South Carolina, 14
South Dakota, 159, 173
Soviet Russia, 156
Spain, 180, 181
Spencer, Selden P , 161
Springfield, Ohio, 109
S S Leviathan, 155-6
Stanton, Mrs E C , 24
State Sanitary Convention in Wichita, 24
Stauffer, Oscar S , 193
Stauffer Publications, Inc and Capper Publications, Inc , 269n49, 225, 226, 231

Stevens County, Kansas, 25
'Stockman-Farmer Publishing Company, 142
Stone, Robert, 176-7
Stratton, Clif, 231, 268n32
Strong, Frank, 248n69
Stubbs, Walter Roscoe, 63, 72, 73, 76, 77, 79, 82, 83, 91, 104, 248n86
Successful Farming, 54, 189
"Sunday Forum" in *Capital*, 108
Sunflower, 45
Supreme Court "packing" bill, 178, 186
Switzerland, 156

Taft, William Howard, 75, 76, 77, 78, 94, 95, 97, 127, 128, 130, 132, 247n43, 254n18
Taft-Hartley Act, 196
Talmage, T DeWitt, 30
Tammany Hall, 30, 34
Tariff, 163-4
Taxes, withholding for, 206
Television station WIBW-TV, 225
Tennessee, 208
Tennessee Farmer, 226
Tennessee Valley Authority, 174
Thirty-fifth Division, 161
Thomas, Dick, 23
Thomas, Elmer, 174
Thomas, R L , 50, 241n41
Thompson, Tom, 234n15
Thompson, William H , 105
Tincher, J N (Polly), 266n64
Topeka, Kansas described in 1884, 19, real estate boom, 21, visited by President and Mrs Wilson, 94, still home for Capper, 105, 23, 27, 28, 31, 40, 42, 111, 124, 141, 143, 145, 172, 182, 187, 191, 194, 195, 197, 214, 217, 224, 226, 231
Topeka Capital Company, 49
Topeka Cemetery, 157, 268n35
Topeka *Daily Capital* description and working conditions, 19, publication schedule, 22, ownership, 26, office of, 54, effort to buy out Capper, 64, on Hodges' administration, 85, on publicizing Capper's political career, 91-2, Juvenile Flower Club, 115, acceptable advertising, 198, 18, 20, 21, 26, 29, 31, 34, 35, 39, 41, 49, 52, 55, 62, 63, 69, 79, 108, 114, 127, 143, 177, 192, 193, 205, 207, 215, 216
Topeka *Mail* description of, 42, advertising and recognition, 43, as official county paper, 44, consolidation with *Kansas Breeze*, 45, business methods, 55, 41, 113, 115, 215, 231
Topeka Newspaper Printing Company, 192, 193, 198
Topeka Orphans' Home, 227
Topeka Post Office, 192
Topeka *State Journal*, 72, 192, 193
Topeka Typographical Union, 19

Toronto, Canada, 30
Townley, Arthur C , 103
Troutman, James A , 257n33
"T R " Republicans, 63, 73
Truman, Harry S, 204, 209, 224, 260n59
"Truthful James" stories by Tom McNeal, 108
"Truth-in-advertising" bill, 197
Tumulty, Joseph, 254n17
Tuttle Creek Dam, 266n52
Twentieth Century Farmer, 60

Ulysses, Kansas, 25
Underground railroad, 2
Union Pacific Railway, 112
United Nations Charter, 134, 209
United States Congress, Sixty-sixth, Special Session, 126
United States Department of Agriculture, 123, 148, 152
United States Department of Agriculture Library, 231
United States Department of Labor, 91
United States District Attorney in Kansas, 101
United States entry into World War I, 98
United States House of Representatives, 148
United States Liberty Bonds, 101
United States Navy Department, 168
United States Secretary of Agriculture, 72, 112, 154, 171
United States Senate, 106, 126, 145-6, 148
United States Supreme Court, 166
University of Kansas, 72
University of Wisconsin, 123
Useful Poultry Culture, 59
Utah, 138

Vandenberg, Arthur, 177, 184, 210, 266n54
Van Natta, Conrad C , 112, 113, 226-7
Van Natta, Constance, 269n51, 270n58
Versailles Treaty early action on, 127, and reservations, 128, and public opinion, 129, blame for defeat, 132, 134, 161
Villard, Oswald Garrison, 94, 247n27
Vineland, New Jersey, 14

Wabaunsee County, Kansas, 80
Wagner, Rogert F , 174
Wall Street Journal, 237n10
Wallace, Henry A , 168, 171, 191
Wallace, Henry C , 152, 154, 222
Wallaces' Farmer, 123
Walsh, Thomas J , 156
Ware, Eugene F , 239n22
Washburn University of Topeka, 268n29
Washington, George, 223
Washington, D C , 28, 29, 33, 34, 105, 116, 124, 139, 141, 185, 204, 214, 224, 231
Waters, Henry J , 242n26
Waters, Joseph G , 239n22

Watson, James, 129
Wayne, Kansas, 23
Welles, Sumner, 182
Wellington *Daily News*, 213
West, Judson S , 80
Westmoreland County, Pennsylvania, 5
White, Wallace H , 266n56
White, William Allen a "T R " booster, 63, linked with Capper, 68, 76, regent of University of Kansas, 72, advice on Capper's Governor race, 75, national committeeman, 77, Progressive party leader, 82, politics in 1914, 83, why Capper won in 1914, 86, and Kansas attitude on League, 128, comments on Capper, 153, recalls the Cappers in the 1890's, 157, anxiety during depression, 169, rating of Capper record, 173, former chairman of the Committee to Defend America by Aiding the Allies, 202, on Kansas' five great Senators, 203, proposes parole for Finney, 207, 207, correspondence with Capper, 236n14, postage stamp honoring him, 267n78, 215, 240n36, 242n18, 244n36, 3, 5, 8, 259n17, 264n3, 7
White, William L , 207, 212, 220, 265n8, 35, 36, 38, 267n68
White House, 155, 158, 218
Whittier, John Greenleaf, 27, 230
Wichita, Kansas, 24, 145, 192
William Allen White Foundation, 218
Willkie, Wendell L , 183-4, 264n4
Wilson, James, 72
Wilson, Woodrow, 93, 94, 95, 99, 126, 127, 128, 129, 132, 133, 134, 248n56, 64, 254n14, 15
Windsor Hotel, 21
Winton automobile, 71
Wisconsin, 53, 64, 120
Woman's Kansas Day Club, 94
Woman suffrage in Kansas, 84, 85
Wood, Leonard, 100, 127, 150, 248n63, 249n89
Wood, Sam N , 25
Woodring, Harry H , 167
Woodsdale, Kansas, 25
World Court, 161, 174
World War I intolerance, 101, "Unconditional Surrender" for, 127, 85, 87, 161
World War I Peace Treaty, 126-34
World War II begins, 181, declaration of war, 185, restrictions on publishers, 198
Wright, Harry, 112, 113
Wyoming, 138

Yale, 28, 33, 34
Yarnell, Ray, 188, 190, 244n23, 261n7, 10, 11, 12
Y M C A , 31, 105, 116
Yugoslavia, 156

Zach, Phil, 196-7, 269n41

CPSIA information can be obtained at www.ICGtesting.com
Printed in the USA
LVOW01s1522260415

436154LV00027B/1494/P

9 781258 172695